INFERNO

DANTE

INFERNO

*Translated, Edited, and with an
Introduction by Anthony Esolen*

Illustrations by Gustave Doré

THE MODERN LIBRARY

NEW YORK

2003 Modern Library Paperback Edition

Biographical note copyright © 1996 by Random House, Inc.
Translation, introduction, and notes copyright © 2002 by Random House, Inc.

Library of Congress Cataloging-in-Publication Data
Dante Alighieri, 1265–1321.
[Inferno. English]
Inferno / Dante Alighieri; translated, edited, and with an introduction by Anthony
Esolen; illustrations by Gustave Doré.
p. cm.
ISBN 0-8129-7006-3 (pbk.)
I. Esolen, Anthony M. II. Doré, Gustave, 1832–1883. III. Title.

PQ4315.2 .E76 2002
851'.1—dc21   2002029511

Modern Library website address: www.modernlibrary.com

Printed in Mexico

20th Printing

DANTE ALIGHIERI

Dante Alighieri, the Italian poet whose great allegory *The Divine Comedy* has exerted a profound effect on Western literature and thought, was born in Florence in May 1265. He came from a noble though impoverished family, descendants of the city's Roman founders. Relatively little is known with certainty about Dante's early life, but it is noteworthy that he grew up during the restless period that followed decades of blood rivalry between two Florentine political groups, the Guelphs and the Ghibellines. His childhood was doubtless colored by stories of this partisan strife from which, as Machiavelli later wrote, "there resulted more murders, banishments, and destruction of families than ever in any city known to history."

Dante probably received his early schooling from the Franciscans and the Dominicans; later, he studied rhetoric with the Guelph statesman and scholar Brunetto Latini. Another significant mentor was the aristocratic poet Guido Cavalcanti, who strongly influenced his early work. For the young Dante, writing poetry became an important expression of his passion for art and learning, and of his abiding concern with the nature of love and spiritual fulfillment. A Florentine woman of exceptional beauty, Beatrice Portinari, provided a powerful stimulus to the poet's artistic development. Dante idealized her as the "bringer of blessings," a beatific guide capable of pointing him toward the inner perfection sought by every noble mind. Following her untimely death in 1290, Dante, overcome with grief, celebrated her grace and virtue in *La vita nuova* (1292–94), a small "book of memory" written in verse and prose. He then sought renewal in an extensive study of theology and philosophy.

In 1295 Dante entered public life and within a few years emerged as a prominent figure in Florentine politics. By then he had entered into an arranged marriage with Gemma Donati, a gentlewoman with whom he had several children. In the summer of 1300 Dante was named one of the six governing magistrates of Florence. During this time he was involved in the clash between two hostile factions of the Guelph party, the Whites and the Blacks. Aligning himself with the White Guelphs, Dante campaigned to preserve the independence of Florence and repeatedly opposed the machinations of Pope Boniface VIII, who was attempting to place all of Tuscany under papal control. In 1301, however, the Black Guelphs seized power, and Dante was banished at once on trumped-up charges of graft, embezzlement, and other transgressions. Later sentenced to death by fire if he returned to Florence, Dante never entered his native city again.

Dante's remaining years were spent with a series of patrons in various courts of Italy. Two uncompleted works date from his early period of exile. *De vulgari eloquentia* (1303–4), a scholarly tract in Latin on the eloquence of the Italian vernacular, is generally acknowledged to be the key to Dante's artistic inquiries. *Il convivio* (1304–7), a glorification of moral philosophy, is viewed as the cornerstone of his investigations into knowledge and wisdom. Perhaps as early as 1306, Dante began to compose *The Divine Comedy,* the greatest poem of the Middle Ages and the first masterpiece of world literature written in a modern European language. The Latin treatise *De monarchia* (1312–13), a practical guide calling for the restoration of peace in Europe under a secular ruler in Rome, is a statement of the poet's political theories. In his final years Dante was given asylum in Ravenna, where he completed *The Divine Comedy* shortly before his death in September 1321.

Contents

LIST OF ILLUSTRATIONS

INTRODUCTION

Anthony Esolen

In Plato's *Phaedrus*, Socrates explains that true love is a passion to behold not just a beautiful face or body but the eternal Form of Beauty itself. To make his point he compares the soul to a charioteer and a team of horses, one obedient and the other unruly. While the unruly horse, representing appetite, strains to leap upon the beloved as soon as he is in sight, the obedient horse, the "spirit" or "ambition," heeds the reins and the whip of the shuddering driver, who recalls that eternal Beauty and beholds its image with awe and reverence. Dante never read the *Phaedrus*, but in a deep sense he is at one with Plato, for he too believes that the goal of human life is to behold Beauty, and he too believes that the way to that beholding is traversed by love. Plato's description of the good horse gives us a clue about what made Dante so great, and why, after so many centuries, we still (perhaps now more than ever) regard his work with wonder:

> He that is on the more honorable side is upright and clean-limbed, carrying his neck high, with something of a hooked nose; in color he is white, with black eyes; a lover of glory, but with temperance and modesty; one that consorts with genuine renown, and needs no whip, being driven by the word of command alone. (253d; trans. R. Hackforth)

He "consorts with genuine renown," our poet does, as a steed longing for glory. Few poets have ever possessed a mind as analytical and as painstakingly precise as Dante's, yet that is not what makes us read the *Comedy*. What Dante sees should allure us, but his striving, his energy, his ambition, his longing to see and to sweep us along and compel us to see likewise, that is what wins us. He carries his neck high, and makes us ashamed of ourselves if we do not.

Dante is the most irascible of poets. By that I do not mean he was prone to peevishness or petty vengeance. There was nothing petty about the man. Rather, I mean to denote that fiery quality of the noble horse, that quick love for what is well done, gracious, brave, and beautiful, and that quick disdain for the foul, craven, ill-ordered, and low. In the *Inferno*, this passion is most often manifest as a love for justice. Now, it is one thing to analyze what justice is: the giving of each his due (as Dante, following Aristotle, would have said), or the treating of everyone identically (as with less complexity and a shakier hold on human affairs we ourselves would say). It is another thing to hunger and thirst for justice, and to put the expression of one's hunger and thirst under such severe artistic restraints that their well-directed force causes one's readers to hunger and thirst for justice too. We can scarce find more than a dusty historian who cares about the Republicans and Democrats in 1904. But when we read about Dante's Guelphs and Ghibellines—and no subject in the poem puts greater strain on our ability to remember who did what—we find ourselves drawn into their local dramas of family intrigue and patriotism and treachery. We are meant almost to feel the hanks of the Guelph traitor Bocca degli Abati as Dante pulls the hair out of his scalp, and to relish it, with zeal; as we are meant to hear, with admiration and gratitude, the words of the noble enemy Farinata, who alone stood up to defend Florence when his Ghibelline allies were determined to destroy her once and forever.

If that were all, it would be much; it would be more than almost any poet gives us. It is not all. For those machinations of Guelphs and Ghibellines touch upon a great question indeed, that of the source and end of true authority. And that returns us to the Beauty Dante is in love with: that vision of God, both Unity and Trinity, and of the incarnate Christ, God and Man, which is the end or goal of all rational beings, as it is the end or goal of the *Comedy* itself. Why must we return to that vision? For one thing, Dante tells us we must. Let us continue with the example of those aristocratic parties of his day. Dante argues that ultimate temporal authority must rest with the Empire, just as ultimate spiritual authority must rest with the papacy, since both were ordained by God and both are gifts to man—the latter as a guide, the former as a curb—to help human beings attain something like peace in this life and beatitude in the next. What concerns us is not the details of Dante's argument but the sheer sweep of it. For Dante sees that human beings act, and as actors they need something to tell them how to act and to inspire them to act rightly, and something to check them when they act wrongly. The will needs both guide and rein. That is the nature of the will, and it is evident from observation. And since God creates nothing in vain, he must have provided for the will's needs; only thus can human society be made beautiful and good. Hence he ordained the spiritual and temporal authorities, whose existence and whose spheres of influence can be deduced from Scripture. The argument proceeds not *from* but *toward* Scripture, starting from assumptions about the validity of observation, the reliability of reason, and the decorousness of all things in the universe, created as they were through Christ, the wisdom of God, and the power of God. Dante's passion for justice, like fire, tends ever toward the stars.

So we find, despite ourselves, that to analyze what we find so attractive about the *Comedy* and its author, we must turn our gaze where he has turned his. And there, if I may venture a guess, the modern reader finds something lovely and appealing. It is not that medieval Christian cosmos, necessarily, which excites his interest, although it may and indeed should—it is surely far nobler than our lazy relativist world, wherein every man creates his own moral order (that is, until he suspects he has been overcharged by his auto mechanic). Rather, what arouses is the intriguing presence of any cosmos at all. For us, the setting sun, the number pi, Seattle, a father's role in the family have nothing to do with one another. Even those who profess the Christian faith live in a dead and silent world: religion has retreated into the foxholes of the heart and says nothing about the stars. It is, I think, refreshing, invigorating, to enter a world of significance—of love and of love's profound consequences.

Many editors will remind their readers of the astronomy of Dante's day, the Ptolemaic system of ten concentric heavenly spheres, beginning with the outermost—First Mover, or Primum Mobile—and ending with our earth. A few words on that system are in order. Each planetary sphere was thought to shed its particular influence upon the earth below, and in particular upon those born when that planet was dominant in the heavens; the signs of the zodiac, too, played their nudging but not determinant role in the life of men. The earth was the center of this universe, physically, but at the same time very small, prone to change and decay, rife with sin, and farthest from God. Dante accepted all of this, and it is a basic structural principle not only in his *Paradiso* (where, of course, one expects to find heavenly spheres) but even in the *Inferno*, with its ten concentric rings of sinners, proceeding inward and downward toward greater wickedness and more complete loss of freedom. But, and I hope it is not literary-critical heresy to say so, we can have something very like Dante's cosmos without that astronomical system. For there are three principles regarding created things that I find fundamental to Dante's view of the world and its beauty; they are also principles that underlie the beauty of Dante's poem and that, for our purposes in the *Inferno*, will help us see the justice that inspired his zeal. They are these: *Things have an end. Things have meaning. Things are connected.*

THINGS HAVE AN END. Aristotle, a biologist by hobby, saw that all living things strive toward some finished state, some perfection of their inherent structure. The acorn possesses a form or principle of organization that, given sufficient water and nourishment, will become realized in the oak tree. That is the acorn's telos, or end; it is the state of completion that it strives (of course, without intention) to attain. What is man's end? That which will fulfill, or bring to its finished state, whatever distinguishes man as a genus. Now, just as the sapling does not grow so that it may use water, but uses water so that it may grow, so man's end must be what man seeks for its own sake, and not for the sake of something else. That end, Aristotle reasons, must be happiness, since all who desire wealth or fame or glory or any other perceived good do so because they believe these things will make them happy; yet no one desires happiness because he thinks it will make him rich or famous or glorious. And the happiness of man must consist in the fulfillment of what makes him man: in particular, his reason, which distinguishes him from all other living things.

Notice that Aristotle's argument does not assume a Creator (Aristotle's famous First Cause is not a Creator per se, much less a providential and personal God), nor does it assume an afterlife. It is, however, an extraordinarily powerful argument, based in observation, applicable to creatures great and small, and quite adaptable by Christianity. Take the human body, for example. Suppose one were to knit one's brows and ask Aristotle, "What on earth can you mean about all things possessing an end? What about the human reproductive system?" I imagine the philosopher would give a quizzical look and reply, "Why, the reproductive system is for reproduction. What did you think?" The charge of obviousness he would find absurd. Of course it is obvious. Most truths observable by the senses are. It is indecorous to walk on one's hands; the human body obviously is not constructed for that. It is indecorous for small children to paddle their parents, since that would vitiate the end, or purpose, of the family, which obviously includes the raising and educating of small children.

This line of reasoning, applied to human behavior, is called the natural law. In Scripture it is codified in the Ten Commandments, but it is also implicit in the account of creation in Genesis. For God created by speaking things into being, distinguishing them from one another, setting limits upon them, and, in the case of living things especially, giving them an aim, an end: "Be fruitful and multiply; fill the earth and subdue it." Since all things created by God are, in themselves, good, they are necessarily endowed with beauty. Now, nothing useless or pointless is either good or beautiful. Therefore, if things are created by God, they must possess ends, goals toward which they strive, as it were—even if the goal is that of inert matter, merely to subsist or to fall. To violate the end or goal of a thing is to act against the structure of its being. It is to violate beauty and, as Dante would argue, to dishonor the Creator of that beauty. Hence sin involves an absurdity, a corruption of what should make lovely sense, and it is an affront against the wise Creator.

An example or two may help. We possess (or are given) minds and tongues. Our minds desire to know, and with our speech we can express what we know. Since that is the case, the lie is an ugly sin against reason itself, against what distinguishes man from beast, and that is why Dante punishes it so severely. The hideous skin diseases of his alchemists are not imposed upon the sinners from without (although one can imagine what working with sal ammoniac and mercuric powders might do to you). The diseases express, in brute corporeal form, the reality of the falsehoods the alchemists committed. Another example: Aristotle believed that, since we do have minds, our highest end, or perfection, must involve the fulfillment of those minds. But for Dante, who read the words in Genesis "Let us make man in our own image and likeness," that fulfillment could be attained only if what is God-like in us were fulfilled. Hence it is no philosophical contemplation man is made for, but the intellectual vision of the One in whose image we were made. To scorn that One, as the blasphemers do, or to deny the possibility of our attaining that end, as the Epicurean heretics do, is to sin against not only God's beauty but our own.

By now it should be clear that if Dante's *Comedy* is to reflect, even distantly, the glory of the Creator, its components must possess ends or purposes just as creatures do. That is not a matter of cleverness but of recognizing patterns of beauty in the created world and incorporating them into one's poem. Number is an obvious example, and, for modern readers, the most difficult to justify. Dante invented his rhyme scheme (terza rima) precisely to give glory to the Trinity; so, too, the threefold division of the poem, reflecting the threefold division of the hereafter into Hell, Purgatory, and Heaven. Since tradition held that Christ died at age thirty-three, each of the sections of the poem contains thirty-three cantos, except for the unworthy *Inferno*, which contains either thirty-four or thirty-two, an excess or a deficiency, depending on whether we consider that Hell begins in the first canto or at the gates in Canto Three. Just as the fall of Adam is the happy fault that brought the Redeemer into the world, so the numerical blemish of the *Inferno* brings the whole *Comedy* to an even one hundred cantos, the square of ten, itself the square of the Trinity plus Unity. And in each of the three canticles of the poem we find the number ten: in the *Inferno*, ten areas of sinners whose deeds grow fouler as we descend farther below, until, in the dead center of the earth, we find Lucifer. And that is only a hint of the complexity of Dante's use of number and mathematics. Dante thought there were four elements; we know there are a hundred or so. The difference is that Dante would have been fascinated by the fact that there was a specific number at all. He knew, better than we, the musicality of order, and even if we resist his numerology, we respond to the order, and find the poem fascinating and beautiful because everything in it and about it has its end and is in its place.

THINGS HAVE MEANING. This principle follows from the first, when one assumes the existence of a providential God. For the same Creator who makes things beautiful as they are may endow them with a beauty not properly their own, either by allowing them to point toward things beyond themselves, or by allowing them a special role in the unfolding story of the universe. For example, it was a good and pious thing for Aeneas, the hero of Virgil's *Aeneid* and the mythological progenitor of the Romans, to visit his father in the underworld and learn from him what he needed to do to settle the Trojan race in Italy. By that action he was fulfilling his duty as a son and as a leader of his people. But what Aeneas could not know was that, as Dante saw it, he was playing a crucial part in the history of salvation, setting the stage for the Roman Empire and the temporal reign of peace under Augustus, itself the stage for what Augustus could not know of, the reign of peace under Christ and the establishment of the spiritual authority, the Church.

This habit of mind is less medieval than Christian. In the Sistine Chapel, surmounting the great painting of the Last Judgment and the resurrection of the dead, stands Michelangelo's dramatic portrayal of the minor prophet Jonah, in distress. Why Jonah, of all the prophets? This passage from the gospels provides the answer:

> Then some of the scribes and Pharisees said to him, "Teacher, we wish to see a sign from you." But he answered them, "An evil and adulterous generation seeks for a sign; but no sign shall be given to it except the sign of the prophet Jonah. For as Jonah was three days and three nights in the belly of the whale, so will the Son of Man be three days and three nights in the heart of the earth. The men of Nineveh will arise at the judgment with this generation and condemn it; for they repented at the preaching of Jonah, and behold, something greater than Jonah is here." (Matt. 12:38–41)

The story of Jonah was not just a convenient source of symbols for the resurrection; it was actually a type, or forerunner, of that resurrection, a harbinger, exactly as in a symphony a composer will subtly introduce a motif whose full flowering will be heard only at the climax of the piece. Jonah was meant to be that harbinger of the resurrected Christ. To view him as such is not felt as whimsical or arbitrary. It is to see how the particular (and Jonah always remains that particular, that recalcitrant prophet with his marine mishap) fits within the whole. It is to see and love the beauty of the universe's story.

Let us observe a few of the implications of this principle for the *Inferno.* Readers may be surprised at first by how little fire there is in Dante's Hell. That is because the *meaning* of fire is incompatible with the punishment of most sins. Lesser portrayers of eternal damnation have fixed upon fire for obvious reasons: fire is often (though by no means exclusively) so used in Scripture, and fire hurts. But Dante, considering the fiery heavens above, the nature of fire to rise, the liveliness of flame, and, of course, such scriptural passages as "Our God is a consuming fire" (Heb. 12:29), will not suffer the indecorous presence of that noble element in Hell. Rather, he reserves it for sinners who most directly affront the nature of the Deity—since it is to the Deity that fire most directly testifies—and also for those who sin most directly against the fire of the human intellect. Hence the rain of fire upon the desert sands, punishing the blasphemers, sodomites, and usurers, and the anti-Pentecostal swathes of flame punishing the evil counselors. Of course, the sodomites of Sodom were punished, in Genesis, by a rain of fire; yet Dante is apparently interested not in the fact of the fire but in the reason behind it. He saw that punishment as appropriate, given the nature of the sin and the nature of fire. (For a discussion of the relationship of that sin to blasphemy, see the note to 14.8.)

Or consider Pope Boniface's temptation of Guido da Montefeltro. It is a reprise, for evil purposes and with roles reversed, of the supposed curing of the emperor Constantine by Pope Sylvester. That pope brought Constantine out of bodily harm, precipitating, as it was thought, his long-delayed entry into the Christian Church. In exchange, Constantine was thought to have granted the papacy temporal power in central Italy—the so-called Donation of Constantine, which Dante saw as a source of great evil in his own day. His vision of events might be described as follows. Because of what the well-intended Constantine did, the papacy was corrupted. Because of that corruption, men like Boniface ascended the throne of Peter, concerned more with temporal power than with the spiritual health of the people. Because Boniface ascended the throne of Peter when he did, he required the astuteness of people like Guido da Montefeltro to assist him. Therefore he went to Guido, sick with the fever of power, desiring a cure in the form of evil counsel, and leading his spiritual charge (not by the promises of baptism but by sly threats of excommunication) into mortal sin and, finally, damnation. It is not that Dante has ironically cast Boniface in the role of the layman and Guido in the role of the cleric, but that Constantine's blunder and all the sins to follow have already done so. Dante does not assign the meanings; he sees them.

One of the happy corollaries of this belief in the meaning of things is that life is tremendously dramatic, with eternal consequences. For in his providence God has allowed human beings free will, and the use of one man's free will, at one moment, can mean life or death for a city, or salvation or damnation for himself and even, ultimately, for countless others. Suppose Mosca dei Lamberti had not said, "A thing that's done with has an end," recommending the killing of a young man who had jilted a young lady of a family close to the Lamberti. Mosca would not now be suffering in Hell, his family would not have disintegrated, and Florence might have been spared decades of civil bloodshed when (as it was thought) the vendetta he began erupted into general warfare between the Guelphs and the Ghibellines. Mosca was a noble man; he need not have said what he said. Yet that warfare might also be fit punishment for a city that had abandoned its devotion to courtesy and valor. To believe that our actions, not accidentally but providentially, point beyond themselves is to believe that some quiet moment of truth may be around the corner, in a tower, in a friar's small cell, in a drawing room with a sister-in-law reading a romance. It is terrible to suppose that Paolo and Francesca, the adulterous lovers of Canto Five, need not have turned the page.

Fittingly enough, then, in an age that saw the reawakening of popular drama, Dante is a supremely dramatic poet. One thinks of his persona's sudden and crushing recognition of Brunetto Latini:

> . . . we met a band
>   of spirits coming toward us, and each one
>   stared at us hard as one is wont to stare
> At someone in the dark of the new moon,
>   knitting their brows to keep us keen in sight
>   as an old tailor threads the needle's eye.
> And while this family was watching us
>   one of them knew me and he seized me by
>   my tunic's hem and cried, "What wonder's this!"
> And I, when he'd stretched out his arm to me,
>   so fixed my eyes upon his crusted looks
>   that even the charred features could not keep
> My intellect from recognizing them,
>   and lowering my hand toward his face
>   I answered, "Ser Brunetto, are *you* here?"

To explain the drama of this scene, it is not enough to note that the place is dark, that the recognitions occur one then the other, or that Dante alternates motifs of intense concentration with surprise. The scene is built upon the foundations of eternal truths. If it does not matter what a man does, we cannot have this scene; if a man has no choice but to follow his impulses, we cannot have this scene. Only if we assume that what we choose really does have meaning, and that therefore the stakes of our actions are infinitely high, can we look with unspeakable disappointment and shock at the ruin of a Brunetto Latini.

THINGS ARE CONNECTED. This last principle follows from the other two. In that beautiful universe created by God, each thing has an end and a significance; therefore each thing reflects the mind and plan of its Architect; and since the Architect has created a world unfolding in time, each thing assumes its place in that unfolding. It is not possible to separate, in this universe, those things which have to do with divinity from those things which do not. After all, oxen and stables and swaddling bands apparently do.

This more than anything else explains the vast range of Dante's language and style. It was more than a wise choice for him to write in the vernacular. It was, finally, the only justifiable choice, since he wished to write a poem about the whole universe, a universe packed with angelic intelligences, true, but also with shipmen caulking up their keels by the boatyards in winter, peasants brushing away mosquitoes as the sun sets, pilgrims jostling their way along a crowded bridge, cooks ordering their boys to keep the meat hunks from floating to the top, men in exile who have to climb other people's stairs to go to bed, and blessed souls remembering what it was like to be children looking upon the faces of Mama and Papa. The glory of God shines in all these things, and connects them intimately to one another. Augustine said that the Scriptures were written in the low style (the style proper to comedies) so that even a child might enter in and learn. But he also said that beneath those humble words lay untold riches and mysteries too deep for the mind to fathom without grace. It is, essentially, the mystery of the Christ child, and the humiliation of the Cross; the mystery of great things revealed in the humblest and least expected places, of the Word made flesh. What do a common thief condemned to die and a bit of unleavened bread have to do with divinity or with each other? Consider this verse from a eucharistic hymn by Thomas Aquinas:

> Godhead alone was hidden on the Cross,
> but here humanity is hidden too.
> Believing and confessing both, I seek
> what the repentant thief then sought from you.

Paradise is what the poet seeks, opened to him by the spiritual nourishment provided by means of a wafer. That is as strange, as surprising, as humble as to seek Paradise from the criminal being executed at one's left.

Somehow it has entered the popular mythology that the Middle Ages were a time of excessively abstract philosophizing and general flight from the earth and from our own humble bodies. No matter how many masons carve scenes of daily activity on the sides of Gothic cathedrals, no matter how many carpenters and smiths and tanners and glaziers put on rollicking town-wide cycles of plays every year on the feast of Corpus Christi from one end of Europe to the other, no matter how many bawdy stories come to us from Chaucer and Boccaccio or love lyrics from unnamed songsters by the hundreds, we persist in thinking that only in the Renaissance were bodies set free. A strange bit of folklore, this; what truth it possesses certainly does not apply to Dante's age. Thomas Aquinas wrote about the essence and nature of God, and the difference between act and potency; he also wrote about food and drink, and the price of money, and whether it is all right to save someone's life by telling an untruth, and the proper use of anger. We have not had, since, a philosopher more attentive to the bodily nature of man. Chaucer has two chickens discuss the prophetic value of dreams, clucking on about one ancient authority after another. As for Dante, there is not a single fact of human experience, from the lowly to the sublime, that cannot find a place in his *Comedy*.

Take the body and its functions. Modern translators are fond of blunting the words of Christ (whose parables and metaphors are fetched from all areas of life—a woman cleaning her house to look for a coin, a mustard seed, a shifty bailiff writing off bad debts, a man lying beaten at the side of a road) when they make him say, "I come not to bring peace but *division*" (Matt. 10:34). Actually, he says "a sword," not "division," but our translators are too squeamish for something so physical. Far from fleeing the body or attenuating it into abstraction, Dante sees other bodies where we would see only legal fictions—for instance, the body of the family and the body of the state. Our own bodies have to do with those bodies. That is why Dante uses the body to punish those who sow discord in the body—and with a real sword, not with some abstract and fussy "division"! Consider the perfectly physical and metaphysical punishment of Mohammed:

> A barrel with the midstave split apart
>   is not—as I saw one there—so burst wide,
>   from the chin severed down to where we fart.
> His bowels and guts dangled between the legs;
>   the organs showed, and that repugnant bag
>   that turns whatever we gobble into shit.

But our bodies are also the vehicles of salvation. That, too, is necessary and is one of the lessons of the enfleshing of Christ. The lady Beatrice begins the action of the *Inferno* by sending Virgil down to help Dante find the true path again. Of course she is a symbol of grace; but she is first a lovely woman, and Virgil himself responds as quickly to that loveliness as would a gallant man on earth:

> When she had finished speaking to me so,
>   she turned her glistening eyes all bright with tears—
>   which made me all the readier to go,
> And so I came to you as she desired,
>   raising you from the beast that faced you down
>   and stole from you the short way up the hill.

And the thought of those eyes stirs the right response in Dante:

> As little flowers shut small and bowed beneath
>   the frost of night, when the sun brightens them,
>   rise open-petaled on their stems upright,
> So did my weary courage surge again,
>   and such sweet boldness rushed into my heart
>   I cried out as a man at last set free,
> "O Lady of compassion and my help!"

By now I hope the reader will see the truth of what surely would have sounded odd at the beginning of this essay. The *Inferno* is not, finally, a poem about wickedness and punishment, but about beauty and love: the terrible beauty of God which should arouse in man the most ardent love, and the ruin of beauty which the soul becomes when it turns that love elsewhere. That love, that longing for beauty, pulses all through the *Comedy*, from the solemn judgments imposed upon the sinners, to sweet reminiscences of rural life, to scenes of camaraderie and pleasant talk, to the rapture of the soul before the unspeakable mysteries of Trinity and Incarnation. Love of Florence, and the fierce desire to see it made just, finds its place there, as does love of a beautiful woman named Beatrice, and love of a wise poet of the ancient days from whose works one first learned the severity of art. Largehearted to a sublime degree, Dante loved greatly, and in Purgatory even described his poetry as the finding of signs for what Love had spoken to him. That description applies to the *Inferno*, too, with its zeal for justice. "God is love," says Saint John, but the writer of the letter to the Hebrews says, "It is a fearful thing to fall into the hands of the living God." To hold both truths at once is to glimpse the majesty of love, and the complexities of Dante's symphony in love's honor.

NOTE ON THE TRANSLATION

The Italians have a saying, *"Traduttore traditore,"* which basically means that everyone in my line of work is an arrant traitor. That may be. I wish that all my students could read Dante in the Italian, as I wish they could all read Virgil in the Latin and *Beowulf* in the Anglo-Saxon, and so forth. Consider translation one of the consequences of Adam's sin.

That said, I think every translator of poetry must decide what he will try to preserve at all costs, what he will take when it is available, and what he will receive only occasionally from the hands of a stubborn Muse. I have decided, for the *Inferno*, that the preservation of Dante's rhyme in any systematic form would so overburden syntax, individual lines, and tercets as to compromise either meaning or music. In the former case the trade is a hard one; in the latter, it is self-defeating. John Ciardi's superb translation compromises some of the meaning to save about half of the rhyme. I do not criticize but merely note the losses any translator must incur. Some contemporary translations have dispensed not only with rhyme but with meter altogether, in an attempt to render Dante's meanings as tersely and accurately as possible. That is an admirable and self-effacing decision, and a student can learn a great deal from such a translation. But memorability and almost all of the power of music are lost.

I have assumed, in this translation, that a sublime poem had better be rendered into a meter capable of hinting now and again at that sublimity. In English, iambic pentameter is the only meter that will do. This translation is in blank verse, with some but not a very great many enjambments, as Dante's own verse is not highly enjambed. If I find a rhyme in my path I will use it, but will not turn things inside out for its sake; some ten percent or more of the lines do rhyme. In diction I have tried to crack English's knuckles to render Dante's striking coinages and constructions; if Dante turns an intransitive into a transitive verb, I attempt to do the same, and hope the reader will forgive the violence. Dante's linguistic range rivals that of any poet besides Shakespeare. No translator can match it; I hope only that the ruggedness and muscularity of his diction will still appear, with some regularity, in these English verses. Finally, the polysyllables of Italian will sometimes leave the English translator with a bit of breathing room, since English is rich in monosyllabic words. I try to use such space to bring out submerged or etymological metaphors, or to cover the range of meanings of a single word; from time to time I use a pair of words to translate one, and use a metaphorical verbal phrase for a single verb. Yet taken all in all, the philosophy underlying this translation is conservative, and, especially for figures of speech, the renderings are quite literal.

As an aid to the reader (who should not interrupt poetry by thumbing back and forth from the text to the notes), this edition provides short glosses at the bottom of the page, designed mainly to explain an elliptical phrase (what is "that wandering light of Heaven"?) so that the reader can move on. Fuller notes are provided in the back of the book, along with appendices.

The Italian text given beside the translation is based on the editions of Giorgio Petrocchi (1965) and Umberto Bosco and Giovanni Reggio (1979).

This book would not have seen the light of day were it not for the encouragement and the suggestions of many people, especially Willis Regier of the University of Illinois Press and my fearless editor, Will Murphy, of the Modern Library. To my colleagues in the English department at Providence College (particularly S. Terrie Curran, who spurred me in this direction), and to my colleagues in the Western Civilization

Program, with whom I have taught Dante and Aquinas and by means of whom I have managed to constrict some of my theological and philosophical gaps, and to the Dominican Fathers at Providence College, who have kept alive a devotion to and a conversation about Aquinas that have helped me in countless ways, I owe the knowledge it required to write this book. Without them, nothing. And to my wife, Debra—it is a mere matter of fact to say that I owe all. For I, too, have my blessed one.

ANTHONY ESOLEN
Providence College
December 30, 2001

INFERNO

Nel mezzo del cammin di nostra vita
   mi ritrovai per una selva oscura,
   che la diritta via era smarrita.
Ahi quanto a dir qual era è cosa dura   4
   esta selva selvaggia e aspra e forte
   che nel pensier rinova la paura!
Tant' è amara che poco è più morte;   7
   ma per trattar del ben ch'i' vi trovai,
   dirò de l'altre cose ch'i' v'ho scorte.
Io non so ben ridir com' i' v'intrai,   10
   tant' era pien di sonno a quel punto
   che la verace via abbandonai.
Ma poi ch'i' fui al piè d'un colle giunto,   13
   là dove terminava quella valle
   che m'avea di paura il cor compunto,
guardai in alto e vidi le sue spalle   16
   vestite già de' raggi del pianeta
   che mena dritto altrui per ogne calle.
Allor fu la paura un poco queta,   19
   che nel lago del cor m'era durata
   la notte ch'i' passai con tanta pieta.
E come quei che con lena affannata,   22
   uscito fuor del pelago a la riva,
   si volge a l'acqua perigliosa e guata,

CANTO ONE

*Lost in a **dark wood** and threatened by **three beasts**, Dante is rescued by **Virgil**, who proposes a journey to the other world.*

Midway upon the journey of our life
    I found myself in a dark wilderness,
    for I had wandered from the straight and true.
How hard a thing it is to tell about,   4
    that wilderness so savage, dense, and harsh,
    even to think of it renews my fear!
It is so bitter, death is hardly more—   7
    but to reveal the good that came to me,
    I shall relate the other things I saw.
How I had entered, I can't bring to mind,   10
    I was so full of sleep just at that point
    when I first left the way of truth behind.
But when I reached the foot of a high hill,   13
    right where the valley opened to its end—
    the valley that had pierced my heart with fear—
I raised my eyes and saw its shoulders robed   16
    with the rays of that wandering light of Heaven°
    that leads all men aright on every road.
That quieted a bit the dread that stirred   19
    trembling within the waters of my heart
    all through that night of misery I endured.
And as a man with labored breathing drags   22
    his legs out of the water and, ashore,
    fixes his eyes upon the dangerous sea,

° *that wandering light of Heaven:* Italian *pianeta,* "planet." It is the sun, considered a planet, or *wandering light,* revolving about the earth.

così l'animo mio, ch'ancor fuggiva,   25
    si volse a retro a rimirar lo passo
    che non lasciò già mai persona viva.

Poi ch'èi posato un poco il corpo lasso,   28
    ripresi via per la piaggia diserta,
    sì che 'l piè fermo sempre era 'l più basso.

Ed ecco, quasi al cominciar de l'erta,   31
    una lonza leggera e presta molto,
    che di pel macolato era coverta;

e non mi si partia dinanzi al volto,   34
    anzi 'mpediva tanto il mio cammino,
    ch'i' fui per ritornar più volte vòlto.

Temp' era dal principio del mattino,   37
    e 'l sol montava 'n sù con quelle stelle
    ch'eran con lui quando l'amor divino

mosse di prima quelle cose belle;   40
    sì ch'a bene sperar m'era cagione
    di quella fiera a la gaetta pelle

l'ora del tempo e la dolce stagione;   43
    ma non sì che paura non mi desse
    la vista che m'apparve d'un leone.

Questi parea che contra me venisse   46
    con la test' alta e con rabbiosa fame,
    sì che parea che l'aere ne tremesse.

Ed una lupa, che di tutte brame   49
    sembiava carca ne la sua magrezza,
    e molte genti fé già viver grame,

questa mi porse tanto di gravezza   52
    con la paura ch'uscia di sua vista,
    ch'io perdei la speranza de l'altezza.

E qual è quei che volontieri acquista,   55
    e giugne 'l tempo che perder lo face,
    che 'n tutti suoi pensier piange e s'attrista;

tal mi fece la bestia sanza pace,   58
    che, venendomi 'ncontro, a poco a poco
    mi ripigneva là dove 'l sol tace.

So too my mind, while still a fugitive,   25
 turned back to gaze again upon that pass
 which never let a man escape alive.
When I had given my weary body rest,   28
 I struck again over the desert slope,
 ever the firmer foot the one below,
And look! just where the steeper rise began,   31
 a leopard light of foot and quick to lunge,
 all covered in a pelt of flecks and spots,
Who stood before my face and would not leave,   34
 but did so check me in the path I trod,
 I often turned to go the way I came.
The hour was morning at the break of dawn;   37
 the sun was mounting higher with those stars°
 that shone beside him when the Love Divine
In the beginning made their beauty move,   40
 and so they were a cause of hope for me
 to get free of that beast of flashy hide—
The waking hour and that sweet time of year;   43
 but hope was not so strong that I could stand
 bold when a lion stepped before my eyes!
This one seemed to be coming straight for me,   46
 his head held high, his hunger hot with wrath—
 seemed to strike tremors in the very air!
Then a she-wolf, whose scrawniness seemed stuffed   49
 with all men's cravings, sluggish with desires,
 who had made many live in wretchedness—
So heavily she weighed my spirit down,   52
 pressing me by the terror of her glance,
 I lost all hope to gain the mountaintop.
And as a gambler, winning with a will,   55
 happening on the time when he must lose,
 turns all his thoughts to weeping and despair,
So I by that relentless beast, who came   58
 against me step by step, and drove me back
 to where the sun is silent evermore.

° *those stars:* the constellation Aries. It is the springtime of the year, recalling the springtime of the universe; see notes.

Mentre ch'i' rovinava in basso loco,   61
   dinanzi a li occhi mi si fu offerto
   chi per lungo silenzio parea fioco.

Quando vidi costui nel gran diserto,   64
   «*Miserere* di me», gridai a lui,
   «qual che tu sii, od ombra od omo certo!».

Rispuosemi: «Non omo, omo già fui,   67
   e li parenti miei furon lombardi,
   mantoani per patrïa ambedui.

Nacqui *sub Iulio*, ancor che fosse tardi,   70
   e vissi a Roma sotto 'l buono Augusto
   nel tempo de li dèi falsi e bugiardi.

Poeta fui, e cantai di quel giusto   73
   figliuol d'Anchise che venne di Troia,
   poi che 'l superbo Ilïón fu combusto.

Ma tu perché ritorni a tanta noia?   76
   perché non sali il dilettoso monte
   ch'è principio e cagion di tutta gioia?».

«Or se' tu quel Virgilio e quella fonte   79
   che spandi di parlar sì largo fiume?»,
   rispuos' io lui con vergognosa fronte.

«O de li altri poeti onore e lume,   82
   vagliami 'l lungo studio e 'l grande amore
   che m'ha fatto cercar lo tuo volume.

Tu se' lo mio maestro e 'l mio autore,   85
   tu se' solo colui da cu' io tolsi
   lo bello stilo che m'ha fatto onore.

Vedi la bestia per cu' io mi volsi;   88
   aiutami da lei, famoso saggio,
   ch'ella mi fa tremar le vene e i polsi».

«A te convien tenere altro vïaggio»,   91
   rispuose, poi che lagrimar mi vide,
   «se vuo' campar d'esto loco selvaggio;

ché questa bestia, per la qual tu gride,   94
   non lascia altrui passar per la sua via,
   ma tanto lo 'mpedisce che l'uccide;

Now while I stumbled to the deepest wood,   61
   before my eyes appeared the form of one
   who seemed hoarse, having held his words so long.

And when I saw him in that endless waste,   64
   "Mercy upon me, mercy!" I cried out,
   "whatever you are, a shade, or man in truth!"

He answered me: "No man; I *was* a man,   67
   and both my parents came from Lombardy,
   and Mantua they called their native land.

In the last days of Julius I was born,   70
   and lived in Rome under the good Augustus
   in the time of the false and cheating gods.

I was a poet, and I sang of how   73
   that just son of Anchises° came from Troy
   when her proud towers and walls were burnt to dust.

But you, why do you turn back to such pain?   76
   Why don't you climb that hill that brings delight,
   the origin and cause of every joy?"

"Then are you—are you Virgil? And that spring   79
   swelling into so rich a stream of verse?"
   I answered him, my forehead full of shame.

"Honor and light of every poet, may   82
   my long study avail me, and the love
   that made me search the volume of your work.

You are my teacher, my authority;   85
   you alone are the one from whom I took
   the style whose loveliness has honored me.

See there the beast that makes me turn aside.   88
   Save me from her, O man renowned and wise!
   She sets the pulses trembling in my veins!"

"It is another journey you must take,"   91
   replied the poet when he saw me weep,
   "if you wish to escape this savage place,

Because this beast that makes you cry for help   94
   never lets any pass along her way,
   but checks his path until she takes his life.

° *that just son of Anchises:* Aeneas, legendary founder of Rome. His piety and his heroic sufferings
are celebrated by Virgil in his epic, the *Aeneid.*

e ha natura sì malvagia e ria,   97
  che mai non empie la bramosa voglia,
  e dopo 'l pasto ha più fame che pria.
Molti son li animali a cui s'ammoglia,   100
  e più saranno ancora, infin che 'l veltro
  verrà, che la farà morir con doglia.
Questi non ciberà terra né peltro,   103
  ma sapïenza, amore e virtute,
  e sua nazion sarà tra feltro e feltro.
Di quella umile Italia fia salute   106
  per cui morì la vergine Cammilla,
  Eurialo e Turno e Niso di ferute.
Questi la caccerà per ogne villa,   109
  fin che l'avrà rimessa ne lo 'nferno,
  là onde 'nvidia prima dipartilla.
Ond' io per lo tuo me' penso e discerno   112
  che tu mi segui, e io sarò tua guida,
  e trarrotti di qui per loco etterno,
ove udirai le disperate strida,   115
  vedrai li antichi spiriti dolenti,
  ch' a la seconda morte ciascun grida;
e vederai color che son contenti   118
  nel foco, perché speran di venire
  quando che sia a le beate genti.
A le quai poi se tu vorrai salire,   121
  anima fia a ciò più di me degna:
  con lei ti lascerò nel mio partire;
ché quello imperador che là sù regna,   124
  perch' i' fu' ribellante a la sua legge,
  non vuol che 'n sua città per me si vegna.
In tutte parti impera e quivi regge;   127
  quivi è la sua città e l'alto seggio:
  oh felice colui cu' ivi elegge!».

So vicious is her nature, so ill-bent,   97
    she never stuffs her ravenous will enough,
    but after feeding hungers all the more.

Many a living soul takes her to wife   100
    and many shall, until the Greyhound comes,
    he who will make her die in misery.

Not land, not lucre will he feed upon,   103
    but wisdom, love, and strength shall be his meat,
    and by the cloth of felt he will be born.

He will bring health to humbled Italy,   106
    the land for which the maid Camilla died,
    and Nisus, Turnus, and Euryalus.

Through every village he will hunt her down   109
    until at last he drives her back to Hell,
    whence envy set her loose upon the world.

And so I judge it would be best for you   112
    to follow me, and I will be your guide,
    leading you out through an eternal place,

Where you will hear the groans of hopeless men,°   115
    will look upon the sorrowing souls of old,
    crying in torment for the second death;

Then you will look upon those souls content   118
    to wait in fire,° because they hope someday
    to come among the nation of the blessed.

Should you then wish to rise and go to them,   121
    another soul° will come, worthier than I—
    with her I'll leave you when I go my way.

For that great Emperor who reigns above,   124
    because I was a rebel to His law,
    will not allow me entry to his realm.

Everywhere he commands, from there he rules,   127
    there stand his city and his lofty throne.
    Happy the man He chooses for His house!"

° *hopeless men:* the souls in Hell, longing for a *second death* that will not come; see notes.

° *content to wait in fire:* the souls in Purgatory, who have all been saved.

° *another soul:* Beatrice, Dante's beloved, who will guide him through Paradise; see notes.

E io a lui: «Poeta, io ti richeggio   130
   per quello Dio che tu non conoscesti,
   acciò ch'io fugga questo male e peggio,
che tu mi meni là dov'or dicesti,   133
   sì ch'io veggia la porta di san Pietro
   e color cui tu fai cotanto mesti».
Allor si mosse, e io li tenni dietro.   136

"Poet," I said to him, "I beg of you,   130
    by that same God you never knew, that I
    may flee this evil and the worse to come,
Lead me now to the place you tell me of,   133
    so I may see Saint Peter's gate,° and those
    you say are dwelling in such misery."
He set on, and I held my pace behind.   136

° *Saint Peter's gate:* the gates of Purgatory (see *Purg.* 9.121–32).

Lo giorno se n'andava, e l'aere bruno
	togliea li animai che sono in terra
	da le fatiche loro; e io sol uno
m'apparecchiava a sostener la guerra		4
	sì del cammino e sì de la pietate,
	che ritrarrà la mente che non erra.
O muse, o alto ingegno, or m'aiutate;		7
	o mente che scrivesti ciò ch'io vidi,
	qui si parrà la tua nobilitate.
Io cominciai: «Poeta che mi guidi,		10
	guarda la mia virtù s'ell' è possente,
	prima ch'a l'alto passo tu mi fidi.
Tu dici che di Silvïo il parente,		13
	corruttibile ancora, ad immortale
	secolo andò, e fu sensibilmente.
Però, se l'avversario d'ogne male		16
	cortese i fu, pensando l'alto effetto
	ch'uscir dovea di lui, e 'l chi e 'l quale,
non pare indegno ad omo d'intelletto,		19
	ch'e' fu de l'alma Roma e di suo impero
	ne l'empireo ciel per padre eletto,

CANTO TWO

To settle Dante's doubts about his worthiness to take the journey, Virgil tells of how **Beatrice** *came down from Heaven to beg his help.*

So the day wore away, and the dark air
   released the living souls that dwell on earth
   from all their labors. I alone remained,
Girding myself to bear and battle through   4
   the journey, and the pity of my heart—
   which memory never straying shall recount.
O Muses, O high genius, help me now!   7
   O memory that engraved the things I saw,
   here shall your worth be manifest to all.
"Poet," I started, "you who guide my steps,   10
   see to my strength, make sure it will suffice,
   before you trust me to so hard a road.
You tell of Silvius' father,° who went down   13
   to the immortal world still in the flesh—
   and with his flesh's senses all aware.
Yet if the Adversary of all evil°   16
   showed him this grace, it does not seem unfit
   to intellects that see the great result,
Both who and what was meant to spring from him;   19
   for he was chosen in the Heaven of heavens
   father of sacred Rome and her command,

° *Silvius' father:* Aeneas. In book 6 of the *Aeneid*, Aeneas goes to the underworld to learn of his own destiny and that of the city Rome, which his people are to found. Virgil's account of that journey provided much of the inspiration for Dante's own poetic journey to the hereafter. Appropriate selections from the *Aeneid* are provided in Appendix A.

° *the Adversary of all evil:* God.

la quale e 'l quale, a voler dir lo vero,   22
  fu stabilita per lo loco santo
  u' siede il successor del maggior Piero.

Per quest' andata onde li dai tu vanto,   25
  intese cose che furon cagione
  di sua vittoria e del papale ammanto.

Andovvi poi lo Vas d'elezïone,   28
  per recarne conforto a quella fede
  ch'è principio a la via di salvazione.

Ma io, perché venirvi? o chi 'l concede?   31
  Io non Enëa, io non Paulo sono;
  me degno a ciò né io né altri 'l crede.

Per che, se del venire io m'abbandono,   34
  temo che la venuta non sia folle.
  Se' savio; intendi me' ch'i' non ragiono».

E qual è quei che disvuol ciò che volle   37
  e per novi pensier cangia proposta,
  sì che dal cominciar tutto si tolle,

tal mi fec' ïo 'n quella oscura costa,   40
  perché, pensando, consumai la 'mpresa
  che fu nel cominciar cotanto tosta.

«S'i' ho ben la parola tua intesa»,   43
  rispuose del magnanimo quell' ombra,
  «l'anima tua è da viltade offesa;

la qual molte fïate l'omo ingombra   46
  sì che d'onrata impresa lo rivolve,
  come falso veder bestia quand' ombra.

Da questa tema acciò che tu ti solve,   49
  dirotti perch' io venni e quel ch'io 'ntesi
  nel primo punto che di te mi dolve.

And these, if we would speak the truth, were set   22
   firmly in place to be the holy throne
   where the successor to great Peter° sits.

Upon this journey which you celebrate   25
   he learned of things which were the cause of both
   his triumph, and the mantle of the pope.

Later, the Chosen Vessel° also went   28
   to bring back comfort, strengthening the faith
   which is the first step on salvation's way.

But I? Who grants my coming? And for what?   31
   I'm not Aeneas, I'm not Saint Paul! No one—
   not I myself—could think me worthy, so

If I should enter on this quest, I fear   34
   it would be mad and foolish. But you're wise,
   you understand more than my words can say."

And as a man who unwills what he wills,   37
   changing his plan for every little thought,
   till he withdraws from any kind of start,

So did I turn my mind on that dark verge,   40
   for thinking ate away the enterprise
   so prompt in the beginning to set forth.

"If I have understood your words aright,"   43
   replied the shade of that greathearted man,
   "your spirit has been bruised by cowardice,

Which many a time so weighs a man's heart down   46
   it turns him from a glorious enterprise—
   as shadows fool the horse that shies away.

That you may slip this worry and go free,   49
   I'll tell you why I came and what I heard
   when first I pitied you your misery.

° *the successor to great Peter:* the pope, tracing his office in a direct line of descent from Saint Peter, the first head of the Church.

° *the Chosen Vessel:* Saint Paul, whom the Lord called his "chosen vessel" for preaching to all nations (Acts 9:15). Paul had a vision of Paradise (2 Cor. 12:1–5); he mentions the vision in order to stir ardent hope and longing for the resurrection. The contents of that vision, naturally, became the subject of much pious imagination. One result, the apocryphal *Vision of Saint Paul,* was widely known, and Dante may have borrowed from it as he borrowed from the *Aeneid.* Selections are provided in Appendix B.

Io era tra color che son sospesi, 52
  e donna mi chiamò beata e bella,
  tal che di comandare io la richiesi.
Lucevan li occhi suoi più che la stella, 55
  e cominciommi a dir soave e piana,
  con angelica voce, in sua favella:
'O anima cortese mantoana, 58
  di cui la fama ancor nel mondo dura,
  e durerà quanto 'l mondo lontana,
l'amico mio, e non de la ventura, 61
  ne la diserta piaggia è impedito
  sì nel cammin, che vòlt' è per paura;
e temo che non sia già sì smarrito, 64
  ch'io mi sia tardi al soccorso levata,
  per quel ch'i' ho di lui nel cielo udito.
Or movi, e con la tua parola ornata 67
  e con ciò c'ha mestieri al suo campare,
  l'aiuta sì ch'i' ne sia consolata.
I' son Beatrice che ti faccio andare. 70
  Vegno del loco ove tornar disio;
  amor mi mosse, che mi fa parlare.
Quando sarò dinanzi al segnor mio, 73
  di te mi loderò sovente a lui'.
  Tacette allora, e poi comincia' io:
'O donna di virtù sola per cui 76
  l'umana spezie eccede ogne contento
  di quel ciel c'ha minor li cerchi sui,
tanto m'aggrada il tuo comandamento, 79
  che l'ubidir, se già fosse, m'è tardi;
  più non t'è uo' ch'aprirmi il tuo talento.
Ma dimmi la cagion che non ti guardi 82
  de lo scender qua giuso in questo centro
  de l'ampio loco ove tornar tu ardi'.

I was among the souls in Limbo° when   52
   so lovely and blest a lady° called to me
   I asked her for the grace of a command.

Her eyes were flashing brighter than the stars,   55
   and she addressed me with an angel's voice,
   sweetly and softly, in such words as these:

'O kind and gracious soul of Mantua,   58
   whom the world still renowns and ever shall,
   whose fame will last as long as earth endures,

The friend I love—and not a fortune-friend—   61
   has been so checked along his journey up
   the desert slope, he has turned back for dread,

And from what I have heard of him in Heaven   64
   I fear he may have wandered so far wrong,
   my rising for his help may come too late.

Go then, and with the beauty of your words,   67
   and any skill you have to set him free,
   help him, that I may be consoled. I am

The blessed Beatrice who bid you go;   70
   love makes me speak, and bade me hasten from
   the place that stirs my longing to return.

When I shall stand before my Lord, I vow   73
   often to speak to him in praise of you.'
   Then she fell silent, and I thus began:

'O lady of that power whereby alone   76
   the human race transcends all mortal things
   dwelling below the circle of the moon,

What you command is such a grace indeed,   79
   it would be late, had I obeyed already!
   Show me your will, for that is all you need.

But tell me why it does not worry you   82
   to descend to this center of the world
   from that vast realm you burn to see again.'

° *Limbo:* Literally, "among the suspended souls." Limbo, deriving from Latin *limbus,* "edge," is a state suspended between salvation and damnation. Dante describes it in Canto Four.
° *so lovely and blest a lady:* Beatrice. Dante puns on her name, which means "the blessed woman." I have brought out the same pun in line 67 below.

'Da che tu vuo' saver cotanto a dentro,   85
   dirotti brievemente', mi rispuose,
   'perch' i' non temo di venir qua entro.

Temer si dee di sole quelle cose   88
   c'hanno potenza di fare altrui male;
   de l'altre no, ché non son paurose.

I' son fatta da Dio, sua mercé, tale,   91
   che la vostra miseria non mi tange,
   né fiamma d'esto 'ncendio non m'assale.

Donna è gentil nel ciel che si compiange   94
   di questo impedimento ov' io ti mando,
   sì che duro giudicio là sù frange.

Questa chiese Lucia in suo dimando   97
   e disse:—Or ha bisogno il tuo fedele
   di te, e io a te lo raccomando—.

Lucia, nimica di ciascun crudele,   100
   si mosse, e venne al loco dov' i' era,
   che mi sedea con l'antica Rachele.

Disse:—Beatrice, loda di Dio vera,   103
   ché non soccorri quei che t'amò tanto,
   ch'uscì per te de la volgare schiera?

Non odi tu la pieta del suo pianto,   106
   non vedi tu la morte che 'l combatte
   su la fiumana ove 'l mar non ha vanto?—.

Al mondo non fur mai persone ratte   109
   a far lor pro o a fuggir lor danno,
   com' io, dopo cotai parole fatte,

venni qua giù del mio beato scanno,   112
   fidandomi del tuo parlare onesto,
   ch'onora te e quei ch'udito l'hanno'.

Poscia che m'ebbe ragionato questo,   115
   li occhi lucenti lagrimando volse,
   per che mi fece del venir più presto,

'Because you wish to know things to the core,'   85
   replied the lady, 'I will tell in brief
   why I am not afraid to enter here.

The only things that justly cause us fear   88
   are those that have the power to do us harm;
   the others, not at all. By the free gift

Of God I have been fashioned in such form,   91
   no misery you feel can touch me now,
   no flame of these hellfires can harrow me.

A gentle Lady in Heaven° was so moved   94
   with pity for that soul whose way is barred,
   she broke the rigid sentence from above.

She called to Lucy,° making this request: 97
   "Your faithful follower now has need of you;
   I give him over to your loving care."

Lucy, the foe of every cruelty,   100
   arose and hastened to the place where I
   sat beside Rachel of the ancient days.

"Beatrice, true praise of God, why do you not   103
   come to the aid of him who loved you so
   that for your sake he left the common crowd?

Do you not hear him weeping piteously?   106
   Do you not see the death he wrestles with
   upon the flood tide violent as the sea?"

No man was ever quicker in the world   109
   to seize his profit or to flee his harm
   than I was, when I heard the words she spoke,

Leaving my blessed seat to come down here   112
   to rest my trust upon your noble speech,
   which honors you and those who heed it well.'

When she had finished speaking to me so,   115
   she turned her glistening eyes all bright with tears—
   which made me all the readier to go,

° *Lady in Heaven:* Mary. In the *Inferno* neither she nor Christ is ever named directly.

° *Lucy:* Saint Lucy (Lucia), a Sicilian virgin martyred under the persecutions of Christians during the reign of Diocletian, in the third century. Perhaps Dante had a special devotion for her, or perhaps he is saying he had a special devotion to the Light of Truth which her name suggests. Lucy assists him in Purgatory, too (*Purg.* 9.52–63).

e venni a te così com' ella volse: 118
   d'inanzi a quella fiera ti levai
   che del bel monte il corto andar ti tolse.

Dunque, che è? perché, perché restai,   121
   perché tanta viltà nel core allette,
   perché ardire e franchezza non hai,

poscia che tai tre donne benedette   124
   curan di te ne la corte del cielo,
   e 'l mio parlar tanto ben ti promette?».

Quali fioretti dal notturno gelo   127
   chinati e chiusi, poi che 'l sol li 'mbianca,
   si drizzan tutti aperti in loro stelo,

tal mi fec' io di mia virtude stanca,   130
   e tanto buono ardire al cor mi corse,
   ch'i' cominciai come persona franca:

«Oh pietosa colei che mi soccorse!   133
   e te cortese ch'ubidisti tosto
   a le vere parole che ti porse!

Tu m'hai con disiderio il cor disposto   136
   sì al venir con le parole tue,
   ch'i' son tornato nel primo proposto.

Or va, ch'un sol volere è d'ambedue: 139
   tu duca, tu segnore e tu maestro».
   Così li dissi; e poi che mosso fue,

intrai per lo cammino alto e silvestro.   142

And so I came to you as she desired, 118
    raising you from the beast that faced you down
    and stole from you the short way up the hill.

What is it, then? Why stand here, why delay? 121
    Why let such cowardice come take your heart?
    Why are you not afire and bold and free,

Seeing that three such ladies blessed in Heaven 124
    care for your healing from their court above,
    and what I tell you holds forth so much good?"

As little flowers shut small and bowed beneath 127
    the frost of night, when the sun brightens them,
    rise open-petaled on their stems upright,

So did my weary courage surge again, 130
    and such sweet boldness rushed into my heart
    I cried out as a man at last set free,

"O lady of compassion and my help! 133
    And you most gracious who obeyed her wish
    soon as you heard the truth she spoke to you!

Your words have put my heart in order now, 136
    kindling so great a longing to set on
    you've turned me to our first intention—go!

Go, for we two now share one will alone: 139
    you are my guide, my teacher, and my lord."
    So did I say to him. Then we set forth,

Taking the deep and savage-wooded path. 142

'PER ME SI VA NE LA CITTÀ DOLENTE,
  PER ME SI VA NE L'ETTERNO DOLORE,
  PER ME SI VA TRA LA PERDUTA GENTE.

GIUSTIZIA MOSSE IL MIO ALTO FATTORE: 4
  FECEMI LA DIVINA PODESTATE,
  LA SOMMA SAPÏENZA E 'L PRIMO AMORE.

DINANZI A ME NON FUOR COSE CREATE   7
  SE NON ETTERNE, E IO ETTERNA DURO.
  LASCIATE OGNE SPERANZA, VOI CH'INTRATE'.

Queste parole di colore oscuro   10
  vid' ïo scritte al sommo d'una porta,
  per ch'io: «Maestro, il senso lor m'è duro».
Ed elli a me, come persona accorta: 13
  «Qui si convien lasciare ogne sospetto;
  ogne viltà convien che qui sia morta.
Noi siam venuti al loco ov' i' t'ho detto   16
  che tu vedrai le genti dolorose
  c'hanno perduto il ben de l'intelletto».
E poi che la sua mano a la mia puose   19
  con lieto volto, ond' io mi confortai,
  mi mise dentro a le segrete cose.

CANTO THREE

*Virgil and Dante enter the **gates of Hell**. There they meet the **small-souled**, those un-named spirits whose cowardice relegates them to the vestibule of the lower world. Pass-ing onward, they come to the **river Acheron**, whose ferryman, **Charon**, ushers the gathered souls to their eternal misery.*

I AM THE WAY INTO THE CITY OF WOE,
I AM THE WAY INTO ETERNAL PAIN,
I AM THE WAY TO GO AMONG THE LOST.

JUSTICE CAUSED MY HIGH ARCHITECT TO MOVE: 4
DIVINE OMNIPOTENCE CREATED ME,
THE HIGHEST WISDOM, AND THE PRIMAL LOVE.

BEFORE ME THERE WERE NO CREATED THINGS   7
BUT THOSE THAT LAST FOREVER—AS DO I.
ABANDON ALL HOPE YOU WHO ENTER HERE.

I saw these words of dark and harsh intent   10
    engraved upon the archway of a gate.
    "Teacher," I said, "their sense is hard for me."
And he to me, as one who read my thoughts: 13
    "Here you must leave distrust and doubt behind,
    here you must put all cowardice to death.
We have come to the place I spoke about,   16
    where you would see the souls who dwell in pain,
    for they have lost the good of intellect."
And after he had laid his hand on mine   19
    with cheerful countenance, strengthening my resolve,
    he led me to the secret things below.

Quivi sospiri, pianti e alti guai 22
 risonavan per l'aere sanza stelle,
 per ch'io al cominciar ne lagrimai.

Diverse lingue, orribili favelle, 25
 parole di dolore, accenti d'ira,
 voci alte e fioche, e suon di man con elle

facevano un tumulto, il qual s'aggira 28
 sempre in quell' aura sanza tempo tinta,
 come la rena quando turbo spira.

E io ch'avea d'orror la testa cinta, 31
 dissi: «Maestro, che è quel ch'i' odo?
 e che gent' è che par nel duol sì vinta?».

Ed elli a me: «Questo misero modo 34
 tegnon l'anime triste di coloro
 che visser sanza 'nfamia e sanza lodo.

Mischiate sono a quel cattivo coro 37
 de li angeli che non furon ribelli
 né fur fedeli a Dio, ma per sé fuoro.

Caccianli i ciel per non esser men belli, 40
 né lo profondo inferno li riceve,
 ch'alcuna gloria i rei avrebber d'elli».

E io: «Maestro, che è tanto greve 43
 a lor che lamentar li fa sì forte?».
 Rispuose: «Dicerolti molto breve.

Questi non hanno speranza di morte, 46
 e la lor cieca vita è tanto bassa,
 che 'nvidïosi son d'ogne altra sorte.

Fama di loro il mondo esser non lassa; 49
 misericordia e giustizia li sdegna:
 non ragioniam di lor, ma guarda e passa».

E io, che riguardai, vidi una 'nsegna 52
 che girando correva tanto ratta,
 che d'ogne posa mi parea indegna;

e dietro le venìa sì lunga tratta 55
 di gente, ch'i' non averei creduto
 che morte tanta n'avesse disfatta.

There sighs and moans and utter wailing swept   22
   resounding through the dark and starless air.
   I heard them for the first time, and I wept.

Shuddering din of strange and various tongues,   25
   sorrowful words and accents pitched with rage,
   shrill and harsh voices, blows of hands with these

Raised up a tumult ever swirling round   28
   in that dark air untinted by a dawn,
   as sand-grains whipping when the whirlwind blows.

Said I—a blind of horror held my brain—   31
   "My Teacher, what are all these cries I hear?
   Who are these people conquered by their pain?"

And he to me: "This state of misery   34
   is clutched by those sad souls whose works in life
   merited neither praise nor infamy.

Here they're thrown in among that petty choir   37
   of angels who were for themselves alone,
   not rebels, and not faithful to the Lord.

Heaven drives them out—to keep its beauty pure,   40
   nor will the deep abyss receive their souls,
   lest they bring glory to the wicked there."

And I: "Teacher, what weighs upon their hearts?   43
   What grief is it that makes them wail so loud?"
   And he responded, "A few words will do.

These souls, immortal, have no hope for death,   46
   and their blind lives crept groveling so low
   they leer with envy at every other lot.

The world allows no rumor of them now.   49
   Mercy and justice hold them in contempt.
   Let's say no more about them. Look, and pass."

And I, beholding, saw a banner fly,   52
   whirling about and racing with such speed
   it seemed that it would scorn to stand, or pause,

And all behind that flag in a long file   55
   so numerous a host of people ran,
   I had not thought death had unmade so many.

Poscia ch'io v'ebbi alcun riconosciuto,   58
   vidi e conobbi l'ombra di colui
   che fece per viltade il gran rifiuto.

Incontanente intesi e certo fui   61
   che questa era la setta d'i cattivi,
   a Dio spiacenti e a' nemici sui.

Questi sciaurati, che mai non fur vivi,   64
   erano ignudi e stimolati molto
   da mosconi e da vespe ch'eran ivi.

Elle rigavan lor di sangue il volto,   67
   che, mischiato di lagrime, a' lor piedi
   da fastidiosi vermi era ricolto.

E poi ch'a riguardar oltre mi diedi,   70
   vidi genti a la riva d'un gran fiume,
   per ch'io dissi: «Maestro, or mi concedi

ch'i' sappia quali sono, e qual costume   73
   le fa di trapassar parer sì pronte,
   com' i' discerno per lo fioco lume».

Ed elli a me: «Le cose ti fier conte   76
   quando noi fermerem li nostri passi
   su la trista riviera d'Acheronte».

Allor con li occhi vergognosi e bassi,   79
   temendo no 'l mio dir li fosse grave,
   infino al fiume del parlar mi trassi.

Ed ecco verso noi venir per nave   82
   un vecchio, bianco per antico pelo,
   gridando: «Guai a voi, anime prave!

Non isperate mai veder lo cielo: 85
   i' vegno per menarvi a l'altra riva
   ne le tenebre etterne, in caldo e 'n gelo.

E tu che se' costì, anima viva,   88
   pàrtiti da cotesti che son morti».
   Ma poi che vide ch'io non mi partiva,

When I had recognized a few of these,   58
    I saw and knew at once the shade of him,
    the craven one,° who made the great denial.

Immediately I understood the truth: 61
    this was the low sect of those paltry souls
    hateful to God and to his enemies.

These worthless wretches who had never lived   64
    were pricked to motion now perpetually
    by flies and wasps that stung their naked limbs

And ran the blood in furrows down their faces,   67
    which, mingled with their tears, fell to their feet,
    where loathsome maggots gathered up the rot.

When I had turned my gaze ahead, I saw   70
    a band of people gathered at the banks
    of a broad river. "Teacher, if you please,

Let me know of those people, and what law   73
    makes them appear so eager to cross over,
    from what I make out through the feeble light."

And he responded, "These things will be made   76
    plain to you when we fix our steps upon
    the melancholy shores of Acheron."°

Then with eyes fallen low and full of shame,   79
    fearing that I had burdened him with talk,
    I held my words until we reached the stream.

And look here—coming at us in a boat,   82
    an old man, hair and lank skin white with age,
    hollering, "Woe to you, you crooked souls!

Give up all hope to look upon the sky!   85
    I come to lead you to the other shore,
    into eternal darkness—fire and ice!

And as for you there, you the living soul,   88
    get away from these others who are dead."
    But when he saw that I would not depart

° *the craven one:* Some critics say it is Pontius Pilate; most agree that it is Pope Celestine V, who abdicated the papacy in 1294. See notes.

° *Acheron:* one of the five rivers of the classical underworld. Three others, Styx, Phlegethon, and Cocytus, Dante will encounter below. All are really stages of the same river (see 14.116–38). The other one, Lethe, he will cross at the top of the Mountain of Purgatory (*Purg.* 28.130).

disse: «Per altra via, per altri porti 91
   verrai a piaggia, non qui, per passare:
   più lieve legno convien che ti porti».

E 'l duca lui: «Caron, non ti crucciare: 94
   vuolsi così colà dove si puote
   ciò che si vuole, e più non dimandare».

Quinci fuor quete le lanose gote 97
   al nocchier de la livida palude,
   che 'ntorno a li occhi avea di fiamme rote.

Ma quell' anime, ch'eran lasse e nude, 100
   cangiar colore e dibattero i denti,
   ratto che 'nteser le parole crude.

Bestemmiavano Dio e lor parenti, 103
   l'umana spezie e 'l loco e 'l tempo e 'l seme
   di lor semenza e di lor nascimenti.

Poi si ritrasser tutte quante insieme, 106
   forte piangendo, a la riva malvagia
   ch'attende ciascun uom che Dio non teme.

Caron dimonio, con occhi di bragia, 109
   loro accennando, tutte le raccoglie;
   batte col remo qualunque s'adagia.

Come d'autunno si levan le foglie 112
   l'una appresso de l'altra, fin che 'l ramo
   vede a la terra tutte le sue spoglie,

similemente il mal seme d'Adamo 115
   gittansi di quel lito ad una ad una,
   per cenni come augel per suo richiamo.

Così sen vanno su per l'onda bruna, 118
   e avanti che sien di là discese,
   anche di qua nuova schiera s'auna.

«Figliuol mio», disse 'l maestro cortese, 121
   «quelli che muoion ne l'ira di Dio
   tutti convegnon qui d'ogne paese,

e pronti sono a trapassar lo rio, 124
   ché la divina giustizia li sprona,
   sì che la tema si volve in disio.

He said, "Another way, another port   91
    will bring your passage to the shore—not here.
    A lighter boat° must carry you across."
"Quit grumbling, Charon," said my guide. "Be still!   94
    No questions—only know that this is willed
    where power is power to do whatever it will."
Then all at once the goatish jowls fell quiet,   97
    those of the rower of that livid swamp,
    whose furious eyes yet flashed with wheels of fire.
But when they heard the old man's cruel words   100
    those naked and exhausted souls turned white,
    gnashing their teeth with fury for their fate—
Hurled blasphemy at God and at their parents,   103
    at the whole human race, the place, the time,
    and the seed of their begetting and their birth.
Then all these people, wailing bitterly,   106
    gathered upon the cursed riverbank
    that awaits each man who does not fear the Lord.
Charon the demon, eyes of fiery coal,   109
    signals them all to get into the boat—
    smacks with his oar the soul that lags behind.
As in the fall when leaves are lifted off,   112
    one drops—another—till the naked branch
    sees all its garment lying on the earth,
So the bad seed of Adam one by one   115
    toss themselves from the shore at Charon's sign,
    as hawks returning to the master's call.
They cross the murky waters, and before   118
    they disembark upon the farther side,
    another throng has gathered at the shore.
My gracious Teacher spoke to me: "My son,   121
    all souls that die beneath the wrath of God
    from every nation here collect in one,
And they are prompt to cross the river, for   124
    Justice Divine so goads and spurs them on,
    that what they fear turns into their desire.

° *a lighter boat:* the ferry from the Tiber's shores to the Mountain of Purgatory (*Purg.* 2.100–5).

Quinci non passa mai anima buona;   127
  e però, se Caron di te si lagna,
  ben puoi sapere omai che 'l suo dir suona».
Finito questo, la buia campagna   130
  tremò sì forte, che de lo spavento
  la mente di sudore ancor mi bagna.
La terra lagrimosa diede vento,   133
  che balenò una luce vermiglia
  la qual mi vinse ciascun sentimento,
e caddi come l'uom cui sonno piglia.   136

No good soul ever passes by these ways,　　　　　　　　　127
　　and so, if Charon rails about you, well—
　　you know how to interpret what he says."
He finished, and the gloomy plains of Hell　　　　　　　130
　　shook with such might that though the terror's past
　　it bathes me in a sweat to think of it.
That tear-drenched land heaved forth a sudden blast,　　133
　　flashing a lightning bolt as red as fire
　　that vanquished all my senses, and I fell
As a man falls whom sleep has overcome.　　　　　　　136

Ruppemi l'alto sonno ne la testa
    un greve truono, sì ch'io mi riscossi
    come persona ch'è per forza desta;
e l'occhio riposato intorno mossi,   4
    dritto levato, e fiso riguardai
    per conoscer lo loco dov' io fossi.
Vero è che 'n su la proda mi trovai   7
    de la valle d'abisso dolorosa
    che 'ntrono accoglie d'infiniti guai.
Oscura e profonda era e nebulosa   10
    tanto che, per ficcar lo viso a fondo,
    io non vi discernea alcuna cosa.
«Or discendiam qua giù nel cieco mondo»,   13
    cominciò il poeta tutto smorto.
    «Io sarò primo, e tu sarai secondo».
E io, che del color mi fui accorto,   16
    dissi: «Come verrò, se tu paventi
    che suoli al mio dubbiare esser conforto?».
Ed elli a me: «L'angoscia de le genti   19
    che son qua giù, nel viso mi dipigne
    quella pietà che tu per tema senti.
Andiam, chè la via lunga ne sospigne».   22
    Così si mise e così mi fé intrare
    nel primo cerchio che l'abisso cigne.

Canto Four

*Dante and Virgil descend into the abyss. They enter the **first of the concentric rings** of Hell, that of **Limbo**, the Rim, where dwell, neither in joy nor in suffering, all unbaptized infants and those men and women who lived virtuously but who lacked the true faith. There they meet **Homer** and the great poets of old, and **Aristotle** and the great philosophers.*

Thunder! a great boom broke into the deep
    sleep in my head and made me shake myself
    as one who is awakened by main force—
Then I stood up and turned my rested eyes   4
    about me, peering steadily, to see
    what kind of place it was where I awoke.
Indeed I found myself upon the brink   7
    of the valley of the sorrowful abyss
    thundering with the roar of endless woe.
So dark it was and deep and bleared with mist,   10
    that though I fixed my gaze upon the bottom
    I still could not discern a single thing.
"Into the blind world let us now descend,"   13
    began the poet, his face as pale as death.
    "I will go first, and you will follow me."
And I—for I had seen his color turn—   16
    replied, "How should I go, when you're afraid,
    you who have been my courage when I doubt?"
"The anguish of the souls who dwell down here,"   19
    he answered me, "has painted in my face
    the pity you have taken to be fear.
We must be moving on. The road is long."   22
    So he set forth, and so he made me enter
    into the first belt circling the abyss.

Quivi, secondo che per ascoltare,   25
    non avea pianto mai che di sospiri
    che l'aura etterna facevan tremare;
ciò avvenia di duol sanza martìri,   28
    ch'avean le turbe, ch'eran molte e grandi,
    d'infanti e di femmine e di viri.
Lo buon maestro a me: «Tu non dimandi   31
    che spiriti son questi che tu vedi?
    Or vo' che sappi, innanzi che più andi,
ch'ei non peccaro; e s'elli hanno mercedi,   34
    non basta, perché non ebber battesmo,
    ch'è porta de la fede che tu credi;
e s'e' furon dinanzi al cristianesmo,   37
    non adorar debitamente a Dio:
    e di questi cotai son io medesmo.
Per tai difetti, non per altro rio,   40
    semo perduti, e sol di tanto offesi
    che sanza speme vivemo in disio».
Gran duol mi prese al cor quando lo 'ntesi,   43
    però che gente di molto valore
    conobbi che 'n quel limbo eran sospesi.
«Dimmi, maestro mio, dimmi, segnore»,   46
    comincia' io per volere esser certo
    di quella fede che vince ogne errore:
«uscicci mai alcuno, o per suo merto   49
    o per altrui, che poi fosse beato?».
    E quei che 'ntese il mio parlar coverto,
rispuose: «Io era nuovo in questo stato,   52
    quando ci vidi venire un possente,
    con segno di vittoria coronato.
Trasseci l'ombra del primo parente,   55
    d'Abèl suo figlio e quella di Noè,
    di Moïsè legista e ubidente;

As far as I could tell from listening, here   25
    there were no wails, but only sighs, that made
    a trembling in the everlasting air.

They rose from sorrow, without punishment,   28
    the sorrow of vast throngs of people there,
    of men and women and of infants too.

"You don't ask," my good Teacher said to me,   31
    "who are these souls you look upon? Before
    you go on in your journey, you must know

They did not sin. If they had merits, these   34
    were not enough—baptism they did not have,
    the one gate to the faith which *you* believe.

And if they lived before the Christian faith,   37
    they did not give God homage as they ought,
    and of these people I myself am one.

For such a falling short, and for no crime,   40
    we all are lost, and suffer only this:
    hopeless, we live forever in desire."

When I heard this, great sorrow seized my heart,   43
    for I saw men of great distinction there
    hovering in Limbo at the edge of Hell.

"Tell me, my Teacher, tell me, my good lord,"   46
    I started—for I wanted to confirm
    the faith that conquers every path that strays,

"Has anyone ever left here by his own   49
    or by another's merits, to be blessed?"
    He heard the meaning mantled by my words

And said, "I had just entered in this state   52
    when I saw coming One° of power and might,
    crowned with the glorious sign of victory.

From us he took the shade of our first father,°   55
    the shades of his son Abel and of Noah,
    of Moses who, obedient, gave the Law,

° *One of power and might:* Christ, in the harrowing of Hell between his death and resurrection. The *sign of victory* is the haloed cross.

° *our first father:* Adam.

Abraàm patrïarca e Davìd re, 58
   Israèl con lo padre e co' suoi nati
   e con Rachele, per cui tanto fé,
e altri molti, e feceli beati. 61
   E vo' che sappi che, dinanzi ad essi,
   spiriti umani non eran salvati».
Non lasciavam l'andar perch' ei dicessi, 64
   ma passavam la selva tuttavia,
   la selva, dico, di spiriti spessi.
Non era lunga ancor la nostra via 67
   di qua dal sonno, quand' io vidi un foco
   ch'emisperio di tenebre vincia.
Di lungi n'eravamo ancora un poco, 70
   ma non sì ch'io non discernessi in parte
   ch'orrevol gente possedea quel loco.
«O tu ch'onori scïenzïa e arte, 73
   questi chi son c'hanno cotanta onranza,
   che dal modo de li altri li diparte?».
E quelli a me: «L'onrata nominanza 76
   che di lor suona sù ne la tua vita,
   grazïa acquista in ciel che sì li avanza».
Intanto voce fu per me udita: 79
   «Onorate l'altissimo poeta;
   l'ombra sua torna, ch'era dipartita».
Poi che la voce fu restata e queta, 82
   vidi quattro grand' ombre a noi venire:
   sembianz' avevan né trista né lieta.
Lo buon maestro cominciò a dire: 85
   «Mira colui con quella spada in mano,
   che vien dinanzi ai tre sì come sire:
quelli è Omero poeta sovrano; 88
   l'altro è Orazio satiro che vene;
   Ovidio è 'l terzo, e l'ultimo Lucano.

Of patriarch Abraham, David the king,   58
    of Israel with his father and his sons
    and Rachel,° whom so long he labored for,
And many others, and he made them blessed.   61
    And I want you to know that, before these,
    salvation came for not one human soul."
We did not leave off walking while he spoke   64
    but went on through the forest all the way—
    I mean the forest thicketed with souls.
We hadn't ventured far from where I'd slept   67
    when there before us blazed a ring of light
    quelling the darkness that surrounded it.
We were still quite a little length away   70
    but close enough for me to see in part
    that people to be honored held that place.
"O you who honor knowledge and all art,   73
    who are these here so favored that they dwell
    distinguished from the manner of the rest?"
And he: "The honored name that still resounds   76
    their glory in your life above has won
    the grace from Heaven that now exalts them here."
And suddenly I heard a voice call out: 79
    "Honor the highest prince of poetry!
    His shade which had departed has returned."
And when the voice had ceased, and all was still,   82
    I saw four mighty shades approaching us
    with neither joy nor sadness in their eyes.
"Behold that shade whose right hand wields the sword,"   85
    my worthy Teacher thus began to say,
    "who comes before the others as their lord.
Homer the sovereign poet is that soul.   88
    Horace the satirist comes after him,
    Ovid comes third, and Lucan is the last.

° *Rachel:* Jacob (*Israel*) worked for Laban for seven years to win his daughter Rachel. But on the wedding night, Laban sent to Jacob's tent Rachel's sister, Leah, instead. The next day Laban agreed to give Rachel to Jacob also, on the condition that he work for him another seven years (Gen. 29:9–30).

Però che ciascun meco si convene 91
   nel nome che sonò la voce sola,
   fannomi onore, e di ciò fanno bene».

Così vid' i' adunar la bella scola 94
   di quel segnor de l'altissimo canto
   che sovra li altri com' aquila vola.

Da ch'ebber ragionato insieme alquanto, 97
   volsersi a me con salutevol cenno,
   e 'l mio maestro sorrise di tanto;

e più d'onore ancora assai mi fenno, 100
   ch'e' sì mi fecer de la loro schiera,
   sì ch'io fui sesto tra cotanto senno.

Così andammo infino a la lumera, 103
   parlando cose che 'l tacere è bello,
   sì com' era 'l parlar colà dov' era.

Venimmo al piè d'un nobile castello, 106
   sette volte cerchiato d'alte mura,
   difeso intorno d'un bel fiumicello.

Questo passammo come terra dura; 109
   per sette porte intrai con questi savi:
   giugnemmo in prato di fresca verdura.

Genti v'eran con occhi tardi e gravi, 112
   di grande autorità ne' lor sembianti:
   parlavan rado, con voci soavi.

Traemmoci così da l'un de' canti, 115
   in loco aperto, luminoso e alto,
   sì che veder si potien tutti quanti.

Colà diritto, sovra 'l verde smalto, 118
   mi fuor mostrati li spiriti magni,
   che del vedere in me stesso m'essalto.

I' vidi Eletra con molti compagni, 121
   tra' quai conobbi Ettor ed Enea,
   Cesare armato con li occhi grifagni.

Vidi Cammilla e la Pantasilea; 124
   da l'altra parte vidi 'l re Latino
   che con Lavina sua figlia sedea.

Because we come together in that name 91
 of 'poet' which the one soul spoke alone,
 they do me honor—and in this do well."
So did I see united that sweet school 94
 of the lord of the most exalted song
 that like an eagle soars above the rest.
When they had talked together for a while 97
 they turned to me, and beckoned me to come,
 bringing a smile unto my Teacher's lips,
And greeted me, and honored me so well 100
 that they included me among their band,
 and made me sixth in that academy.
So we proceeded till we reached the light, 103
 speaking of things best kept in silence here,
 as in that place to speak of them was right.
Before a noble castle then we came. 106
 Seven times it was ringed with lofty walls,
 defended all around by a lovely stream.
Over this stream we passed as on dry land; 109
 then with those sages through the seven gates
 I entered, and we reached a fresh green field,
Where I saw souls whose eyes were grave and slow, 112
 whose looks were marked with great authority.
 Seldom they spoke, and held their voices low.
We drew away to one side of the plain 115
 to a place high and free and filled with light,
 that we might see them all. And there before me
On meadows bright as fine-enameled green, 118
 the spirits of the great were shown to me—
 glory it is, to see what I have seen!
I saw Electra with a numerous train— 121
 among them I knew Hector and Aeneas,
 and, in arms, Caesar with his falcon eye.
I saw Penthesilea and Camilla 124
 there on the other side, and King Latinus,
 who sat beside his child Lavinia.

Vidi quel Bruto che cacciò Tarquino,   127
   Lucrezia, Iulia, Marzïa e Corniglia;
   e solo, in parte, vidi 'l Saladino.

Poi ch'innalzai un poco più le ciglia,   130
   vidi 'l maestro di color che sanno
   seder tra filosofica famiglia.

Tutti lo miran, tutti onor li fanno: 133
   quivi vid' ïo Socrate e Platone,
   che 'nnanzi a li altri più presso li stanno;

Democrito che 'l mondo a caso pone,   136
   Dïogenès, Anassagora e Tale,
   Empedoclès, Eraclito e Zenone;

e vidi il buono accoglitor del quale,   139
   Dïascoride dico; e vidi Orfeo,
   Tulïo e Livio e Seneca morale;

Euclide geomètra e Tolomeo,   142
   Ipocràte, Avicenna e Galïeno,
   Averoìs che 'l gran comento feo.

Io non posso ritrar di tutti a pieno,   145
   però che sì mi caccia il lungo tema,
   che molte volte al fatto il dir vien meno.

La sesta compagnia in due si scema: 148
   per altra via mi mena il savio duca,
   fuor de la queta, ne l'aura che trema.

E vegno in parte ove non è che luca.   151

I saw that Brutus who drove Tarquin out,   127
    Lucretia, Julia, Martia, and Cornelia;
    and sitting by himself, the Saladin.
And when I raised the lashes of my eye   130
    I saw the master of all those who know°
    among his wisdom-seeking family.
All look upon him there, all honor him;   133
    I saw the souls of Socrates and Plato
    where they stood nearer to him than the rest;
Democritus, who posits that the world   136
    is ruled by chance; Thales, Empedocles,
    Zeno, Diogenes, and Heraclitus,
And Anaxagoras, and the good collector   139
    of herbals Dioscorides, and Orpheus,
    Cicero, Livy, moral Seneca,
Geometrician Euclid, Ptolemy,   142
    Hippocrates and Galen, Avicenna,
    and the great Commenter, Averroes.
I give no reckoning of them all—the length   145
    of what I have to do so drives me on,
    often my words fall short of the event.
The company of six is cut by two,   148
    and my wise guide leads me another way,
    out of the quiet, into the trembling air—
Into a place where nothing ever shines.   151

° *the Master of all those who know:* Aristotle, whom Dante considered the greatest of philosophers.

Così discesi del cerchio primaio
     giù nel secondo, che men loco cinghia
     e tanto più dolor, che punge a guaio.
Stavvi Minòs orribilmente, e ringhia: 4
     essamina le colpe ne l'intrata;
     giudica e manda secondo ch'avvinghia.
Dico che quando l'anima mal nata   7
     li vien dinanzi, tutta si confessa,
     e quel conoscitor de le peccata
vede qual loco d'inferno è da essa;   10
     cignesi con la coda tante volte
     quantunque gradi vuol che giù sia messa.
Sempre dinanzi a lui ne stanno molte: 13
     vanno a vicenda ciascuna al giudizio,
     dicono e odono e poi son giù volte.
«O tu che vieni al doloroso ospizio»,   16
     disse Minòs a me quando mi vide,
     lasciando l'atto di cotanto offizio,
«guarda com' entri e di cui tu ti fide.   19
     Non t'inganni l'ampiezza de l'intrare!».
     E 'l duca mio a lui: «Perché pur gride?
Non impedir lo suo fatale andare: 22
     vuolsi così colà dove si puote
     ciò che si vuole, e più non dimandare».

CANTO FIVE

*Now the poets descend into the realm of the damned. After they meet and defy **Minos**, the monstrous judge over all of the entering souls, they enter the **second circle**, that of the lustful. Here they listen to the tale of **Paolo and Francesca**, noble young people murdered in the act of adulterous love.*

So I descended from the outer ring
    down to the next, which belts less space about
    but stings the souls to greater agony.
Horrible Minos grunts there like a bull,   4
    weighs all the sins and sends the wicked down
    according to how far he winds his tail.
I mean that when one born in evil hour   7
    appears before him, he confesses all,
    and then judge Minos, the sin-connoisseur,
Discerns what place in Hell is fit for him: 10
    belts himself with his tail as many times
    as there are grades the sinner must descend.
Ever before him stand a crowd of souls.   13
    They step up one by one to testify,
    they speak and hear and then are flung below.
"You who come to this sanctuary of pain,"   16
    said Minos when he saw me, leaving off
    the duties of so great a role, "beware!
"Watch how you enter and in whom you trust!   19
    Don't be fooled by the broad and easy gate."
    My guide to him: "Enough! Why must you shout?
You shall not bar him, for he comes by fate.   22
    No questions—only know that this is willed
    where power is power to do whatever it will."

PAOLO AND FRANCESCA

Or incomincian le dolenti note   25
    a farmisi sentire, or son venuto
    là dove molto pianto mi percuote.

Io venni in loco d'ogne luce muto,   28
    che mugghia come fa mar per tempesta,
    se da contrari venti è combattuto.

La bufera infernal, che mai non resta,   31
    mena li spirti con la sua rapina;
    voltando e percotendo li molesta.

Quando giungon davanti a la ruina,   34
    quivi le strida, il compianto, il lamento;
    bestemmian quivi la virtù divina.

Intesi ch'a così fatto tormento   37
    enno dannati i peccator carnali,
    che la ragion sommettono al talento.

E come li stornei ne portan l'ali   40
    nel freddo tempo, a schiera larga e piena,
    così quel fiato li spiriti mali

di qua, di là, di giù, di sù li mena;   43
    nulla speranza li conforta mai,
    non che di posa, ma di minor pena.

E come i gru van cantando lor lai,   46
    faccendo in aere di sé lunga riga,
    così vid' io venir, traendo guai,

ombre portate da la detta briga;   49
    per ch'i' dissi: «Maestro, chi son quelle
    genti che l'aura nera sì gastiga?».

«La prima di color di cui novelle   52
    tu vuo' saper», mi disse quelli allotta,
    «fu imperadrice di molte favelle.

I now begin to hear arising wails 25
    of sorrow; I have come where the great cries
    batter me like a wave pounding the shore.
It is a place where all light is struck dumb, 28
    moaning as when high winds from east and west
    wrestle upon the sea in a fierce storm.
That hellish cyclone that can never rest 31
    snatches the spirits up in its driving whirl,
    whisks them about and beats and buffets them,
And when they fall before the ruined slope,° 34
    ah then the shrieking, the laments, the cries!
    then they hurl curses at the power of God.
I learned that such a torment was designed 37
    for the damned who were wicked in the flesh,
    who made their reason subject to desire.
And as a flock of starlings winter-beaten 40
    founder upon their wings in widening turns,
    so did that whirlwind whip those evil souls,
Flinging them here and there and up and down; 43
    nor were they ever comforted by hope—
    no hope for rest, or even lesser pain.
And as the cranes go cawing out their songs, 46
    forming a long streak in the air, I saw
    approaching us and trailing cries of woe
Shades blown our way by the great battling winds, 49
    so I said, "Teacher, tell me, who are those
    spirits so lashed and scourged in the black air?"
"The first among those souls whose history 52
    you wish to hear," he then responded, "was
    empress of men of many languages.

° *the ruined slope:* possibly the gap in the ring through which they once entered into their eternal loss. When they are blown past it, they are reminded of the dreadful first experience of the pain they have chosen. The ruins of Hell are the result of the earthquake that accompanied Christ's death and the harrowing of Hell that followed: "The earth quaked, and the rocks were rent, and the tombs were opened, and many bodies of the saints who had fallen asleep arose" (Matt. 27:51–52).

A vizio di lussuria fu sì rotta,   55
    che libito fé licito in sua legge,
    per tòrre il biasmo in che era condotta.
Ell' è Semiramìs, di cui si legge   58
    che succedette a Nino e fu sua sposa:
    tenne la terra che 'l Soldan corregge.
L'altra è colei che s'ancise amorosa,   61
    e ruppe fede al cener di Sicheo;
    poi è Cleopatràs lussurïosa.
Elena vedi, per cui tanto reo   64
    tempo si volse, e vedi 'l grande Achille,
    che con amore al fine combatteo.
Vedi Parìs, Tristano»; e più di mille   67
    ombre mostrommi e nominommi a dito,
    ch'amor di nostra vita dipartille.
Poscia ch'io ebbi 'l mio dottore udito   70
    nomar le donne antiche e ' cavalieri,
    pietà mi giunse, e fui quasi smarrito.
I' cominciai: «Poeta, volontieri   73
    parlerei a quei due che 'nsieme vanno,
    e paion sì al vento esser leggieri».
Ed elli a me: «Vedrai quando saranno   76
    più presso a noi; e tu allor li priega
    per quello amor che i mena, ed ei verranno».
Sì tosto come il vento a noi li piega,   79
    mossi la voce: «O anime affannate,
    venite a noi parlar, s'altri nol niega!».
Quali colombe dal disio chiamate   82
    con l'ali alzate e ferme al dolce nido
    vegnon per l'aere, dal voler portate,
cotali uscir de la schiera ov' è Dido,   85
    a noi venendo per l'aere maligno,
    sì forte fu l'affettüoso grido.

She had so rotted with the lecher's vice   55
   she altered 'lust' to 'just' by her decree,
   to bleach the scandal that she brought herself.

Semiramis is she, of whom we read   58
   that she was Ninus' heir, his whorish wife;
   she held the land where now the Sultan rules.

Next is that amorous soul° who slew herself   61
   and to Sychaeus' ashes broke her vow;
   then Cleopatra, steeped in lechery.

Helen of Troy then see, for whom ten years   64
   of ill revolved; and see the great Achilles,
   who fell in his last combat, all for love.

See Paris, Tristan . . ." And he pointed out   67
   innumerable shades and named them all,
   whom love had severed from our life on earth.

When I had heard my learned Teacher name   70
   the courtly ladies and the knights of old,
   a whelm of pity left me at a loss,

And "Poet," I began, "I greatly long   73
   to speak to those two shades who fly as one
   and seem so lightly carried on the wind."

And he responded: "You shall see them when   76
   they sail nearer to us; then beg them by
   the love that drives them on, and they will come."

Soon as the wind had swerved their flight our way,   79
   I cried, "O weary spirits, if Another°
   does not forbid it, come and speak with us!"

As turtledoves who heed the loving call—   82
   with firm and lifted wings they shear the air
   and fly to the sweet dovecote, swift of will—

So did they veer away from Dido's flock   85
   and come to us through that malignant air,
   such force had the affection of my cry.

° *that amorous soul:* Dido, queen of Carthage, who fell in love with Aeneas and committed suicide when, at the command of the gods, he left her to journey to Italy. She had vowed to remain loyal to the memory of her murdered husband, *Sychaeus.* Her tragedy is told by Virgil in *Aeneid* 4.
° *Another:* God.

«O animal grazïoso e benigno   88
   che visitando vai per l'aere perso
   noi che tignemmo il mondo di sanguigno,

se fosse amico il re de l'universo,   91
   noi pregheremmo lui de la tua pace,
   poi c'hai pietà del nostro mal perverso.

Di quel che udire e che parlar vi piace,   94
   noi udiremo e parleremo a voi,
   mentre che 'l vento, come fa, ci tace.

Siede la terra dove nata fui   97
   su la marina dove 'l Po discende
   per aver pace co' seguaci sui.

Amor, ch'al cor gentil ratto s'apprende,   100
   prese costui de la bella persona
   che mi fu tolta; e 'l modo ancor m'offende.

Amor, ch'a nullo amato amar perdona,   103
   mi prese del costui piacer sì forte,
   che, come vedi, ancor non m'abbandona.

Amor condusse noi ad una morte.   106
   Caina attende chi a vita ci spense».
   Queste parole da lor ci fuor porte.

Quand' io intesi quell' anime offense,   109
   china' il viso, e tanto il tenni basso,
   fin che 'l poeta mi disse: «Che pense?».

Quando rispuosi, cominciai: «Oh lasso,   112
   quanti dolci pensier, quanto disio
   menò costoro al doloroso passo!».

Poi mi rivolsi a loro e parla' io,   115
   e cominciai: «Francesca, i tuoi martìri
   a lagrimar mi fanno tristo e pio.

Ma dimmi: al tempo d'i dolci sospiri,   118
   a che e come concedette amore
   che conosceste i dubbiosi disiri?».

"O living spirit, courteous and good,   88
    traveling the black night to visit us
    who left the world dyed purple with our blood,
Were He who rules the universe our friend,   91
    we would entreat him, praying for your peace,
    for you have pitied us our twisted fate.
All that you please to hear and speak about   94
    we two will hear and speak with you, as long
    as the wind falls in silence. Where the Po
Rushes with all its tributaries down   97
    to its sea harbor, that it may have peace,
    in that place lies the town where I was born.
Love that flames soonest in the gentle heart   100
    seized him for that sweet body which was snatched
    from me—and how it happened hurts me still.
Love, which allows no loved one not to love,   103
    seized me with such a strong delight in him
    that, as you see, it will not leave me yet.
Love led us to one death. The realm of Cain°   106
    waits for the man who quenched us of our lives."
    Such were the words they offered. And I bowed
My head to hear the story of those souls   109
    and what they suffered, bowed so low, at last
    the poet said, "What are you thinking of?"
When I could speak I thus began, "Alas,   112
    what great desire, what sweet and tender thoughts
    have led these lovers to this woeful pass!"
Turning to them once more, I spoke again.   115
    "Francesca," I began, "your torments move
    my heart to weep in pity for your pain.
But tell me, in the season of sweet sighs,   118
    how did it happen, what made Love give way
    that you should know the truth of your desires?"

° *Cain:* Cain, who slew his brother Abel (Gen. 4:1–16), lends his name to Caina, a region near the bottom of Hell where those who betrayed their kinsmen are punished (Canto Thirty-two, below).

E quella a me: «Nessun maggior dolore 121
   che ricordarsi del tempo felice
   ne la miseria; e ciò sa 'l tuo dottore.

Ma s'a conoscer la prima radice 124
   del nostro amor tu hai cotanto affetto,
   dirò come colui che piange e dice.

Noi leggiavamo un giorno per diletto 127
   di Lancialotto come amor lo strinse;
   soli eravamo e sanza alcun sospetto.

Per più fiate li occhi ci sospinse 130
   quella lettura, e scolorocci il viso;
   ma solo un punto fu quel che ci vinse.

Quando leggemmo il disïato riso 133
   esser basciato da cotanto amante,
   questi, che mai da me non fia diviso,

la bocca mi basciò tutto tremante. 136
   Galeotto fu 'l libro e chi lo scrisse!
   Quel giorno più non vi leggemmo avante».

Mentre che l'uno spirto questo disse, 139
   l'altro piangëa sì che di pietade
   io venni men così com' io morisse,

e caddi come corpo morto cade. 142

And she to me: "There is no greater grief 121
    than to recall a time of happiness
    while plunged in misery—as your Teacher knows.

But if so great a longing urges you 124
    to know about the first root of our love,
    then I will tell you, speaking through my tears.

One day we two were reading for delight 127
    about how love had mastered Lancelot;
    we were alone and innocent and felt

No cause to fear. And as we read, at times 130
    we went pale, as we caught each other's glance,
    but we were conquered by one point alone.

For when we read that the much-longed-for smile° 133
    accepted such a gentle lover's kiss,
    this man, whom nothing will divide from me,

Trembled to place his lips upon my mouth. 136
    A pander was that author, and his book!
    That day we did not read another page."

And all the while one spirit told their tale, 139
    the other wept so sadly that I fell
    for pity of it to a deathlike faint—

and I dropped like a body stricken dead. 142

° *smile:* that of Guinevere, wife of King Arthur.

Al tornar de la mente, che si chiuse
    dinanzi a la pietà d'i due cognati,
    che di trestizia tutto mi confuse,

novi tormenti e novi tormentati   4
    mi veggio intorno, come ch'io mi mova
    e ch'io mi volga, e come che io guati.

Io sono al terzo cerchio, de la piova   7
    etterna, maladetta, fredda e greve;
    regola e qualità mai non l'è nova.

Grandine grossa, acqua tinta e neve   10
    per l'aere tenebroso si riversa;
    pute la terra che questo riceve.

Cerbero, fiera crudele e diversa,   13
    con tre gole caninamente latra
    sovra la gente che quivi è sommersa.

Li occhi ha vermigli, la barba unta e atra,   16
    e 'l ventre largo, e unghiate le mani;
    graffia li spirti ed iscoia ed isquatra.

Urlar li fa la pioggia come cani;   19
    de l'un de' lati fanno a l'altro schermo;
    volgonsi spesso i miseri profani.

Quando ci scorse Cerbero, il gran vermo,   22
    le bocche aperse e mostrocci le sanne;
    non avea membro che tenesse fermo.

Canto Six

After eluding **Cerberus,** *the triple-headed beast of Hell, the poets enter the* **third ring,** *where the* **gluttonous** *are punished in a storm of cold rain. There Dante speaks with* **Ciacco,** *a fellow Florentine, who foretells strife for a city divided by injustice and greed.*

In coming to—my mind had shut its door,
    pitying those two kinsmen and their tale,
    confounding me and covering me with sadness—
I see new forms of torment all about   4
    and new tormented souls wherever I move,
    wherever I turn, wherever I set my gaze.
At the third ring am I, where the rain falls   7
    eternally, accursed, ponderous, cold—
    changeless in rhythm, changeless in quality.
Thick knobs of hail, snow, water foul as ink   10
    pour down forever through the gloomy air
    and soak into the ground to make it stink.
Cerberus the bizarre and cruel beast   13
    with his three gullets barks like a great dog
    over the spirits drowning in that paste.
His eyes are bloody, his scruff is slick and black,   16
    his paunch is huge, his paw-hands clawed like hooks
    to snatch and skin and shred the souls to bits.
The downpour makes the spirits yowl like dogs.   19
    They roll upon one side to shield the other—
    those desecrating wretches turn and turn!
When Cerberus that great worm caught sight of us   22
    he bared his fangs and opened his maws wide,
    his muscles taut and not one holding still.

The Gluttons—Ciacco

E 'l duca mio distese le sue spanne,   25
   prese la terra, e con piene le pugna
   la gittò dentro a le bramose canne.

Qual è quel cane ch'abbaiando agogna,   28
   e si racqueta poi che 'l pasto morde,
   ché solo a divorarlo intende e pugna,

cotai si fecer quelle facce lorde   31
   de lo demonio Cerbero, che 'ntrona
   l'anime sì, ch'esser vorrebber sorde.

Noi passavam su per l'ombre che adona   34
   la greve pioggia, e ponavam le piante
   sovra lor vanità che par persona.

Elle giacean per terra tutte quante,   37
   fuor d'una ch'a seder si levò, ratto
   ch'ella ci vide passarsi davante.

«O tu che se' per questo 'nferno tratto»,   40
   mi disse, «riconoscimi, se sai:
   tu fosti, prima ch'io disfatto, fatto».

E io a lui: «L'angoscia che tu hai   43
   forse ti tira fuor de la mia mente,
   sì che non par ch'i' ti vedessi mai.

Ma dimmi chi tu se' che 'n sì dolente   46
   loco se' messo, e hai sì fatta pena,
   che, s'altra è maggio, nulla è sì spiacente».

Ed elli a me: «La tua città, ch'è piena   49
   d'invidia sì che già trabocca il sacco,
   seco mi tenne in la vita serena.

Voi cittadini mi chiamaste Ciacco.   52
   Per la dannosa colpa de la gola,
   come tu vedi, a la pioggia mi fiacco.

E io anima trista non son sola,   55
   ché tutte queste a simil pena stanno
   per simil colpa». E più non fé parola.

Io li rispuosi: «Ciacco, il tuo affanno   58
   mi pesa sì, ch'a lagrimar mi 'nvita.
   Ma dimmi, se tu sai, a che verranno

My guide spread out his palms and shoveled up   25
    two big fistfuls of mud and chucked them down
    the monster's ravenous funnels. As a dog

Yammering in an agony of greed,   28
    straining to eat and nothing else, shuts up
    soon as he sinks his fangs into his feed,

So did those greasy mugs of Cerberus   31
    the demon, who so thunders at the souls
    they wish they could go deaf. We took our way,

Passing above the shadows in the press   34
    of that thick rain; and fixed our soles upon
    what seemed their persons, but was emptiness.

Each one of them, flat on the earth, lay prone,   37
    until one jerked himself up to a sit
    as soon as he perceived us passing by.

"O you, led through this low world," said the shade,   40
    "look at me well! You may know who I am—
    for you were made before I was unmade."

And I: "Perhaps the anguish you endure   43
    has cast you from my memory, for it seems
    I've never looked upon your face before.

But tell me who you are, sent to a place   46
    so painful, and with such a punishment—
    though some are harsher, none is so unpleasant."

And he to me: "Your city,° so stuffed full   49
    with envy that the sack's mouth spews it up,
    once held me in the calm and sunlit life.

You fellow citizens called me Ciacco—'Hog.'   52
    For that sin of the throat that damns the soul,
    as you can see, I'm flattened by the rain.

And I am not the only sad soul here,   55
    for all these others suffer the same pain
    for the same fault." And he spoke nothing more.

And I responded: "Ciacco, your distress   58
    weighs on my heart and summons me to tears.
    But tell me, if you know, where they will end,

° *Your city:* Florence. Here follows the first of Dante's many invectives against that city.

li cittadin de la città partita;   61
   s'alcun v'è giusto; e dimmi la cagione
   per che l'ha tanta discordia assalita».

E quelli a me: «Dopo lunga tencione   64
   verranno al sangue, e la parte selvaggia
   caccerà l'altra con molta offensione.

Poi appresso convien che questa caggia   67
   infra tre soli, e che l'altra sormonti
   con la forza di tal che testé piaggia.

Alte terrà lungo tempo le fronti,   70
   tenendo l'altra sotto gravi pesi,
   come che di ciò pianga o che n'aonti.

Giusti son due, e non vi sono intesi;   73
   superbia, invidia e avarizia sono
   le tre faville c'hanno i cuori accesi».

Qui puose fine al lagrimabil suono.   76
   E io a lui: «Ancor vo' che mi 'nsegni
   e che di più parlar mi facci dono.

Farinata e 'l Tegghiaio, che fuor sì degni,   79
   Iacopo Rusticucci, Arrigo e 'l Mosca
   e li altri ch'a ben far puoser li 'ngegni,

dimmi ove sono e fa ch'io li conosca,   82
   ché gran disio mi stringe di savere
   se 'l ciel li addolcia o lo 'nferno li attosca».

E quelli: «Ei son tra l'anime più nere;   85
   diverse colpe giù li grava al fondo.
   Se tanto scendi, là i potrai vedere.

Ma quando tu sarai nel dolce mondo,   88
   priegoti ch'a la mente altrui mi rechi:
   più non ti dico e più non ti rispondo».

Li diritti occhi torse allora in biechi;   91
   guardommi un poco e poi chinò la testa:
   cadde con essa a par de li altri ciechi.

Our party-riven city and its people.   61
    Have we a single man of justice there?
    Say why such discord has assailed the town."
And he: "After a struggle long and tense   64
    they'll come to bloodshed, and the backwoods side
    will chase the other out with great offense.
Then by his force° who waits his chance to strike,   67
    that party will collapse within three years.
    The other one then climbs to power again,
And long they hold their foreheads high for pride,   70
    and despite all the cries and accusations,
    they heap great burdens on the other side.
Two men are just, but no one heeds their words.   73
    Avarice, pride, and envy are the three
    principal flames that set their hearts afire."
He put an end here to his grievous speech.   76
    And I to him: "I wish to learn yet—please,
    do me the favor, speak a little more.
Those worthy men Tegghiaio, Farinata,   79
    Jacopo Rusticucci, Arrigo, Mosca,
    the rest who set their minds to merit well,
Say where they are and let me know their state,   82
    for a great longing presses me to know
    if Heaven sweetens or Hell poisons them."
"They dwell among the blackest souls below,"   85
    said he, "weighed to the pit by different faults.
    Go far enough and you will find them all.
But when you have returned to the sweet world,   88
    I beg, remember me to someone there.
    I say no more, and no more will respond."
His eyes that held me rolled a-squint—he stared   91
    at me a moment, hung his head, and fell
    flat with the other sinners, blind as they.

° *by his force:* that of Pope Boniface VIII, lurking in the background, interfering in Florentine politics. See notes for line 65 above.

E 'l duca disse a me: «Più non si desta   94
  di qua dal suon de l'angelica tromba,
  quando verrà la nimica podesta:

ciascun rivederà la trista tomba,   97
  ripiglierà sua carne e sua figura,
  udirà quel ch'in etterno rimbomba».

Sì trapassammo per sozza mistura   100
  de l'ombre e de la pioggia, a passi lenti,
  toccando un poco la vita futura,

per ch'io dissi: «Maestro, esti tormenti   103
  crescerann' ei dopo la gran sentenza,
  o fier minori, o saran sì cocenti?».

Ed elli a me: «Ritorna a tua scïenza,   106
  che vuol, quanto la cosa è più perfetta,
  più senta il bene, e così la doglienza.

Tutto che questa gente maladetta   109
  in vera perfezion già mai non vada,
  di là più che di qua essere aspetta».

Noi aggirammo a tondo quella strada,   112
  parlando più assai ch'i' non ridico;
  venimmo al punto dove si digrada.

Quivi trovammo Pluto, il gran nemico.   115

And my guide said to me: "He wakes no more 94
    till roused by the angelic trump of doom
    when he will go to face the hostile Power.°
Each man shall see again his woeful tomb, 97
    shall reassume his flesh and form, and hear
    his sentence thundering through eternity."
So we passed on through that polluted mix 100
    of soul and slush, with slow and thoughtful steps,
    touching awhile upon the life to come,
And I said, "Teacher, for these torments here— 103
    after the final sentence will they grow,
    or ease a bit, or stew as sharp as now?"
He: "Turn to your philosophy again, 106
    which shows that when a thing at last is whole
    it feels more pleasure—so it feels more pain.
For all that these accursed folk cannot 109
    come to their true perfection and man's end,
    they look to be more 'perfect' then than now."
Down that wide-bending road we took our way, 112
    saying a great deal more than I repeat,
    until we reached the edge of the descent.
There we found Plutus,° the great enemy. 115

° *hostile Power:* Christ, as judge, given authority by the Father (John 5:27).
° *Plutus:* God of wealth, confused even in ancient times with Pluto, king of the underworld. *Enemy* (Italian *nemico*) translates the Hebrew *satan,* "adversary."

«Pape Satàn, pape Satàn aleppe!»,
     cominciò Pluto con la voce chioccia,
     e quel savio gentil, che tutto seppe,

disse per confortarmi: «Non ti noccia   4
     la tua paura; ché, poder ch'elli abbia,
     non ci torrà lo scender questa roccia».

Poi si rivolse a quella 'nfiata labbia,   7
     e disse: "Taci, maledetto lupo!
     consuma dentro te con la tua rabbia.

Non è sanza cagion l'andare al cupo.   10
     Vuolsi ne l'alto, là dove Michele
     fé la vendetta del superbo strupo».

Quali dal vento le gonfiate vele   13
     caggiono avvolte, poi che l'alber fiacca,
     tal cadde a terra la fiera crudele.

Così scendemmo ne la quarta lacca,   16
     pigliando più de la dolente ripa
     che 'l mal de l'universo tutto insacca.

Ahi giustizia di Dio! tante chi stipa   19
     nove travaglie e pene quant' io viddi?
     e perché nostra colpa sì ne scipa?

CANTO SEVEN

*Passing by the jabbering **Plutus**, guardian of the **fourth circle**, Dante and Virgil see where the unnamed **avaricious**, in teams of misers and squanderers, roll huge boulders at one another while jeering at one another's vices. Virgil explains to Dante the role of **Fortune** in the governance of the world. Continuing, they reach the **fifth circle**, the river Styx, where the **wrathful** and the **sullen** are punished.*

"*Pape Satan, pape Satan aleppe!*"
    So Plutus chopped out with his clucking voice,
    and that most gracious sage, aware of all,
Strengthened my heart. "Though he has power enough,   4
    let your fears never lead you to dismay.
    He won't prevent our going down this bluff."
Then he turned back to face those blood-puffed lips   7
    and said, "Shut up, you cursed wolf of Hell!
    Swallow your rage and let it gnaw your guts!
His passage to the hollows has its cause.   10
    It is willed from on high, whence Michael brought
    vengeance against the arrogant revolt."°
As in a fresh breeze when a ship's mast snaps,   13
    the sails once puffed and stretched fall in a heap;
    so did that cruel beast drop to the earth.
So we descended into the fourth purse,   16
    taking more of that sad embankment which
    bags all the evil of the universe.
Justice of God! Who else but you crams in   19
    all of the strange new toils and pains I saw?
    And why are we so laid to waste in sin?

° *the arrogant revolt:* led by Satan and punished by the archangel Michael (Rev. 12:7–12).

Come fa l'onda là sovra Cariddi, 22
   che si frange con quella in cui s'intoppa,
   così convien che qui la gente riddi.

Qui vid' i' gente più ch'altrove troppa, 25
   e d'una parte e d'altra, con grand' urli,
   voltando pesi per forza di poppa.

Percotëansi 'ncontro; e poscia pur lì 28
   si rivolgea ciascun, voltando a retro,
   gridando: «Perché tieni?» e «Perché burli?».

Così tornavan per lo cerchio tetro 31
   da ogne mano a l'opposito punto,
   gridandosi anche loro ontoso metro;

poi si volgea ciascun, quand' era giunto, 34
   per lo suo mezzo cerchio a l'altra giostra.
   E io, ch'avea lo cor quasi compunto,

dissi: «Maestro mio, or mi dimostra 37
   che gente è questa, e se tutti fuor cherci
   questi chercuti a la sinistra nostra».

Ed elli a me: «Tutti quanti fuor guerci 40
   sì de la mente in la vita primaia,
   che con misura nullo spendio ferci.

Assai la voce lor chiaro l'abbaia, 43
   quando vegnono a' due punti del cerchio
   dove colpa contraria li dispaia.

Questi fuor cherci, che non han coperchio 46
   piloso al capo, e papi e cardinali,
   in cui usa avarizia il suo soperchio».

E io: «Maestro, tra questi cotali 49
   dovre' io ben riconoscere alcuni
   che furo immondi di cotesti mali».

Ed elli a me: «Vano pensiero aduni. 52
   La sconoscente vita che i fé sozzi,
   ad ogne conoscenza or li fa bruni.

As at Charybdis° when two sea waves wheel   22
   head-on and smash over the whirlpool—so
   the people in this ring must dance their reel.

I saw far more than I had elsewhere seen,   25
   howling on one side, howling on the other,
   popping their chests to roll enormous weights.

They slammed those stones together front to front,   28
   then straight off each side turned about and yelled,
   "Why do you fritter?" "Why the fists so tight?"

So in the dismal circle they went round   31
   on either hand to the point opposite,
   bellowing out their poetry of shame,

And when they'd gotten halfway round the ring,   34
   they turned around to have another joust.
   And I said, for my heart was nearly pierced,

"My Teacher, show me who these people are,   37
   and let me know if they were all ordained,
   those on our left with hair clipped like a clerk's."°

And he to me: "In the first life, each soul   40
   you see here was so cross-eyed in his mind,
   he held no measure when he saved or spent.

Their voices yap that judgment loud enough   43
   when they come to the two points of the ring,
   where their opposing vices split them off.

Those whose heads have no cap of hair to crop   46
   were all clerks, even popes and cardinals,
   whom avarice browbeats, bullying to the top."

"Teacher," said I, "among this mob of such,   49
   I'll wager I can recognize a few
   who got their fingers dirty in this sin!"

And he: "Forget it, it's an empty thought.   52
   The nothing-knowing life that made them foul
   dims them beyond all recognition now.

° *Charybdis:* the fabulous monster inhabiting a whirlpool in the straits between Italy and Sicily; see notes.

° *hair clipped like a clerk's:* the tonsure of a cleric, leaving the top of the head bald.

In etterno verranno a li due cozzi: 55
  questi resurgeranno del sepulcro
  col pugno chiuso, e questi coi crin mozzi.

Mal dare e mal tener lo mondo pulcro   58
  ha tolto loro, e posti a questa zuffa:
  qual ella sia, parole non ci appulcro.

Or puoi, figliuol, veder la corta buffa   61
  d'i ben che son commessi a la fortuna,
  per che l'umana gente si rabuffa;

ché tutto l'oro ch'è sotto la luna   64
  e che già fu, di quest' anime stanche
  non poterebbe farne posare una».

«Maestro mio», diss' io, «or mi dì anche: 67
  questa fortuna di che tu mi tocche,
  che è, che i ben del mondo ha sì tra branche?».

E quelli a me: «Oh creature sciocche,   70
  quanta ignoranza è quella che v'offende!
  Or vo' che tu mia sentenza ne 'mbocche.

Colui lo cui saver tutto trascende,   73
  fece li cieli e diè lor chi conduce
  sì, ch'ogne parte ad ogne parte splende,

distribuendo igualmente la luce.   76
  Similemente a li splendor mondani
  ordinò general ministra e duce

che permutasse a tempo li ben vani   79
  di gente in gente e d'uno in altro sangue,
  oltre la difension d'i senni umani;

per ch'una gente impera e l'altra langue,   82
  seguendo lo giudicio di costei,
  che è occulto come in erba l'angue.

Vostro saver non ha contasto a lei: 85
  questa provede, giudica, e persegue
  suo regno come il loro li altri dèi.

They will butt head to head forevermore.   55
    From the tomb these will rise with their fists shut,
    and these with half the hair ripped from their scalps.

Ill-giving and ill-keeping snatched from them   58
    the lovely world, and set them in this brawl.
    I will not prettify it by my words.

Now you can see, my son, how short a jest   61
    are the good things assigned to Fortune's care—
    for which the human race squabble and squall,

For all the gold that lies beneath the moon   64
    and all that has, could never give a moment
    of rest to one of these exhausted souls."

"My Teacher," I said then, "tell me this too.   67
    What is that Fortune you have touched upon,
    that holds the world's goods in so fierce a clutch?"

And he: "Oh you are simpletons indeed!   70
    How deep the ignorance that injures you!
    I'll give you the bare truth, that you may feed.

He whose transcendent wisdom passes all   73
    fashioned the heavens and gave each sphere a guide°
    that every part might shine to every part,

Distributing the splendor equally.   76
    Similarly for things that shine on earth
    He chose a general minister° and guide

To scramble now and then the empty goods   79
    from race to race, from one blood to another,
    past all defense man's shrewdness might devise,

And so this nation rises to command   82
    and that one droops, just as her judgments please—
    as hidden as a serpent in the grass.

Your wisdom cannot duel hers: she sees   85
    ahead, she judges, and she follows through
    in her realm as the other heavenly powers

° *guide:* a so-called intelligence, which Dante identifies as an angel, to govern each of the planetary spheres and the influences that those spheres were thought to shed upon the worlds below.
° *general minister:* Fortune.

Le sue permutazion non hanno triegue: 88
   necessità la fa esser veloce;
   sì spesso vien chi vicenda consegue.
Quest' è colei ch'è tanto posta in croce   91
   pur da color che le dovrien dar lode,
   dandole biasmo a torto e mala voce;
ma ella s'è beata e ciò non ode.   94
   Con l'altre prime creature lieta
   volve sua spera e beata si gode.
Or discendiamo omai a maggior pieta;   97
   già ogne stella cade che saliva
   quand' io mi mossi, e 'l troppo star si vieta».
Noi ricidemmo il cerchio a l'altra riva   100
   sovr' una fonte che bolle e riversa
   per un fossato che da lei deriva.
L'acqua era buia assai più che persa;   103
   e noi, in compagnia de l'onde bige,
   intrammo giù per una via diversa.
In la palude va c'ha nome Stige   106
   questo tristo ruscel, quand' è disceso
   al piè de le maligne piagge grige.
E io, che di mirare stava inteso,   109
   vidi genti fangose in quel pantano,
   ignude tutte, con sembiante offeso.
Queste si percotean non pur con mano,   112
   ma con la testa e col petto e coi piedi,
   troncandosi co' denti a brano a brano.
Lo buon maestro disse: «Figlio, or vedi   115
   l'anime di color cui vinse l'ira;
   e anche vo' che tu per certo credi
che sotto l'acqua è gente che sospira,   118
   e fanno pullular quest' acqua al summo,
   come l'occhio ti dice, u' che s'aggira.

In theirs. Her many changes know no truce;   88
    she must go swiftly, by necessity—
    so many men step up to take their turn!

She is the one so cursed and crucified   91
    by the same people who should give her praise,
    slanderously accusing her of wrong,

But she is blessed, and she does not hear.   94
    With all the other creatures fashioned first°
    she dwells in gladness and she turns her sphere.

Let us descend to greater misery now,   97
    for every star is sinking which had climbed
    when I set out. We must not stay too long."

We cut the circle to the other bank,   100
    passing a spring that boiled and bubbled over
    into a trench that led the stream away.

Dark was that water, of a purplish black,   103
    and we companions of its murky waves
    walked down below along its cursed track.

It flows into a swamp whose name is Styx,°   106
    this gloomy little brook, descending to
    the bottom of the gray, malignant slope.

And I, who gazed intently as I stood,   109
    saw people in that slough all slimed with mud,
    stripped naked, and their faces torn with rage.

They thumped each other not with hands alone   112
    but with the head, the chest, the feet, the teeth!—
    snapping to rip each other limb from limb.

"Son," my good Teacher said, "now you may see   115
    the souls of those whom wrath has overcome,
    and you should take it for a certainty

That underwater here are souls who sigh   118
    and make the river bubble to the top,
    as you may see wherever you turn your eye.

° *creatures fashioned first:* the angels. God created Fortune even before He created the earthly things at her disposal.

° *Styx:* one of the rivers of the classical underworld.

Fitti nel limo dicon: "Tristi fummo   121
   ne l'aere dolce che dal sol s'allegra,
   portando dentro accidïoso fummo:
or ci attristiam ne la belletta negra".   124
   Quest' inno si gorgoglian ne la strozza,
   ché dir nol posson con parola integra».
Così girammo de la lorda pozza   127
   grand' arco, tra la ripa secca e 'l mézzo,
   con li occhi vòlti a chi del fango ingozza.
Venimmo al piè d'una torre al da sezzo.   130

Stuck in the mire they say: 'Sullen we were   121
   up in the sweet air gladdened by the sun,
   bearing a sluggish smoke within our hearts.
Now we are sullen in this black bog here.'   124
   Such is the hymn they gargle in the throat.
   They cannot get the words out whole and clear."
So in a wide arc we walked round that pond   127
   between the dry slope and the rotten squelch,
   eyes turned upon the souls who gulped down mud.
To the foot of a tower at last we came.   130

Io dico, seguitando, ch'assai prima
   che noi fossimo al piè de l'alta torre,
   li occhi nostri n'andar suso a la cima
per due fiammette che i vedemmo porre,   4
   e un'altra da lungi render cenno,
   tanto ch'a pena il potea l'occhio tòrre.
E io mi volsi al mar di tutto 'l senno;   7
   dissi: «Questo che dice? e che risponde
   quell' altro foco? e chi son quei che 'l fenno?».
Ed elli a me: «Su per le sucide onde   10
   già scorgere puoi quello che s'aspetta,
   se 'l fummo del pantan nol ti nasconde».
Corda non pinse mai da sé saetta   13
   che sì corresse via per l'aere snella,
   com' io vidi una nave piccioletta
venir per l'acqua verso noi in quella,   16
   sotto 'l governo d'un sol galeoto,
   che gridava: «Or se' giunta, anima fella!».
«Flegïàs, Flegïàs, tu gridi a vòto»,   19
   disse lo mio segnore, «a questa volta:
   più non ci avrai che sol passando il loto».

Canto Eight

*The poets are ferried over the **Styx** by the boatman **Phlegyas**. On their way they meet the angry **Filippo Argenti**, drive him off when he tries to harass them, and watch in pleasure as the others rip him to pieces. Finally they land at the shores of inner Hell, outside the walls of the city of **Dis**, where they are refused entry by the fallen angels.*

Continuing, I say that long before
 we'd arrived at the foot of the high tower,
 we raised our eyes up to the top—for there
Were placed two little lights, and in reply   4
 another signal flickered far away,
 so far the eye could hardly make it out.
To the sea of all wisdom° then I turned: 7
 "What does this signal mean? That other fire,
 what answer does it give? Who's sending them?"
"Over the nasty water you can find   10
 already what we're waiting for," said he,
 "if the bog's fumes don't hide it from your sight."
No arrow shot a-whistling from the cord   13
 could ever fly so swiftly through the air
 as in that instant a small boat I saw
Coming in our direction on the water,   16
 one oarsman only at her helm, who cried,
 "Traitor! I've got you now, you wicked soul!"
"Phlegyas, Phlegyas, holler all you want!"   19
 my lord replied. "This time it's all in vain.
 You'll have us only while we cross the slough."

° *the sea of all wisdom:* Virgil. Dante puns on Italian *mare,* "sea," and *Maro,* Virgil's clan name.

THE STYX—PHLEGYAS

Qual è colui che grande inganno ascolta 22
   che li sia fatto, e poi se ne rammarca,
   fecesi Flegïàs ne l'ira accolta.

Lo duca mio discese ne la barca, 25
   e poi mi fece intrare appresso lui;
   e sol quand' io fui dentro parve carca.

Tosto che 'l duca e io nel legno fui, 28
   segando se ne va l'antica prora
   de l'acqua più che non suol con altrui.

Mentre noi corravam la morta gora, 31
   dinanzi mi si fece un pien di fango,
   e disse: «Chi se' tu che vieni anzi ora?».

E io a lui: «S'i' vegno, non rimango. 34
   Ma tu chi se', che sì se' fatto brutto?».
   Rispuose: «Vedi che son un che piango».

E io a lui: «Con piangere e con lutto, 37
   spirito maladetto, ti rimani,
   ch'i' ti conosco, ancor sie lordo tutto».

Allor distese al legno ambo le mani; 40
   per che 'l maestro accorto lo sospinse,
   dicendo: «Via costà con li altri cani!».

Lo collo poi con le braccia mi cinse; 43
   basciommi 'l volto e disse: «Alma sdegnosa,
   benedetta colei che 'n te s'incinse!

Quei fu al mondo persona orgogliosa; 46
   bontà non è che sua memoria fregi:
   così s'è l'ombra sua qui furïosa.

Quanti si tegnon or là sù gran regi 49
   che qui staranno come porci in brago,
   di sé lasciando orribili dispregi!».

E io: «Maestro, molto sarei vago 52
   di vederlo attuffare in questa broda
   prima che noi uscissimo del lago».

Ed elli a me: «Avante che la proda 55
   ti si lasci veder, tu sarai sazio:
   di tal disïo convien che tu goda».

As when a man who hears of a big fraud   22
    pulled off on him resents it, seethes with grief—
    so Phlegyas chafed, his anger shut inside.

After my guide went down into the boat   25
    he bade me enter too, and only then
    did the craft seem to carry any weight.

Soon as my guide and I were in the skiff   28
    that ancient prow went cutting through more water
    than when it ferried other souls across.

While we were racing over the dead pond,   31
    before me rose a spirit full of slime—
    "And who are you, who come before your hour?"

And I to him: "I've come, but not to stay.   34
    But who are you, made ugly by such filth?"
    "Look for yourself!" said he. "I'm one who weeps."

And I to him: "Well, then, accursed spirit,   37
    keep to your weeping and your misery!
    I know you, fouled and mucked though you may be."

Then he flung out both hands to grab the skiff—   40
    at that my wary Teacher shoved him off,
    "Get out of here! Run with the other dogs!"

Then round my neck he clasped me in his arms   43
    and kissed my face and said, "Indignant soul!
    Blessed be she whose womb bore fruit in you!

That man on earth was full of arrogance.   46
    No good or gracious deed adorns his name—
    and so his shade is full of fury here.

Up there how many think themselves great kings   49
    who will be stuck like swine here in this sty,
    leaving a name to spit on in contempt."

"Teacher, I've got a hankering," said I,   52
    "to see them dunk that spirit in this swill
    before we leave the lake and disembark."

And he replied, "You will enjoy your fill   55
    before the farther beach comes into sight.
    Such a desire is good to satisfy."

Dopo ciò poco vid' io quello strazio   58
  far di costui a le fangose genti,
  che Dio ancor ne lodo e ne ringrazio.
Tutti gridavano: «A Filippo Argenti!»;   61
  e 'l fiorentino spirito bizzarro
  in sé medesmo si volvea co' denti.
Quivi il lasciammo, che più non ne narro;   64
  ma ne l'orecchie mi percosse un duolo,
  per ch'io avante l'occhio intento sbarro.
Lo buon maestro disse: «Omai, figliuolo,   67
  s'appressa la città c'ha nome Dite,
  coi gravi cittadin, col grande stuolo».
E io: «Maestro, già le sue meschite   70
  là entro certe ne la valle cerno,
  vermiglie come se di foco uscite
fossero». Ed ei mi disse: «Il foco etterno   73
  ch'entro l'affoca le dimostra rosse,
  come tu vedi in questo basso inferno».
Noi pur giugnemmo dentro a l'alte fosse   76
  che vallan quella terra sconsolata:
  le mura mi parean che ferro fosse.
Non sanza prima far grande aggirata,   79
  venimmo in parte dove il nocchier forte
  «Usciteci», gridò: «qui è l'intrata».
Io vidi più di mille in su le porte   82
  da ciel piovuti, che stizzosamente
  dicean: «Chi è costui che sanza morte
va per lo regno de la morta gente?».   85
  E 'l savio mio maestro fece segno
  di voler lor parlar segretamente.
Allor chiusero un poco il gran disdegno   88
  e disser: «Vien tu solo, e quei sen vada
  che sì ardito intrò per questo regno.
Sol si ritorni per la folle strada: 91
  pruovi, se sa; ché tu qui rimarrai,
  che li ha' iscorta sì buia contrada».

Soon after that I saw the mud-melee   58
    rake him apart just as I could have wished—
    for which I praise and thank God to this day.

"Get Filippo Argenti!" they all yelled,   61
    and that short-tempered shade from Florence turned
    gnashing his teeth against his peevish self.

We left him there—of him I tell no more,   64
    but such a cry of grief pounded my ears
    I fixed my gaze wide-eyed to see the shore.

The good Teacher advised me, "Now, my son,   67
    we draw near to the city they call Dis,
    with its great hosts, with its grave citizens."

"Teacher," said I, "already I discern   70
    the turrets of its mosques behind the moat.
    Like iron from the forge they glow and burn."

And he replied, "The everlasting flames   73
    its heart ignites make it as red as fire,
    flaring within these nether depths of Hell."

We sped along into the deep-trenched moats   76
    that fortify that never-solaced land;
    the city seemed to loom with iron walls.

Not without taking first a long turn round   79
    we came to where the strapping boatman cried,
    "Out! Here's the entrance—here's where you get off!"

More than a thousand of those angels rained   82
    from Heaven I saw upon the garrison,
    jeering, "Who's this who has no death to show

But travels through the kingdom of the dead?"   85
    And my wise Teacher made a sign to say
    that he desired to speak with them aside.

More closely then they played their mighty scorn   88
    and said, "You come alone, and let him go
    who was so hot to come into this reign.

Let him go back alone on his mad way!   91
    Let him try, if he can. For you who've led
    him down so dark a country—here you'll stay."

Pensa, lettor, se io mi sconfortai 94
   nel suon de le parole maladette,
   ché non credetti ritornarci mai.

«O caro duca mio, che più di sette 97
   volte m'hai sicurtà renduta e tratto
   d'alto periglio che 'ncontra mi stette,

non mi lasciar», diss' io, «così disfatto; 100
   e se 'l passar più oltre ci è negato,
   ritroviam l'orme nostre insieme ratto».

E quel segnor che lì m'avea menato, 103
   mi disse: «Non temer; ché 'l nostro passo
   non ci può tòrre alcun: da tal n'è dato.

Ma qui m'attendi, e lo spirito lasso 106
   conforta e ciba di speranza buona,
   ch'i' non ti lascerò nel mondo basso».

Così sen va, e quivi m'abbandona 109
   lo dolce padre, e io rimagno in forse,
   che sì e no nel capo mi tenciona.

Udir non potti quello ch'a lor porse; 112
   ma ei non stette là con essi guari,
   che ciascun dentro a pruova si ricorse.

Chiuser le porte que' nostri avversari 115
   nel petto al mio segnor, che fuor rimase
   e rivolsesi a me con passi rari.

Li occhi a la terra e le ciglia avea rase 118
   d'ogne baldanza, e dicea ne' sospiri:
   «Chi m'ha negate le dolenti case!».

E a me disse: «Tu, perch' io m'adiri, 121
   non sbigottir, ch'io vincerò la prova,
   qual ch'a la difension dentro s'aggiri.

Questa lor tracotanza non è nova; 124
   ché già l'usaro a men segreta porta,
   la qual sanza serrame ancor si trova.

Consider, Reader, whether I was not   94
   distressed on hearing those accursed words!
   For I believed I never would return.
"Beloved guide, you who have given me   97
   assurance seven times and more and saved
   me from the greatest dangers in my way,"
Said I, "don't leave me so undone and lost!   100
   If we are not permitted to go on,
   let's trace our footsteps back again at once!"
And that lord who had guided me so far   103
   said, "Have no fear. No one can take from us
   our passage on—granted by One° so great.
Wait for me here, and feed upon good hope   106
   to fortify your soul in its fatigue.
   I will not leave you in the lower world."
So saying, the sweet father goes his way,   109
   leaves me behind, while I remain in doubt,
   with yes and no at combat in my head.
I couldn't hear the words he put to them,   112
   but not long would they stand with him in place
   when back inside the gates they scrambled, where
Our adversaries slammed them in the face   115
   of my good master, who remained outside
   and turned to me with slow and measured steps.
His eyes were bowed to earth, his brow was shorn   118
   of all his boldness as he sighed and said,
   "Who are these here to block my going down
To the houses of pain? But you"—to me—   121
   "ignore my anger. No dismay. They'll bustle
   to fight it, but I'll have the victory.
This insolence of theirs is nothing new.   124
   They showed it once at a less secret gate,°
   whose locks and bars stand broken even now.

° *One:* God; perhaps also Beatrice, as permitted by God. See Rom. 8:31: "If God is for us, who is against us?"
° *a less secret gate:* the gates of Hell; see notes.

Sovr' essa vedestù la scritta morta: 127
    e già di qua da lei discende l'erta,
    passando per li cerchi sanza scorta,
tal che per lui ne fia la terra aperta».   130

On it are etched those words of death you saw.   127
   Already someone's° coming down the slope,
   passing through all the rings without a guide—
One who will breach these city gates for us."   130

° *someone:* the angel of the next canto.

Quel color che viltà di fuor mi pinse
   veggendo il duca mio tornare in volta,
   più tosto dentro il suo novo ristrinse.
Attento si fermò com' uom ch'ascolta;   4
   ché l'occhio nol potea menare a lunga
   per l'aere nero e per la nebbia folta.
«Pur a noi converrà vincer la punga»,   7
   cominciò el, «se non . . . Tal ne s'offerse.
   Oh quanto tarda a me ch'altri qui giunga!».
I' vidi ben sì com' ei ricoperse   10
   lo cominciar con l'altro che poi venne,
   che fur parole a le prime diverse;
ma nondimen paura il suo dir dienne,   13
   perch' io traeva la parola tronca
   forse a peggior sentenzia che non tenne.
«In questo fondo de la trista conca   16
   discende mai alcun del primo grado,
   che sol per pena ha la speranza cionca?».
Questa question fec' io; e quei «Di rado   19
   incontra», mi rispuose, «che di noi
   faccia il cammino alcun per qual io vado.

Canto Nine

*Waiting for the **angel from Heaven**, the poets see the **Furies** upon the ramparts and hear them call for the Gorgon, **Medusa**, the sight of whom would turn a man to stone. Virgil shields Dante from looking at her. At last the angel arrives and opens the gates. Dante and Virgil now enter the **sixth circle**, where the **heretics** are confined to tombs of fire.*

That hue of cowardice which blanched upon
    my countenance when I saw my leader turn,
    all the more swiftly checked it in his own.
He held himself as one who listens hard,   4
    for the eye could not travel very far
    through that black air and through those briars of fog.
"Yet it must be—we have to win this fight.   7
    If not—but such a person offered it!
    How long it seems before our helper comes!"
I saw well how he covered up again,   10
    veiling his start with what came afterward,
    choosing words very different from the first,
But still I was dismayed by what he said.   13
    It could be that I drew from his clipped speech
    a meaning darker than its true intent.
"Down to the bottom of this dismal shell   16
    has anyone descended from the rim,
    whose severed hope° is his sole pain in Hell?"
I asked this question. "Rarely," he replied,   19
    "it comes about that one of us will make
    the journey here along the path I take.

° *severed hope:* more literally, "hobbled" or "crippled." Dante refers to those who dwell in Limbo, where one is punished only by hopelessness. He is trying to ask Virgil, tactfully, whether the journey is new to him, too.

Ver è ch'altra fïata qua giù fui,   22
 congiurato da quella Eritón cruda
 che richiamava l'ombre a' corpi sui.

Di poco era di me la carne nuda,   25
 ch'ella mi fece intrar dentr' a quel muro,
 per trarne un spirto del cerchio di Giuda.

Quell' è 'l più basso loco e 'l più oscuro,   28
 e 'l più lontan dal ciel che tutto gira:
 ben so 'l cammin, però ti fa sicuro.

Questa palude che 'l gran puzzo spira   31
 cigne dintorno la città dolente,
 u' non potemo intrare omai sanz' ira».

E altro disse, ma non l'ho a mente,   34
 però che l'occhio m'avea tutto tratto
 ver' l'alta torre a la cima rovente,

dove in un punto furon dritte ratto   37
 tre furïe infernal di sangue tinte,
 che membra feminine avieno e atto,

e con idre verdissime eran cinte;   40
 serpentelli e ceraste avien per crine,
 onde le fiere tempie erano avvinte.

E quei, che ben conobbe le meschine   43
 de la regina de l'etterno pianto,
 «Guarda», mi disse, «le feroci Erine.

Quest' è Megera dal sinistro canto;   46
 quella che piange dal destro è Aletto;
 Tesifón è nel mezzo»; e tacque a tanto.

Con l'unghie si fendea ciascuna il petto;   49
 battiensi a palme e gridavan sì alto,
 ch'i' mi strinsi al poeta per sospetto.

It's true that I've come down here once before,   22
    conjured to by the cruel witch Erichtho,
    who summoned souls to animate the corpse.

My flesh had not been stripped of me for long   25
    when I was forced to come inside these walls
    to drag a spirit back from Judas' ring.

That is the lowest and the blackest place,   28
    the farthest from the Heaven that turns all things.°
    I know the journey well, so rest assured.

This quagmire which exhales so great a stink   31
    runs like a belt around the city of woe,
    which we can't enter without anger now."

He said more, which my mind cannot recall,   34
    because my eyes were wholly focused on
    the lofty tower up to the searing top,

Where in a moment there had risen erect   37
    three hellish Furies dyed and stained in blood,
    members and gestures of the female sex,

Gartered with greenest hydras° round their waists;   40
    adders and small horned vipers formed their hair,
    twisting about the temples of those beasts.

And he, who knew those shabby handmaids of   43
    Hecate, queen of everlasting woe,
    said to me, "See the fierce Erinyes° there!

Mègara is the Fury on the left;   46
    she is Alecto wailing on the right;
    Tisiphone in the center." That was all.

And each one clawed her nails to cleave her chest,   49
    beat her breasts with her palms and shrieked so loud
    I flinched, and to the poet's side I pressed.

° *the Heaven that turns all things:* the Primum Mobile, or First Mover, the sphere that, in the Ptole-
maic system adopted by Christianity, imparts its motion to all the heavenly spheres beneath. The
center of the earth is the farthest point from it, and thus the furthest from blessedness.

° *hydras:* in ancient lore, lovely and venomous serpents that lived in the sea.

° *Erinyes:* the Furies; see note on line 38 above.

«Vegna Medusa: sì 'l farem di smalto»,   52
   dicevan tutte riguardando in giuso;
   «mal non vengiammo in Tesëo l'assalto».

«Volgiti 'n dietro e tien lo viso chiuso,   55
   ché se 'l Gorgón si mostra e tu 'l vedessi,
   nulla sarebbe di tornar mai suso».

Così disse 'l maestro, ed elli stessi   58
   mi volse, e non si tenne a le mie mani,
   che con le sue ancor non mi chiudessi.

O voi ch'avete li 'ntelletti sani,   61
   mirate la dottrina che s'asconde
   sotto 'l velame de li versi strani.

E già venìa su per le torbide onde   64
   un fracasso d'un suon, pien di spavento,
   per cui tremavano amendue le sponde,

non altrimenti fatto che d'un vento   67
   impetüoso per li avversi ardori,
   che fier la selva e sanz' alcun rattento

li rami schianta, abbatte e porta fori;   70
   dinanzi polveroso va superbo,
   e fa fuggir le fiere e li pastori.

Li occhi mi sciolse e disse: «Or drizza il nerbo   73
   del viso su per quella schiuma antica
   per indi ove quel fummo è più acerbo».

Come le rane innanzi a la nimica   76
   biscia per l'acqua si dileguan tutte,
   fin ch'a la terra ciascuna s'abbica,

vid' io più di mille anime distrutte   79
   fuggir così dinanzi ad un ch'al passo
   passava Stige con le piante asciutte.

Dal volto rimovea quell' aere grasso,   82
   menando la sinistra innanzi spesso;
   e sol di quell' angoscia parea lasso.

"Medusa, come! Let's turn this one to stone!"   52
    they cried together, staring down at us.
    "We blundered, letting Theseus get away."°
"Quick, turn your back and cover up your face,   55
    for should you see the Gorgon° if she shows,
    there would be no returning up above!"
So did my Teacher say, and he himself   58
    turned me around, and since he didn't trust
    my own, he shut my eyes with his hands too.
O you whose intellects see clear and whole,   61
    gaze on the doctrine that is hidden here
    beneath the unfamiliar verses' veil.
And now above the water churned with scum   64
    broke such a fearful crash it sent the shakes
    through either shore—the roarings such as come
Whenever a headstrong gale is raised by war   67
    of heat and cold massed in the atmosphere:
    it batters the woods with nothing to hold it back,
Slashes and beats limbs down and sweeps them off,   70
    drives onward in its arrogance of dust,
    and sets the shepherds and the beasts to flee.
He freed my eyes and said, "Now strain the nerve   73
    of your sight there above the ancient sludge
    where the smoke is the bitterest." As frogs
Are quick to vanish in the water when   76
    they see their enemy the serpent come,
    and squat and crouch all quiet at the bottom,
I saw more than a thousand souls destroyed°   79
    scurry away before the steps of one
    who passed the waters of the Styx, dry shod.
He swept his left arm out in front of him,   82
    clearing the gross air from before his face—
    and that alone for him seemed wearisome.

° *letting Theseus get away:* Theseus descended below to rescue Persephone, who had been ravished by Hades (Pluto) that she might become his queen. Theseus failed and was imprisoned, but at last Hercules came and rescued him.
° *the Gorgon:* Medusa.
° *souls destroyed:* the devils.

Ben m'accorsi ch'elli era da ciel messo, 85
  e volsimi al maestro; e quei fé segno
  ch'i' stessi queto ed inchinassi ad esso.

Ahi quanto mi parea pien di disdegno! 88
  Venne a la porta e con una verghetta
  l'aperse, che non v'ebbe alcun ritegno.

«O cacciati del ciel, gente dispetta», 91
  cominciò elli in su l'orribil soglia,
  «ond' esta oltracotanza in voi s'alletta?

Perché recalcitrate a quella voglia 94
  a cui non puote il fin mai esser mozzo,
  e che più volte v'ha cresciuta doglia?

Che giova ne le fata dar di cozzo? 97
  Cerbero vostro, se ben vi ricorda,
  ne porta ancor pelato il mento e 'l gozzo».

Poi si rivolse per la strada lorda, 100
  e non fé motto a noi, ma fé sembiante
  d'omo cui altra cura stringa e morda

che quella di colui che li è davante; 103
  e noi movemmo i piedi inver' la terra,
  sicuri appresso le parole sante.

Dentro li 'ntrammo sanz' alcuna guerra; 106
  e io, ch'avea di riguardar disio
  la condizion che tal fortezza serra,

com' io fui dentro, l'occhio intorno invio, 109
  e veggio ad ogne man grande campagna,
  piena di duolo e di tormento rio.

Sì come ad Arli, ove Rodano stagna, 112
  sì com' a Pola, presso del Carnaro
  ch'Italia chiude e suoi termini bagna,

fanno i sepulcri tutt' il loco varo, 115
  così facevan quivi d'ogne parte,
  salvo che 'l modo v'era più amaro;

ché tra li avelli fiamme erano sparte, 118
  per le quali eran sì del tutto accesi,
  che ferro più non chiede verun' arte.

I saw he was a herald sent from Heaven,   85
    turned to my Teacher, but he made a sign
    that I should hold my peace, and bow to him.
How full of scorn did he appear to me!   88
    Came to the gate, and with a little wand
    opened it; there was nothing to resist.
"O you despicable race cast out from Heaven,"   91
    upon the horrible threshold he began,
    "whence do you fetch this pride that feeds on you!
Why do you kick your heels against the will   94
    of Him whose ends can never be cut short,
    who many a time has made your torments grow?
What good is it to butt your heads at fate?   97
    Your Cerberus did so, if you may recall,
    and he still wears his chin and jowls skinned bald."
Then he turned back along the filthy road   100
    without a word to us, as if he were
    someone with other business on his mind
Than what may press and sting the man before him;   103
    and so we made our way into that city—
    his holy words had made us confident.
Without a battle then we went inside,   106
    and I, who had a wish to scout the site
    and the condition of the spirits barred
Within that stronghold, saw a stretching plain   109
    wherever I turned my gaze, on every side,
    full of the cruelest punishments and pain.
As at Arles, near the mudflats of the Rhône,   112
    or as at Pola, near Quarnero Bay
    which bathes and shuts the bounds of Italy,
The crammed-in tombs make all the ground uneven,   115
    so did the tombs in this place, everywhere,
    save that the manner made it crueler,
For flames were sown among those open graves   118
    and fired them to so great a temperature
    that iron forged red-hot requires no more.

Tutti li lor coperchi eran sospesi,   121
 e fuor n'uscivan sì duri lamenti,
 che ben parean di miseri e d'offesi.
E io: «Maestro, quai son quelle genti   124
 che, seppellite dentro da quell' arche,
 si fan sentir coi sospiri dolenti?».
E quelli a me: «Qui son li eresïarche   127
 con lor seguaci, d'ogne setta, e molto
 più che non credi son le tombe carche.
Simile qui con simile è sepolto,   130
 e i monimenti son più e men caldi».
 E poi ch'a la man destra si fu vòlto,
passammo tra i martìri e li alti spaldi.   133

All of their slabs hung open, and there came   121
    laments so bitter from within, that they
    who made them seemed in misery indeed.

"Teacher," I said, "who are those people there   124
    entombed within the arks, who can be heard
    by the great sighs of woe they give inside?"

"These are the patriarchs of heresy,"   127
    he said, "with all their followers, every sect.
    More than you'd think lie packed into these tombs.

Heretics here are buried like with like,   130
    and hot and less hot are their monuments."
    And after he turned right, we took our path

Between the tortures and the battlements.   133

Ora sen va per un secreto calle,
   tra 'l muro de la terra e li martìri,
   lo mio maestro, e io dopo le spalle.
«O virtù somma, che per li empi giri   4
   mi volvi», cominciai, «com' a te piace,
   parlami, e sodisfammi a' miei disiri.
La gente che per li sepolcri giace   7
   potrebbesi veder? già son levati
   tutt' i coperchi, e nessun guardia face».
E quelli a me: «Tutti saran serrati   10
   quando di Iosafàt qui torneranno
   coi corpi che là sù hanno lasciati.
Suo cimitero da questa parte hanno   13
   con Epicuro tutti suoi seguaci,
   che l'anima col corpo morta fanno.
Però a la dimanda che mi faci   16
   quinc' entro satisfatto sarà tosto,
   e al disio ancor che tu mi taci».
E io: «Buon duca, non tegno riposto   19
   a te mio cuor se non per dicer poco,
   e tu m'hai non pur mo a ciò disposto».

Canto Ten

*In the **sixth circle**, Dante speaks to the Epicurean heretic **Farinata**, valorous leader of one of the Florentine factions. They are interrupted by **Cavalcante de' Cavalcanti**, the father of Dante's friend and fellow poet Guido Cavalcanti; he is dismayed to hear, as he thinks, that Guido is dead. Dante resumes speaking with Farinata, who prophesies **Dante's exile from Florence** and explains to Dante the limits of the **knowledge of the damned**.*

Now he proceeded down a secret track
    between the torments and the city wall,
    my Teacher, with me close behind his back.
"O highest peak of virtue," I began,   4
    "who lead me at your pleasure round these rings,
    speak to me, let my wish be satisfied.
The people who are lying in these graves,   7
    can they be seen? The lids have all been raised
    and no one seems on guard." And he to me:
"These will be bolted on the day of doom   10
    when from the Valley of Jehosophat
    the souls bring back their bodies to the tomb.
On this side, in his cemetery, lies   13
    that Epicurus with his followers who
    put it that spirit dies when body dies.
Now as for your request, soon it will be   16
    fulfilled for you in here—that, and another
    desire you silently withhold from me."
"Good leader, if I hide my heart from you,"   19
    said I, "I do it only to speak less.
    That's what you've often said that I should do."

Farinata

«O Tosco che per la città del foco 22
   vivo ten vai così parlando onesto,
   piacciati di restare in questo loco.

La tua loquela ti fa manifesto 25
   di quella nobil patrïa natio,
   a la qual forse fui troppo molesto».

Subitamente questo suono uscìo 28
   d'una de l'arche; però m'accostai,
   temendo, un poco più al duca mio.

Ed el mi disse: «Volgiti! Che fai? 31
   Vedi là Farinata che s'è dritto:
   da la cintola in sù tutto 'l vedrai».

Io avea già il mio viso nel suo fitto; 34
   ed el s'ergea col petto e con la fronte
   com' avesse l'inferno a gran dispitto.

E l'animose man del duca e pronte 37
   mi pinser tra le sepulture a lui,
   dicendo: «Le parole tue sien conte».

Com' io al piè de la sua tomba fui, 40
   guardommi un poco, e poi, quasi sdegnoso,
   mi dimandò: «Chi fuor li maggior tui?».

Io ch'era d'ubidir disideroso, 43
   non gliel celai, ma tutto gliel' apersi;
   ond' ei levò le ciglia un poco in suso;

poi disse: «Fieramente furo avversi 46
   a me e a miei primi e a mia parte,
   sì che per due fïate li dispersi».

«S'ei fur cacciati, ei tornar d'ogne parte», 49
   rispuos' io lui, «l'una e l'altra fïata;
   ma i vostri non appreser ben quell'arte».

Allor surse a la vista scoperchiata 52
   un'ombra, lungo questa, infino al mento:
   credo che s'era in ginocchie levata.

Dintorno mi guardò, come talento 55
   avesse di veder s'altri era meco;
   e poi che 'l sospecciar fu tutto spento,

"O Tuscan, you who speak with modest grace,   22
    alive and traveling through the city of fire,
    may it please you to pause here in this place.

Your speech and accent make it clear to me   25
    you were born in the noble fatherland°
    I may have punished once too bitterly."

This sound suddenly burst forth from inside   28
    one of the arks of stone, and in some fear
    I drew a little closer to my guide.

"What are you doing? Turn around!" said he.   31
    "Look upon Farinata risen there!
    His full height from the waist up you will see."

I had already fixed my eyes on his;   34
    who raised himself with great chest and great brow,
    surging as if he held all Hell in scorn.

And with his prompt and spirited hand my guide   37
    pushed me toward him among the sepulchers,
    saying, "Make sure each word you utter counts."

At the foot of his tomb I stood, and he   40
    looked at me for a little, till he asked,
    with some disdain, "Who were your family?"

I who was eager to obey him did   43
    not hide the matter, but revealed it all,
    at which he raised his eyebrow just a bit

And said, "They were bold enemies of mine,   46
    fierce to my party and my ancestors,
    for which twice over I sent them scattering."

"If they were twice cast out, they twice returned"—   49
    I thus responded—"and from every side,
    an art which yours, it seems, have not well learned."

Then next to him out of the lidless tomb   52
    arose a shadow visible to the chin;
    I think he must have risen to his knees.

He looked around me, searched, as if he longed   55
    to see if someone else was there with me,
    and when his little hope was doused, he wept

° *fatherland:* Tuscany; specifically, Florence.

piangendo disse: «Se per questo cieco   58
   carcere vai per altezza d'ingegno,
   mio figlio ov' è? e perché non è teco?».

E io a lui: «Da me stesso non vegno.   61
   Colui ch'attende là, per qui mi mena
   forse cui Guido vostro ebbe a disdegno».

Le sue parole e 'l modo de la pena   64
   m'avean di costui già letto il nome;
   però fu la risposta così piena.

Di sùbito drizzato gridò: «Come   67
   dicesti 'elli ebbe'? non viv' elli ancora?
   non fiere li occhi suoi lo dolce lume?».

Quando s'accorse d'alcuna dimora   70
   ch'io facëa dinanzi a la risposta,
   supin ricadde e più non parve fora.

Ma quell' altro magnanimo, a cui posta   73
   restato m'era, non mutò aspetto,
   né mosse collo, né piegò sua costa,

e sé continüando al primo detto,   76
   «S'elli han quell' arte», disse, «male appresa,
   ciò mi tormenta più che questo letto.

Ma non cinquanta volte fia raccesa   79
   la faccia de la donna che qui regge,
   che tu saprai quanto quell' arte pesa.

E se tu mai nel dolce mondo regge,   82
   dimmi perché quel popolo è sì empio
   incontr' a' miei in ciascuna sua legge?».

Ond' io a lui: «Lo strazio e 'l grande scempio   85
   che fece l'Arbia colorata in rosso,
   tal orazion fa far nel nostro tempio».

Poi ch'ebbe sospirando il capo mosso,   88
   «A ciò non fu' io sol», disse, «né certo
   sanza cagion con li altri sarei mosso.

Ma fu' io solo, là dove sofferto   91
   fu per ciascun di tòrre via Fiorenza,
   colui che la difesi a viso aperto».

And said, "If through this dungeon of the blind   58
    you go by means of genius at its height,
    where is my son?° Why is he not with you?"

And I: "I haven't come here on my own.   61
    He who stands waiting leads me through this place
    for one° your Guido, maybe, held in scorn."

I'd read his name already by his words   64
    and by the manner of his punishment,
    so I replied in full. But suddenly

He drew upright and cried, "What do you mean?   67
    You said 'he held'—isn't he still alive?
    Has the sweet sunlight ceased to strike his eyes?"

And when he noticed I was hesitant   70
    and didn't answer him immediately,
    he fell back, and did not come out again.

But he at whose request I'd stopped to speak,   73
    that man of great soul, never turned his neck,
    or bent his trunk, or changed his countenance,

But went on speaking as he had at first.   76
    "If they have badly learned that art, that wrings
    more pain from me than does this bed of fire.

Yet fifty times the moon will not re-burn—   79
    that face of Hecate, the queen of Hell—
    before you find how hard that is to learn.

As you hope to go back to the sweet world,   82
    tell me, why are those people pitiless
    against my side in every law they pass?"

Said I, "The great rout and the massacre   85
    that blushed the river Arbia red with blood—
    that's why our temple sounds with such a prayer."

He shook his head a little, with a sigh.   88
    "There I was not alone—nor would have moved
    with all the others, had there been no cause.

But when each man agreed to wipe away   91
    Florence from off the earth, I was alone,
    her sole defender in the sight of all."

° *my son:* the poet Guido Cavalcanti; see notes.

° *one:* Beatrice, as I read it; see notes.

«Deh, se riposi mai vostra semenza»,   94
   prega' io lui, «solvetemi quel nodo
   che qui ha 'nviluppata mia sentenza.

El par che voi veggiate, se ben odo,   97
   dinanzi quel che 'l tempo seco adduce,
   e nel presente tenete altro modo».

«Noi veggiam, come quei c'ha mala luce,   100
   le cose», disse, «che ne son lontano;
   cotanto ancor ne splende il sommo duce.

Quando s'appressano o son, tutto è vano   103
   nostro intelletto; e s'altri non ci apporta,
   nulla sapem di vostro stato umano.

Però comprender puoi che tutta morta   106
   fia nostra conoscenza da quel punto
   che del futuro fia chiusa la porta».

Allor, come di mia colpa compunto,   109
   dissi: «Or direte dunque a quel caduto
   che 'l suo nato è co' vivi ancor congiunto;

e s'i' fui, dianzi, a la risposta muto,   112
   fate i saper che 'l fei perché pensava
   già ne l'error che m'avete soluto».

E già 'l maestro mio mi richiamava;   115
   per ch'i' pregai lo spirto più avaccio
   che mi dicesse chi con lu' istava.

Dissemi: «Qui con più di mille giaccio.   118
   Qua dentro è 'l secondo Federico
   e 'l Cardinale; e de li altri mi taccio».

Indi s'ascose; e io inver' l'antico   121
   poeta volsi i passi, ripensando
   a quel parlar che mi parea nemico.

Elli si mosse, e poi, così andando,   124
   mi disse: «Perché se' tu sì smarrito?».
   E io li sodisfeci al suo dimando.

«La mente tua conservi quel ch'udito   127
   hai contra te», mi comandò quel saggio;
   «e ora attendi qui», e drizzò 'l dito:

"Ah, as your seed may ever hope for peace,"   94
    I begged him, "please, untie this knot for me
    which twists my judgment all in tangles here.
If I've heard right, it seems that you can see   97
    what time will bring before it comes to pass—
    not so for things that happen currently."
"As a man with bad vision," he replied,   100
    "we dimly see things far away. So much
    splendor the sovereign Lord still shines on us.
When things draw near, or happen, emptiness   103
    is all we see. If no one brings us news,
    we can know nothing of your human state.
Now you can understand that evermore   106
    dead will be all our knowledge from the time
    the future ends, and Judgment shuts the door."
Then I said—for I felt remorse's sting—   109
    "Will you now tell that soul who fell away,
    his son is still on earth among the living?
If at first I was silent in reply,   112
    let him know I was caught in that mistake,
    dwelling upon the doubt you've solved for me."
And now my Teacher called me to return,   115
    so I besought the soul to hurry on
    and tell me who stood with him in that tomb.
"More," he said, "than a thousand lie with me;   118
    "Frederick the Second and the Cardinal.
    About the rest I have no more to say."
At that he hid his form within. So toward   121
    the ancient poet I turned my steps, and mulled
    the spirit's speech to me, his hostile words.
And as we walked in silence, by and by   124
    the poet said, "Why are you lost in thought?"
    And so I satisfied him in reply.
"Save in your memory everything you've heard   127
    against you," that wise man commanded me,
    "and now listen to this," he said and pointed.

«quando sarai dinanzi al dolce raggio 130
    di quella il cui bell' occhio tutto vede,
    da lei saprai di tua vita il vïaggio».
Appresso mosse a man sinistra il piede: 133
    lasciammo il muro e gimmo inver' lo mezzo
    per un sentier ch'a una valle fiede,
che 'nfin là sù facea spiacer suo lezzo. 136

"When you shall come before the radiance 130
    of that sweet soul° whose lovely eye sees all,
    from her you'll learn the journey of your life."
Then straight to the left hand he took his way; 133
    we left the walls and toward the center walked
    along a path that struck into a pit
Whose loathsome stench rose to the very top. 136

° *that sweet soul:* Beatrice. She will lead Dante to his ancestor Cacciaguida, who will actually be
the one to foretell Dante's future (*Par.* 17.46–99).

In su l'estremità d'un'alta ripa
    che facevan gran pietre rotte in cerchio,
    venimmo sopra più crudele stipa;
e quivi, per l'orribile soperchio   4
    del puzzo che 'l profondo abisso gitta,
    ci raccostammo, in dietro, ad un coperchio
d'un grand' avello, ov' io vidi una scritta   7
    che dicea: 'Anastasio papa guardo,
    lo qual trasse Fotin de la via dritta'.
«Lo nostro scender conviene esser tardo,   10
    sì che s'ausi un poco in prima il senso
    al tristo fiato; e poi no i fia riguardo».
Così 'l maestro; e io «Alcun compenso»,   13
    dissi lui, «trova che 'l tempo non passi
    perduto». Ed elli: «Vedi ch'a ciò penso».
«Figliuol mio, dentro da cotesti sassi»,   16
    cominciò poi a dir, «son tre cerchietti
    di grado in grado, come que' che lassi.
Tutti son pien di spirti maladetti;   19
    ma perché poi ti basti pur la vista,
    intendi come e perché son costretti.
D'ogne malizia, ch'odio in cielo acquista,   22
    ingiuria è 'l fine, ed ogne fin cotale
    o con forza o con frode altrui contrista.

CANTO ELEVEN

*At the inner rim of the **sixth circle**, the poets find the tombstone of **Pope Anastasius**. Before they descend, Virgil explains to Dante the **structure of lower Hell**. The last three rings punish **violence, fraud**, and **treachery**, with the ring of violence subdivided according to the one violated: one's neighbor, oneself, or God—either in God's own person or in His handmaid Nature.*

At the edge of a ring of broken stones
    heaped in a tumble down to the steep pit,
    we came upon a crueler pack of woe,
Where for the horrid overwhelming stink   4
    belched up out of the depths of the abyss,
    we drew away a bit, and made our screen
The great slab of a tomb, on which I read   7
    these words engraved: "I guard Pope Anastasius.
    Photinus drew him from the straight and true."
"We should take our descent a little slow,   10
    letting our sense grow used to the foul air
    a little—then we will not mind it so."
That from the Teacher. "Let's not lose the time,"   13
    said I to him, "but find some recompense."
    "That's just what I've been thinking of," said he.
"My son, down in the pit below these rocks,"   16
    he began, "there are three rings, small and smaller
    as you go down, like those you've left above.
They are all filled with spirits of the damned.   19
    So that the sight of them will be enough,
    hear how and why Hell stows them where they're crammed.
All malice meriting the hate of God   22
    has, for its end, injustice. All such ends
    afflict the sufferer by force, or fraud.

Ma perché frode è de l'uom proprio male,   25
    più spiace a Dio; e però stan di sotto
    li frodolenti, e più dolor li assale.

Di vïolenti il primo cerchio è tutto;   28
    ma perché si fa forza a tre persone,
    in tre gironi è distinto e costrutto.

A Dio, a sé, al prossimo si pòne   31
    far forza, dico in loro e in lor cose,
    come udirai con aperta ragione.

Morte per forza e ferute dogliose   34
    nel prossimo si danno, e nel suo avere
    ruine, incendi e tollette dannose;

onde omicide e ciascun che mal fiere,   37
    guastatori e predon, tutti tormenta
    lo giron primo per diverse schiere.

Puote omo avere in sé man vïolenta   40
    e ne' suoi beni; e però nel secondo
    giron convien che sanza pro si penta

qualunque priva sé del vostro mondo,   43
    biscazza e fonde la sua facultade,
    e piange là dov' esser de' giocondo.

Puossi far forza ne la deïtade,   46
    col cor negando e bestemmiando quella,
    e spregiando natura e sua bontade;

e però lo minor giron suggella   49
    del segno suo e Soddoma e Caorsa
    e chi, spregiando Dio col cor, favella.

La frode, ond' ogne coscïenza è morsa,   52
    può l'omo usare in colui che 'n lui fida
    e in quel che fidanza non imborsa.

Since fraud's a sin peculiar to mankind,   25
    God hates it more; and so the fraudulent
    sink farther down, assailed by greater pain.

The violent fill the first ring, but because   28
    there are three persons force is used against,
    the ring is delved with three rounds, each distinct.

Against one's neighbor or oneself or God   31
    one can use force—against their persons or
    their property, as I shall now explain.

Violent death and vicious wounds are sins   34
    against one's neighbor; and his property
    may suffer arson, ruin, and forced loss,

So homicides and all who strike for hate,°   37
    spoilers and beasts of prey, are tortured there
    in the first round, in all their separate packs.

Men can raise violent hands against themselves   40
    and their own goods, so in the second round
    it's fit that they repent—to no avail—

Who robbed themselves of life on earth above,   43
    gambled their substance, melted all their wealth,
    or wept for things that should have brought them joy.

One can use force against the Deity,   46
    cursing it, or denying it in one's heart,
    or scorning Nature and her generous goods;

And so the narrowest round seals with its mark   49
    Sodomites,° and the usurers of Cahors,°
    and those who speak their scorn of God at heart.

Now fraud—which bites at every conscience°—can   52
    be used on one who puts his faith in you
    or one who pockets no such confidence.

° *who strike for hate:* premeditatedly, that is, and not in the throes of wrath.

° *Sodomites:* those who act upon unnatural sexual desires; particularly, homosexuals. They are named for the city of Sodom, where such sins were practiced. God destroyed Sodom and its neighbor Gomorrah with a rain of fire (Gen. 19:1–29).

° *Cahors:* a French town in Provence, proverbial in the Middle Ages for its usurers.

° *which bites at every conscience:* Since fraud employs reason, the liar must be conscious of his evil. Hence fraud must always be accompanied by some remorse—the "biting back" of conscience.

Questo modo di retro par ch'incida   55
    pur lo vinco d'amor che fa natura;
    onde nel cerchio secondo s'annida
ipocresia, lusinghe e chi affattura,   58
    falsità, ladroneccio e simonia,
    ruffian, baratti e simile lordura.
Per l'altro modo quell' amor s'oblia   61
    che fa natura, e quel ch'è poi aggiunto,
    di che la fede spezïal si cria;
onde nel cerchio minore, ov' è 'l punto   64
    de l'universo in su che Dite siede,
    qualunque trade in etterno è consunto».
E io: «Maestro, assai chiara procede   67
    la tua ragione, e assai ben distingue
    questo baràtro e 'l popol ch'e' possiede.
Ma dimmi: quei de la palude pingue,   70
    che mena il vento, e che batte la pioggia,
    e che s'incontran con sì aspre lingue,
perché non dentro da la città roggia   73
    sono ei puniti, se Dio li ha in ira?
    e se non li ha, perché sono a tal foggia?».
Ed elli a me «Perché tanto delira»,   76
    disse, «lo 'ngegno tuo da quel che sòle?
    o ver la mente dove altrove mira?
Non ti rimembra di quelle parole   79
    con le quai la tua Etica pertratta
    le tre disposizion che 'l ciel non vole,
incontenenza, malizia e la matta   82
    bestialitade? e come incontenenza
    men Dio offende e men biasimo accatta?
Se tu riguardi ben questa sentenza,   85
    e rechiti a la mente chi son quelli
    che sù di fuor sostegnon penitenza,
tu vedrai ben perché da questi felli   88
    sien dipartiti, e perché men crucciata
    la divina vendetta li martelli».

This latter type of fraud appears to cut   55
    only that bond of love which Nature makes;°
    thus to the second circle for their nest

Go flatterers, swindling sorcerers, hypocrites,   58
    impostors, pickers of purses, simonists,
    panders and greasy palms and all such filth.

The other fraud forgets two bonds of love,   61
    one made by Nature and one added on,
    from which a special faith to keep is born;

So at the bottom of the universe   64
    where Satan sits, in the lowest ring of all,
    traitors are laid to waste eternally."

"Teacher, your explanation is quite clear,   67
    and you've pieced out this chasm very well,"
    said I, "with all the people it confines.

But tell me, those up there in the swamp's slime,   70
    those windswept spirits, those the rain beats down,
    those tongues that jeer when they collide each time,

Why aren't they also in this city of rust   73
    to suffer, if God holds them in His wrath?
    If He does not, how is their suffering just?"

And he to me: "How is it that your mind   76
    goes madly wandering so far from itself?
    In what direction have you turned its gaze?

Don't you remember your Philosopher°—   79
    the *Ethics,* where he treats at length the three
    propensities that Heaven does not will,

Incontinence and malice and deranged   82
    bestiality? And how incontinence
    offends God less, is taxed with lesser blame?

So if you study his conclusion well,   85
    and bring back to your mind who those souls are
    who bear their penalties in upper Hell,

You will perceive why they are parted from   88
    these villains here, and why less angrily
    Heaven's vengeance brings on them its hammering blows."

° *that bond of love which Nature makes:* By Nature all men are to be friends with one another.
° *your Philosopher:* my gloss. Dante refers to Aristotle; see *Nicomachean Ethics* 7.1 and notes.

«O sol che sani ogne vista turbata,   91
    tu mi contenti sì quando tu solvi,
    che, non men che saver, dubbiar m'aggrata.
Ancora in dietro un poco ti rivolvi»,   94
    diss'io, «là dove di' ch'usura offende
    la divina bontade, e 'l groppo solvi».
«Filosofia», mi disse, «a chi la 'ntende,   97
    nota, non pure in una sola parte,
    come natura lo suo corso prende
dal divino 'ntelletto e da sua arte;   100
    e se tu ben la tua Fisica note,
    tu troverai, non dopo molte carte,
che l'arte vostra quella, quanto pote,   103
    segue, come 'l maestro fa 'l discente;
    sì che vostr' arte a Dio quasi è nepote.
Da queste due, se tu ti rechi a mente   106
    lo Genesì dal principio, convene
    prender sua vita e avanzar la gente;
e perché l'usuriere altra via tene,   109
    per sé natura e per la sua seguace
    dispregia, poi ch'in altro pon la spene.
Ma seguimi oramai che 'l gir mi piace;   112
    ché i Pesci guizzan su per l'orizzonta,
    e 'l Carro tutto sovra 'l Coro giace,
e 'l balzo via là oltra si dismonta».   115

"O sun who clear and cure all troubled sight, 91
    you please me so much when you solve these things—
    no less than knowledge, doubt is a delight!

Could you go back a little, though," said I, 94
    "when you said usury's an offense against
    God's bounty? There's a riddle to untie."

"Whoever understands philosophy 97
    and heeds it, notes, not in one place alone,
    how Nature takes her course," he said to me,

"From Intellect Divine and from its art, 100
    and in your *Physics*,° if you gloss it well,
    you'll find, not many pages from the start,

That your art strives to follow, as it may, 103
    Nature—you are the pupil, she the teacher.
    So we might say that human industry

Is the grandchild of God. From these two things— 106
    remember the first part of Genesis—
    man must derive his life and his advance,

And since the usurer takes a different path, 109
    setting his hope in something else, he sins,
    despising Nature and her follower.

But now I'd like to move, so follow me, 112
    for the Fish flash their tails on the horizon,
    the Bear is full northwest,° and still ahead

There lies our way to venture down the slope." 115

° *your Physics:* again, that of Aristotle (2.2). Dante has studied these works closely, and Virgil is reminding him of what he should already know.

° *the Bear is full northwest:* The Fish are Pisces and *the Bear* is Ursa Major. Since the sun is in Aries, the constellation that follows Pisces, it is almost dawn of the next day, Holy Saturday.

Era lo loco ov' a scender la riva
　　venimmo, alpestro e, per quel che v'er' anco,
　　tal, ch'ogne vista ne sarebbe schiva.
Qual è quella ruina che nel fianco　　　　　　　　　　　　　　4
　　di qua da Trento l'Adice percosse,
　　o per tremoto o per sostegno manco,
che da cima del monte, onde si mosse,　　　　　　　　　　　　7
　　al piano è sì la roccia discoscesa,
　　ch'alcuna via darebbe a chi sù fosse:
cotal di quel burrato era la scesa;　　　　　　　　　　　　　　10
　　e 'n su la punta de la rotta lacca
　　l'infamïa di Creti era distesa
che fu concetta ne la falsa vacca;　　　　　　　　　　　　　13
　　e quando vide noi, sé stesso morse,
　　sì come quei cui l'ira dentro fiacca.
Lo savio mio inver' lui gridò: «Forse　　　　　　　　　　　　16
　　tu credi che qui sia 'l duca d'Atene,
　　che sù nel mondo la morte ti porse?

CANTO TWELVE

*The poets descend into the **seventh circle**, which is guarded by the **Minotaur**. At the base of the embankment they meet the **Centaurs**, led by **Chiron**, who shoot arrows at murderers standing in the **river Phlegethon**, a boiling stream as red as blood. The centaur **Nessus** identifies the sinners and carries Dante across the ford.*

This descent was a jagged-bouldered one,
    and, for the loathsome thing before the bank,
    a place which any eye would gladly shun.
As at the Slips of Mark° that struck the flank   4
    of the river Adige this side of Trent,
    because of earthquake or support too weak,
To the plain from the very mountaintop   7
    the rock face is so smashed-in and destroyed
    it makes a path for someone up above;
Such was the way to go down this gorge here,   10
    and at the ruptured margin of the ditch
    there lay sprawled out the infamy of Crete°
Conceived within the counterfeited cow;   13
    and when he saw us two, he champed his lips
    as one who's crushed and half consumed with wrath.
Turning to him, my wise one cried, "Perhaps   16
    you think you've got the duke of Athens° here,
    the one who slew you in the world above?

° *the Slips of Mark:* a gloss on the text. Dante refers to a rock slide near the *Adige* River, probably the slide known as the Slavini di Marco.
° *the infamy of Crete:* the Minotaur, "the unspeakable thing" of Crete. See notes.
° *the duke of Athens:* Theseus.

Pàrtiti, bestia, ché questi non vene   19
   ammaestrato da la tua sorella,
   ma vassi per veder le vostre pene».

Qual è quel toro che si slaccia in quella   22
   c'ha ricevuto già 'l colpo mortale,
   che gir non sa, ma qua e là saltella,

vid' io lo Minotauro far cotale;   25
   e quello accorto gridò: «Corri al varco;
   mentre ch'e' 'nfuria, è buon che tu ti cale».

Così prendemmo via giù per lo scarco   28
   di quelle pietre, che spesso moviensi
   sotto i miei piedi per lo novo carco.

Io gia pensando; e quei disse: «Tu pensi   31
   forse a questa ruina, ch'è guardata
   da quell' ira bestial ch'i' ora spensi.

Or vo' che sappi che l'altra fïata   34
   ch'i' discesi qua giù nel basso inferno,
   questa roccia non era ancor cascata.

Ma certo poco pria, se ben discerno,   37
   che venisse colui che la gran preda
   levò a Dite del cerchio superno,

da tutte parti l'alta valle feda   40
   tremò sì, ch'i' pensai che l'universo
   sentisse amor, per lo qual è chi creda

più volte il mondo in caòsso converso;   43
   e in quel punto questa vecchia roccia,
   qui e altrove, tal fece riverso.

Ma ficca li occhi a valle, ché s'approccia   46
   la riviera del sangue in la qual bolle
   qual che per vïolenza in altrui noccia».

Oh cieca cupidigia e ira folle,   49
   che sì ci sproni ne la vita corta,
   e ne l'etterna poi sì mal c'immolle!

Clear away, beast! For this man has not come 19
    taught by your clever sister and her clue,
    but goes about to view your punishments."
And as a bull who's snapped his harness ropes 22
    when the deathblow's already set him reeling—
    he cannot charge, but bucks this way and that—
So did I see the furious Minotaur. 25
    "Run to the gap," the wary poet cried,
    "Better go down while he is blind with rage!"
We picked our way then down that garbage dump 28
    of fallen rocks, which slid and shifted as
    I trod on them with unaccustomed weight.
He noticed I was thinking as I walked. 31
    "This ruin guarded by the bestial wrath
    I doused just now—perhaps you're wondering
How it collapsed. Know then, that other time° 34
    when I descended to the deepest Hell,
    the cliff had not yet crumbled. But not long,
As far as I can judge, before He° came 37
    who made the glorious raid on Lucifer
    and raised up spirits from the highest ring,
Every side of this deep and stinking hole 40
    shivered as if the universe felt love—
    which some believe has often turned the world
Back to the chaos of its origin; 43
    and at that instant this old cliff side, here
    and elsewhere, shook and toppled. But look down,
Fix your eyes on the valley, for we draw 46
    near to the river of blood which seethes all men
    who injured others by their violence."
O foolish wrath and blind cupidity, 49
    that dig their spurs in us through our short lives,
    then cruelly drench us for eternity!

° *that other time:* when the witch Erichtho used him to retrieve a soul from the lowest circle of Hell; see 9.22–27 above.
° *He:* Christ, in the harrowing of Hell. See 4.52–63.

Io vidi un'ampia fossa in arco torta,   52
   come quella che tutto 'l piano abbraccia,
   secondo ch'avea detto la mia scorta;
e tra 'l piè de la ripa ed essa, in traccia   55
   corrien centauri, armati di saette,
   come solien nel mondo andare a caccia.
Veggendoci calar, ciascun ristette,   58
   e de la schiera tre si dipartiro
   con archi e asticciuole prima elette;
e l'un gridò da lungi: «A qual martiro   61
   venite voi che scendete la costa?
   Ditel costinci; se non, l'arco tiro».
Lo mio maestro disse: «La risposta   64
   farem noi a Chirón costà di presso:
   mal fu la voglia tua sempre sì tosta».
Poi mi tentò, e disse: «Quelli è Nesso,   67
   che morì per la bella Deianira,
   e fé di sé la vendetta elli stesso.
E quel di mezzo, ch'al petto si mira,   70
   è il gran Chirón, il qual nodrì Achille;
   quell' altro è Folo, che fu sì pien d'ira.
Dintorno al fosso vanno a mille a mille,   73
   saettando qual anima si svelle
   del sangue più che sua colpa sortille».
Noi ci appressammo a quelle fiere isnelle: 76
   Chirón prese uno strale, e con la cocca
   fece la barba in dietro a le mascelle.
Quando s'ebbe scoperta la gran bocca,   79
   disse a' compagni: «Siete voi accorti
   che quel di retro move ciò ch'el tocca?
Così non soglion far li piè d'i morti».   82
   E 'l mio buon duca, che già li er' al petto,
   dove le due nature son consorti,
risupose: «Ben è vivo, e sì soletto   85
   mostrar li mi convien la valle buia;
   necessità 'l ci 'nduce, e non diletto.

I saw a deep moat bent into an arc 52
  so that its arms encircled the whole plain,
  as my escort had said. Between this moat
And the foot of the cliff, hot on the trace 55
  ran centaurs, armed with arrows for their bows,
  as in the world they galloped at the chase.
When they saw us come down, they stopped at once 58
  and three of their platoon approached us with
  bows slung, and arrows picked to fly. And one
Cried from afar, "You who descend the banks, 61
  which of the tortures have you come for? Tell
  from where you stand—if not, I draw my bow."
"We will make our response," my Teacher said, 64
  "to Chiron, when we reach him. As for you,
  your will was always hot—to your own harm."
He nudged me, saying, "That one's Nessus, who 67
  died for his theft of lovely Deianira,
  and made himself a vengeance for himself.
He in the middle, gazing at his chest, 70
  is great Chiron, who nursed and raised Achilles;
  the other, Pholus, ever filled with wrath.
They go by thousands round about the moat, 73
  shooting the souls who try to pluck themselves
  out of the blood more than their faults allot."
So we approached those quick and sleek-limbed beasts. 76
  Chiron took out a dart, and with the fledge
  smoothed back the beard from both sides of his jaws.
When he had thus uncovered his large mouth 79
  he said to his companions, "Have you marked
  how things move at the touch of him in back?
The feet of dead men are not known for that." 82
  And my good guide, beside his chest by now
  where the two natures meld in company,
Replied, "He is alive indeed, and I 85
  must show him the dark valley all alone,
  not for delight, but by necessity.

Tal si partì da cantare alleluia 88
 che mi commise quest' officio novo:
 non è ladron, né io anima fuia.

Ma per quella virtù per cu' io movo 91
 li passi miei per sì selvaggia strada,
 danne un de' tuoi, a cui noi siamo a provo,

e che ne mostri là dove si guada, 94
 e che porti costui in su la groppa,
 ché non è spirto che per l'aere vada».

Chirón si volse in su la destra poppa, 97
 e disse a Nesso: «Torna, e sì li guida,
 e fa cansar s'altra schiera v'intoppa».

Or ci movemmo con la scorta fida 100
 lungo la proda del bollor vermiglio,
 dove i bolliti facieno alte strida.

Io vidi gente sotto infino al ciglio, 103
 e 'l gran centauro disse: «E' son tiranni
 che dier nel sangue e ne l'aver di piglio.

Quivi si piangon li spietati danni; 106
 quivi è Alessandro, e Dïonisio fero
 che fé Cicilia aver dolorosi anni.

E quella fronte c'ha 'l pel così nero, 109
 è Azzolino; e quell' altro ch'è biondo,
 è Opizzo da Esti, il qual per vero

fu spento dal figliastro sù nel mondo». 112
 Allor mi volsi al poeta, e quei disse:
 «Questi ti sia or primo, e io secondo».

Poco più oltre il centauro s'affisse 115
 sovr' una gente che 'nfino a la gola
 parea che di quel bulicame uscisse.

Mostrocci un'ombra da l'un canto sola, 118
 dicendo: «Colui fesse in grembo a Dio
 lo cor che 'n su Tamisi ancor si cola».

Poi vidi gente che di fuor del rio 121
 tenean la testa e ancor tutto 'l casso;
 e di costoro assai riconobb' io.

One° left her song of alleluia to   88
    give me this strange commission I fulfill;
    he is no thief, nor I a thieving soul.

But by that power through which I move my steps   91
    along so wild a trail of savagery,
    give us one of your troop to keep beside us,

To show us where to wade across the stream,   94
    and carry this one here upon his croup—
    he is no spirit walking through the air."

Chiron then turned aside by his right breast   97
    and said to Nessus, "Go back, be their guide.
    If troops get in your way, make them clear out."

Along the bubbling of the bloodred stream   100
    now with the trusty escort we moved on,
    where all the boiling spirits shriek and scream.

I saw some people plunged up to the brow.   103
    "These are the tyrants," the huge centaur said,
    "who thrust their hands for plunder and for blood.

Here they wail for their ruthlessness in crime;   106
    here's Alexander and fierce Dionysius
    who grieved his Sicily so long a time.

That forehead there whose fur is so jet black   109
    is Azzolino, and the blond one there,
    Obizzo of the Estes. For a fact,

He was snuffed by his bastard son above."   112
    At that I turned to the poet, but he said,
    "Let him speak to you first now. I will follow."

A little farther on the centaur stopped   115
    beside a band who stuck out to the throat
    above that seething river. To one side

He pointed out a solitary shade.   118
    "That spirit° sabered, in the lap of God,
    the heart that still drips blood beside the Thames."

Then I saw people lifting from the brew   121
    the head and all the trunk besides; of these
    I recognized the forms of quite a few.

° *One:* Beatrice; see 2.52–120.

° *That spirit:* Guy de Montfort, who slew Henry, brother of the English king Edward I; see notes.

Così a più a più si facea basso 124
  quel sangue, sì che cocea pur li piedi;
  e quindi fu del fosso il nostro passo.
«Sì come tu da questa parte vedi 127
  lo bulicame che sempre si scema»,
  disse 'l centauro, «voglio che tu credi
che da quest' altra a più a più giù prema 130
  lo fondo suo, infin ch'el si raggiunge
  ove la tirannia convien che gema.
La divina giustizia di qua punge 133
  quell' Attila che fu flagello in terra,
  e Pirro e Sesto; e in etterno munge
le lagrime, che col bollor diserra, 136
  a Rinier da Corneto, a Rinier Pazzo,
  che fecero a le strade tanta guerra».
Poi si rivolse e ripassossi 'l guazzo. 139

At every step the blood subsided so,   124
     until it cooked only the spirit's feet.
     That was our crossing for the realms below.
"Just as you see the bubbling river here   127
     grow shallower as we go," the centaur said,
     "you should know too that farther down the moat
The riverbed sinks lower, step by step,   130
     until you reach the deeper holes again,
     where they who practiced tyranny must groan.
The divine justice skewers on that side   133
     Attila the Hun, who was a scourge on earth,
     Pyrrhus and Sextus, and perpetually
Squeezes the tears these boiling waves unbar   136
     from Rinier Pazzo and Rinier Corneto,
     who waged their bitter war as highwaymen."
We reached the banks; he turned and crossed the ford.   139

Non era ancor di là Nesso arrivato,
   quando noi ci mettemmo per un bosco
   che da neun sentiero era segnato.

Non fronda verde, ma di color fosco;   4
   non rami schietti, ma nodosi e 'nvolti;
   non pomi v'eran, ma stecchi con tòsco.

Non han sì aspri sterpi né sì folti   7
   quelle fiere selvagge che 'n odio hanno
   tra Cecina e Corneto i luoghi cólti.

Quivi le brutte Arpie lor nidi fanno,   10
   che cacciar de le Strofade i Troiani
   con tristo annunzio di futuro danno.

Ali hanno late, e colli e visi umani,   13
   piè con artigli, e pennuto 'l gran ventre;
   fanno lamenti in su li alberi strani.

E 'l buon maestro «Prima che più entre,   16
   sappi che se' nel secondo girone»,
   mi cominciò a dire, «e sarai mentre

CANTO THIRTEEN

*Dante and Virgil enter a dark, thorny forest. It is the second round of the **seventh circle**, that of the **suicides** and the **spoilers** of their own substance. Here the suicides are imprisoned in thorn trees, and the spoilers are hunted through the forest by snapping dogs. Dante speaks to **Pier della Vigna**, a poet and courtier who slew himself rather than endure slander. Then they encounter the spoilers **Lano da Siena** and **Jacopo da Sant' Andrea**—the latter disturbing the tree of an **unnamed Florentine.***

Nessus had not arrived at the far shore
    when we had made our way into a wood,
    a place unmarked by any kind of path.
Its leaves not green, but dingy and dull black;   4
    no slender limbs, but hunched with knots and gnarls;
    no hanging fruit, but sticks and poisonous thorns.
Not those fierce beasts that hate the harrowed farms   7
    between Corneto and Cecina find
    such tangled boles and thickets harsh with brush.
Here the disgusting Harpies° build their nests   10
    who chased the Trojans from the Strophades
    with sad announcement of the harm to come.
They have broad wings, a human face and neck,   13
    claws on the foot and feathers on the paunch.
    They cry their wailing from those alien trees.
"Before you enter farther, you should know   16
    that you are now within the second round,"
    said my good Teacher, "and you shall be so

° *Harpies:* in mythology, ministers of divine vengeance, part woman, part vulture. They snatched or befouled the food of those they punished. The Harpies predicted famine for the Trojans when Aeneas and his men unwittingly slew some of the cattle of the sun god, Apollo (*Aen.* 3.210–35).

THE SUICIDES

che tu verrai ne l'orribil sabbione.   19
   Però riguarda ben; sì vederai
   cose che torrien fede al mio sermone».

Io sentia d'ogne parte trarre guai   22
   e non vedea persona che 'l facesse;
   per ch'io tutto smarrito m'arrestai.

Cred' ïo ch'ei credette ch'io credesse   25
   che tante voci uscisser, tra quei bronchi,
   da gente che per noi si nascondesse.

Però disse 'l maestro: «Se tu tronchi   28
   qualche fraschetta d'una d'este piante,
   li pensier c'hai si faran tutti monchi».

Allor porsi la mano un poco avante   31
   e colsi un ramicel da un gran pruno;
   e 'l tronco suo gridò: «Perché mi schiante?».

Da che fatto fu poi di sangue bruno,   34
   ricominciò a dir: «Perché mi scerpi?
   non hai tu spirto di pietade alcuno?

Uomini fummo, e or siam fatti sterpi: 37
   ben dovrebb' esser la tua man più pia,
   se state fossimo anime di serpi».

Come d'un stizzo verde ch'arso sia   40
   da l'un de' capi, che da l'altro geme
   e cigola per vento che va via,

sì de la scheggia rotta usciva insieme   43
   parole e sangue; ond' io lasciai la cima
   cadere, e stetti come l'uom che teme.

«S'elli avesse potuto creder prima»,   46
   rispuose 'l savio mio, «anima lesa,
   ciò c'ha veduto pur con la mia rima,

non averebbe in te la man distesa;   49
   ma la cosa incredibile mi fece
   indurlo ad ovra ch'a me stesso pesa.

Until you reach the horrifying sand.°   19
   Keep your eyes open, then, and you'll see things
   which if I told you of, you'd not believe."

I heard from all sides heaving cries of woe   22
   but saw no one to make them anywhere,
   so I stood lost, bewildered. I believe

That he believed that I believed they came,   25
   so many voices, from behind those trunks,
   from people hiding on account of us.

And so the Teacher said, "If you should snap   28
   some little twig from off one of these plants,
   the thoughts you're thinking will be left like stumps."

At that I reached my hand out gingerly   31
   and from a thorn-tree plucked a little branch,
   and its trunk cried, "Why do you hack at me?"

When it had darkened with its dripping blood   34
   it cried anew, "Why do you mangle me?
   Isn't there any pity in your soul?

Once we were men, now we are stubs and stakes.   37
   Your hand might well have felt more sympathy
   even if we had been the souls of snakes."

As when you light one end of a green log,   40
   the air inside that forces its way out
   will squeak and sputter at the other end,

So from the splintered limb came forth at once   43
   both blood and speech; at which I let it drop
   and stood there like a man in fear. "If he

Could have believed at first, O injured soul,"   46
   my guide so wise responded, "what he has
   read about only in my poetry,°

Never would he have stretched his hand against you.   49
   But since the thing was unbelievable,
   I made him do what I myself regret.

° *the horrifying sand:* in the next ring, described in Cantos Fourteen–Seventeen.
° *in my poetry:* Virgil had written about a similar bleeding tree in the *Aeneid;* see notes to line 35 above.

Ma dilli chi tu fosti, sì che 'n vece 52
    d'alcun' ammenda tua fama rinfreschi
    nel mondo sù, dove tornar li lece».

E 'l tronco: «Sì col dolce dir m'adeschi, 55
    ch'i' non posso tacere; e voi non gravi
    perch' ïo un poco a ragionar m'inveschi.

Io son colui che tenni ambo le chiavi 58
    del cor di Federigo, e che le volsi,
    serrando e diserrando, sì soavi,

che dal secreto suo quasi ogn' uom tolsi; 61
    fede portai al glorïoso offizio,
    tanto ch'i' ne perde' li sonni e 'polsi.

La meretrice che mai da l'ospizio 64
    di Cesare non torse li occhi putti,
    morte comune e de le corti vizio,

infiammò contra me li animi tutti, 67
    e li 'nfiammati infiammar sì Augusto,
    che ' lieti onor tornaro in tristi lutti.

L'animo mio, per disdegnoso gusto, 70
    credendo col morir fuggir disdegno,
    ingiusto fece me contra me giusto.

Per le nove radici d'esto legno 73
    vi giuro che già mai non ruppi fede
    al mio segnor, che fu d'onor sì degno.

E se di voi alcun nel mondo riede, 76
    conforti la memoria mia, che giace
    ancor del colpo che 'nvidia le diede».

Un poco attese, e poi «Da ch'el si tace», 79
    disse 'l poeta a me, «non perder l'ora;
    ma parla, e chiedi a lui, se più ti piace».

Ond' ïo a lui: «Domandal tu ancora 82
    di quel che credi ch'a me satisfaccia;
    ch'i' non potrei, tanta pietà m'accora».

But tell him who you were. To mend the deed   52
 maybe he'll make your memory green again
 back in the world above, when he returns."

"You speak so sweetly, I must take the bait,"   55
 the trunk replied. "May it not weigh you down
 if I should lime myself and speak a bit.

I was the guardian of Frederick's° heart,   58
 the Emperor's trusted man who held the keys,
 locking, unlocking with so soft an art

I stole most of the other courtiers from   61
 his secrets. In that glorious duty I
 kept faith so well, I lost my sleep, and wore

My pulse away. But she who never turns   64
 her eyes from Caesar's house—the harlot Envy,
 vice of the court and death for all mankind,

Inflamed against me every other soul,   67
 and the inflamed inflamed Augustus° so,
 that my glad honors turned to mournful gloom.

My spirit, relishing the taste of scorn,   70
 thinking that I could flee their scorn in death,
 made me against myself, though just, unjust.

By the bizarre roots of this tree I swear   73
 I never broke the faith I owed my lord,
 so worthy to be honored by all men.

If either of you goes back to the world,   76
 prop up my reputation, which still lies
 beneath the blow that Envy dealt it then."

The poet paused awhile, then turned to me.   79
 "Since he is silent now, don't lose the time,
 but speak, if you would like to ask him more."

But I replied, "Whatever you believe   82
 will satisfy me, ask it—I cannot,
 such is the pity pressing on my heart."

° *Frederick:* Frederick II, Holy Roman Emperor.
° *Augustus:* that is, Frederick.

Perciò ricominciò: «Se l'om ti faccia   85
   liberamente ciò che 'l tuo dir priega,
   spirito incarcerato, ancor ti piaccia
di dirne come l'anima si lega   88
   in questi nocchi; e dinne, se tu puoi,
   s'alcuna mai di tai membra si spiega».

Allor soffiò il tronco forte, e poi   91
   si convertì quel vento in cotal voce:
   «Brievemente sarà risposto a voi.

Quando si parte l'anima feroce   94
   dal corpo ond' ella stessa s'è disvelta,
   Minòs la manda a la settima foce.

Cade in la selva, e non l'è parte scelta;   97
   ma là dove fortuna la balestra,
   quivi germoglia come gran di spelta.

Surge in vermena e in pianta silvestra: 100
   l'Arpie, pascendo poi de le sue foglie,
   fanno dolore, e al dolor fenestra.

Come l'altre verrem per nostre spoglie,   103
   ma non però ch'alcuna sen rivesta,
   ché non è giusto aver ciò ch'om si toglie.

Qui le strascineremo, e per la mesta   106
   selva saranno i nostri corpi appesi,
   ciascuno al prun de l'ombra sua molesta».

Noi eravamo ancora al tronco attesi,   109
   credendo ch'altro ne volesse dire,
   quando noi fummo d'un romor sorpresi,

similemente a colui che venire   112
   sente 'l porco e la caccia a la sua posta,
   ch'ode le bestie, e le frasche stormire.

Ed ecco due da la sinistra costa,   115
   nudi e graffiati, fuggendo sì forte,
   che de la selva rompieno ogne rosta.

Quel dinanzi: «Or accorri, accorri, morte!».   118
   E l'altro, cui pareva tardar troppo,
   gridava: «Lano, sì non furo accorte

So he began, "O soul locked in this cell— 85
    so may he freely do you the good turn
    you have requested—may it please you, tell

How the soul's grafted here inside these knobs, 88
    and if you can, if ever anyone
    will shuck such knotted members and go free."

Then the trunk gusted out a sigh of grief, 91
    turning the breath into a voice, and spoke.
    "The answer to your question will be brief.

When the ferocious soul that plucks itself 94
    from its own body leaves it and departs,
    judge Minos sends it to this seventh shelf.

Into the woods it falls, no chosen place. 97
    Wherever Fortune's crossbow slings it, there
    it puts its roots down like the rankest weed.

It shoots into a sapling, a wild plant. 100
    The Harpies chew its foliage for their feed,
    cause pain, and for that pain create a vent.

We too will come to take our sloughed-off skins, 103
    but none of us will put them on again:
    it is not just to have what one has stripped.

Here we will drag our bodies through the dust, 106
    and on this sad wood's branches they will hang,
    each by the thorns of its assaulting soul."

We were still waiting for the broken branch, 109
    believing that he wanted to say more,
    when we were startled by a sudden noise,

As when a hunter posting in the woods 112
    senses at once the wild boar and the chase
    come near—he hears the beast, the trampled brush—

So look there now, two spirits at our left, 115
    naked and clawed to ribbons, hard in flight,
    smashing through all the thickets in the woods.

The one in front: "Run quickly, quickly, death!" 118
    The other one, who seemed to lag too far,
    cried out, "Lano, your legs were not so deft

le gambe tue a le giostre dal Toppo!». 121
   E poi che forse li fallia la lena,
   di sé e d'un cespuglio fece un groppo.

Di rietro a loro era la selva piena 124
   di nere cagne, bramose e correnti
   come veltri ch'uscisser di catena.

In quel che s'appiattò miser li denti, 127
   e quel dilaceraro a brano a brano;
   poi sen portar quelle membra dolenti.

Presemi allor la mia scorta per mano, 130
   e menommi al cespuglio che piangea
   per le rotture sanguinenti in vano.

«O Iacopo», dicea, «da Santo Andrea, 133
   che t'è giovato di me fare schermo?
   che colpa ho io de la tua vita rea?».

Quando 'l maestro fu sovr' esso fermo, 136
   disse: «Chi fosti, che per tante punte
   soffi con sangue doloroso sermo?».

Ed elli a noi: «O anime che giunte 139
   siete a veder lo strazio disonesto
   c'ha le mie fronde sì da me disgiunte,

raccoglietele al piè del tristo cesto. 142
   I' fui de la città che nel Batista
   mutò 'l primo padrone, ond' ei per questo

sempre con l'arte sua la farà trista; 145
   e se non fosse che 'n sul passo d'Arno
   rimane ancor di lui alcuna vista,

que' cittadin che poi la rifondarno 148
   sovra 'l cener che d'Attila rimase,
   avrebber fatto lavorare indarno.

Io fei gibetto a me de le mie case». 151

In the tilt at the Toppo riverbank!"°   121
    Then—failing in his breath perhaps—he made
    himself a tangled hideout with a bush.
Behind were all the forest could contain   124
    of black bitches running in ravenous greed,
    as fast as greyhounds that have slipped the chain.
Into the squatting soul they sank their teeth   127
    and tore apart his muscles into shreds;
    then carried off those members ripped in pain.
And then my escort took me by the hand   130
    and led me to the little shrub that wept
    for all its bloody branches, torn in vain.
"O Jacopo," said he, "of Sant' Andrea!   133
    How did it help to make a screen of me?
    Is it my fault you led a wicked life?"
My teacher then approached the soul, and said,   136
    "Who were you, who through all your broken sticks
    puff out your sorrowing speech with drops of blood?"
And he to us: "O souls who have arrived   139
    to witness the dishonor done to me,
    the slaughter that has torn my leaves away,
Gather them at the foot of this sad bush.   142
    My city° changed its patron from the god
    of war to John the Baptist, on its coins—
So Mars' art will ever make her grieve.   145
    And had there been no fragments of him left
    in stone upon the bridge over the Arno,
Those citizens who built her base anew   148
    upon the ashes that Attila left
    would have found all their labor was in vain.
I made myself a gallows of my house."   151

° *the tilt at the Toppo riverbank:* a battle in 1288, in which Lano is said to have sought his own death because he had squandered all his means.
° *My city:* Florence; see notes.

Poi che la carità del natio loco
  mi strinse, raunai le fronde sparte
  e rende'le a colui, ch'era già fioco.
Indi venimmo al fine ove si parte   4
  lo secondo giron dal terzo, e dove
  si vede di giustizia orribil arte.
A ben manifestar le cose nove,   7
  dico che arrivammo ad una landa
  che dal suo letto ogne pianta rimove.
La dolorosa selva l'è ghirlanda   10
  intorno, come 'l fosso tristo ad essa;
  quivi fermammo i passi a randa a randa.
Lo spazzo era una rena arida e spessa,   13
  non d'altra foggia fatta che colei
  che fu da' piè di Caton già soppressa.
O vendetta di Dio, quanto tu dei   16
  esser temuta da ciascun che legge
  ciò che fu manifesto a li occhi mei!
D'anime nude vidi molte gregge   19
  che piangean tutte assai miseramente,
  e parea posta lor diversa legge.

CANTO FOURTEEN

*Taking leave of the Florentine, Dante and Virgil enter the third round of the **seventh circle**, that of the **violent against God**. These are punished in a **rain of fire** that kindles the desert sands beneath them. They are also divided into three groups, the first of which, the **blasphemers**, lie flat. After Virgil rebukes the blasphemer **Capaneus**, he identifies the five rivers of the other world and describes how the four that flow in Hell spring from the tears of the **Old Man of Crete**.*

The love I cherished for my native land
    so wrung my heart, I gathered the strewn fronds
    and gave them back to him, whose voice had grown

Already faint. Then to the edge we came,   4
    passing the second to the third round, where
    a fearful work of justice could be seen.

To show most clearly these unheard-of things,   7
    I say we had arrived at a flat moor
    whose bed was bare, refusing every plant.

The woeful forest garlands it about,   10
    as it was circled by the dismal moat.
    We halted in our steps right at the rim.

Its floor was all one packed and parched expanse   13
    of sand—a desert like the Libyan plains
    pressed by the feet of Cato long ago.

Vengeance of God! How much should you be feared   16
    by everyone who reads my tale and learns
    of what was made so clear before my eyes!

For there I saw great flocks of naked souls   19
    mightily weeping in their misery,
    subject, apparently, to different rules:

Supin giacea in terra alcuna gente,   22
   alcuna si sedea tutta raccolta,
   e altra andava continüamente.

Quella che giva 'ntorno era più molta,   25
   e quella men che giacëa al tormento,
   ma più al duolo avea la lingua sciolta.

Sovra tutto 'l sabbion, d'un cader lento,   28
   piovean di foco dilatate falde,
   come di neve in alpe sanza vento.

Quali Alessandro in quelle parti calde   31
   d'Indïa vide sopra 'l süo stuolo
   fiamme cadere infino a terra salde,

per ch'ei provide a scalpitar lo suolo   34
   con le sue schiere, acciò che lo vapore
   mei si stingueva mentre ch'era solo:

tale scendeva l'etternale ardore;   37
   onde la rena s'accendea, com' esca
   sotto focile, a doppiar lo dolore.

Sanza riposo mai era la tresca   40
   de le misere mani, or quindi or quinci
   escotendo da sè l'arsura fresca.

I' cominciai: «Maestro, tu che vinci   43
   tutte le cose, fuor che ' demon duri
   ch'a l'intrar de la porta incontra uscinci,

chi è quel grande che non par che curi   46
   lo 'ncendio e giace dispettoso e torto,
   sì che la pioggia non par che 'l maturi?».

E quel medesmo, che si fu accorto   49
   ch'io domandava il mio duca di lui,
   gridò: «Qual io fui vivo, tal son morto.

Se Giove stanchi 'l suo fabbro da cui   52
   crucciato prese la folgore aguta
   onde l'ultimo dì percosso fui;

o s'elli stanchi li altri a muta a muta   55
   in Mongibello a la focina negra,
   chiamando 'Buon Vulcano, aiuta, aiuta!',

Some lay flat on their backs upon the ground,   22
    and some were sitting huddled at the knees,
    and others roved about continually.
The greatest number were of those who ran;   25
    the least, who took their tortures lying down—
    but their tongues were the freest in their cries.
Over the desert, in a gentle fall,   28
    there rained broad flakes of fire, as in the Alps
    the snow comes falling on a windless day.
As in those torrid parts of India   31
    over his army Alexander saw
    flames fall from heaven and strike the earth still strong,
And so, looking ahead, he had his troops   34
    trample them out before they fed each other—
    easier to extinguish one by one—
So the eternal fire descended here,   37
    sparking the sand like fuel beneath the flint,
    doubling the sorrows of the damned. Without
A moment's pause their miserable hands   40
    jittered their polka here there everywhere
    brushing the burns of fresh flakes from their skin.
"Teacher," I started, "you who overcome   43
    all things, except the stubborn demons who
    came out against us at their kingdom's gate,
Who's that huge one who doesn't seem to mind   46
    the fire, but lies and twists his face for spite,
    so that the rains don't seem to ripen him?"
And he himself, who picked up what I said,   49
    hearing me ask my guide about him, cried,
    "What I was living, so am I still, dead!
Jove can go break his blacksmith's° back with work,   52
    from whom in wrath he took the thunderbolt
    that ran me through on my last day on earth—
Or wear the others out in endless shifts   55
    under Mount Aetna at the pitch-black forge,
    hollering, 'Vulcan, help, I need your help!'

° *blacksmith:* Vulcan, crippled smith of the Greco-Roman gods. His forge was said to lie beneath the volcanic Mount Aetna in Sicily.

sì com' el fece a la pugna di Flegra,   58
    e me saetti con tutta sua forza,
    non ne potrebbe aver vendetta allegra».

Allora il duca mio parlò di forza   61
    tanto, ch'i' non l'avea sì forte udito:
    «O Capaneo, in ciò che non s'ammorza

la tua superbia, se' tu più punito;   64
    nullo martiro, fuor che la tua rabbia,
    sarebbe al tuo furor dolor compito».

Poi si rivolse a me con miglior labbia,   67
    dicendo: «Quei fu l'un d'i sette regi
    ch'assiser Tebe; ed ebbe e par ch'elli abbia

Dio in disdegno, e poco par che 'l pregi;   70
    ma, com' io dissi lui, li suoi dispetti
    sono al suo petto assai debiti fregi.

Or mi vien dietro, e guarda che non metti,   73
    ancor, li piedi ne la rena arsiccia,
    ma sempre al bosco tien li piedi stretti».

Tacendo divenimmo là 've spiccia   76
    fuor de la selva un picciol fiumicello,
    lo cui rossore ancor mi raccapriccia.

Quale del Bulicame esce ruscello   79
    che parton poi tra lor le peccatrici,
    tal per la rena giù sen giva quello.

Lo fondo suo e ambo le pendici   82
    fatt' era 'n pietra, e ' margini dallato;
    per ch'io m'accorsi che 'l passo era lici.

«Tra tutto l'altro ch'i' t'ho dimostrato,   85
    poscia che noi intrammo per la porta
    lo cui sogliare a nessuno è negato,

cosa non fu da li tuoi occhi scorta   88
    notabile com' è 'l presente rio,
    che sovra sè tutte fiammelle ammorta».

Queste parole fuor del duca mio;   91
    per ch'io 'l pregai che mi largisse 'l pasto
    di cui largito m'avëa il disio.

As he did on the Phlegran battlefield,   58
 and hurl his lance through me with all his force—
 he'd get from me no joy in his revenge."
At that my guide spoke out so loud and strong,   61
 I had not heard him speak so loud before:
 "Your pride has not cooled off, O Capaneus,
And in that you are punished all the more!   64
 No other torture than your own mad rage
 would bring your fury its most fitting pain."
He turned to me then, with his lips composed,   67
 and said, "One of the seven kings was he
 who besieged Thebes. The man held God in scorn,
Still thinks Him worthless, as his words attest—   70
 but, as I told him, his despisings are
 the fittest decorations for his chest.
Now follow me, and watch that you don't set   73
 your feet upon the scorching sand, but keep
 a straight path at the margin of the wood."
We walked in silence, till we came upon   76
 a narrow river gushing from the forest.
 It makes me shiver yet, so red it was!
As hot springs bubble up at Bulicame,   79
 where whores divide the water for their use,
 so did that stream cut through the desert sand.
Both its embankments and its bed were stone,   82
 as were the channel's margins on each side,
 so I surmised we'd cross the desert here.
"Of all the things I've shown you up to now,   85
 from when we entered through the gate of Hell,
 crossing whose threshold no one is refused,
Nothing you've seen is as remarkable   88
 as is this river here before your eyes,
 which cools and quenches all the flames above it."
This from my guide; at which I begged him to   91
 let me partake more largely of that food
 for which he had aroused the appetite.

«In mezzo mar siede un paese guasto»,   94
  diss' elli allora, «che s'appella Creta,
  sotto 'l cui rege fu già 'l mondo casto.

Una montagna v'è che già fu lieta   97
  d'acqua e di fronde, che si chiamò Ida;
  or è diserta come cosa vieta.

Rëa la scelse già per cuna fida   100
  del suo figliuolo, e per celarlo meglio,
  quando piangea, vi facea far le grida.

Dentro dal monte sta dritto un gran veglio,   103
  che tien volte le spalle inver' Dammiata
  e Roma guarda come süo speglio.

La sua testa è di fin oro formata,   106
  e puro argento son le braccia e 'l petto,
  poi è di rame infino a la forcata;

da indi in giuso è tutto ferro eletto,   109
  salvo che 'l destro piede è terra cotta;
  e sta 'n su quel, più che 'n su l'altro, eretto.

Ciascuna parte, fuor che l'oro, è rotta   112
  d'una fessura che lagrime goccia,
  le quali, accolte, fóran quella grotta.

Lor corso in questa valle si diroccia;   115
  fanno Acheronte, Stige e Flegetonta;
  poi sen van giù per questa stretta doccia,

infin, là dove più non si dismonta,   118
  fanno Cocito; e qual sia quello stagno
  tu lo vedrai, però qui non si conta».

E io a lui: «Se 'l presente rigagno   121
  si diriva così dal nostro mondo,
  perché ci appar pur a questo vivagno?».

"Far in the sea a country lies in waste,"   94
    the poet then began, "whose name is Crete.
    Under its ancient king° the world was chaste.
There stood a mountain lush with leaf and spring,   97
    Mount Ida, as they called it in those days;
    now it is barren, like an aged thing.
The goddess Rhea chose it for a crib   100
    to trust her son° to, and to hide him better,
    her followers made a racket when he wailed.
Deep in that hill a huge Old Man stands tall.   103
    His back turned to the delta of the Nile,
    he stares at Rome as at his looking glass.
His head is fashioned all of finest gold;   106
    his arms and chest are silver unalloyed;
    then he is bronze down to the torso's fork,
Below which all is iron, choice and pure,   109
    except his right foot, which is mere baked clay.
    He leans more weight on that than on the other.
Each part, except the gold, is rotted through   112
    by a long fissure made by trickling tears,
    which form a stream, and tunnel through that cave.
They fall into this valley, rock to rock;   115
    make Acheron, and Styx, and Phlegethon,
    then they go lower by this narrow duct
Till there are no more mountains to descend,   118
    where they make Cocytus.° What that dead pool is,
    you will soon see. Here let the matter end."
And I to him: "Then if this present stream   121
    comes guttering down from our world up above,
    why do we see it only at this hem?"

° *its ancient king:* Saturn, in the so-called Golden Age. Crete was thought to lie in the dead center of the inhabited world, between Europe, Africa, and Asia.

° *her son:* Jupiter. Saturn (Cronos) had heard a prophecy that he would be overthrown by one of his offspring. To prevent that, he swallowed them as soon as they were born. But Rhea hid her baby in the mountains of Crete, her devotees singing and banging the cymbals to drown out his crying.

° *Cocytus: Acheron, Styx, Phlegethon,* and *Cocytus* are the four rivers of Hell.

Ed elli a me: «Tu sai che 'l loco è tondo;   124
   e tutto che tu sie venuto molto,
   pur a sinistra, giù calando al fondo,
non se' ancor per tutto 'l cerchio vòlto;   127
   per che, se cosa n'apparisce nova,
   non de' addur maraviglia al tuo volto».
E io ancor: «Maestro, ove si trova   130
   Flegetonta e Letè? ché de l'un taci,
   e l'altro di' che si fa d'esta piova».
«In tutte tue question certo mi piaci»,   133
   rispuose, «ma 'l bollor de l'acqua rossa
   dovea ben solver l'una che tu faci.
Letè vedrai, ma fuor di questa fossa,   136
   là dove vanno l'anime a lavarsi
   quando la colpa pentuta è rimossa».
Poi disse: «Omai è tempo da scostarsi   139
   dal bosco; fa che di retro a me vegne:
   li margini fan via, che non son arsi,
e sopra loro ogne vapor si spegne».   142

And he to me: "You know this place is round,   124
    and even though you've traveled a long way
    and tended to the left while going down,

You have not yet gone all around the ring.   127
    So let it not bring wonder to your face
    should there appear before us some new thing."

"Teacher, where are the Lethe° and the Phlegethon?   130
    You say the one springs from this rain of tears,
    and you've said nothing of the other one."

"All of your questions bring delight to me,   133
    but the boiling red stream,"° he said, "should solve
    your first one with no trouble. You shall see

The river Lethe, but not in this gulch—   136
    you'll see it where the spirits go to bathe
    when their repented sins are wiped away.

But now it's time for us to leave these woods.   139
    Follow behind me on the walk of stone;
    there is no burning sand upon the rim,

And the flames are extinguished overhead."   142

° *Lethe:* classical river of forgetfulness; Dante will find it at the top of the Mountain of Purgatory
(*Purg.* 28.130).
° *boiling red stream:* the Phlegethon of Canto Twelve, above, in the first round of the violent.

Ora cen porta l'un de' duri margini,
    e 'l fummo del ruscel di sopra aduggia,
    sì che dal foco salva l'acqua e li argini.
Qual i Fiamminghi tra Guizzante e Bruggia,   4
    temendo 'l fiotto che 'nver' lor s'avventa,
    fanno lo schermo perché 'l mar si fuggia;
e qual i Padoan lungo la Brenta,   7
    per difender lor ville e lor castelli,
    anzi che Carentana il caldo senta:
a tale imagine eran fatti quelli,   10
    tutto che né sì alti né sì grossi,
    qual che si fosse, lo maestro félli.
Già eravam da la selva rimossi   13
    tanto, ch'i' non avrei visto dov' era,
    perch' io in dietro rivolto mi fossi,
quando incontrammo d'anime una schiera   16
    che venian lungo l'argine, e ciascuna
    ci riguardava come suol da sera

CANTO FIFTEEN

*Still in the third round of the **seventh circle**, walking along the channel's wall, Dante and Virgil meet the second group of the **violent against God: the Sodomites,** who run continually through the hailing fire. One of their group, a Florentine politician and poet named **Brunetto Latini,** recognizes his protégé Dante and discusses with him Dante's own future and that of Florence. After naming some of the others who share his sin, Brunetto must hurry away.*

Along one of the rims of stone we came,
    where the mist of the river makes a shade,
    shielding the water and the banks from flame.
As do the Dutch who fear the hurling tide   4
    smashing the coast between Bruges and Wissant°—
    they build a dike to shunt the sea aside;
And as the Paduans along the Brent   7
    defend their towns and villages before
    the mountains of Carinthia feel the heat,°
In such a fashion were these bulwarks made,   10
    although their master builder made them not
    so thick or tall—whoever he might be.
We had already left the woods behind   13
    so far that even had I turned to look,
    I never could have made out where it was,
When following the dike we met a band   16
    of spirits coming toward us, and each one
    stared at us hard as one is wont to stare

° *between Bruges and Wissant:* cities at the eastern and western ends of what was known as Flanders in Dante's time.
° *feel the heat:* before the melting snows from the Dolomite Alps cause the streams to flood.

Brunetto Latini

guardare uno altro sotto nuova luna; 19
    e sì ver' noi aguzzavan le ciglia
    come 'l vecchio sartor fa ne la cruna.

Così adocchiato da cotal famiglia, 22
    fui conosciuto da un, che mi prese
    per lo lembo e gridò: «Qual maraviglia!».

E io, quando 'l suo braccio a me distese, 25
    ficcaï li occhi per lo cotto aspetto,
    sì che 'l viso abbrusciato non difese

la conoscenza süa al mio 'ntelletto; 28
    e chinando la mano a la sua faccia,
    rispuosi: «Siete voi qui, ser Brunetto?».

E quelli: «O figliuol mio, non ti dispiaccia 31
    se Brunetto Latino un poco teco
    ritorna 'n dietro e lascia andar la traccia».

I' dissi lui: «Quanto posso, ven preco; 34
    e se volete che con voi m'asseggia,
    faròl, se piace a costui che vo seco».

«O figliuol», disse, «qual di questa greggia 37
    s'arresta punto, giace poi cent' anni
    sanz' arrostarsi quando 'l foco il feggia.

Però va oltre: i' ti verrò a' panni; 40
    e poi rigiugnerò la mia masnada,
    che va piangendo i suoi etterni danni».

Io non osava scender de la strada 43
    per andar par di lui; ma 'l capo chino
    tenea com' uom che reverente vada.

El cominciò: «Qual fortuna o destino 46
    anzi l'ultimo dì qua giù ti mena?
    e chi è questi che mostra 'l cammino?».

«Là sù di sopra, in la vita serena», 49
    rispuos' io lui, «mi smarri' in una valle,
    avanti che l'età mia fosse piena.

Pur ier mattina le volsi le spalle: 52
    questi m'apparve, tornand' ïo in quella,
    e reducemi a ca per questo calle».

At someone in the dark of the new moon,   19
    knitting their brows to keep us keen in sight
    as an old tailor threads the needle's eye.
And while this family was watching us,   22
    one of them knew me and he seized me by
    my tunic's hem and cried, "What wonder's this!"
And I, when he'd stretched out his arm to me,   25
    so fixed my eyes upon his crusted looks
    that even the charred features could not keep
My intellect from recognizing them,   28
    and lowering my hand toward his face
    I answered, "Ser Brunetto, are *you* here?"
Said he, "May it not trouble you, my son,   31
    if Brunetto Latini turns awhile
    to walk with you, and lets the file go on."
And I: "I beg you, please, with all my heart!   34
    And if you wish me to sit down with you,
    if he with whom I go is pleased, I shall."
"My son," said he, "whoever of this flock   37
    stops for an instant, lies a hundred years
    and cannot fan away the flames that strike.
So let's go on, I'll follow at your feet,   40
    then will I join my company again,
    who go and mourn their everlasting loss."
I did not dare to come down from that road   43
    to walk beside him, but I bowed my head
    as one who, walking, shows his reverence.
And he began, "What chance or destiny   46
    has brought you here before your final day?
    And who is he who leads your pilgrimage?"
"Up there in life beneath the quiet stars   49
    I lost my way," I answered, "in a valley,
    before I'd reached the fullness of my age.
I turned my shoulders on it yesterday: 52
    this soul appeared as I was falling back,
    and by the road through Hell he leads me home."

Ed elli a me: «Se tu segui tua stella,   55
   non puoi fallire a glorïoso porto,
   se ben m'accorsi ne la vita bella;
e s'io non fossi sì per tempo morto,   58
   veggendo il cielo a te così benigno,
   dato t'avrei a l'opera conforto.
Ma quello ingrato popolo maligno   61
   che discese di Fiesole *ab* antico,
   e tiene ancor del monte e del macigno,
ti si farà, per tuo ben far, nimico;   64
   ed è ragion, ché tra li lazzi sorbi
   si disconvien fruttare al dolce fico.
Vecchia fama nel mondo li chiama orbi;   67
   gent' è avara, invidiosa e superba:
   dai lor costumi fa che tu ti forbi.
La tua fortuna tanto onor ti serba,   70
   che l'una parte e l'altra avranno fame
   di te; ma lungi fia dal becco l'erba.
Faccian le bestie fiesolane strame   73
   di lor medesme, e non tocchin la pianta,
   s'alcuna surge ancora in lor letame,
in cui riviva la sementa santa   76
   di que' Roman che vi rimaser quando
   fu fatto il nido di malizia tanta».
«Se fosse tutto pieno il mio dimando»,   79
   rispuos' io lui, «voi non sareste ancora
   de l'umana natura posto in bando;
ché 'n la mente m'è fitta, e or m'accora,   82
   la cara e buona imagine paterna
   di voi quando nel mondo ad ora ad ora
m'insegnavate come l'uom s'etterna: 85
   e quant' io l'abbia in grado, mentr' io vivo
   convien che ne la mia lingua si scerna.

"Follow your star and you will never fail   55
    to find your glorious port," he said to me,
    "if in that lovely life I judged you well.

And if I hadn't died when you were young,   58
    seeing the heavens smile on you so kindly,
    I would have given you strength to do your work.

But those ungrateful people of ill will,   61
    who in old days came down from Fiesole°
    and smack still of the granite and the hill,

Will grow to hate you for your doing good—   64
    justly so, for among the bitter sorbs
    the sweet fig should not bloom. About their brood,

The world has long reported them as blind—   67
    a people greedy, envious, and proud.
    Clean yourself of the customs of their kind!

Such honor will your fortune hold for you   70
    that both sides will be hungry for your life,
    but let the grass be far from the goat's tooth.

Let the beasts of Fiesole provender   73
    upon themselves, and never touch the plant,
    if any can still sprout in their manure,

Wherein there lives again the holy seed   76
    of those old Romans who remained behind
    when men had built that nest of vice and greed."°

"If I could have my wishes heard in full,"   79
    I answered him, "you would not even now
    be banished from our life. It moves my heart,

But in my mind your image is set firm,   82
    how like a father, gentle and beloved,
    you taught me in the world from time to time

How man achieves an everlasting name,   85
    and in my words as long as I may live
    I shall declare my gratitude to you.

° *Fiesole:* mountain town above Florence; see notes.
° *that nest of vice and greed:* Florence.

Ciò che narrate di mio corso scrivo,   88
   e serbolo a chiosar con altro testo
   a donna che saprà, s'a lei arrivo.

Tanto vogl' io che vi sia manifesto,   91
   pur che mia coscïenza non mi garra,
   ch'a la Fortuna, come vuol, son presto.

Non è nuova a li orecchi miei tàl arra: 94
   però giri Fortuna la sua rota
   come le piace, e 'l villan la sua marra».

Lo mio maestro allora in su la gota   97
   destra si volse in dietro e riguardommi;
   poi disse: «Bene ascolta chi la nota».

Né per tanto di men parlando vommi   100
   con ser Brunetto, e dimando chi sono
   li suoi compagni più noti e più sommi.

Ed elli a me: «Saper d'alcuno è buono;   103
   de li altri fia laudabile tacerci,
   ché 'l tempo saria corto a tanto suono.

In somma sappi che tutti fur cherci   106
   e litterati grandi e di gran fama,
   d'un peccato medesmo al mondo lerci.

Priscian sen va con quella turba grama,   109
   e Francesco d'Accorso anche; e vedervi,
   s'avessi avuto di tal tigna brama,

colui potei che dal servo de' servi   112
   fu trasmutato d'Arno in Bacchiglione,
   dove lasciò li mal protesi nervi.

Di più direi; ma 'l venire e 'l sermone   115
   più lungo esser non può, però ch'i' veggio
   là surger nuovo fummo del sabbione.

I'll write down what you tell of my life's course   88
    and save it, with the other prophecies,
    to be glossed by a lady° who will know—

If I arrive to see her. Let this much   91
    be clear to you: unless my conscience scolds me,
    I'm ready for whatever Fortune wills.

My ears have heard such pledges made before.   94
    Let Fortune turn her wheel which way she likes
    for all that—and the peasant turn his hoe!"

And then my Teacher turned his cheek to me,   97
    catching my glance behind him on the right.
    "One who takes note has listened well," said he.

Continuing with Ser Brunetto, I   100
    walk on and ask him of the worthiest
    and the most famous of his company.

And he to me: "To know of some is well;   103
    it merits praise to pass the rest in silence;
    the time's too short for such a tale to tell.

Know, in a word, that they were scholars all,   106
    great men of letters, clerks of wide renown,
    made filthy in the world by the same fall.

Pedagogue Priscian's with that wretched mob,   109
    Francis d'Accorso with him; and note there,
    in case you hanker after such a scab,

Him whom the Servant of all Servants° switched   112
    from Arno's see to Bacchiglione's, where
    he left his sinews stretched in wickedness.

I'd tell of more, but can't go further on   115
    talking and walking with you, for I see
    fresh smoke arising from the sands ahead.

° *lady:* Beatrice.
° *the Servant of all Servants:* the pope, one of whose titles is *servus servorum,* "the servant of the ser-
vants," for "he who is greatest among you shall be your servant" (Matt. 23:11). The pope here
is Boniface VIII, compelled by scandal to transfer the sodomite bishop Andrea da Mozzi from
Florence, on the Arno River, to Vicenza, on the Bacchiglione.

Gente vien con la quale esser non deggio. 118
    Sieti raccomandato il mio Tesoro,
    nel qual io vivo ancora, e più non cheggio».
Poi si rivolse, e parve di coloro 121
    che corrono a Verona il drappo verde
    per la campagna; e parve di costoro
quelli che vince, non colui che perde. 124

People approach with whom I must not be.   118
    In one thing I still live: I ask no more,
    but trust my *Treasure*° to your memory."
Then he turned round, and seemed like those who strip   121
    to race for the green banner through the fields
    about Verona; and of those he seemed
The one who wins, and not the one who loses.   124

° *my* Treasure: Brunetto's most enduring literary work; see note on line 30 above. The words of Christ render the title of that work most poignant: "Lay up for yourselves treasures in heaven, where neither rust nor moth consumes, nor thieves break in and steal. For where thy treasure is, there also will thy heart be" (Matt. 6:20–21).

Già era in loco onde s'udia 'l rimbombo
de l'acqua che cadea ne l'altro giro,
simile a quel che l'arnie fanno rombo,

quando tre ombre insieme si partiro, 4
correndo, d'una torma che passava
sotto la pioggia de l'aspro martiro.

Venian ver' noi, e ciascuna gridava: 7
«Sòstati tu ch'a l'abito ne sembri
esser alcun di nostra terra prava».

Ahimè, che piaghe vidi ne' lor membri, 10
ricenti e vecchie, da le fiamme incese!
Ancor men duol pur ch'i' me ne rimembri.

A le lor grida, il mio dottor s'attese; 13
volse 'l viso ver' me, e «Or aspetta»,
disse, «a costor si vuole esser cortese.

E se non fosse il foco che saetta 16
la natura del loco, i' dicerei
che meglio stesse a te che a lor la fretta».

Ricominciar, come noi restammo, ei 19
l'antico verso; e quando a noi fuor giunti,
fenno una rota di sé tutti e trei.

Qual sogliono i campion far nudi e unti, 22
avvisando lor presa e lor vantaggio,
prima che sien tra lor battuti e punti,

Canto Sixteen

*Continuing in the third round of the **seventh ring**, that of the **violent against God**, the poets meet **three noble Florentines** who discuss with Dante the corruption of their native city. Moving on toward the precipice that forms the edge of this ring, Virgil asks Dante for his belt and casts it into the chasm below, summoning the monster **Geryon**, symbol of **fraud**.*

By now we'd come where you can hear the tumble
    of waters rushing into the next ring,
    as bees about the beehive hum and rumble;
When three shades hastening all together went   4
    off from a squad of spirits passing by
    under the rain of bitter punishment.
They came toward us and cried out this demand: 7
    "Stop, you who in your habit seem to be
    another citizen of our crooked land!"
Alas, what scars I saw on every member,   10
    old and fresh wounds, carved into them by fire!
    It gives me sadness even to remember.
My learned master waited on their cries.   13
    Turning his eyes to me, "Hold on," he said.
    "One should be courteous to men like these.
And if this place's nature sent no flame   16
    arrowing down, I'd say it was less fit
    that they should run to you, than you to them."
They recommenced their ancient litany   19
    while we were waiting; when they reached our side,
    a wheel they fashioned of themselves all three.
As naked champions, muscles slicked with oil,   22
    warily searching where and when to seize
    their chance before the jabs and punches fly—

così rotando, ciascuno il visaggio   25
   drizzava a me, sì che 'n contraro il collo
   faceva ai piè continüo vïaggio.

E «Se miseria d'esto loco sollo   28
   rende in dispetto noi e nostri prieghi»,
   cominciò l'uno, «e 'l tinto aspetto e brollo,

la fama nostra il tuo animo pieghi   31
   a dirne chi tu se', che i vivi piedi
   così sicuro per lo 'nferno freghi.

Questi, l'orme di cui pestar mi vedi,   34
   tutto che nudo e dipelato vada,
   fu di grado maggior che tu non credi:

nepote fu de la buona Gualdrada;   37
   Guido Guerra ebbe nome, e in sua vita
   fece col senno assai e con la spada.

L'altro, ch'appresso me la rena trita,   40
   è Tegghiaio Aldobrandi, la cui voce
   nel mondo sù dovria esser gradita.

E io, che posto son con loro in croce,   43
   Iacopo Rusticucci fui, e certo
   la fiera moglie più ch'altro mi nuoce».

S'i' fossi stato dal foco coperto,   46
   gittato mi sarei tra lor di sotto,
   e credo che 'l dottor l'avria sofferto;

ma perch' io mi sarei brusciato e cotto,   49
   vinse paura la mia buona voglia
   che di loro abbracciar mi facea ghiotto.

Poi cominciai: «Non dispetto, ma doglia   52
   la vostra condizion dentro mi fisse,
   tanta che tardi tutta si dispoglia,

tosto che questo mio segnor mi disse   55
   parole per le quali i' mi pensai
   che qual voi siete, tal gente venisse.

Di vostra terra sono, e sempre mai   58
   l'ovra di voi e li onorati nomi
   con affezion ritrassi e ascoltai.

So these wheeled in a ring; each turned his eye 25
    in my direction, cocked his neck to go
    opposite to his feet, continually.

And, "If the miseries of this shifting sand 28
    cause you to hold our prayers and us in scorn,"
    began one, "and our features scorched and skinned,

Still, let our reputations bend your soul 31
    to tell us who you are, with living feet
    scraping securely through the pit of Hell.

The man whose tracks you see me trample on, 34
    though he goes naked, scalded of his hair,
    was of a higher rank than you believe:

The grandson of the womanly Gualdrada, 37
    Guido Guerra his name; and in his life
    he achieved much by judgment, and the sword.

He who comes after me to thresh the sand 40
    was Tegghiaio Aldobrandi, whose advice
    should have been welcomed in the world above.

I who am crucified with them, in life 43
    was Jacopo Rusticucci. Far the worst
    was the harm done me by my shrewish wife."

Had I a covering from the rain of fire 46
    I'd have leapt off and cast myself among them,
    and think my Teacher would have suffered it—

But since I'd have been burnt and baked, my fear 49
    overpowered the good will that made me crave
    to clasp within my arms the three down there.

"Sorrow, not loathing," I began to say, 52
    "had fixed itself so deep within my heart
    it will be long before it's stripped away,

And did so just as soon as he, my lord, 55
    uttered the words that made me think that men
    of honor, such as you, were coming near.

I am your countryman, and ever have 58
    heard tell of your good works and honored names—
    heard, and recounted them with reverent love.

Lascio lo fele e vo per dolci pomi   61
   promessi a me per lo verace duca;
   ma 'nfino al centro pria convien ch'i' tomi».

«Se lungamente l'anima conduca   64
   le membra tue», rispuose quelli ancora,
   «e se la fama tua dopo te luca,

cortesia e valor dì se dimora   67
   ne la nostra città sì come suole,
   o se del tutto se n'è gita fora;

ché Guglielmo Borsiere, il qual si duole   70
   con noi per poco e va là coi compagni,
   assai ne cruccia con le sue parole».

«La gente nuova e i sùbiti guadagni   73
   orgoglio e dismisura han generata,
   Fiorenza, in te, sì che tu già ten piagni».

Così gridai con la faccia levata;   76
   e i tre, che ciò inteser per risposta,
   guardar l'un l'altro com' al ver si guata.

«Se l'altre volte sì poco ti costa»,   79
   rispuoser tutti, «il satisfare altrui,
   felice te se sì parli a tua posta!

Però, se campi d'esti luoghi bui   82
   e torni a riveder le belle stelle,
   quando ti gioverà dicere 'I' fui',

fa che di noi a la gente favelle».   85
   Indi rupper la rota, e a fuggirsi
   ali sembiar le gambe loro isnelle.

Un amen non saria possuto dirsi   88
   tosto così com' e' fuoro spariti;
   per ch'al maestro parve di partirsi.

Io lo seguiva, e poco eravam iti,   91
   che 'l suon de l'acqua n'era sì vicino,
   che per parlar saremmo a pena uditi.

Come quel fiume c'ha proprio cammino   94
   prima dal Monte Viso 'nver' levante,
   da la sinistra costa d'Apennino,

I leave the chaff and go for the sweet fruit   61
    promised me by my guide, whose word is true;
    but I must fall to Hell's dead center first."

"May your limbs long enjoy your soul as guide,"   64
    the spirit then responded, "and your fame
    shine forth its light long after you have died,

Tell us if courtesy and valor dwell   67
    within our city as they used to do,
    or if they have departed from them all.

Borsiere, who came to suffer here with us   70
    recently, and who goes there with his troop,
    troubles us deeply with the bitter news."

"Outsiders and their sudden wash of wealth   73
    beget in you such arrogance and excess,
    Florence, you feel already your ill health."

So I cried out, with proud and lifted head.   76
    As men change glances when they meet the truth,
    so did those three, on hearing what I said.

"If you shall ever pay so slight a fee   79
    to satisfy a question," all replied,
    "happy are you whose speech is bold and free!

Yet if you do escape this murky lair   82
    and turn to see the lovely stars again,
    when you'll rejoice in saying, 'I was there,'

Please, speak about us to the living." Then   85
    they broke their wheel and fled on feet as swift
    as slender wings. One could not say "amen"

As quickly as the three had disappeared,   88
    so to my Teacher also it seemed time
    for us to take our leave. I followed him,

And not long had we ventured when so near   91
    was the roar of the water's cataract,
    words were almost impossible to hear.

As that stream° in the western Apennines,   94
    first among those that from Mount Viso fall
    in the direction of the rising sun,

° *that stream:* the Montone, called the Acquacheta (*Quietwater*) near its source.

che si chiama Acquacheta suso, avante 97
   che si divalli giù nel basso letto,
   e a Forlì di quel nome è vacante,
rimbomba là sovra San Benedetto 100
   de l'Alpe per cadere ad una scesa
   ove dovria per mille esser recetto;
così, giù d'una ripa discoscesa, 103
   trovammo risonar quell'acqua tinta,
   sì che 'n poc' ora avria l'orecchia offesa.
Io avea una corda intorno cinta, 106
   e con essa pensai alcuna volta
   prender la lonza a la pelle dipinta.
Poscia ch'io l'ebbi tutta da me sciolta, 109
   sì come 'l duca m'avea comandato,
   porsila a lui aggroppata e ravvolta.
Ond' ei si volse inver' lo destro lato, 112
   e alquanto di lunge da la sponda
   la gittò giuso in quell'alto burrato.
«E' pur convien che novità risponda», 115
   dicea fra me medesmo, «al novo cenno
   che 'l maestro con l'occhio sì seconda».
Ahi quanto cauti li uomini esser dienno 118
   presso a color che non veggion pur l'ovra,
   ma per entro i pensier miran col senno!
El disse a me: «Tosto verrà di sovra 121
   ciò ch'io attendo e che il tuo pensier sogna;
   tosto convien ch'al tuo viso si scovra».
Sempre a quel ver c'ha faccia di menzogna 124
   de' l'uom chiuder le labbra fin ch'el puote,
   però che sanza colpa fa vergogna;
ma qui tacer nol posso; e per le note 127
   di questa comedìa, lettor, ti giuro,
   s'elle non sien di lunga grazia vòte,

Called Quietwater in the hills above   97
   before it tumbles down the valleys to
   its bed at Forlì, where that name is gone,
Thunders at Saint Benedict of the Alps   100
   because it plummets at a single leap
   where it should brim over a thousand steps—
So too down from a shattered side of cliff   103
   echoed the crash of that polluted brook.
   Much longer, and it would have drummed us deaf.
About my waist I wore a rope for belt   106
   and once or twice considered using it
   to snare the leopard with the gaudy pelt.
But when I'd loosened it and slipped it off,   109
   as my guide had commanded me to do,
   I gave it to him, knotted and wound up,
And then he swung about on his right side   112
   and flung it far away over the edge
   of the deep chasm before us. To myself
I said, "Some strange new thing must correspond   115
   to the strange gesture my good Teacher makes
   and seconds with his gaze." Ah, men, beware!
How watchful you must be when you are near   118
   one who not only sees the action but
   can peer beneath and read your very thoughts!
He said to me: "You will soon see arise   121
   what I await, and what you only dream.
   Soon it will be unveiled before your eyes."
Knowing a truth whose face appears a lie,   124
   a man should always keep his lips shut tight
   as long as he can, lest he be tagged with shame
Though he has told the truth; but I cannot   127
   keep silent here; and, Reader, by the notes
   of this my Comedy,° I swear—and may

° *Comedy:* Dante names his poem here. For writers of the Middle Ages, a comedy is a song written in the humble style (Dante is writing in the vernacular), wherein the main character begins in grief and trouble and ends in happiness.

ch'i' vidi per quell' aere grosso e scuro   130
   venir notando una figura in suso,
   maravigliosa ad ogne cor sicuro,
sì come torna colui che va giuso   133
   talora a solver l'àncora ch'aggrappa
   o scoglio o altro che nel mare è chiuso,
che 'n sù si stende e da piè si rattrappa.   136

They keep in favor long—through that thick air 130
    I saw a figure swimming in the night,
    such as would stun the surest heart with wonder,
Just as a diver surfacing, who's gone 133
    below to pry an anchor loose from rocks
    or something hidden in the sea, will stretch
His arms and tuck his legs to thrust again. 136

«Ecco la fiera con la coda aguzza,
    che passa i monti e rompe i muri e l'armi!
    Ecco colei che tutto 'l mondo appuzza!».
Sì cominciò lo mio duca a parlarmi;   4
    e accennolle che venisse a proda,
    vicino al fin d'i passeggiati marmi.
E quella sozza imagine di froda   7
    sen venne, e arrivò la testa e 'l busto,
    ma 'n su la riva non trasse la coda.
La faccia sua era faccia d'uom giusto,   10
    tanto benigna avea di fuor la pelle,
    e d'un serpente tutto l'altro fusto;
due branche avea pilose insin l'ascelle;   13
    lo dosso e 'l petto e ambedue le coste
    dipinti avea di nodi e di rotelle.
Con più color, sommesse e sovraposte   16
    non fer mai drappi Tartari né Turchi,
    né fuor tai tele per Aragne imposte.
Come talvolta stanno a riva i burchi,   19
    che parte sono in acqua e parte in terra,
    e come là tra li Tedeschi lurchi

CANTO SEVENTEEN

*The monster of fraud, **Geryon**, lands on the brink. Virgil instructs Dante to walk far-*
*ther along the stone dike to witness the last group of the **violent against God**: the name-*
*less **usurers**, who take the rain of fire sitting down, and who can be identified only by the*
insignia of the purses hung around their necks. When Dante returns, the poets descend
*into the circle of the **fraudulent**, flying on the back of Geryon.*

"Behold the beast with the barbed tail, who flies
    past mountains, scattering armies, smashing walls!
    Behold the beast whose stench sickens the world!"
So did my guide begin, speaking to me   4
    and signaling the thing to come to land
    at the end of the stone walk on the dike.
And that disgusting likeness of deceit   7
    arrived, and lugged his head and chest ashore,
    but did not draw his tail onto the beach.
He had the features of an honest man,   10
    so kindly was his countenance at the skin,
    but the trunk down below was serpentine;
His paws were furry to the shoulder tops,   13
    and his back and his breast and both his sides
    were particolored all in whorls and knots.
Not Turks nor Tartars weaving carpets weave   16
    more colors for their groundwork or their fringe;
    Arachne never set them on her loom.
As barges sometimes mooring at the shore   19
    stand part within the water, part on land,
    and as among those Germans swilling beer

lo bivero s'assetta a far sua guerra,   22
　　così la fiera pessima si stava
　　su l'orlo ch' e di pietra e 'l sabbion serra.

Nel vano tutta sua coda guizzava,   25
　　torcendo in sù la venenosa forca
　　ch'a guisa di scorpion la punta armava.

Lo duca disse: «Or convien che si torca   28
　　la nostra via un poco insino a quella
　　bestia malvagia che colà si corca».

Però scendemmo a la destra mammella,   31
　　e diece passi femmo in su lo stremo,
　　per ben cessar la rena e la fiammella.

E quando noi a lei venuti semo,   34
　　poco più oltre veggio in su la rena
　　gente seder propinqua al loco scemo.

Quivi 'l maestro «Acciò che tutta piena   37
　　esperïenza d'esto giron porti»,
　　mi disse, «va, e vedi la lor mena.

Li tuoi ragionamenti sian là corti;   40
　　mentre che torni, parlerò con questa,
　　che ne conceda i suoi omeri forti».

Così ancor su per la strema testa   43
　　di quel settimo cerchio tutto solo
　　andai, dove sedea la gente mesta.

Per li occhi fora scoppiava lor duolo;   46
　　di qua, di là soccorrien con le mani
　　quando a' vapori, e quando al caldo suolo:

non altrimenti fan di state i cani   49
　　or col ceffo or col piè, quando son morsi
　　o da pulci o da mosche o da tafani.

Poi che nel viso a certi li occhi porsi,   52
　　ne' quali 'l doloroso foco casca,
　　non ne conobbi alcun; ma io m'accorsi

che dal collo a ciascun pendea una tasca   55
　　ch'avea certo colore e certo segno,
　　e quindi par che 'l loro occhio si pasca.

The beaver dips his tail into the brook   22
    to seize his prey,° this worst of beasts stood here
    on the stone rim, the cutoff of the sand.
Out into empty space he flicked his tail,   25
    coiling the venomous fork to keep it high,
    which armed his bone point like a scorpion's flail.
"Now we must veer a little," said my guide,   28
    "and take our way down to that vicious beast
    who waits there, crouching." So to the right side
We turned, descending down the bank of stone,   31
    and took nine or ten steps upon its verge
    to keep clear of the sand and hailing flame.
And when we had come up to it, I saw   34
    souls sitting a bit farther up the dunes
    near the edge of the chasm. My teacher then:
"In order that you may bring back with you   37
    the full experience of this round," he said,
    "go and observe the habits of that crew.
But clip your conversation, keep it short.   40
    While you are gone I'll haggle with this beast
    that he may yield the use of his strong back."
And so along the seventh circle's cape   43
    I went on, all alone, until I came
    to where the mournful people sat in pain.
Sorrowing streams broke from their eyes, and here   46
    and there with restless hands they tried to find
    relief from fire-flakes or the scalding ground,
Not unlike dogs who in the sweltering days   49
    snap with the snout or scratch with flurrying paw
    when they are bit by fleas or gnats or flies.
When I had turned my eyes to stare at some   52
    upon whose faces fell the dolorous fire,
    not one could I make out; yet I observed
That round the neck of each one hung a pouch   55
    of its own color and insignia.
    Each seemed to gorge his eyes upon that feast.

° *to seize his prey:* Beavers were thought to lure fish by dipping their tails in the water and secreting an oil.

E com' io riguardando tra lor vegno,   58
   in una borsa gialla vidi azzurro
   che d'un leone avea faccia e contegno.

Poi, procedendo di mio sguardo il curro,   61
   vidine un'altra come sangue rossa,
   mostrando un'oca bianca più che burro.

E un che d'una scrofa azzurra e grossa   64
   segnato avea lo suo sacchetto bianco,
   mi disse: «Che fai tu in questa fossa?

Or te ne va; e perché se' vivo anco,   67
   sappi che 'l mio vicin Vitalïano
   sederà qui dal mio sinistro fianco.

Con questi Fiorentin son padoano: 70
   spesse fïate mi 'ntronan li orecchi
   gridando: "Vegna 'l cavalier sovrano,

che recherà la tasca con tre becchi!"».   73
   Qui distorse la bocca e di fuor trasse
   la lingua, come bue che 'l naso lecchi.

E io, temendo no 'l più star crucciasse   76
   lui che di poco star m'avea 'mmonito,
   torna'mi in dietro da l'anime lasse.

Trova' il duca mio ch'era salito   79
   già su la groppa del fiero animale,
   e disse a me: «Or sie forte e ardito.

Omai si scende per sì fatte scale;   82
   monta dinanzi, ch'i' voglio esser mezzo,
   sì che la coda non possa far male».

Qual è colui che sì presso ha 'l riprezzo   85
   de la quartana, c'ha già l'unghie smorte,
   e triema tutto pur guardando 'l rezzo,

tal divenn' io a le parole porte;   88
   ma vergogna mi fé le sue minacce,
   che innanzi a buon segnor fa servo forte.

And as I walked beside them, noting well,   58
    I saw in azure on a purse of gold
    a face and rampant figure of a lion.°

The chariot of my vision rolling on,   61
    I saw another purse as red as blood
    showing a goose whiter than butter.° One

Who bore a fat and farrowing sow of blue   64
    for the insignia of his silver sack°
    said, "What are you doing in this gutter, you?

Get lost. And just because you're still alive,   67
    know that Vitaliano from my town
    will someday sit in Hell at my left side.

I am a Paduan with these Florentines.   70
    They thunder and they thunder in my ears,
    'Salute the coming of the sovereign knight

Who brings the bag with the three goats!'" He made   73
    a face then, screwing up his mouth and sticking
    his tongue out, like an ox that licks its nose.

Fearing that if I stayed much longer there   76
    I'd irk the man who warned me to be quick,
    I turned my back on those defeated souls,

And found my leader had already climbed   79
    upon the hunch of that fierce animal.
    He said to me, "Be fearless now and strong.

Now we go down the pit by stairs like these.   82
    Climb on in front—I want to stay between
    to guard you from the venom of its tail."

As one who shudders with the four-day chills   85
    of quartan fever, nails already blue,
    shivers all over at the sight of shade,

So did I shudder at his words, but shame   88
    rose up against me with its threats which make
    a servant brave before his valiant lord.

° *figure of a lion:* arms of the Gianfigliazzi family of Florence.

° *a goose whiter than butter:* arms of the Ubriachi family of Florence.

° *silver sack:* arms of the Scrovegni family of Padua.

I' m'assettai in su quelle spallacce;   91
    sì volli dir, ma la voce non venne
    com' io credetti: «Fa che tu m'abbracce».

Ma esso, ch'altra volta mi sovvenne   94
    ad altro forse, tosto ch'i' montai
    con le braccia m'avvinse e mi sostenne;

e disse: «Gerïon, moviti omai: 97
    le rote larghe, e lo scender sia poco;
    pensa la nova soma che tu hai».

Come la navicella esce di loco   100
    in dietro in dietro, sì quindi si tolse;
    e poi ch'al tutto si sentì a gioco,

là 'v' era 'l petto, la coda rivolse,   103
    e quella tesa, come anguilla, mosse,
    e con le branche l'aere a sé raccolse.

Maggior paura non credo che fosse   106
    quando Fetonte abbandonò li freni,
    per che 'l ciel, come pare ancor, si cosse;

né quando Icaro misero le reni   109
    sentì spennar per la scaldata cera,
    gridando il padre a lui «Mala via tieni!»,

che fu la mia, quando vidi ch'i' era   112
    ne l'aere d'ogne parte, e vidi spenta
    ogne veduta fuor che de la fera.

Ella sen va notando lenta lenta;   115
    rota e discende, ma non me n'accorgo
    se non che al viso e di sotto mi venta.

Io sentia già da la man destra il gorgo   118
    far sotto noi un orribile scroscio,
    per che con li occhi 'n giù la testa sporgo.

Allor fu' io più timido a lo stoscio,   121
    però ch'i' vidi fuochi e senti' pianti;
    ond' io tremando tutto mi raccoscio.

E vidi poi, chè nol vedea davanti,   124
    lo scendere e 'l girar per li gran mali
    che s'appressavan da diversi canti.

I took my seat upon its cursed back,   91
    trying, trying to say, but my voice couldn't
    come as I thought, "Please, hold on to me tight."

But he who'd come so often to my aid   94
    in times of doubt and peril, when I mounted,
    secured me with his arms and bore me up

And called out, "You can go now, Geryon.   97
    Be slow on the descent, keep the turns wide.
    Remember the new weight you carry down."

And as a little boat from off the quay   100
    slips steadily backward, so he shoved away,
    and when he felt himself entirely free

He swung his tail around to meet his chest,   103
    swerved and stretched out and darted like an eel,
    sweeping the air behind him with his paws.

I don't think Phaëthon felt greater fright   106
    when he let drop his chariot's reins, and seared
    that streak into the sky, still seen at night,

Nor Icarus when he felt the melting wax   109
    unfeathering himself about the loins,
    his father crying, "You're going the wrong way!"

Than was the fear I felt when I saw air   112
    on every side of me, and every sight
    extinguished but the savage serpent there.

Slowly, slowly it swam and took its course   115
    wheeling, descending, as I could not tell
    but for the breeze below, and on my cheek.

Now on the right hand I could hear the gorge   118
    thunder beneath us with a horrible crash,
    and so I leaned and stared into the gulf.

Then I was more afraid of falling off   121
    for I saw flames below and heard the wails,
    trembled, and huddled tighter with my thighs.

Now I saw what could not be seen before,   124
    marking our turning and our plummeting
    by the great evils nearing on all sides.

Come 'l falcon ch'è stato assai su l'ali,   127
  che sanza veder logoro o uccello
  fa dire al falconiere «Omè, tu cali!»,
discende lasso onde si move isnello,   130
  per cento rote, e da lunge si pone
  dal suo maestro, disdegnoso e fello;
così ne puose al fondo Gerïone   133
  al piè al piè de la stagliata rocca,
  e, discarcate le nostre persone,
si dileguò come da corda cocca.   136

As the trained falcon long upon the wing   127
    causes the falconer to cry, "You fall!"
    when without catching sight of call or prey

It droops down in a hundred languid turns   130
    where it had taken off with speed, and perches
    far from its master, peevish and dismayed,

So by the very foot of the sheer rock   133
    Geryon landed at the bottom and—
    free of the burden of our persons—shot

Vanishing like an arrow from the string.   136

Luogo è in inferno detto Malebolge,
  tutto di pietra di color ferrigno,
  come la cerchia che dintorno il volge.
Nel dritto mezzo del campo maligno   4
  vaneggia un pozzo assai largo e profondo,
  di cui *suo loco* dicerò l'ordigno.
Quel cinghio che rimane adunque è tondo   7
  tra 'l pozzo e 'l piè de l'alta ripa dura,
  e ha distinto in dieci valli il fondo.
Quale, dove per guardia de le mura   10
  più e più fossi cingon li castelli,
  la parte dove son rende figura,
tale imagine quivi facean quelli;   13
  e come a tai fortezze da' lor sogli
  a la ripa di fuor son ponticelli,
così da imo de la roccia scogli   16
  movien che ricidien li argini e ' fossi
  infino al pozzo che i tronca e raccogli.
In questo luogo, de la schiena scossi   19
  di Gerïon, trovammoci; e 'l poeta
  tenne a sinistra, e io dietro mi mossi.

Canto Eighteen

*Dante and Virgil enter the **eighth circle**, that of the **fraudulent**. Called **Malebolge**, this*
circle is divided into ten pockets, or ditches, each punishing a different sort of fraud. In
*the **first ditch**, Dante sees **seducers** and **panderers** whipped by demons; there he meets*
***Venedico Caccianemico**, and Virgil directs his attention to **Jason** the Argonaut.*
*Crossing to the **second ditch** by means of a rock formation that runs like a bridge from*
*end to end of Malebolge, they see the **flatterers**, plunged in excrement, among whom they*
*identify **Alessio Interminei** and the whore **Thaïs**.*

There is a place in Hell called Malebolge,
    "Pouches of Evil," all of iron-gray stone,
    just like the ring that circles it above.

Right in the center of this wicked plain   4
    a broad and plummeting basin drops from sight—
    its structure I will speak of, in its place.

This strip of Hell that thus remains goes round   7
    between the hole and the hard precipice.
    Into ten separate pockets it is split.

As where defenders of a city's walls   10
    dig trench on trench about the fortresses,
    the rings of ditches form a pattern there

Similar to the pattern made by these;   13
    and as from sill to the next stronghold's sill
    small bridges lead the way to the last edge,

So from the cliff's base rock-ribs cut their way   16
    across the gutters here and up their banks,
    converging at the hole that chops them short.

Here, shaken from the monster Geryon's back,   19
    we found ourselves; the poet then set out
    to the left, and I followed in his track.

A la man destra vidi nova pieta,   22
   novo tormento e novi frustatori,
   di che la prima bolgia era repleta.

Nel fondo erano ignudi i peccatori;   25
   dal mezzo in qua ci venien verso 'l volto,
   di là con noi, ma con passi maggiori,

come i Roman per l'essercito molto,   28
   l'anno del giubileo, su per lo ponte
   hanno a passar la gente modo colto,

che da l'un lato tutti hanno la fronte   31
   verso 'l castello e vanno a Santo Pietro,
   da l'altra sponda vanno verso 'l monte.

Di qua, di là, su per lo sasso tetro   34
   vidi demon cornuti con gran ferze,
   che li battien crudelmente di retro.

Ahi come facean lor levar le berze   37
   a le prime percosse! già nessuno
   le seconde aspettava né le terze.

Mentr' io andava, li occhi miei in uno   40
   furo scontrati; e io sì tosto dissi:
   «Già di veder costui non son digiuno».

Per ch'ïo a figurarlo i piedi affissi;   43
   e 'l dolce duca meco si ristette,
   e assentio ch'alquanto in dietro gissi.

E quel frustato celar si credette   46
   bassando 'l viso; ma poco li valse,
   ch'io dissi: «O tu che l'occhio a terra gette,

se le fazion che porti non son false,   49
   Venedico se' tu Caccianemico.
   Ma che ti mena a sì pungenti salse?».

Ed elli a me: «Mal volontier lo dico;   52
   ma sforzami la tua chiara favella,
   che mi fa sovvenir del mondo antico.

I' fui colui che la Ghisolabella   55
   condussi a far la voglia del marchese,
   come che suoni la sconcia novella.

On our right hand we saw new misery,   22
    new torments, and new handlers of the lash,
    and this first pocket was stuffed full with them.

The sinners at the bottom were all nude: 25
    those near approached us while the far ones went
    in our direction, but with greater strides,

As Romans in the year of jubilee,   28
    for the great hosts of pilgrims on the bridge,
    found a way to move traffic steadily,

For on one side the travelers had to face   31
    Castle Sant' Angelo, going toward Saint Peter's,
    while those upon the other faced the hill.

Over the blackish stone and everywhere   34
    I saw horned devils ply their thick-boled whips,
    thirsty for blood, lashing the sinners' backs.

Ah how the first strokes made them lift their heels!   37
    Yes, no one stood and waited for another
    or yet a third! And as I walked along,

My glance happened to light on one of them   40
    and I broke out directly, "For a fact,
    I haven't fasted from the sight of him."

To get a better view I set my feet,   43
    and my guide, sweet and courteous, halted too,
    permitting me to walk a short way back.

And that scourged spirit thought to hide himself,   46
    lowering his brow. It did him little good!
    "O you who cast your eyes upon the earth,

If your face and its features aren't false,   49
    you're Venedico Caccianemico.
    But what has dipped you in so sharp a sauce?"

And he to me: "Against my will I'll tell,   52
    for your clear speech recalls that world of old
    and has a power upon me to compel.

I was the man who pushed Ghisolabella   55
    my sister to the bed of the Marchese,
    no matter how they tell the dirty tale.

E non pur io qui piango bolognese;   58
   anzi n'è questo loco tanto pieno,
   che tante lingue non son ora apprese
a dicer 'sipa' tra Sàvena e Reno;   61
   e se di ciò vuoi fede o testimonio,
   rècati a mente il nostro avaro seno».
Così parlando il percosse un demonio   64
   de la sua scurïada, e disse: «Via,
   ruffian! qui non son femmine da conio».
I' mi raggiunsi con la scorta mia;   67
   poscia con pochi passi divenimmo
   là 'v' uno scoglio de la ripa uscia.
Assai leggeramente quel salimmo;   70
   e vòlti a destra su per la sua scheggia,
   da quelle cerchie etterne ci partimmo.
Quando noi fummo là dov' el vaneggia   73
   di sotto per dar passo a li sferzati,
   lo duca disse: «Attienti, e fa che feggia
lo viso in te di quest' altri mal nati,   76
   ai quali ancor non vedesti la faccia
   però che son con noi insieme andati».
Del vecchio ponte guardavam la traccia   79
   che venìa verso noi da l'altra banda,
   e che la ferza similmente scaccia.
E 'l buon maestro, sanza mia dimanda,   82
   mi disse: «Guarda quel grande che vene,
   e per dolor non par lagrime spanda:
quanto aspetto reale ancor ritene!   85
   Quelli è Iasón, che per cuore e per senno
   li Colchi del monton privati féne.
Ello passò per l'isola di Lenno   88
   poi che l'ardite femmine spietate
   tutti li maschi loro a morte dienno.

I'm not the only Bolognese who weeps 58
 here in this ditch—the place is full of us!
 More than the tongues that learn to answer *sipa*°
Between the Reno and the Savena. 61
 Want witness for it, something you can trust?
 Only recall the avarice of our hearts."
So he spoke, but a demon slashed at him 64
 with his rough horsewhip, crying, "Off with you,
 pimp! We're no whores for you to swindle here!"
Then I rejoined my leader and my guide, 67
 and soon we came upon a place where juts
 a stone reef from the chasm's rocky side.
We scrambled up this bridge quite easily, 70
 and turning right upon its jagged back
 we left those endless circlings all behind.
When we were at the summit of its arch, 73
 where it gapes underneath and gives the flogged
 a passage through, my guide said, "Stop and let
Sight of these others born in evil hour 76
 strike you. You haven't seen their faces yet,
 for they were walking the same way we walked."
So from that ancient bridge we watched the track 79
 of sinners from the other band; here too
 the lash made sure their paces were not slack.
And my good Teacher, though I did not ask, 82
 said, "Look at that great figure coming there,
 who does not seem to shed a tear for pain.
What kingliness his image still retains! 85
 He's Jason—who with his brave heart and wits
 deprived the Colchians of the golden fleece.
He came ashore upon the isle of Lemnos 88
 after the ruthless women boldly put
 their fathers, sons, and brothers all to death.

° *sipa:* Bolognese dialect for *si,* "yes." The *Savena* and *Reno* are rivers that flow in the vicinity of Bologna. The sinner says there are more Bolognese pimps already damned than there are people alive in the whole district.

Ivi con segni e con parole ornate 91
  Isifile ingannò, la giovinetta
  che prima avea tutte l'altre ingannate.

Lasciolla quivi, gravida, soletta; 94
  tal colpa a tal martiro lui condanna;
  e anche di Medea si fa vendetta.

Con lui sen va chi da tal parte inganna; 97
  e questo basti de la prima valle
  sapere e di color che 'n sé assanna».

Già eravam là 've lo stretto calle 100
  con l'argine secondo s'incrocicchia,
  e fa di quello ad un altr' arco spalle.

Quindi sentimmo gente che si nicchia 103
  ne l'altra bolgia e che col muso scuffa,
  e sé medesma con le palme picchia.

Le ripe eran grommate d'una muffa, 106
  per l'alito di giù che vi s'appasta,
  che con li occhi e col naso facea zuffa.

Lo fondo è cupo sì, che non ci basta 109
  loco a veder sanza montare al dosso
  de l'arco, ove lo scoglio più sovrasta.

Quivi venimmo; e quindi giù nel fosso 112
  vidi gente attuffata in uno sterco
  che da li uman privadi parea mosso.

E mentre ch'io là giù con l'occhio cerco, 115
  vidi un col capo sì di merda lordo,
  che non parëa s'era laico o cherco.

Quei mi sgridò: «Perché se' tu sì gordo 118
  di riguardar più me che li altri brutti?».
  E io a lui: «Perché, se ben ricordo,

già t'ho veduto coi capelli asciutti, 121
  e se' Alessio Interminei da Lucca:
  però t'adocchio più che li altri tutti».

Ed elli allor, battendosi la zucca: 124
  «Qua giù m'hanno sommerso le lusinghe
  ond'io non ebbi mai la lingua stucca».

With acts of love and words of sweetest skill 91
    he fooled the pretty girl Hypsipyle,
    who'd fooled the rest in leading them to kill.

He left her great with child and all alone; 94
    such fault condemns him to such punishment.
    What he did to Medea also earns

Its vengeance here. Seducers go with him, 97
    all liars. That's enough for you to know
    of this first ditch and those clamped in its fangs."

Our narrow path over the bridge now met 100
    the second bank, and where they crossed they made
    a buttress for another arch beyond.

Here in the second pouch we came upon 103
    people who whimpered, sniveling, runny-nosed,
    who slapped and smacked themselves with open palms.

The walls were fungus-crusted, thick with mold 106
    which rose in vapors from below and clung,
    making a nauseous brawl with eyes and nose.

So hollow was the bottom of this pouch 109
    we had no vantage point to see a soul
    until we climbed the summit of the arch.

So there we climbed, and in the trench I saw 112
    people plunged deep in just the sort of dung
    you dump from human privies and latrines.

And while I searched the bottom with my eyes 115
    I saw a man, his head so shit-besmeared
    you couldn't tell if he were lay or priest,

Who yelled: "Why does your hunger make you choke 118
    to stare at me and not the other filth?"
    And I: "Because, if I remember well,

I saw you when you wore your haircut dry, 121
    Alessio Interminei, from Lucca!
    That's why I gaze upon you more than all."

Then he, smacking himself about the pate: 124
    "They've sunk me down here, all my flatteries,
    with which my tongue was never tuckered out."

Appresso ciò lo duca «Fa che pinghe»,   127
    mi disse, «il viso un poco più avante,
    sì che la faccia ben con l'occhio attinghe
di quella sozza e scapigliata fante   130
    che là si graffia con l'unghie merdose,
    e or s'accoscia e ora è in piedi stante.
Taïde è, la puttana che rispuose   133
    al drudo suo quando disse "Ho io grazie
    grandi apo te?": "Anzi maravigliose!".
E quinci sian le nostre viste sazie».   136

And after that my guide, "Pray, stretch your gaze,"   127
    he said to me, "a little farther on,
    until your eye can reach the filthy face
Of that hair-rumpled and disgusting wench   130
    who claws herself with shit beneath her nails,
    now standing up, now squatting on her haunch.
She's Thaïs, she's the whore whose lover asked,   133
    'Have I found lots of favor in your eyes?'
    and she replied, 'And how! You're marvelous.'
I think our sights have had their fill of this."   136

O Simon mago, o miseri seguaci
   che le cose di Dio, che di bontate
   deon essere spose, e voi rapaci
per oro e per argento avolterate,   4
   or convien che per voi suoni la tromba,
   però che ne la terza bolgia state.
Già eravamo, a la seguente tomba,   7
   montati de lo scoglio in quella parte
   ch'a punto sovra mezzo 'l fosso piomba.
O somma sapïenza, quanta è l'arte   10
   che mostri in cielo, in terra e nel mal mondo,
   e quanto giusto tua virtù comparte!
Io vidi per le coste e per lo fondo   13
   piena la pietra livida di fóri,
   d'un largo tutti e ciascun era tondo.
Non mi parean men ampi né maggiori   16
   che que' che son nel mio bel San Giovanni,
   fatti per loco d'i battezzatori;

Canto Nineteen

*Dante and Virgil pass to the **third ditch of Malebolge**, where the **simonists**—those who use church offices for profiteering—are plunged headfirst in fontlike holes in the stone, with the soles of their feet anointed and set afire. Here Dante finds **Pope Nicholas III**, who first mistakes him for **Boniface VIII**, then prophesies Boniface's damnation and that of a succeeding pope, **Clement V**. Dante replies with a vigorous attack against the corruption of the papacy.*

O Simon Magus,° O you wretched crew
   of his disciples! The things of God should be
   espoused to righteousness and love, and you
Rapacious wolves, you pander them for gold,   4
   foul them for silver! Sound the trumpet now
   for you—for this third pocket is your place.
We had already reached the following tomb,   7
   climbing the ledge until the spot we gained
   hung plumb above the middle of the moat.
O highest Wisdom, how much art you show   10
   in Heaven, on earth, and in the evil world!
   How justly does your power apportion all!
I saw that on both walls and on the ground   13
   the livid iron stone was full of holes,
   all of a size, and every one was round.
No bigger, and no narrower they appeared   16
   than the holes in my lovely baptistery
   of San Giovanni, made for holy fonts,

° *Simon Magus:* a magician who wished to purchase from the apostles the gifts of the Holy Spirit (Acts 8:9–24). He lends his name to the sin of turning church offices to profit.

THE SIMONISTS

l'un de li quali, ancor non è molt' anni,   19
    rupp' io per un che dentro v'annegava:
    e questo sia suggel ch' ogn'omo sganni.

Fuor de la bocca a ciascun soperchiava   22
    d'un peccator li piedi e de le gambe
    infino al grosso, e l'altro dentro stava.

Le piante erano a tutti accese intrambe;   25
    per che sì forte guizzavan le giunte,
    che spezzate averien ritorte e strambe.

Qual suole il fiammeggiar de le cose unte   28
    muoversi pur su per la strema buccia,
    tal era lì dai calcagni a le punte.

«Chi è colui, maestro, che si cruccia   31
    guizzando più che li altri suoi consorti»,
    diss' io, «e cui più roggia fiamma succia?».

Ed elli a me: «Se tu vuo' ch'i' ti porti   34
    là giù per quella ripa che più giace,
    da lui saprai di sé e de' suoi torti».

E io: «Tanto m'è bel, quanto a te piace: 37
    tu se' segnore, e sai ch'i' non mi parto
    dal tuo volere, e sai quel che si tace».

Allor venimmo in su l'argine quarto;   40
    volgemmo e discendemmo a mano stanca
    là giú nel fondo foracchiato e arto.

Lo buon maestro ancor de la sua anca   43
    non mi dipuose, sì mi giunse al rotto
    di quel che sì piangeva con la zanca.

«O qual che se' che 'l di sù tien di sotto,   46
    anima trista come pal commessa»,
    comincia' io a dir, «se puoi, fa motto».

Io stava come 'l frate che confessa   49
    lo perfido assessin, che, poi ch'è fitto,
    richiama lui per che la morte cessa.

Ed el gridò: «Se' tu già costì ritto,   52
    se' tu già costì ritto, Bonifazio?
    Di parecchi anni mi mentì lo scritto.

One of which, and not many years ago,   19
    I had to break to save a boy from drowning—
    and let men take that for the stamp of truth.

Out of the mouth of every hole there stuck   22
    a sinner's feet and legs up to the fat
    above the knee; the rest remained inside.

And everywhere the soles were set afire,   25
    making them kick and wrench their joints so hard
    they'd have snapped twisted ropes or cords in two.

As flame upon a thing anointed goes   28
    darting and dancing on the peel, so here
    flames flickered from their heels up to the toes.

"Who's that one, Teacher, in his painful wrath,   31
    kicking more than the others of his lot,"
    said I, "whose soles are licked by redder flame?"

"Come with me, if you like," he said, "along   34
    that farther bank, which slopes more easily.
    You'll learn of him and of his twisted wrong."

"As a thing pleases you, it pleases me.   37
    You are my lord, you know I never part
    from your will, and you know my silent thoughts."

And so we crossed to the fourth bank and turned,   40
    descending by the weaker hand until
    we reached the narrow-walked and riddled base.

My gentle Teacher held me at his hip   43
    until he set me down beside the hole
    of him who was lamenting with his shanks.

"Whoever you may be whose up is down,   46
    O wretched spirit planted like a stake,"
    said I, "give us a few words, if you can."

There I stood like a friar who hears the sins   49
    of a faithless assassin, head in grave,°
    who calls him back to hold death off awhile,

And he cried, "Are you standing there already,   52
    you standing there already, Boniface?°
    The writing has deceived me by some years!

° *head in grave:* Assassins were executed by being "planted," or buried alive, upside down.
° *Boniface:* Pope Boniface VIII.

Se' tu sì tosto di quell' aver sazio   55
   per lo qual non temesti tòrre a 'nganno
   la bella donna, e poi di farne strazio?».

Tal mi fec' io, quai son color che stanno,   58
   per non intender ciò ch'è lor risposto,
   quasi scornati, e risponder non sanno.

Allor Virgilio disse: «Dilli tosto: 61
   "Non son colui, non son colui che credi"»;
   e io rispuosi come a me fu imposto.

Per che lo spirto tutti storse i piedi;   64
   poi, sospirando e con voce di pianto,
   mi disse: «Dunque che a me richiedi?

Se di saper ch'i' sia ti cal cotanto,   67
   che tu abbi però la ripa corsa,
   sappi ch'i' fui vestito del gran manto,

e veramente fui figliuol de l'orsa,   70
   cupido sì per avanzar li orsatti,
   che sù l'avere e qui me misi in borsa.

Di sotto al capo mio son li altri tratti   73
   che precedetter me simoneggiando,
   per le fessure de la pietra piatti.

Là giù cascherò io altresì quando   76
   verrà colui ch'i' credea che tu fossi,
   allor ch'i' feci 'l sùbito dimando.

Ma più è 'l tempo già che i piè mi cossi   79
   e ch'i' son stato così sottosopra,
   ch'el non starà piantato coi piè rossi:

chè dopo lui verrà di più laida opra,   82
   di ver' ponente, un pastor sanza legge,
   tal che convien che lui e me ricuopra.

Nuovo Iasón sarà, di cui si legge   85
   ne' Maccabei; e come a quel fu molle
   suo re, così fia lui chi Francia regge».

Io non so s'i' mi fui qui troppo folle,   88
   ch'i' pur rispuosi lui a questo metro:
   «Deh, or mi dì, quanto tesoro volle

So quickly glutted, are you, with the wealth 55
    for which you didn't fear to wed by guile
    the lovely Bride,° then rend and sell her flesh?"
I was as one who takes for mockery 58
    someone's response he does not understand,
    and cannot fathom how he should reply.
Then Virgil said, "Say this to him at once: 61
    'I am not he, I am not he you think.'"
    As he instructed, so was my response.
At that the spirit writhed and wrenched his feet 64
    and, sighing, with a voice of grief and tears,
    replied, "Well then what do you want from me?
If you're so hot to know just who I was 67
    that you've come down the banks for that alone,
    know that I wore the mantle of the pope,
And was Orsini, 'the bear's son,' indeed, 70
    so eager to advance my cubs, on earth
    I stashed great wealth and here I stash myself.
Under my head the others all are crammed— 73
    my predecessor popes in simony,
    squashed flat into the fissure of the stone.
I in my turn will tumble lower when 76
    he comes, the one whom I mistook you for
    when I asked what I asked so suddenly.
But longer is the time that I'll have spent 79
    with my feet cooked and body upside down
    than he'll be planted with his feet on fire,
For after him will come a filthier work° 82
    out of the west, a shepherd without laws,
    such as must top both him and me together.
A modern Jason, he, from Maccabees: 85
    and as the first one's king was pliable,
    so he who governs France will bend for him."
I may have been too bold, I just don't know, 88
    or mad, when in this measure I replied:
    "Oh, tell me, how much treasure did He want

° *the lovely Bride:* the Church; see note to line 5 above.
° *a filthier work:* Pope Clement V; see notes.

Nostro Segnore in prima da san Pietro   91
  ch'ei ponesse le chiavi in sua balìa?
  Certo non chiese se non "Viemmi retro".
Né Pier né li altri tolsero a Matia   94
  oro od argento, quando fu sortito
  al loco che perdé l'anima ria.
Però ti sta, ché tu se' ben punito;   97
  e guarda ben la mal tolta moneta
  ch'esser ti fece contra Carlo ardito.
E se non fosse ch'ancor lo mi vieta   100
  la reverenza de le somme chiavi
  che tu tenesti ne la vita lieta,
io userei parole ancor più gravi;   103
  ché la vostra avarizia il mondo attrista,
  calcando i buoni e sollevando i pravi.
Di voi pastor s'accorse il Vangelista,   106
  quando colei che siede sopra l'acque
  puttaneggiar coi regi a lui fu vista;
quella che con le sette teste nacque,   109
  e da le diece corna ebbe argomento,
  fin che virtute al suo marito piacque.
Fatto v'avete dio d'oro e d'argento;   112
  e che altro è da voi a l'idolatre,
  se non ch'elli uno, e voi ne orate cento?
Ahi, Costantin, di quanto mal fu matre,   115
  non la tua conversion, ma quella dote
  che da te prese il primo ricco patre!».
E mentr' io li cantava cotai note,   118
  o ira o coscïenza che 'l mordesse,
  forte spingava con ambo le piote.

Out of Saint Peter, did our Lord, before   91
    he placed the keys in his authority?
    Surely he asked no more than 'Follow me.'

And neither Peter nor the others squeezed   94
    cash from Matthias when he drew the lot
    to take the place the wicked Judas lost.

Then stay right where you are, you're punished well!   97
    Make sure you guard those evil-gotten coins
    that made you bold to battle with Anjou!°

And were it not that even here in Hell   100
    I'm ruled by reverence for those highest keys°
    you once held in the happy life above,

I would use words still heavier than these—   103
    for the world is made dismal by your greed,
    raising the crooked, trampling down the good.

About you shepherds was the prophecy   106
    of the Evangelist,° when he saw her
    who sits upon the seas, whoring with kings:

The woman who was born with seven heads,   109
    who from ten horns, the Ten Commandments, took
    her strength, so long as virtue pleased her spouse.°

Silver and gold you've made into your god!   112
    How can we tell you from the idolater?
    He prays to one god—to a hundred, you.

How great the evil it was mother to—   115
    not your conversion, Constantine, but that
    dowry the first rich papa took from you!"

And while I sang the notes of such a song,   118
    anger or conscience bit him to the quick
    and made him kick his soles with violence.

° *Anjou:* Charles of Anjou; see notes.
° *highest keys:* symbols of papal authority; see Matt. 16:19.
° *the Evangelist:* Saint John, who described this woman, the Whore of Babylon (Rev. 17), using her as a symbol for Rome. Dante reinterprets her as a symbol for the corrupt Roman Church.
° *her spouse:* the Pope, in his role as Vicar of Christ; hence, wedded to the Church.
° *Donation:* the so-called Donation of Constantine, whereby the emperor gave temporal authority in Italy to the pope; see notes.

I' credo ben ch'al mio duca piacesse,   121
   con sì contenta labbia sempre attese
   lo suon de le parole vere espresse.

Però con ambo le braccia mi prese;   124
   e poi che tutto su mi s'ebbe al petto,
   rimontò per la via onde discese.

Né si stancò d'avermi a sé distretto,   127
   sì men portò sovra 'l colmo de l'arco
   che dal quarto al quinto argine è tragetto.

Quivi soavemente spuose il carco,   130
   soave per lo scoglio sconcio ed erto
   che sarebbe a le capre duro varco.

Indi un altro vallon mi fu scoperto.   133

But those words pleased my guide, I well believe,   121
    for all the while he listened to the sound
    of spoken truth, his lips were calm and glad.
Taking me in his arms, he helped me up,   124
    and, holding me against his breast, he climbed
    back up the bank the same way we went down.
It did not weary him to clutch me tight,   127
    bearing me to the summit of the arch,
    the ferry from the fourth to the fifth rim.
Here he set down his burden, tenderly,   130
    for here the rock was battered in and steep,
    a strenuous crossing for a mountain goat.
From there another valley came in sight.   133

Di nova pena mi conven far versi
    e dar matera al ventesimo canto
    de la prima canzon, ch'è d'i sommersi.
Io era già disposto tutto quanto   4
    a riguardar ne lo scoperto fondo,
    che si bagnava d'angoscioso pianto;
e vidi gente per lo vallon tondo   7
    venir, tacendo e lagrimando, al passo
    che fanno le letane in questo mondo.
Come 'l viso mi scese in lor più basso,   10
    mirabilmente apparve esser travolto
    ciascun tra 'l mento e 'l principio del casso,
ché da le reni era tornato 'l volto,   13
    e in dietro venir li convenia,
    perché 'l veder dinanzi era lor tolto.
Forse per forza già di parlasia   16
    si travolse così alcun del tutto;
    ma io nol vidi, né credo che sia.
Se Dio ti lasci, lettor, prender frutto   19
    di tua lezione, or pensa per te stesso
    com' io potea tener lo viso asciutto,

CANTO TWENTY

*In the **fourth ditch of Malebolge**, the poets see the **diviners**, who weep from heads wrenched backward on their shoulders. After pointing out some of the notable soothsayers of ancient myth, Virgil tells the story of the witch **Manto**, who gave her name to his native city, Mantua. Finally, he shows Dante the fraudulent magicians of the present age.*

Now of new punishment my verse must tell,
    lending the matter for the twentieth canto
    of my first song,° of spirits drowned in Hell.

I was disposed already to look down   4
    upon the bottom of the pouch in sight,
    bathed as it was in anguish and laments,

And I saw people in that rounding vale   7
    silently weeping, walking at a pace
    as slow and solemn as a litany.°

And when my eyes observed them farther down,   10
    they seemed miraculously screwed about
    between the chin and where the torso starts,

For backward to the kidneys turned the face,   13
    and backward always did they have to go,
    as they had lost the sight of things ahead.

Maybe in wrenchings of paralysis   16
    a man may be so wholly twisted round;
    I've never seen it, and I have my doubts.

Reader, so may God let you gather fruit   19
    from this your reading, place yourself with me
    and think how I could keep my own face dry

° *my first song:* or "canticle," one of the three divisions of the *Comedy*.
° *a litany:* a religious procession.

quando la nostra imagine di presso   22
   vidi sì torta, che 'l pianto de li occhi
   le natiche bagnava per lo fesso.
Certo io piangea, poggiato a un de' rocchi   25
   del duro scoglio, sì che la mia scorta
   mi disse: «Ancor se' tu de li altri sciocchi?
Qui vive la pietà quand' è ben morta.   28
   Chi è più scellerato che colui
   che al giudicio divin passion comporta?
Drizza la testa, drizza, e vedi a cui   31
   s'aperse a li occhi d'i Teban la terra;
   per ch'ei gridavan tutti: "Dove rui,
Anfïarao? perché lasci la guerra?".   34
   E non restò di ruinare a valle
   fino a Minòs che ciascheduno afferra.
Mira c'ha fatto petto de le spalle;   37
   perché volse veder troppo davante,
   di retro guarda e fa retroso calle.
Vedi Tiresia, che mutò sembiante   40
   quando di maschio femmina divenne,
   cangiandosi le membra tutte quante;
e prima, poi, ribatter li convenne   43
   li duo serpenti avvolti, con la verga,
   che rïavesse le maschili penne.
Aronta è quel ch'al ventre li s'atterga,   46
   che ne' monti di Luni, dove ronca
   lo Carrarese che di sotto alberga,
ebbe tra' bianchi marmi la spelonca   49
   per sua dimora; onde a guardar le stelle
   e 'l mar non li era la veduta tronca.
E quella che ricuopre le mammelle,   52
   che tu non vedi, con le trecce sciolte,
   e ha di là ogne pilosa pelle,
Manto fu, che cercò per terre molte;   55
   poscia si puose là dove nacqu' io;
   onde un poco mi piace che m'ascolte.

When I looked on our human image there 22
    so gone awry and twisted, that the eyes
    shed tears that trickled down the buttocks' crack.

I leaned upon an outcrop of the bridge 25
    and surely wept; I wept so, that my guide
    said, "Even now, with all the other fools!

Here pity lives the best when it is dead. 28
    Who is more wicked than the man who longs
    to make God's judgment yield to human force?

Lift up your head, lift it up, look at him 31
    for whom the Thebans saw the earth yawn open,
    at which they cried, 'Where are you tumbling to,

Amphiaraus? Leaving the war so soon?' 34
    Who tumbled to the pit until he came
    to Minos, he who snatches everyone.

See how he's made a breast out of his back. 37
    Because he wished to see too far ahead,
    now he looks back and walks a backward path.

See there Tiresias, he whose figure changed 40
    when he became a female from a male,
    converting every member, every limb,

Who had to beat apart, first, with a stick, 43
    two serpents twined about in intercourse,
    before he gained his manly quills again.

Aruns is he, his back to the Greek's° belly, 46
    who in the hills of Luni, harrowed by
    the Carrarese who live down in the valley,

Dwelt in a cave among those marble cliffs, 49
    and spent his nights watching the sea and stars,
    with not a thing to cut his vision short.

The woman there who covers up her breasts— 52
    her back's to you—with tresses loosed and wild,
    and on that side wears all her hairy parts,

Was Manto, who went searching many lands 55
    till settling in the place where I was born.
    Please, hear me on this topic for a bit.

° *the Greek:* Tiresias. Aruns follows him.

Poscia che 'l padre suo di vita uscìo   58
   e venne serva la città di Baco,
   questa gran tempo per lo mondo gio.

Suso in Italia bella giace un laco,   61
   a piè de l'Alpe che serra Lamagna
   sovra Tiralli, c'ha nome Benaco.

Per mille fonti, credo, e più si bagna   64
   tra Garda e Val Camonica e Pennino
   de l'acqua che nel detto laco stagna.

Loco è nel mezzo là dove 'l trentino   67
   pastore e quel di Brescia e 'l veronese
   segnar poria, s'e' fesse quel cammino.

Siede Peschiera, bello e forte arnese   70
   da fronteggiar Bresciani e Bergamaschi,
   ove la riva 'ntorno più discese.

Ivi convien che tutto quanto caschi   73
   ciò che 'n grembo a Benaco star non può,
   e fassi fiume giù per verdi paschi.

Tosto che l'acqua a correr mette co,   76
   non più Benaco, ma Mencio si chiama
   fino a Governol, dove cade in Po.

Non molto ha corso, ch'el trova una lama,   79
   ne la qual si distende e la 'mpaluda;
   e suol di state talor esser grama.

Quindi passando la vergine cruda   82
   vide terra nel mezzo del pantano,
   sanza coltura e d'abitanti nuda.

Lì, per fuggire ogne consorzio umano,   85
   ristette coi suoi servi a far sue arti,
   e visse, e vi lasciò suo corpo vano.

Li uomini poi che 'ntorno erano sparti   88
   s'accolsero a quel loco, ch'era forte
   per lo pantan ch'avea da tutte parti.

After Tiresias her father died,   58
    and Bacchus' city, Thebes, became a slave,
    this woman roved a long time through the world.
A lake above in lovely Italy   61
    lies at the foot of the Alps that cut the Tyrol
    from German lands: its name is Benaco.°
All of the hills from Garda to Pennino   64
    to Val Camonica are watered by
    the thousand springs that flow into that lake.
There in the middle is a spot° the bishops   67
    from Brescia and from Trent and from Verona
    could bless as theirs, if they should go that way.
Peschiera, strong and handsome front for war   70
    against the Brescians and the Bergamasks,
    lies to the south, on the more level shore.
Here all the water which cannot be held   73
    within the lap of Benaco must fall,
    forming a river flowing through green fields.
From the point where that stream begins to flow,   76
    they call it Mincio, and not Benaco,
    all the way to Governolo and the Po.
Not far on in its course it finds the flats   79
    and spreads itself and turns into a marsh;
    and sometimes in the summer it grows rank.
Passing by here the brutish virgin saw   82
    an island in the middle of the swamp,
    untilled, and naked of inhabitants.
And there, to flee all human intercourse,   85
    she settled with her slaves to ply her arts,
    and lived, and left her empty corpse behind.
The men who then were scattered roundabout   88
    gathered upon that island, rendered strong
    by the marsh circling round it like a moat.

° *Benaco:* the Lago di Garda.
° *a spot:* Some say that a small island in the middle of the lake lay at the boundaries of the three bishoprics.

Fer la città sovra quell'ossa morte;   91
   e per colei che 'l loco prima elesse,
   Mantüa l'appellar sanz' altra sorte.

Già fuor le genti sue dentro più spesse,   94
   prima che la mattia da Casalodi
   da Pinamonte inganno ricevesse.

Però t'assenno che, se tu mai odi   97
   originar la mia terra altrimenti,
   la verità nulla menzogna frodi».

E io: «Maestro, i tuoi ragionamenti   100
   mi son sì certi e prendon sì mia fede,
   che li altri mi sarien carboni spenti.

Ma dimmi, de la gente che procede,   103
   se tu ne vedi alcun degno di nota;
   ché solo a ciò la mia mente rifiede».

Allor mi disse: «Quel che da la gota   106
   porge la barba in su le spalle brune.
   fu—quando Grecia fu di maschi vòta,

sì ch'a pena rimaser per le cune—   109
   augure, e diede 'l punto con Calcanta
   in Aulide a tagliar la prima fune.

Euripilo ebbe nome, e così 'l canta   112
   l'alta mia tragedìa in alcun loco:
   ben lo sai tu che la sai tutta quanta.

Quell'altro che ne' fianchi è così poco,   115
   Michele Scotto fu, che veramente
   de le magiche frode seppe 'l gioco.

Vedi Guido Bonatti; vedi Asdente,   118
   ch'avere inteso al cuoio e a lo spago
   ora vorrebbe, ma tardi si pente.

Vedi le triste che lasciaron l'ago,   121
   la spuola e 'l fuso, e fecersi 'ndivine;
   fecer malie con erbe e con imago.

They built a city over those dead bones,   91
    and from her name who first picked out the place,
    drawing no lots, they called it Mantua.
Its citizens were once more numerous,   94
    before the mad and stupid Casalodi
    let Pinamonte play him for a fool.
And so I warn you, if you ever hear   97
    of any other founding of my town,
    let no deception cheat you of the truth."
"Teacher," I said, "for me your arguments   100
    possess such certainty and seize my trust,
    that all the others are extinguished coals.
But tell me of these people in procession: 103
    do you see any soul worthy of note?
    My mind keeps coming back to that alone."
And so he said, "That one who from the cheek   106
    spreads his beard down upon his swarthy back
    was a diviner, when the men of Greece
Waged war,° with hardly a boy left in the crib—   109
    and scanned the heavens with Calchas for that point
    to cut the ropes in Aulis and set sail.
Eurypylus was his name, as I have sung   112
    in my high tragedy, in a certain place,
    as you know well, because you know it all.
That other who's so skinny in the flanks   115
    was Michael Scot, and he without a doubt
    knew how to play the tricks of sorcery.
Bonatti, there; and see Toothless the cobbler   118
    who now would like to have attended more
    to string and leather; his regrets come late.
See the sad women there who left the loom,   121
    the thread and spindle, to be fortune-tellers,
    casting their spells with herbs and waxen dolls.

° *Waged war:* the Trojan War.

Ma vienne omai, ché già tiene 'l confine   124
    d'amendue li emisperi e tocca l'onda
    sotto Sobilia Caino e le spine;
e già iernotte fu la luna tonda: 127
    ben ten de' ricordar, ché non ti nocque
    alcuna volta per la selva fonda».
Sì mi parlava, e andavamo introcque.   130

But come now, for the figure in the moon—   124
    Cain° and his bush of thorns—is in the west,
    setting into the sea south of Seville,
And last night it was round and at the full.   127
    You should recall it, for from time to time
    it did not hurt you in those endless woods."
So we continued walking as he spoke.   130

° *Cain:* In Italian folklore, Cain is the man in the moon. Since the moon, nearly full, is setting, it is early in the morning.

Così di ponte in ponte, altro parlando
   che la mia comedìa cantar non cura,
   venimmo; e tenavamo 'l colmo, quando
restammo per veder l'altra fessura   4
   di Malebolge e li altri pianti vani;
   e vidila mirabilmente oscura.
Quale ne l'arzanà de' Viniziani   7
   bolle l'inverno la tenace pece
   a rimpalmare i legni lor non sani,
ché navicar non ponno—in quella vece   10
   chi fa suo legno novo e chi ristoppa
   le coste a quel che più vïaggi fece,
chi ribatte da proda e chi da poppa;   13
   altri fa remi e altri volge sarte;
   chi terzeruolo e artimon rintoppa—:
tal, non per foco ma per divin' arte,   16
   bollia là giuso una pegola spessa,
   che 'nviscava la ripa d'ogne parte.
I' vedea lei, ma non vedëa in essa   19
   mai che le bolle che 'l bollor levava,
   e gonfiar tutta, e riseder compressa.

Canto Twenty-one

*Here at the **fifth ditch of Malebolge,** where the **grafters** are punished, Dante sees a lake of **boiling tar** into which an **unnamed demon,** shouting to his fellows the **Evilclaws,** pitches the **alderman of Lucca.** Virgil instructs Dante to hide while he speaks to **Eviltail,** the leader of the platoon of Evilclaws. Finally, Eviltail assigns a troop of ten demons, led by **Curlybeard,** to escort Dante and Virgil to the next bridge, which, as we will learn, does not exist.*

And so from one bridge to the next we came,
    talking of things I do not care to sing
    within my Comedy, and reached the top,
And rested there to see the other crack   4
    of Evil Pouches, and their useless cries;
    and what we looked upon was wondrous black.
As sailors in the Arsenal of Venice   7
    boil the whole winter long the tight-grip tar
    to caulk the loosened planks of hulls and keels,
For there's no sailing then—so this one builds   10
    himself a brand-new boat, that one stops up
    the ribs of his that's made a lot of trips;
They hammer at the prow or at the poop,   13
    and some carve oars and some twist cords for rope,
    some stitch the jib or patch the mainsail up—
So boiled below us a thick pot of pitch,   16
    never by fire but by the art of God,
    leaving the banks all sticky in this ditch.
I saw the tar, but in it I could see   19
    nothing but bubbles that the boiling raised,
    puffing and swelling big until they popped.

Mentr' io là giù fisamente mirava,   22
   lo duca mio, dicendo «Guarda, guarda!»
   mi trasse a sé del loco dov' io stava.

Allor mi volsi come l'uom cui tarda   25
   di veder quel che li convien fuggire
   e cui paura sùbita sgagliarda,

che, per veder, non indugia 'l partire: 28
   e vidi dietro a noi un diavol nero
   correndo su per lo scoglio venire.

Ahi quant' elli era ne l'aspetto fero!   31
   e quanto mi parea ne l'atto acerbo,
   con l'ali aperte e sovra i piè leggero!

L'omero suo, ch'era aguto e superbo,   34
   carcava un peccator con ambo l'anche,
   e quei tenea de' piè ghermito 'l nerbo.

Del nostro ponte disse: «O Malebranche,   37
   ecco un de li anzïan di Santa Zita!
   Mettetel sotto, ch'i' torno per anche

a quella terra, che n'è ben fornita: 40
   ogn' uom v'è barattier, fuor che Bonturo.
   Del no, per li denar, vi si fa *ita*».

La giù 'l buttò, e per lo scoglio duro   43
   si volse; e mai non fu mastino sciolto
   con tanta fretta a seguitar lo furo.

Quel s'attuffò, e tornò sù convolto;   46
   ma i demon che del ponte avean coperchio,
   gridar: «Qui non ha loco il Santo Volto!

qui si nuota altrimenti che nel Serchio!   49
   Però, se tu non vuo' di nostri graffi,
   non far sopra la pegola soverchio».

Poi l'addentar con più di cento raffi,   52
   disser: «Coverto convien che qui balli,
   sì che, se puoi, nascosamente accaffi».

While down below attentively I gazed,   22
    my guide hollered to me, "Look out, look out!"
    and grabbed me from the spot where I was standing.

I turned as one who can't just wait to see   25
    (although his valor fails for sudden fear)
    whatever thing it is that he must flee,

Who looks but takes no time in getting out—   28
    and there behind us, scrambling up the ridge,
    I saw a devil coming, black as Hell.

Ah, how his face was fiercer than a beast's!   31
    How cruel his behavior seemed to me,
    his wings spread open and his feet that flew!

Over his shoulder, spiked and hunched for pride,   34
    he slung a sinner by the ankles both
    and snagged him by the sinews of his feet.

He shouted from our bridge, "Hey, Evilclaws!   37
    One of the aldermen of Santa Zita!°
    Stick this one under while I go for more,

For that's a town that's got 'em stocked in force.   40
    Everyone takes a bribe except Bonturo!
    A 'no,' for money, turns into 'of course.' "

He flung him down, and over the rough ridge   43
    he sped—no mastiff ever ran so fast,
    snapping his chain to catch the fleeing thief.

That soul plunged in and bobbed up with his rear.   46
    Sneaking behind the bridge the demons cried,
    "The Holy Face° has got no business here!

The Serchio° is no swimming hole like this!   49
    Unless you want to taste our hooks, make sure
    no part of you sticks up out of the pitch."

When they'd harpooned him with a hundred prongs   52
    they jeered, "You do your jigs here undercover,
    so grab the cash in hiding, if you can!"

° *Santa Zita:* the city of Lucca. Santa Zita was a thirteenth-century holy woman of Lucca. Although the Church had not yet affirmed her sainthood, she had a devoted following in her native city.
° *The Holy Face:* A dark wooden icon of Christ, in the Byzantine style, kept in the Church of San Martino.
° *The Serchio:* a river near Lucca.

Non altrimenti i cuoci a' lor vassalli   55
   fanno attuffare in mezzo la caldaia
   la carne con li uncin, perché non galli.

Lo buon maestro «Acciò che non si paia   58
   che tu ci sia», mi disse, «giù t'acquatta
   dopo uno scheggio, ch'alcun schermo t'aia;

e per nulla offension che mi sia fatta,   61
   non temer tu, ch'i' ho le cose conte,
   perch' altra volta fui a tal baratta».

Poscia passò di là dal co del ponte;   64
   e com' el giunse in su la ripa sesta,
   mestier li fu d'aver sicura fronte.

Con quel furore e con quella tempesta   67
   ch'escono i cani a dosso al poverello
   che di sùbito chiede ove s'arresta,

usciron quei di sotto al ponticello,   70
   e volser contra lui tutt' i runcigli;
   ma el gridò: «Nessun di voi sia fello!

Innanzi che l'uncin vostro mi pigli,   73
   traggasi avante l'un di voi che m'oda,
   e poi d'arruncigliarmi si consigli».

Tutti gridaron: «Vada Malacoda!»;   76
   per ch'un si mosse—e li altri stetter fermi—
   e venne a lui dicendo: «Che li approda?».

«Credi tu, Malacoda, qui vedermi   79
   esser venuto», disse 'l mio maestro,
   «sicuro già da tutti vostri schermi,

sanza voler divino e fato destro?   82
   Lascian' andar, ché nel cielo è voluto
   ch'i' mostri altrui questo cammin silvestro».

Allor li fu l'orgoglio sì caduto,   85
   ch'e' si lasciò cascar l'uncino a' piedi,
   e disse a li altri: «Omai non sia feruto».

E 'l duca mio a me: «O tu che siedi   88
   tra li scheggion del ponte quatto quatto,
   sicuramente omai a me ti riedi».

Just so, the cooks will make their scullery boys   55
    stick forks into a pot of stew to keep
    the hunks of meat from bobbing to the top.

Said my good Teacher then, "So that they don't   58
    know that you're here, go squat behind some rock
    and get yourself a hideout, and remember,

No matter what offense they do to me,   61
    don't be afraid—I've got things reckoned up,
    for I've been through this wrangling place before."

Then he passed over from the bridge's head,   64
    and as he reached the bank of the sixth ditch
    he had to show some boldness in his brow.

With just such storm and such a frenzied rage   67
    dogs race out in the track of the poor soul
    who stands stock-still and begs from where he is

As rushed the demons from beneath the pier   70
    and turned their grappling hooks against his face,
    but he cried, "Better make no mischief here!

Before you snag me on your hooks, you'd best   73
    get one of you to come and hear me out,
    and then decide to stick the fork in me."

And they all cried out, "Eviltail should go!"   76
    One of them stepped up—all the rest stood pat—
    saying, "What good does he think this will do?"

"Eviltail, do you really think you see   79
    me coming here," my Teacher said, "secure
    from every obstacle you've put before me,

Without the favor and the will of God?   82
    So let me go, since it is willed in Heaven
    that I should show someone this savage road."

At that, so disappointed was his pride   85
    he let the hook fall clanking to his feet
    and said, "There won't be any stabbing now."

And then my guide to me: "O you who sit   88
    among the rocks all crouched and huddled up,
    you can come back to me now, safe and sound."

Per ch'io mi mossi e a lui venni ratto;   91
   e i diavoli si fecer tutti avanti,
   sì ch'io temetti ch'ei tenesser patto;
così vid' ïo già temer li fanti   94
   ch'uscivan patteggiati di Caprona,
   veggendo sé tra nemici cotanti.
I' m'accostai con tutta la persona   97
   lungo 'l mio duca, e non torceva li occhi
   da la sembianza lor ch'era non buona.
Ei chinavan li raffi e «Vuo' che 'l tocchi»,   100
   diceva l'un con l'altro, «in sul groppone?».
   E rispondien: «Sì, fa che gliel' accocchi».
Ma quel demonio che tenea sermone   103
   col duca mio, si volse tutto presto
   e disse: «Posa, posa, Scarmiglione!».
Poi disse a noi: «Più oltre andar per questo   106
   iscoglio non si può, però che giace
   tutto spezzato al fondo l'arco sesto.
E se l'andare avante pur vi piace,   109
   andatevene su per questa grotta;
   presso è un altro scoglio che via face.
Ier, più oltre cinqu' ore che quest' otta,   112
   mille dugento con sessanta sei
   anni compié che qui la via fu rotta.
Io mando verso là di questi miei   115
   a riguardar s'alcun se ne sciorina;
   gite con lor, che non saranno rei».
«Tra'ti avante, Alichino, e Calcabrina»,   118
   cominciò elli a dire, «e tu, Cagnazzo;
   e Barbariccia guidi la decina.
Libicocco vegn' oltre e Draghignazzo,   121
   Cirïatto sannuto e Graffiacane
   e Farfarello e Rubicante pazzo.
Cercate 'ntorno le boglienti pane;   124
   costor sian salvi infino a l'altro scheggio
   che tutto intero va sovra le tane».

So I came out and hurried up to him, 91
   and all the devils made as if to lunge,
   so that I feared they wouldn't keep the deal,

As once I saw foot soldiers grow afraid 94
   when they marched with safe conduct from Caprona,
   surrounded by so many enemies.

I pressed myself close to my leader's side 97
   from head to toe, and never let my eyes
   turn from their faces, for they were not kind.

They cocked their hooks and said, one to the next, 100
   "Want I should touch him on the rump a bit?"
   And they replied, "Go on and give it to him!"

The demon who was speaking to my guide 103
   heard it and wheeled around immediately
   and said, "At ease, at ease there, Crumplehead!"

Then said to us: "There's no way down this ridge. 106
   The arch is smashed and toppled to the ground
   that used to serve the sixth ditch for a bridge.

But if you do still want to go on down, 109
   come along by this bank. It's not too far
   before you'll find another ridge to cross.

Yesterday, five hours later than this hour, 112
   one thousand and two hundred sixty-six
   years were completed since the road collapsed.

I'm sending some of these my boys down there 115
   to check if someone's airing himself out.
   Go on with them. They won't do any harm.

Step forward, Tramplefrost and Harlequin!"— 118
   so he began to them—"and Larddog, you,
   and Curlybeard, you lead the troop of ten.

And Stormbreath, march along, and Dragonsnout, 121
   Dogscratcher and tusky Swinetooth too,
   and Gobgoblin and Redfroth howling mad.

Go all around to search the boiling glue; 124
   keep these men safe until that other ridge,
   the one that crosses all the dens intact."

«Omè, maestro, che è quel ch'i' veggio?»,   127
   diss' io, «deh, sanza scorta andianci soli,
   se tu sa' ir, ch'i' per me non la cheggio!
Se tu se' sì accorto come suoli,   130
   non vedi tu ch'e' digrignan li denti
   e con le ciglia ne minaccian duoli?».
Ed elli a me: «Non vo' che tu paventi.   133
   Lasciali digrignar pur a lor senno,
   ch'e' fanno ciò per li lessi dolenti».
Per l'argine sinistro volta dienno;   136
   ma prima avea ciascun la lingua stretta
   coi denti, verso lor duca, per cenno;
ed elli avea del cul fatto trombetta.   139

"Oh no, Teacher!" said I. "What's this I see?　　　　127
　　Let's go alone, if you can find the way,
　　without an escort—I don't want one, me!
If you're as wary as you've ever been,　　　　　130
　　don't you see how they grin and grit their teeth
　　and arch their brows to threaten us with pain?"
And he to me: "You mustn't be afraid.　　　　　133
　　Let them go grit their teeth if they think best.
　　They do it for the boiled meat in the pitch."
Then the platoon turned sharp left on the bank,　　136
　　but first they'd stuck their tongues between their teeth
　　and blown it at their sergeant for a sign,
And he had made a bugle of his arse.　　　　　139

Io vidi già cavalier muover campo,
    e cominciare stormo e far lor mostra,
    e talvolta partir per loro scampo;
corridor vidi per la terra vostra,   4
    o Aretini, e vidi gir gualdane,
    fedir torneamenti e correr giostra;
quando con trombe, e quando con campane,   7
    con tamburi e con cenni di castella,
    e con cose nostrali e con istrane;
né già con sì diversa cennamella   10
    cavalier vidi muover né pedoni,
    né nave a segno di terra o di stella.
Noi andavam con li diece demoni.   13
    Ahi fiera compagnia! ma ne la chiesa
    coi santi, e in taverna coi ghiottoni.
Pur a la pegola era la mia 'ntesa,   16
    per veder de la bolgia ogne contegno
    e de la gente ch'entro v'era incesa.
Come i dalfini, quando fanno segno   19
    a' marinar con l'arco de la schiena
    che s'argomentin di campar lor legno,
talor così, ad alleggiar la pena,   22
    mostrav' alcun de' peccatori 'l dosso
    e nascondea in men che non balena.

CANTO TWENTY-TWO

*Still in the **fifth ditch of Malebolge**, the demons harpoon a **Navarrese bribe taker**,
who names others in the lake and escapes from the Evilclaws by pretending to trick some
of his comrades into coming out. Enraged, the demon Harlequin flies after him, to no
avail, and becomes entangled in a scuffle with his fellow Tramplefrost. They both fall
into the boiling pitch.*

I've seen, in my day, cavalry break camp,
 storm to attack, and muster for parade,
 and sometimes beat retreat to save their lives;
I have seen scouts ride horseback through your lands, 4
 O Aretines, and raiding parties rush,
 and clashing tournaments and galloping jousts;
Sometimes with trumpet blasts, sometimes with bells, 7
 with drums, with signals from the battlements,
 with native gear and that of other lands;
But never a mounted knight or squad afoot 10
 or boat that waits the lantern or the stars
 have I seen move for so bizarre a flute.
With the ten demons then we took our way. 13
 What savage company! But as they say,
 "In church with saints, and in the stews with swine."
For all that, I attended to the tar, 16
 to witness each particular of this pouch
 and of the people it must stew and char.
As do the dolphins when they make a sign 19
 to sailors by the arching of their backs
 that they should save their ship before it storms,
So, sometimes, to alleviate the pain, 22
 one of the sinners showed his backside up,
 then hid it like a lightning flash again.

E come a l'orlo de l'acqua d'un fosso   25
   stanno i ranocchi pur col muso fuori,
   sì che celano i piedi e l'altro grosso,
sì stavan d'ogne parte i peccatori;   28
   ma come s'appressava Barbariccia,
   così si ritraén sotto i bollori.
I' vidi, e anco il cor me n'accapriccia,   31
   uno aspettar così, com' elli 'ncontra
   ch'una rana rimane e l'altra spiccia;
e Graffiacan, che li era più di contra,   34
   li arruncigliò le 'mpegolate chiome
   e trassel sù, che mi parve una lontra.
I' sapea già di tutti quanti 'l nome,   37
   sì li notai quando fuorono eletti,
   e poi ch'e' si chiamaro, attesi come.
«O Rubicante, fa che tu li metti   40
   li unghioni a dosso, sì che tu lo scuoi!»,
   gridavan tutti insieme i maladetti.
E io: «Maestro mio, fa, se tu puoi,   43
   che tu sappi chi è lo sciagurato
   venuto a man de li avversari suoi».
Lo duca mio li s'accostò allato;   46
   domandollo ond' ei fosse, e quei rispuose:
   «I' fui del regno di Navarra nato.
Mia madre a servo d'un segnor mi puose,   49
   che m'avea generato d'un ribaldo,
   distruggitor di sé e di sue cose.
Poi fui famiglia del buon re Tebaldo;   52
   quivi mi misi a far baratteria,
   di ch'io rendo ragione in questo caldo».
E Ciriatto, a cui di bocca uscia   55
   d'ogne parte una sanna come a porco,
   li fé sentir come l'una sdruscia.
Tra male gatte era venuto 'l sorco;   58
   ma Barbariccia il chiuse con le braccia
   e disse: «State in là, mentr' io lo 'nforco».

As at the water's edge beside a ditch   25
    the bullfrogs perch with muzzle sticking out,
    and hide the legs and all the bulging paunch,
So stood these sinners everywhere you'd scout,   28
    but soon as they saw Curlybeard draw near,
    so too they dunked beneath the bubbling pitch.
I saw—it makes my heart shake to this day—   31
    one wait too long, as it can happen that
    this frog stays out while that frog darts away,
And Dogscratcher, right there in front of him,   34
    hooked him and dragged him by the tar-clogged locks,
    and pulled him like an otter from a pond.
(I knew the names of every devil there,   37
    for I had noted them when they were picked,
    and later heard what they would call themselves.)
"Hey, Redfroth, set your nails in this one here!   40
    Claw him and strip the leather from his back!"
    the cursed demons hollered all together.
"My Teacher, please," I asked him, "if you can,   43
    discover who he is whose wretched luck
    has put him in his adversaries' hands."
My guide then walked up to the man in tar   46
    and asked him where he came from, and he answered,
    "I was born in the kingdom of Navarre.
My mother made me servant to a lord.   49
    She'd gotten pregnant by a worthless rogue,
    one who destroyed himself and all his wealth.
Then I was a valet for the good king   52
    Thibault, and there I started to take bribes,
    and in this heat I pay the reckoning."
And Swinetooth, from whose mouth on each side stuck   55
    a tusk like a wild boar's, gave him to feel
    how one of them could rip his stitches out.
The rat had fallen in with wicked cats!   58
    Curlybeard fenced him with his arms stretched wide—
    "Keep clear, you! Mine's the fork for this one here."

E al maestro mio volse la faccia: 61
   «Domanda», disse, «ancor, se più disii
   saper da lui, prima ch'altri 'l disfaccia».
Lo duca dunque: «Or dì: de li altri rii   64
   conosci tu alcun che sia latino
   sotto la pece?». E quelli: «I' mi partii,
poco è, da un che fu di là vicino.   67
   Così foss' io ancor con lui coperto,
   ch'i' non temerei unghia né uncino!».
E Libicocco «Troppo avem sofferto»,   70
   disse, e preseli 'l braccio col runciglio,
   sì che, stracciando, ne portò un lacerto.
Draghignazzo anco i volle dar di piglio   73
   giuso a le gambe; onde 'l decurio loro
   si volse intorno intorno con mal piglio.
Quand' elli un poco rappaciati fuoro,   76
   a lui, ch'ancor mirava sua ferita,
   domandò 'l duca mio sanza dimoro:
«Chi fu colui da cui mala partita   79
   di' che facesti per venire a proda?».
   Ed ei rispuose: «Fu frate Gomita,
quel di Gallura, vasel d'ogne froda,   82
   ch'ebbe i nemici di suo donno in mano,
   e fé sì lor, che ciascun se ne loda.
Danar si tolse e lasciolli di piano,   85
   sì com' e' dice; e ne li altri offici anche
   barattier fu non picciol, ma sovrano.
Usa con esso donno Michel Zanche   88
   di Logodoro; e a dir di Sardigna
   le lingue lor non si sentono stanche.
Omè, vedete l'altro che digrigna!   91
   I' direi anche, ma i' temo ch'ello
   non s'apparecchi a grattarmi la tigna».
E 'l gran proposto, vòlto a Farfarello   94
   che stralunava li occhi per fedire,
   disse: «Fatti 'n costà, malvagio uccello!».

And to my Teacher then he turned his face: 61
    "Ask him what else you'd like to know of him,
    before somebody else rips him apart."
So then the guide: "Now tell us if you know   64
    if there are any souls from Italy
    under the tar?" And that one said, "Just now
I left a spirit from a land nearby.   67
    I wish I were still covered up with him,
    I wouldn't have to fear the hook or claw!"
Said Stormbreath, "We've put up with this too long!"   70
    and with his grappler snagged him by the arm,
    yanked it and tore away a muscle whole.
Dragonsnout also wanted to join in   73
    and give it to him in the legs—but their
    sergeant wheeled round and round with angry eye.
When they had held their peace a little while,   76
    my leader did not pause, but asked the sinner,
    who was still gazing on his open wound,
"Who was that man you say you left behind   79
    unluckily, to come upon the shore?"
    "That was Friar Gomita," he replied,
"He of Sardinia, vessel of all fraud,   82
    who had his master's enemies in hand
    and treated them to earn the praise of all.
For he took bribes and let them off scot-free—   85
    those are his words. In other duties too
    no small-time, but the king of grafters, he.
And Michel Zanche, lord of Logodoro,   88
    hangs with him, and their tongues are never tired
    of talking of their damned Sardinia.
Oh no, that other demon bares his fangs!   91
    I'd tell you a lot more, but I'm afraid
    he's setting up to scratch me on the mange!"
The big commander turned to Gobgoblin,   94
    who rolled his crazy eyes before he struck,
    and said, "Get over there, you filthy crow!"

«Se voi volete vedere o udire»,   97
   ricominciò lo spaürato appresso,
   «Toschi o Lombardi, io ne farò venire;
ma stieno i Malebranche un poco in cesso,   100
   sì ch'ei non teman de le lor vendette;
   e io, seggendo in questo loco stesso,
per un ch'io son, ne farò venir sette   103
   quand' io suffolerò, com' è nostro uso
   di fare allor che fori alcun si mette».
Cagnazzo a cotal motto levò 'l muso,   106
   crollando 'l capo, e disse: «Odi malizia
   ch'elli ha pensata per gittarsi giuso!».
Ond' ei, ch'avea lacciuoli a gran divizia,   109
   rispuose: «Malizioso son io troppo.
   quand' io procuro a' miei maggior trestizia».
Alichin non si tenne e, di rintoppo   112
   a li altri, disse a lui: «Se tu ti cali,
   io non ti verrò dietro di gualoppo,
ma batterò sovra la pece l'ali.   115
   Lascisi 'l collo, e sia la ripa scudo,
   a veder se tu sol più di noi vali».
O tu che leggi, udirai nuovo ludo: 118
   ciascun da l'altra costa li occhi volse,
   quel prima, ch'a ciò fare era più crudo.
Lo Navarrese ben suo tempo colse: 121
   fermò le piante a terra, e in un punto
   saltò e dal proposto lor si sciolse.
Di che ciascun di colpa fu compunto,   124
   ma quei più che cagion fu del difetto;
   però si mosse e gridò: «Tu se' giunto!».
Ma poco i valse: ché l'ali al sospetto   127
   non potero avanzar; quelli andò sotto,
   e quei drizzò volando suso il petto,
non altrimenti l'anitra di botto,   130
   quando 'l falcon s'appressa, giù s'attuffa,
   ed ei ritorna sù crucciato e rotto.

"If you would like to see or hear some more,"   97
    the spirit, terrified, resumed at once,
      "Tuscans, Lombards, I'll make 'em all come out,

But have the Evilclaws step back a bit   100
    so they won't be afraid of their revenge,
      and I, while standing in this very spot,

For one of me, I'll see that seven appear!   103
    I'll whistle, which is what we always do
      whenever we can see the coast is clear."

The Larddog raised his muzzle at those words   106
    and shook his head and said, "It's all a trick,
      a nasty trick so he can jump back in!"

And he, who had a wealth of shifts and snares: 109
    "Now I'm an evil trickster, yes I am,
      conniving greater sorrow for my friends."

Harlequin couldn't hold back, so he said,   112
    contrary to the rest, "You go and dive,
      I won't come at your traces at a gallop—

I'll be batting my wings above the pitch!   115
    Let's leave the edge and hide behind the slope
      and see if you can beat us by yourself."

O Reader, hear this new sport! Each one turned   118
    his eyes an instant to the farther shore—
      Larddog the first, who had resisted most.

He chose his moment well, that Navarrese: 121
    planted his heels and at a single leap
      slipped from the plotting of his enemies.

Each of the devils was stung with shame for that,   124
    he most of all who brought on the mistake,
      so he set off and cried, "I've got you now!"

But to no good: his wings could never fly   127
    as fast as fear. So that one went below
      and this one flapped his wings to pull up short,

Just as a duck who sees the hawk swoop down   130
    aiming for her—she dives at once, and he
      has to return above, ruffled and vexed.

Irato Calcabrina de la buffa,   133
   volando dietro li tenne, invaghito
   che quei campasse per aver la zuffa;
e come 'l barattier fu disparito,   136
   così volse li artigli al suo compagno,
   e fu con lui sopra 'l fosso ghermito.
Ma l'altro fu bene sparvier grifagno   139
   ad artigliar ben lui, e amendue
   cadder nel mezzo del bogliente stagno.
Lo caldo sghermitor sùbito fue;   142
   ma però di levarsi era neente,
   sì avieno inviscate l'ali sue.
Barbariccia, con li altri suoi dolente,   145
   quattro ne fé volar da l'altra costa
   con tutt' i raffi, e assai prestamente
di qua, di là discesero a la posta;   148
   porser li uncini verso li 'mpaniati,
   ch'eran già cotti dentro da la crosta.
E noi lasciammo lor così 'mpacciati.   151

Tramplefrost took the joke in rage, and flew 133
    right after Harlequin, eager to see
    that soul escape so he could start a brawl,
And when the barterer had disappeared 136
    he turned his talons to his fellow demon
    and clutched him in a hold above the trench.
The other was a full-grown falcon too 139
    if it should come to talons, and they both
    fell in the middle of the boiling pool.
The heat did its dis-grappling pretty quick, 142
    but for all that, there was no getting up
    with wings so limed in tar and clotted thick.
Curlybeard, groaning with the rest of them, 145
    commanded four to fly to the far side,
    harpoons and all, and with the greatest speed
The demons flew to man the posts assigned, 148
    and stuck their hooks into their glued-up fellows,
    who were already cooked beneath the crust.
And so we left them in that tangled mess. 151

Taciti, soli, sanza compagnia
     n'andavam l'un dinanzi e l'altro dopo,
     come frati minor vanno per via.
Vòlt' era in su la favola d'Isopo   4
     lo mio pensier per la presente rissa,
     dov' el parlò de la rana e del topo;
ché più non si pareggia 'mo' e 'issa'   7
     che l'un con l'altro fa, se ben s'accoppia
     principio e fine con la mente fissa.
E come l'un pensier de l'altro scoppia,   10
     così nacque di quello un altro poi,
     che la prima paura mi fé doppia.
Io pensava così: «Questi per noi   13
     sono scherniti con danno e con beffa
     sì fatta, ch'assai credo che lor nòi.
Se l'ira sovra 'l mal voler s'aggueffa,   16
     ei ne verranno dietro più crudeli
     che 'l cane a quella lievre ch'elli acceffa».
Già mi sentia tutti arricciar li peli   19
     de la paura e stava in dietro intento,
     quand' io dissi: «Maestro, se non celi

CANTO TWENTY-THREE

Virgil and Dante escape from the Evilclaws by sliding down the steep bank into the
sixth ditch of Malebolge. *Here, walking with gilded cloaks of lead, go the* **hypocrites.**
Dante speaks to two friars, **Catalano** *and* **Loderingo,** *whose hypocrisy set the stage*
for civil bloodshed in Florence. While speaking to them, he observes the high priest
Caiaphas, *crucified to the floor of Hell. From Catalano, Virgil finally learns of the*
treachery of the Evilclaws in the ditch above.

Silent, alone, no escort at our side,
   we set out, one before and one behind,
   as Friars Minor° walk in single file.
The skirmish we'd just seen reminded me   4
   of one of Aesop's fables, where he tells
   about the frog and mouse who crossed the stream,
For "presently" and "soon" are not so close   7
   as those are, if you fix your mind on them
   and pair them from beginning to the end.
And as one thought will jump into the next,   10
   so from this thought another one was born,
   which made me twice as frightened as before.
"These demons took a hurt on our account   13
   and were well mocked," so I thought to myself,
   "and you can bet it rankles a good deal.
If you wind wrath around the spool with hate,   16
   they should be coming back thirstier for blood
   than a dog who snaps a rabbit in his teeth."
Then I could feel the hair curl on my flesh,   19
   and standing back a bit, intent with fear,
   I said, "Please, Teacher, if you don't move fast

° *Friars Minor:* Franciscans, the "little friars," walking in slow procession at their prayers.

THE HYPOCRITES—CRUCIFIED PHARISEE

te e me tostamente, i' ho pavento 22
    d'i Malebranche. Noi li avem già dietro;
    io li 'magino sì, che già li sento».

E quei: «S'i' fossi di piombato vetro, 25
    l'imagine di fuor tua non trarrei
    più tosto a me, che quella dentro 'mpetro.

Pur mo venieno i tuo' pensier tra' miei, 28
    con simile atto e con simile faccia,
    sì che d'intrambi un sol consiglio fei.

S'elli è che sì la destra costa giaccia, 31
    che noi possiam ne l'altra bolgia scendere,
    noi fuggirem l'imaginata caccia».

Già non compié di tal consiglio rendere, 34
    ch'io li vidi venir con l'ali tese
    non molto lungi, per volerne prendere.

Lo duca mio di sùbito mi prese, 37
    come la madre ch'al romore è desta
    e vede presso a sé le fiamme accese,

che prende il figlio e fugge e non s'arresta, 40
    avendo più di lui che di sé cura,
    tanto che solo una camiscia vesta;

e giù dal collo de la ripa dura 43
    supin si diede a la pendente roccia,
    che l'un de' lati a l'altra bolgia tura.

Non corse mai sì tosto acqua per doccia 46
    a volger ruota di molin terragno,
    quand' ella più verso le pale approccia,

come 'l maestro mio per quel vivagno, 49
    portandosene me sovra 'l suo petto,
    come suo figlio, non come compagno.

A pena fuoro i piè suoi giunti al letto 52
    del fondo giù, ch'e' furon in sul colle
    sovresso noi; ma non li era sospetto:

ché l'alta provedenza che lor volle 55
    porre ministri de la fossa quinta,
    poder di partirs' indi a tutti tolle.

And hide yourself and me, I'm fearful of 22
 the Evilclaws—they're gaining on us now!
 What I imagine, I can almost feel!"
And he: "Were I a pane of leaded glass° 25
 your outer form would not reflect as soon
 as I receive the image of your thoughts.
Now more than ever they walk along with mine; 28
 their gestures and expressions are the same.
 So I've devised a single plan from both.
If the slope at the right bank will allow, 31
 we can descend into the other ditch
 and flee the hunting you imagine now."
He'd hardly got two words out for his plan 34
 when I caught sight of them not far away,
 their wings spread wide to overtake and snatch.
All of a sudden my guide seized me—as 37
 a mother who is wakened by a noise
 and sees the leaping flames beside her bed
Seizes her child and flees and does not stop, 40
 having more care for him than for herself,
 without even a smock to cover up—
And from the neck of the rough slope of rock 43
 he took flat on his back the tumbled scarp
 that plugs the near side of the ditch beyond.
Water that gushes down the sluice to turn 46
 the wheel of a great grindstone at a mill
 not even at the paddles falls so fast
As fell my master down that bordering stone, 49
 bearing me on his chest as he slid down—
 not as his fellow or friend, but as his son.
And hardly had his feet touched at the base 52
 when they had reached the summit over us,
 but now we need have no more doubts of them.
For though high Providence has willed that they 55
 be ministers of pain in the fifth ditch,
 all power to leave that ditch it takes away.

° *a pane of leaded glass:* a mirror.

Là giù trovammo una gente dipinta   58
    che giva intorno assai con lenti passi,
    piangendo e nel sembiante stanca e vinta.

Elli avean cappe con cappucci bassi   61
    dinanzi a li occhi, fatte de la taglia
    che in Clugnì per li monaci fassi.

Di fuor dorate son, sì ch'elli abbaglia;   64
    ma dentro tutte piombo, e gravi tanto,
    che Federigo le mettea di paglia.

Oh in etterno faticoso manto!   67
    Noi ci volgemmo ancor pur a man manca
    con loro insieme, intenti al tristo pianto;

ma per lo peso quella gente stanca   70
    venìa sì pian, che noi eravam nuovi
    di compagnia ad ogne mover d'anca.

Per ch'io al duca mio: «Fa che tu trovi   73
    alcun ch'al fatto o al nome si conosca,
    e li occhi, sì andando, intorno movi».

E un che 'ntese la parola tosca,   76
    di retro a noi gridò: «Tenete i piedi,
    voi che correte sì per l'aura fosca!

Forse ch'avrai da me quel che tu chiedi».   79
    Onde 'l duca si volse e disse: «Aspetta,
    e poi secondo il suo passo procedi».

Ristetti, e vidi due mostrar gran fretta   82
    de l'animo, col viso, d'esser meco;
    ma tardavali 'l carco e la via stretta.

Quando fuor giunti, assai con l'occhio bieco   85
    mi rimiraron sanza far parola;
    poi si volsero in sé, e dicean seco:

«Costui par vivo a l'atto de la gola;   88
    e s'e' son morti, per qual privilegio
    vanno scoperti de la grave stola?».

Poi disser me: «O Tosco, ch'al collegio   91
    de l'ipocriti tristi se' venuto,
    dir chi tu se' non avere in dispregio».

Down there we found a painted populace   58
   who walked about with slow, slow steps, and wept;
   exhaustion and defeat dwelt in each face.

They all wore hooded capes with cowls that hung   61
   over their eyes, cut in the ample style
   they like to use at Cluny for the monks.

The outsides all were gilt in blinding gold;   64
   inside, all lead, so heavy, the lead cloaks
   Frederick made felons wear were light as straw.

O weary mantle for eternity!   67
   Still we turned to the left and walked with them,
   and listened to their moans attentively.

But for that heavy burden the tired crew   70
   went slow, so slow, that when we moved the hip
   the company we walked beside was new.

"Please, find someone," I therefore asked my guide,   73
   "whom we might recognize by deed or name.
   We can walk still, and look from side to side."

And one who heard the Tuscan in my speech   76
   cried from behind us, "Hold your feet a bit,
   you who go racing through the troubled air.

It may be I can give you what you need."   79
   At that, my guide turned round to me to say,
   "Wait, and then at the sinner's pace proceed."

So there I stood, and saw two spirits show   82
   great haste to reach me—haste of will, seen in
   their faces; for their burdens made them slow,

As did the crowded way. They came; they looked   85
   sidelong at me, and did not say a word.
   Turned to each other then, and commented:

"This one's alive, it seems. His throat, it moves.   88
   And if they *are* dead, by what privilege
   can they go on without the leaden stole?"

To me: "O Tuscan, who have come unto   91
   the brotherhood of long-faced hypocrites,
   do not think ill to tell us who you are."

E io a loro: «I' fui nato e cresciuto   94
    sovra 'l bel fiume d'Arno a la gran villa,
    e son col corpo ch'i' ho sempre avuto.

Ma voi chi siete, a cui tanto distilla   97
    quant' i' veggio dolor giù per le guance?
    e che pena è in voi che sì sfavilla?».

E l'un rispuose a me: «Le cappe rance   100
    son di piombo sì grosse, che li pesi
    fan così cigolar le lor bilance.

Frati godenti fummo, e bolognesi;   103
    io Catalano e questi Loderingo
    nomati, e da tua terra insieme presi

come suole esser tolto un uom solingo,   106
    per conservar sua pace; e fummo tali,
    ch'ancor si pare intorno dal Gardingo».

Io cominciai: «O frati, i vostri mali . . . »;   109
    ma più non dissi, ch'a l'occhio mi corse
    un, crucifisso in terra con tre pali.

Quando mi vide, tutto si distorse,   112
    soffiando ne la barba con sospiri;
    e 'l frate Catalan, ch'a ciò s'accorse,

mi disse: «Quel confitto che tu miri,   115
    consigliò i Farisei che convenia
    porre un uom per lo popolo a' martìri.

Attraversato è, nudo, ne la via,   118
    come tu vedi, ed è mestier ch'el senta
    qualunque passa, come pesa, pria.

E a tal modo il socero si stenta   121
    in questa fossa, e li altri dal concilio
    che fu per li Giudei mala sementa».

Allor vid' io maravigliar Virgilio   124
    sovra colui ch'era disteso in croce
    tanto vilmente ne l'etterno essilio.

And I to them: "In the great town that stands 94
   on the sweet Arno I was born and bred.
   This is the body I have always had.

But who are you, distilled in drops of woe, 97
   so many drops that fall along the cheek?
   What is your punishment that glitters so?"

And one replied to me: "Our yellow capes 100
   are made of lead so heavy that the weight,
   as you can hear, causes the scales to creak.

We two were Jolly Friars, Bolognese: 103
   I Catalano, Loderingo he.
   Your city called us in to keep the peace.

They took us both at once to fill a place 106
   a single man would hold, and what we were,
   the ruins on the Gardingo leave a trace."

"O friars," I began, "your evil deeds—" 109
   but said no more, for suddenly I caught
   sight of one crucified upon the ground,

Nailed with three stakes. He saw me—and he wrenched 112
   and writhed, and puffed his sobs into his beard,
   and brother Catalan, who noticed, said,

"That soul° you wonder at, who lies transfixed, 115
   advised the Pharisees that it was fit
   to martyr one man for the people's sake.

Naked he lies, spreadeagled in the road, 118
   as you may see, and by necessity
   he feels the weight of all the passing souls.

His father-in-law is racked in this same ditch 121
   along with all the other councillors
   who sowed the seeds of evil for the Jews."

Then I saw Virgil in astonishment 124
   stare at the spirit stretched out in a cross,
   humiliated in the banishment

° *that soul:* Caiaphas, the high priest who advised the Jews to hand *one man,* Jesus, over to the Romans for execution; his *father-in-law,* Annas, took part in the same fraud. See notes.

Poscia drizzò al frate cotal voce: 127
   «Non vi dispiaccia, se vi lece, dirci
   s'a la man destra giace alcuna foce
onde noi amendue possiamo uscirci,   130
   sanza costrigner de li angeli neri
   che vegnan d'esto fondo a dipartirci».

Rispuose adunque: «Più che tu non speri   133
   s'appressa un sasso che da la gran cerchia
   si move e varca tutt' i vallon feri,
salvo che 'n questo è rotto e nol coperchia.   136
   Montar potreste su per la ruina,
   che giace in costa e nel fondo soperchia».

Lo duca stette un poco a testa china;   139
   poi disse: «Mal contava la bisogna
   colui che i peccator di qua uncina».

E 'l frate: «Io udi' già dire a Bologna   142
   del diavol vizi assai, tra ' quali udi'
   ch'elli è bugiardo e padre di menzogna».

Appresso il duca a gran passi sen gì,   145
   turbato un poco d'ira nel sembiante;
   ond' io da li 'ncarcati mi parti'
dietro a le poste de le care piante.   148

That never ends. And to the friar he turned: 127
    "Let it not displease you, if you may,
    tell me if there's a passage on the right
Over which we can both get out of here,   130
    so that we needn't call on the black angels°
    and make them come to take us from this hole."
And he responded: "Nearer than you hope   133
    there is a ridge that starts at Dis's wall
    and arches over all the savage pits
But one, because it's broken at this point   136
    and can't be crossed. You can climb up the ruins
    on that side there, heaped over the next ditch."
My guide stood still a moment, his head bowed,   139
    then said, "He gave a bad account of things,
    that one who hooks the sinners."° And the friar:
"When I was at Bologna° I heard tell   142
    of all the devil's vices, and I heard
    he was a liar and the father of lies."
At that my guide set out with greater strides,   145
    some anger darkening in his countenance,
    and I too left the heavy-laden souls
And followed after his beloved feet.   148

° *the black angels:* the Evilclaws of the previous two cantos.
° *that one who hooks the sinners:* Eviltail lied: there was no other bridge farther along the way.
° *Bologna:* the University of Bologna.

In quella parte del giovanetto anno
  che 'l sole i crin sotto l'Aquario tempra
  e già le notti al mezzo dì sen vanno,
quando la brina in su la terra assempra   4
  l'imagine di sua sorella bianca,
  ma poco dura a la sua penna tempra,
lo villanello a cui la roba manca,   7
  si leva, e guarda, e vede la campagna
  biancheggiar tutta; ond' ei si batte l'anca,
ritorna in casa, e qua e là si lagna,   10
  come 'l tapin che non sa che si faccia;
  poi riede, e la speranza ringavagna,
veggendo 'l mondo aver cangiata faccia   13
  in poco d'ora, e prende suo vincastro
  e fuor le pecorelle a pascer caccia.
Così mi fece sbigottir lo mastro   16
  quand' io li vidi sì turbar la fronte,
  e così tosto al mal giunse lo 'mpiastro;

CANTO TWENTY-FOUR

*The poets climb over to the **seventh ditch of Malebolge**, where they see the **thieves**,*
*harried and transmuted by serpents. Dante recognizes a church robber, **Vanni Fucci**,*
who, for sheer spite, prophesies hardship for Dante and his party in Florence.

When the year's young in season, and the spray
    washes the sunbeams in Aquarius,
    and the nights dwindle south toward half a day,°
When the frost paints a copy on the ground   4
    of her white sister's snowy image, but
    her feather's sharpness doesn't last for long,
The peasant lad who finds his fodder's low   7
    gets up and takes a look, and smacks his thigh,
    thinking the countryside's all white with snow,
Goes inside grumbling, fretting up and down,   10
    like a poor wretch who can't tell what to do,
    comes back out, and puts new hope in his pack,
Seeing the world has changed its face so soon,   13
    and takes his staff and drives his little flock
    to forage in the fields. So too with me:
My Teacher made me downcast for a while   16
    when I perceived the trouble in his brow,
    but then he laid the plaster on the sore,

° *half a day:* the spring equinox, when day and night are each twelve hours. In the Northern
Hemisphere, after the winter solstice, the sun's path arches higher in the sky each day, as the sun
rises and sets farther toward the north. Thus the nights *dwindle south.* The sun is in *Aquarius* from
January 21 to February 21. Dante is describing a late winter frost, which looks like a snowfall but
does not last long.

ché, come noi venimmo al guasto ponte,   19
    lo duca a me si volse con quel piglio
    dolce ch'io vidi prima a piè del monte.

Le braccia aperse, dopo alcun consiglio   22
    eletto seco riguardando prima
    ben la ruina, e diedemi di piglio.

E come quei ch'adopera ed estima,   25
    che sempre par che 'nnanzi si proveggia,
    così, levando me sù ver' la cima

d'un ronchione, avvisava un'altra scheggia   28
    dicendo: «Sovra quella poi t'aggrappa;
    ma tenta pria s'è tal ch'ella ti reggia».

Non era via da vestito di cappa,   31
    ché noi a pena, ei lieve e io sospinto,
    potavam sù montar di chiappa in chiappa.

E se non fosse che da quel precinto   34
    più che da l'altro era la costa corta,
    non so di lui, ma io sarei ben vinto.

Ma perché Malebolge inver' la porta   37
    del bassissimo pozzo tutta pende,
    lo sito di ciascuna valle porta

che l'una costa surge e l'altra scende;   40
    noi pur venimmo al fine in su la punta
    onde l'ultima pietra si scoscende.

La lena m'era del polmon sì munta   43
    quand' io fui sù, ch'i' non potea più oltre,
    anzi m'assisi ne la prima giunta.

«Omai convien che tu così ti spoltre»,   46
    disse 'l maestro; «ché, seggendo in piuma,
    in fama non si vien, né sotto coltre;

sanza la qual chi sua vita consuma,   49
    cotal vestigio in terra di sé lascia,
    qual fummo in aere e in acqua la schiuma.

E però leva sù; vinci l'ambascia   52
    con l'animo che vince ogne battaglia,
    se col suo grave corpo non s'accascia.

For when we reached the ruined bridge, my guide   19
   turned to me with that sweet and gracious look
   which I'd first seen below the mountainside.
He looked upon the ruins quietly,   22
   considering in himself which way to go,
   then spread his arms, and took me by the hand.
And like a man who judges while he works   25
   and therefore always seems to see ahead,
   so, as he helped me to the summit of
A jutting rock, he saw another crag   28
   and said, "Cling tight to that one and climb up,
   but test it first to see if it will hold."
That was no way for those with cowls of lead,   31
   for we—he lightly, I with struggle—could
   hardly mount up the ridge from jag to jag.
And if it weren't that the belt that rings   34
   this ditch was shorter than the one before,
   I cannot speak for him, but I'd have been
Defeated. But since Evil Pouches tilt   37
   down toward the lowest sink in the abyss,
   the lie of every valley makes it so
That one side rises higher than the next;   40
   and so at last we reached where the last stone
   had tumbled from the shattered bridge. My breath
Had been milked dry out of the lungs, so hard   43
   that when I scrambled up, I could do nothing
   but sit at the first level place. "You must
Shake off your sluggishness," the Teacher said,   46
   "for no one comes to fame who sits in soft
   pillows of down, or lies at ease in bed,
And when his life is wasted utterly   49
   he leaves such traces of himself behind
   as smoke in air or foam upon the sea.
Get up, then! Conquer your distress with that   52
   brave soul that wins through every fight, unless
   it should turn weak beneath the flesh's weight.

Più lunga scala convien che si saglia;   55
   non basta da costoro esser partito.
   Se tu mi 'ntendi, or fa sì che ti vaglia».

Leva'mi allor, mostrandomi fornito   58
   meglio di lena ch'i' non mi sentia,
   e dissi: «Va, ch'i' son forte e ardito».

Su per lo scoglio prendemmo la via,   61
   ch'era ronchioso, stretto e malagevole,
   ed erto più assai che quel di pria.

Parlando andava per non parer fievole;   64
   onde una voce uscì de l'altro fosso,
   a parole formar disconvenevole.

Non so che disse, ancor che sovra 'l dosso   67
   fossi de l'arco già che varca quivi;
   ma chi parlava ad ire parea mosso.

Io era vòlto in giù, ma li occhi vivi   70
   non poteano ire al fondo per lo scuro;
   per ch'io: «Maestro, fa che tu arrivi

da l'altro cinghio e dismontiam lo muro;   73
   ché, com' i' odo quinci e non intendo,
   così giù veggio e neente affiguro».

«Altra risposta», disse, «non ti rendo   76
   se non lo far; ché la dimanda onesta
   si de' seguir con l'opera tacendo».

Noi discendemmo il ponte da la testa   79
   dove s'aggiugne con l'ottava ripa,
   e poi mi fu la bolgia manifesta:

e vidivi entro terribile stipa   82
   di serpenti, e di sì diversa mena
   che la memoria il sangue ancor mi scipa.

Più non si vanti Libia con sua rena;   85
   ché se chelidri, iaculi e faree
   produce, e cencri con anfisibena,

né tante pestilenzie né sì ree   88
   mostrò già mai con tutta l'Etïopia
   né con ciò che di sopra al Mar Rosso èe.

It won't suffice for you to leave the damned.   55
    For you shall have to climb a longer stair:°
    turn that to profit, if you understand."

At that I rose, and made myself appear   58
    furnished with better breathing than I felt,
    and said, "Let's go, for I am bold and strong."

Over the arching reef we took our way;   61
    rocky and narrow and difficult it was,
    and pitched more steeply than the last. And as

We walked I spoke a bit, not to seem faint,   64
    when came a voice out of the seventh ditch,
    ill suited to form words. But what it said

I do not know, though I was on the hump   67
    of the stone arch that makes the crossing there.
    Whoever it was seemed quick to get away.

I leaned to look below, but living eyes   70
    could not pierce to the bottom through the dark,
    so I said, "Teacher, please, let's go across

To the next belt and then climb down the wall.   73
    I hear from here but I can't understand—
    look down, but can't make out a thing at all."

"No other answer will I give," said he,   76
    "than to comply. An honorable request
    ought to be met with action, silently."

Then we descended from the bridge's head   79
    where it adjoins the slope of the eighth pit,
    and then the pouch was manifest to me,

For there I saw a terrifying mass   82
    of serpents, of such different shapes and sorts,
    the thought still wastes the color in my face.

Let Libya with its deserts boast no more!   85
    If it breeds spearers, slitherers, hot chelydri,
    cencri erect and twin-head amphisboenes,

Never so many nor so venomous pests   88
    has it and all of Ethiopia borne,
    and all the land that looms on the Red Sea.

° *a longer stair:* probably the arduous climb up the Mountain of Purgatory.

Tra questa cruda e tristissima copia   91
   corrëan genti nude e spaventate,
   sanza sperar pertugio o elitropia:
con serpi le man dietro avean legate;   94
   quelle ficcavan per le ren la coda
   e 'l capo, ed eran dinanzi aggroppate.
Ed ecco a un ch'era da nostra proda,   97
   s'avventò un serpente che 'l trafisse
   là dove 'l collo a le spalle s'annoda.
Né O sì tosto mai né I si scrisse,   100
   com' el s'accese e arse, e cener tutto
   convenne che cascando divenisse;
e poi che fu a terra sì distrutto,   103
   la polver si raccolse per sé stessa
   e 'n quel medesmo ritornò di butto.
Così per li gran savi si confessa   106
   che la fenice more e poi rinasce,
   quando al cinquecentesimo anno appressa;
erba né biado in sua vita non pasce,   109
   ma sol d'incenso lagrime e d'amomo,
   e nardo e mirra son l'ultime fasce.
E qual è quel che cade, e non sa como,   112
   per forza di demon ch'a terra il tira,
   o d'altra oppilazion che lega l'omo,
quando si leva, che 'ntorno si mira   115
   tutto smarrito de la grande angoscia
   ch'elli ha sofferta, e guardando sospira:
tal era 'l peccator levato poscia.   118
   Oh potenza di Dio, quant' è severa,
   che cotai colpi per vendetta croscia!
Lo duca il domandò poi chi ello era;   121
   per ch'ei rispuose: «Io piovvi di Toscana,
   poco tempo è, in questa gola fiera.
Vita bestial mi piacque e non umana,   124
   sì come a mul ch'i' fui; son Vanni Fucci
   bestia, e Pistoia mi fu degna tana».

Through this most wretched and malignant throng 91
    ran people, naked, frightened, without hope
    to find a hiding hole or antidote.

Their wrists were strapped behind their backs by snakes, 94
    which round the kidneys squeezed the head and tail
    and formed a bulging knot above the groin.

And look—right at a sinner near our ledge 97
    there flashed a snake who fixed him with its fangs
    just where the neck is knotted to the back.

A man can't scrawl an I or O as fast 100
    as he ignited and went up in flames
    and disappeared in a collapse of ash;

And after he lay strewn and thus destroyed, 103
    his body's dust collected on its own
    and suddenly returned to what it was.

So the great wise men of the ancient days 106
    held that the Phoenix died and was reborn
    at the approach of the five-hundredth year,

Who in her life feeds not on herb or grain, 109
    but balsamum and tears of frankincense,
    and myrrh and spikenard make her funeral bed.

And as a man who falls° and can't say how— 112
    by demon's force that yanks him to the earth,
    or other blockage binding a man's powers—

When he comes to, he gazes round, all lost, 115
    bewildered by the suffocating fit
    he has endured, and as he looks, breathes deep:

Such was the sinner when he stood once more. 118
    O power of God, how stern your rigor is,
    which deals such blows and lets the vengeance pour!

My guide then asked the spirit who he was, 121
    and he replied, "I rained from Tuscany
    not long ago, into this savage throat.

I loved the life of beasts and not of men, 124
    bastard mule that I was. I'm Vanni Fucci—
    Beast—and Pistoia was my worthy den."

° *a man who falls:* a man afflicted with the "falling disease," epilepsy. Such people were long thought to be troubled, perhaps, by *a demon's force;* see Lk. 4:35, Mk. 1:26.

E ïo al duca: «Dilli che non mucci,   127
   e domanda che colpa qua giù 'l pinse;
   ch'io 'l vidi omo di sangue e di crucci».

E 'l peccator, che 'ntese, non s'infinse,   130
   ma drizzò verso me l'animo e 'l volto,
   e di trista vergogna si dipinse;

poi disse: «Più mi duol che tu m'hai colto   133
   ne la miseria dove tu mi vedi,
   che quando fui de l'altra vita tolto.

Io non posso negar quel che tu chiedi;   136
   in giù son messo tanto perch' io fui
   ladro a la sagrestia d'i belli arredi,

e falsamente già fu apposto altrui.   139
   Ma perché di tal vista tu non godi,
   se mai sarai di fuor da' luoghi bui,

apri li orecchi al mio annunzio, e odi.   142
   Pistoia in pria d'i Neri si dimagra;
   poi Fiorenza rinova gente e modi.

Tragge Marte vapor di Val di Magra   145
   ch'è di torbidi nuvoli involuto;
   e con tempesta impetüosa e agra

sovra Campo Picen fia combattuto;   148
   ond' ei repente spezzerà la nebbia,
   sì ch'ogne Bianco ne sarà feruto.

E detto l'ho perché doler ti debbia!».   151

I to my guide: "Tell him not to sneak off,   127
   and ask of him what fault shoved him down here.
   I knew him as a man of wrath and blood."°

The sinner heard, and did not stall for time,   130
   but turned the focus of his sight to me,
   and his face reddened with a sullen shame.

Said he: "It pains me that you've caught me here   133
   thrust in the misery where you see me now,
   more than it pained me to be snatched from life.

I can't refuse to answer what you ask.   136
   I'm put down here because I was a thief,
   filched the fair vestments from the sacristy—

The blame was wrongly laid on someone else.   139
   But if you get outside this dungeon's night,
   so that the sight of me won't bring you pleasure,

Open your ears and hear what I foretell.   142
   Pistoia first will slim itself of Blacks;°
   Florence changes her families and ways,

Then will the war god draw his thunderbolt   145
   from Val di Magra, wrapped in darkening clouds,
   and with a headlong and tempestuous surge

Do battle on the plains of Piceno,   148
   where he will split the clouds with sudden fire
   and strike down every White upon the field.

I've told you this for spite, to bring you grief."   151

° *I knew him as a man of wrath and blood:* Dante wonders why this spirit is here and not with the cen-
taurs, where the violent against neighbors are punished.

° *Blacks:* The Blacks and Whites were rival families of the Guelph party in Florence. Vanni fore-
tells what will result in the exile of Dante, a member of the Whites. For more details, see notes.

Al fine de le sue parole il ladro
    le mani alzò con amendue le fiche,
    gridando: «Togli, Dio, ch'a te le squadro!».
Da indi in qua mi fuor le serpi amiche,   4
    perch' una li s'avvolse allora al collo,
    come dicesse 'Non vo' che più diche';
e un'altra a le braccia, e rilegollo,   7
    ribadendo sé stessa sì dinanzi,
    che non potea con esse dare un crollo.
Ahi Pistoia, Pistoia, ché non stanzi   10
    d'incenerarti sì che più non duri,
    poi che 'n mal fare il seme tuo avanzi?
Per tutt' i cerchi de lo 'nferno scuri   13
    non vidi spirto in Dio tanto superbo,
    non quel che cadde a Tebe giù da' muri.
El si fuggì che non parlò più verbo;   16
    e io vidi un centauro pien di rabbia
    venir chiamando: «Ov' è, ov' è l'acerbo?».
Maremma non cred' io che tante n'abbia,   19
    quante bisce elli avea su per la groppa
    infin ove comincia nostra labbia.

CANTO TWENTY-FIVE

Vanni Fucci is led away in punishment by serpents. The poets continue among the **Thieves,** *in the* **seventh ditch of Malebolge.** *There they see the thieving centaur* **Cacus,** *and witness the strange* **metamorphoses** *of three of the thieves.*

At the end of his prophecy the thief
    raised up his hands with the two figs° pricked out—
    "Take that, O God—I fling them in your face!"
From that point on the snakes were friends to me,   4
    for one snake wound itself around his neck
    as if it said, "I want you to shut up,"
And then a second slithered through his arms   7
    and noosed them with so tight a knot in front
    he couldn't give those arms a jerk or jolt.
Pistoia, Pistoia! Why should you not decide   10
    once and for all to burn yourself to ash—
    since you surpass your seed in wickedness!
In all the circles of the darkest Hell   13
    I'd seen no soul so haughty against God—
    not him who tumbled from the walls of Thebes.°
He fled—he could not speak another word;   16
    and then there came a centaur mad with rage,
    bellowing, "Where's that rebel, where's he gone!"
I don't believe the marsh flats of Maremma   19
    bring forth as many vipers as his hunch
    had crawling up to where our mouth begins.

° *figs:* an obscene gesture made by sticking the thumb between the index and middle fingers; called the "fig" for that fruit's supposed resemblance to the female genitals.
° *him who tumbled from the walls of Thebes:* Capaneus. See 14.43–72.

Sovra le spalle, dietro da la coppa,   22
    con l'ali aperte li giacea un draco;
    e quello affuoca qualunque s'intoppa.

Lo mio maestro disse: «Questi è Caco,   25
    che, sotto 'l sasso di monte Aventino,
    di sangue fece spesse volte laco.

Non va co' suoi fratei per un cammino,   28
    per lo furto che frodolente fece
    del grande armento ch'elli ebbe a vicino;

onde cessar le sue opere biece   31
    sotto la mazza d'Ercule, che forse
    gliene diè cento, e non sentì le diece».

Mentre che sì parlava, ed el trascorse,   34
    e tre spiriti venner sotto noi,
    de' quai né io né 'l duca mio s'accorse,

se non quando gridar: «Chi siete voi?»;   37
    per che nostra novella si ristette,
    e intendemmo pur ad essi poi.

Io non li conoscea; ma ei seguette,   40
    come suol seguitar per alcun caso,
    che l'un nomar un altro convenette,

dicendo: «Cianfa dove fia rimaso?»;   43
    per ch'io, acciò che 'l duca stesse attento,
    mi puosi 'l dito su dal mento al naso.

Se tu se' or, lettore, a creder lento   46
    ciò ch'io dirò, non sarà maraviglia,
    ché io che 'l vidi, a pena il mi consento.

Com' io tenea levate in lor le ciglia,   49
    e un serpente con sei piè si lancia
    dinanzi a l'uno, e tutto a lui s'appiglia.

Co' piè di mezzo li avvinse la pancia   52
    e con li anterïor le braccia prese;
    poi li addentò l'una e l'altra guancia;

li diretani a le cosce distese,   55
    e miseli la coda tra 'mbedue
    e dietro per le ren sù la ritese.

Upon his shoulders, right behind the neck,   22
   there perched a dragon with his wings spread wide,
   scorching whatever soul he hit upon.
My Teacher said, "This one is Cacus, who   25
   dwelt in the cave beneath the Aventine°
   and there left many a pool of human blood.
He does not share his brother centaurs' walk,   28
   on account of the sneaking theft he made
   of the great herd of cattle near his rock;
But all his shifty deeds came to an end   31
   under the club of Hercules, who gave him
   a hundred blows. He didn't feel the tenth."
While he spoke and the centaur galloped by,   34
   three spirits suddenly appeared below.
   My guide was not aware of them, nor I,
Until they shouted at us, "Who are you!"   37
   at which we broke our conversation off,
   and our attention turned to them alone.
I didn't recognize them, but it happened,   40
   as it does sometimes follow by mere chance,
   one of them had to name another one
And said, "Where is that Cianfa lurking now?"   43
   Whereupon, that my guide would stand and watch,
   I laid my finger to my lips. O Reader,
It's no great cause for wonder if you're slow   46
   to trust what I'm about to tell you now,
   for I, who saw it, hardly can believe.
I held my eyebrows raised to look their way,   49
   and there! a snake with six feet flings itself
   and clings to one of them with all his length.
It strapped the belly with its middle feet   52
   and clutched the arms by the anterior,
   then sank its fangs to bite through either cheek;
It stretched its hind feet straight along the thighs   55
   and flipped its tail between them and on up
   the sinner's loins to clamp behind his back.

° *the Aventine:* the Roman hill where the monster Cacus dwelt; see notes.

Ellera abbarbicata mai non fue   58
   ad alber sì, come l'orribil fiera
   per l'altrui membra avviticchiò le sue.

Poi s'appiccar, come di calda cera   61
   fossero stati, e mischiar lor colore,
   né l'un né l'altro già parea quel ch'era:

come procede innanzi da l'ardore,   64
   per lo papiro suso, un color bruno
   che non è nero ancora e 'l bianco more.

Li altri due 'l riguardavano, e ciascuno   67
   gridava: «Omè, Agnel, come ti muti!
   Vedi che già non se' né due né uno».

Già eran li due capi un divenuti,   70
   quando n'apparver due figure miste
   in una faccia, ov' eran due perduti.

Fersi le braccia due di quattro liste;   73
   le cosce con le gambe e 'l ventre e 'l casso
   divenner membra che non fuor mai viste.

Ogne primaio aspetto ivi era casso: 76
   due e nessun l'imagine perversa
   parea, e tal sen gio con lento passo.

Come 'l ramarro sotto la gran fersa   79
   dei dì canicular, cangiando sepe,
   folgore par se la via attraversa,

sì pareva, venendo verso l'epe   82
   de li altri due, un serpentello acceso,
   livido e nero come gran di pepe;

e quella parte onde prima è preso   85
   nostro alimento, a l'un di lor trafisse;
   poi cadde giuso innanzi lui disteso.

Lo trafitto 'l mirò, ma nulla disse;   88
   anzi, co' piè fermati, sbadigliava
   pur come sonno o febbre l'assalisse.

Elli 'l serpente e quei lui riguardava;   91
   l'un per la piaga e l'altro per la bocca
   fummavan forte, e 'l fummo si scontrava.

No ivy ever gripped its barbs about   58
    a tree so tightly as that horrible beast
    twisted the other's members with its own.

They glued and fused together, as if formed   61
    out of hot wax, and saw their colors melt
    so neither one seemed what it was before,

As when a flame is set below a scrap   64
    of parchment, and a brownish hue appears,
    which, while the white is dying, is not black.

The other two cried out as they looked on: 67
    "Alas, Agnel, how you have changed yourself!
    Already, see, you're neither two nor one!"

Already indeed their two heads had formed one,   70
    and there appeared two figures mingled in
    one face, where the two faces had been lost.

Out of four bands of flesh they formed two arms;   73
    the thighs and calves, the belly and the chest
    made members that no man has ever seen.

Each former countenance was canceled out;   76
    the image in perversion seemed both two
    and nothing—and as such it slunk away.

As the green lizard under the sharp lash   79
    of the dog days, darting from hedge to hedge,
    crosses the road quick as a lightning flash,

So came a little serpent lit with wrath   82
    after the bellies of the other two,
    as black and livid as a peppercorn.

In that part where the fetus takes its food   85
    it fixed itself on one of them and bit,
    then fell stretched out before him on the ground.

The bitten man then stared, but did not speak: 88
    rather, with feet set firm, he yawned, as if
    assailed by fever or by drowsiness.

The man glared at the snake, the snake at him.   91
    This through the wound and that one through its mouth
    sent violent clouds of smoke that rose and merged.

Taccia Lucano omai là dov' e' tocca   94
   del misero Sabello e di Nasidio,
   e attenda a udir quel ch'or si scocca.

Taccia di Cadmo e d'Aretusa Ovidio,   97
   ché se quello in serpente e quella in fonte
   converte poetando, io non lo 'nvidio;

ché due nature mai a fronte a fronte   100
   non trasmutò sì ch'amendue le forme
   a cambiar lor matera fosser pronte.

Insieme si rispuosero a tai norme,   103
   che 'l serpente la coda in forca fesse,
   e 'l feruto ristrinse insieme l'orme.

Le gambe con le cosce seco stesse   106
   s'appiccar sì, che 'n poco la giuntura
   non facea segno alcun che si paresse.

Togliea la coda fessa la figura   109
   che si perdeva là, e la sua pelle
   si facea molle, e quella di là dura.

Io vidi intrar le braccia per l'ascelle,   112
   e i due piè de la fiera, ch'eran corti,
   tanto allungar quanto accorciavan quelle.

Poscia li piè di rietro, insieme attorti,   115
   diventaron lo membro che l'uom cela,
   e 'l misero del suo n'avea due porti.

Mentre che 'l fummo l'uno e l'altro vela   118
   di color novo, e genera 'l pel suso
   per l'una parte e da l'altra il dipela,

l'un si levò e l'altro cadde giuso,   121
   non torcendo però le lucerne empie,
   sotto le quai ciascun cambiava muso.

Quel ch'era dritto, il trasse ver' le tempie,   124
   e di troppa matera ch'in là venne
   uscir li orecchi de le gote scempie;

ciò che non corse in dietro e si ritenne   127
   di quel soverchio, fé naso a la faccia
   e le labbra ingrossò quanto convenne.

Be silent, Lucan, where you touch upon 94
    wretched Sabellus and Nasidius,
    and listen to the arrow I shoot now.

Be silent, Ovid, with your Arethusa 97
    and Cadmus, where your poem turns
    this to a serpent, that one to a spring;

I hold no grudge, for never front to front 100
    did you transmute two natures so their forms
    were ready to change matter with each other.

They corresponded in the following way, 103
    for the snake split his tail into a fork
    while the man pressed his feet together tight.

The legs all the way up the thigh began 106
    to cling together, so that soon no trace
    appeared of any juncture. The forked tail

Assumed in turn the figure that was lost 109
    by the man there; his scaly hide grew soft
    as flesh, while the man's hardened. Then I saw

His arms recede into the shoulder pits 112
    while the two short feet of the serpent stretched
    and grew as long as the man's limbs had shrunk.

Then its hind feet, twisted and wound in one, 115
    became the member which a man must hide,
    while the wretch saw two paws sprout from his own.

As the smoke veiled the one soul and the other 118
    with a new color, and on this side made
    the hair shoot up and stripped the hair from that,

The one got up, the other fell to earth, 121
    but never turned their evil flashing eyes
    beneath whose gaze they interchanged their snouts:

He who was standing drew his face-flesh in 124
    toward the temples, and with the extra matter
    the ears protruded from his hollow cheeks,

And what did not run backward to the ears 127
    composed a nose out of the excess flesh
    and swelled the lips as fat as lips must swell.

Quel che giacëa, il muso innanzi caccia,   130
   e li orecchi ritira per la testa
   come face le corna la lumaccia;

e la lingua, ch'avëa unita e presta   133
   prima a parlar, si fende, e la forcuta
   ne l'altro si richiude; e 'l fummo resta.

L'anima ch'era fiera divenuta,   136
   suffolando si fugge per la valle,
   e l'altro dietro a lui parlando sputa.

Poscia li volse le novelle spalle,   139
   e disse a l'altro: «I' vo' che Buoso corra,
   com' ho fatt' io, carpon per questo calle».

Così vid' io la settima zavorra   142
   mutare e trasmutare; e qui mi scusi
   la novità se fior la penna abborra.

E avvegna che li occhi miei confusi   145
   fossero alquanto e l'animo smagato,
   non poter quei fuggirsi tanto chiusi,

ch'i' non scorgessi ben Puccio Sciancato;   148
   ed era quel che sol, di tre compagni
   che venner prima, non era mutato.

L'altr' era quel che tu, Gaville, piagni.   151

He who lay on the ground lengthens his snout 130
   and draws the two ears back into his head,
   just as a snail retracts its horns inside,
And the tongue, which was single and well made 133
   for speech, now cleaves in two, while the tongue's fork
   closes within the other, and the smoke
Subsides. The soul who had become a beast 136
   slithered across the valley with a hiss
   and he behind the serpent spoke and spat.°
He turned his brand-new shoulders on the snake 139
   and to the third one said: "Let Buoso go
   creeping on all fours down the road, like me!"
So did I see the seventh ballast change 142
   and change again; and if my pen has left
   matters a little tangled, let the strange
Nature of it excuse me. And though my eye 145
   was slightly dazed and my mind somewhat faint,
   they could not sneak away so secretly
That I could overlook Puccio the Lame, 148
   the only soul that did not suffer change
   out of the three companions. And the third
Was he, Gaville, on whose account you mourn. 151

° *spat:* Human saliva was thought poisonous to snakes.

Godi, Fiorenza, poi che se' sì grande
   che per mare e per terra batti l'ali,
   e per lo 'nferno tuo nome si spande!
Tra li ladron trovai cinque cotali   4
   tuoi cittadini onde mi ven vergogna,
   e tu in grande orranza non ne sali.
Ma se presso al mattin del ver si sogna,   7
   tu sentirai, di qua da picciol tempo,
   di quel che Prato, non ch'altri, t'agogna.
E se già fosse, non saria per tempo.   10
   Così foss' ei, da che pur esser dee!
   ché più mi graverà, com' più m'attempo.
Noi ci partimmo, e su per le scalee   13
   che n'avean fatto i borni a scender pria,
   rimontò 'l duca mio e trasse mee;
e proseguendo la solinga via,   16
   tra le schegge e tra ' rocchi de lo scoglio
   lo piè sanza la man non si spedia.
Allor mi dolsi, e ora mi ridoglio   19
   quando drizzo la mente a ciò ch'io vidi,
   e più lo 'ngegno affreno ch'i' non soglio,

CANTO TWENTY-SIX

*After an invective against the corruption of Florence, Dante resumes his account. The poets proceed to the **eighth ditch of Malebolge,** where the **evil counselors** are wholly swathed in flames, and speak through the tongue of fire at the top. Dante asks Virgil to call upon one twin-tongued flame, where dwell the souls of **Ulysses and Diomedes.** Ulysses recounts how he and his men died on their voyage into the Southern Hemisphere, far beyond the Pillars of Hercules.*

Florence, rejoice! Your fame's so great to tell,
    you beat your wings over the land and seas
    and spread your name throughout the deeps of Hell!
Among the thieves I found five citizens,   4
    five of your finest, and that brings me shame,
    nor do you climb in greater reverence.
But if our dreams before the dawn come true,   7
    shortly you'll feel what Prato (not to mention
    the other towns) longs to have fall on you.
It would be fine had it already come.   10
    Then let it, since it must! The more I age,
    the more your punishment will sadden me.
We took our leave up the projecting rocks   13
    that left us pale as ivory, going down;
    my guide climbed up, and pulled me after him,
And following the solitary way   16
    among the shards and boulders of the ridge,
    we couldn't move the foot without the hand.
Then did I grieve and now I grieve again   19
    when I direct my mind to what I saw,
    and hold my genius under tighter rein

perché non corra che virtù nol guidi;   22
     sì che, se stella bona o miglior cosa
     m'ha dato 'l ben, ch'io stessi nol m'invidi.
Quante 'l villan ch'al poggio si riposa,   25
     nel tempo che colui che 'l mondo schiara
     la faccia sua a noi tien meno ascosa,
come la mosca cede a la zanzara,   28
     vede lucciole giù per la vallea,
     forse colà dov' e' vendemmia e ara:
di tante fiamme tutta risplendea   31
     l'ottava bolgia, sì com' io m'accorsi
     tosto che fui là 've 'l fondo parea.
E qual colui che si vengiò con li orsi   34
     vide 'l carro d'Elia al dipartire,
     quando i cavalli al cielo erti levorsi,
che nol potea sì con li occhi seguire,   37
     ch'el vedesse altro che la fiamma sola,
     sì come nuvoletta, in sù salire:
tal si move ciascuna per la gola   40
     del fosso, ché nessuna mostra 'l furto,
     e ogne fiamma un peccatore invola.
Io stava sovra 'l ponte a veder surto,   43
     sì che s'io non avessi un ronchion preso,
     caduto sarei giù sanz' esser urto.
E 'l duca, che mi vide tanto atteso,   46
     disse: «Dentro dai fuochi son li spirti;
     catun si fascia di quel ch'elli è inceso».
«Maestro mio», rispuos' io, «per udirti   49
     son io più certo; ma già m'era avviso
     che così fosse, e già voleva dirti:

Lest without virtue's guidance it run loose: 22
    that if my stars,° or grace, has given me good,
    I won't begrudge myself in its abuse.

But as a peasant resting on a hill   25
    in that warm time of year when he who sheds
    light on the world hides less than usual,

When the mosquito follows on the fly,   28
    sees crowds of fireflies in the twilight dell
    down by the vineyard or the fields he's tilled;

With just so many flickering firelights shone   31
    the eighth pouch, as I was aware as soon
    as I could see the bottom of the pit.

And as that prophet° who avenged himself   34
    with murderous bears beheld the chariot of
    Elijah, horses galloping steep to heaven:

He couldn't follow its parting with his eyes   37
    but saw no more than one bright burst of fire
    like a small cloud, ascending higher and higher—

So every flame moves through this trench's throat   40
    and not one flickering light reveals the theft,
    for each one stows away a sinner's soul.

I stood erect upon the bridge to look,   43
    and would have fallen headlong with no push
    had I not kept a handhold on the rock.

Seeing me so intent to learn, my guide   46
    explained, "In every flame there dwells a soul.
    The fires that light them swaddle them inside."

"My Teacher," I responded, "what you say   49
    makes me more certain, but I'd thought already
    that it was so, and wished to ask you this:

° *my stars:* Dante was born under the sign of Gemini, whose influence was thought to bestow eloquence and intellectual vigor. That influence is not inconsistent with divine *grace.*

° *that prophet:* After his master Elijah was taken up into Heaven by a chariot of fire (2 Kings 2:9–12), Elisha was taunted by boys, crying out, "Go up, thou bald head!" He cursed them, and they were torn to pieces by bears from the woods (2 Kings 2:23–24). Since Elisha had just requested, from his departing master, a double portion of his power, the whole scene may be interpreted as showing Elisha's reverential awe for the gifts of the Spirit, as opposed to the Israelites' scorn for them, evinced by their children's mockery.

chi è 'n quel foco che vien sì diviso   52
   di sopra, che par surger de la pira
   dov' Eteòcle col fratel fu miso?»

Rispuose a me: «Là dentro si martira   55
   Ulisse e Dïomede, e così insieme
   a la vendetta vanno come a l'ira;

e dentro da la lor fiamma si geme   58
   l'agguato del caval che fé la porta
   onde uscì de' Romani il gentil seme.

Piangevisi entro l'arte per che, morta,   61
   Deïdamìa ancor si duol d'Achille,
   e del Palladio pena vi si porta».

«S'ei posson dentro da quelle faville   64
   parlar», diss' io, «maestro, assai ten priego
   e ripriego, che 'l priego vaglia mille,

che non mi facci de l'attender niego   67
   fin che la fiamma cornuta qua vegna.
   Vedi che del disio ver' lei mi piego!».

Ed elli a me: «La tua preghiera è degna   70
   di molta loda, e io però l'accetto;
   ma fa che la tua lingua si sostegna.

Lascia parlare a me, ch'i' ho concetto   73
   ciò che tu vuoi; ch'ei sarebbero schivi,
   perch' e' fuor greci, forse del tuo detto».

Poi che la fiamma fu venuta quivi   76
   dove parve al mio duca tempo e loco,
   in questa forma lui parlare audivi:

«O voi che siete due dentro ad un foco,   79
   s'io meritai di voi mentre ch'io vissi,
   s'io meritai di voi assai o poco

What spirit dwells within that double fire 52
   divided at the top as if it rose
   from Polynices' and his brother's pyre?"°
And he replied: "That flame tortures Ulysses 55
   and Diomedes, and as two they meet
   God's vengeance, as they sinned and met His wrath.
For they bemoan their ambush in that flame, 58
   their wooden horse in Troy, which was the gate
   through which the noble seed of Rome first came;
There they weep for the artful trick which brought 61
   sorrow to Deidamia° even in death,
   and bear the punishment for Pallas' shrine."°
"If they can speak from there inside those flares," 64
   said I, "Teacher, I pray with all my heart,
   and pray again up to a thousand prayers
That you will not decline to let me stay 67
   until the twin-horned fire comes near—you see
   what great desire has made me bend their way!"
And he to me: "Your prayer is worthy of 70
   the highest praise, and therefore I agree:
   but you must hold your own tongue in restraint.
I understand your wish, so let me speak, 73
   for they might take your language in disdain
   and shy away from us, since they were Greek."
And when the flame at last had come our way 76
   and it seemed to my guide the time and place,
   in such a form as this I heard him say,
"O you who are two souls within one fire, 79
   if ever I earned your favor while I lived,
   if ever I earned your favor, great or small,

° *from Polynices' and his brother's pyre:* These are the sons of Oedipus, Polynices and Eteocles, who fought for the rule of Thebes after their father died. They slew each other in battle. The flames above their common pyre parted, evincing the brothers' lasting hatred of each other (see Statius, *Thebaid* 12.429–32).

° *Deidamia:* the girl who loved Achilles. Ulysses and Diomedes employed a trick to have Achilles jilt her and join them in the Trojan War (the story is told by Statius in the *Achilleid*).

° *Pallas' shrine:* the Palladium, tutelary image of the goddess Pallas Athena. It was stolen from Troy by Ulysses and Diomedes (see *Aen.* 2.162–70).

quando nel mondo li alti versi scrissi,   82
   non vi movete, ma l'un di voi dica
   dove, per lui, perduto a morir gissi».
Lo maggior corno de la fiamma antica   85
   cominciò a crollarsi mormorando,
   pur come quella cui vento affatica;
indi la cima qua e là menando,   88
   come fosse la lingua che parlasse,
   gittò voce di fuori e disse: «Quando
mi diparti' da Circe, che sottrasse   91
   me più d'un anno là presso a Gaeta,
   prima che sì Enëa la nomasse,
né dolcezza di figlio, né la pieta   94
   del vecchio padre, né 'l debito amore
   lo qual dovea Penelopè far lieta,
vincer potero dentro a me l'ardore   97
   ch'i' ebbi a divenir del mondo esperto
   e de li vizi umani e del valore;
ma misi me per l'alto mare aperto   100
   sol con un legno e con quella compagna
   picciola da la qual non fui diserto.
L'un lito e l'altro vidi infin la Spagna,   103
   fin nel Morrocco, e l'isola d'i Sardi,
   e l'altre che quel mare intorno bagna.
Io e ' compagni eravam vecchi e tardi   106
   quando venimmo a quella foce stretta
   dov' Ercule segnò li suoi riguardi
acciò che l'uom più oltre non si metta;   109
   da la man destra mi lasciai Sibilia,
   da l'altra già m'avea lasciata Setta.
"O frati", dissi, "che per cento milia   112
   perigli siete giunti a l'occidente,
   a questa tanto picciola vigilia

When in the world I wrote my lofty verse,   82
   do not depart, but tell us, one of you,
     where you were lost, and where you went to die."
The greater horn upon the ancient flame   85
   began to quiver into murmuring,
     just like a torchlight wearied by the wind,
And then, leading the flame-tip here and there,   88
   as if that were the very tongue that spoke,
     it flung a voice without, and said, "When I
Left Circe,° who had lured away from me   91
   more than a year on her isle near Gaeta,
     before Aeneas gave that cape its name,
Neither the sweet affection for my son,   94
   nor piety due my father, nor the love
     I owed Penelope to bring her joy
Could drive from me the burning to go forth   97
   to gain experience of the world, and learn
     of every human vice, and human worth.
I sent myself on the deep open sea   100
   with only a boat and that small troop of men,
     my friends, who never had abandoned me.
I saw the shores of either continent   103
   up to Spain and Morocco, saw Sardinia,
     and all the other isles that ocean bathes.
I and my comrades were stiff-limbed and old   106
   when we arrived within the narrow mouth°
     where Hercules once set his warning signs
Lest man should dare to venture past the mark: 109
   on the right hand I left Seville behind,
     and on the left, Ceuta. Then I spoke:
'O brothers, who have borne innumerable   112
   dangers to reach the setting of the sun,
     from these few hours remaining to our watch,

° *Circe:* the sorceress who had detained Ulysses on his journey home to Ithaca; see notes.
° *narrow mouth:* the Straits of Gibraltar, symbol of the bounds beyond which human reason and achievement, unaided by grace, cannot go.

d'i nostri sensi ch'è del rimanente 115
   non vogliate negar l'esperïenza,
   di retro al sol, del mondo sanza gente.

Considerate la vostra' semenza: 118
   fatti non foste a viver come bruti,
   ma per seguir virtute e canoscenza".

Li miei compagni fec' io sì aguti, 121
   con questa orazion picciola, al cammino,
   che a pena poscia li avrei ritenuti;

e volta nostra poppa nel mattino, 124
   de' remi facemmo ali al folle volo,
   sempre acquistando dal lato mancino.

Tutte le stelle già de l'altro polo 127
   vedea la notte, e 'l nostro tanto basso,
   che non surgëa fuor del marin suolo.

Cinque volte racceso e tante casso 130
   lo lume era di sotto da la luna,
   poi che 'ntrati eravam ne l'alto passo,

quando n'apparve una montagna, bruna 133
   per la distanza, e parvemi alta tanto
   quanto veduta non avëa alcuna.

Noi ci allegrammo, e tosto tornò in pianto; 136
   ché de la nova terra un turbo nacque
   e percosse del legno il primo canto.

Tre volte il fé girar con tutte l'acque; 139
   a la quarta levar la poppa in suso
   e la prora ire in giù, com' altrui piacque,

infin che 'l mar fu sovra noi richiuso». 142

From time so short in which to live and feel, 115
    do not refuse experience of the lands
    beyond the sun, the world where no one dwells.

Think well upon your nation and your seed! 118
    For you were never made to live like brutes,
    but to pursue the good in mind and deed.'

I made my comrades' appetites so keen 121
    to take the journey, by this little speech,
    I hardly could have held them after that.

Turning our aft-side to the morning sun, 124
    we made wings of our oars for the mad flight,
    gradually gaining to the left, so far

That nightfall now revealed the southern pole 127
    and all its stars, while ours were sunk so low
    they never rose above the ocean's rim.

Five times the light of the moon's underside 130
    was kindled for the earth, and five times quenched,
    since we'd set out upon the arduous pass,

When far off there appeared a mountain shore,° 133
    hazy and dark, which seemed to loom so high,
    no man had seen so high a peak before.

We cheered, but soon that cheering turned to woe, 136
    for then a whirlwind born from the strange land
    battered our little vessel on the prow.

Three times the boat and all the sea were whirled, 139
    and at the fourth, to please Another's° will,
    the aft tipped in the air, the prow went down,

Until the ocean closed above our bones." 142

° *a mountain shore:* that of the Mountain of Purgatory, whose approach is here shown to be forbidden to any living man.
° *Another:* God. Yet for the description of the shipwreck itself, Dante is indebted to Virgil, *Aeneid* 1.113–17.

Già era dritta in sù la fiamma e queta
　　per non dir più, e già da noi sen gia
　　con la licenza del dolce poeta,
quand' un'altra, che dietro a lei venìa,　　　　　　　　　　　4
　　ne fece volger li occhi a la sua cima
　　per un confuso suon che fuor n'uscia.
Come 'l bue cicilian che mugghiò prima　　　　　　　　　　7
　　col pianto di colui, e ciò fu dritto,
　　che l'avea temperato con sua lima,
mugghiava con la voce de l'afflitto,　　　　　　　　　　　10
　　sì che, con tutto che fosse di rame,
　　pur el pareva dal dolor trafitto;
così, per non aver via né forame　　　　　　　　　　　　13
　　dal principio nel foco, in suo linguaggio
　　si convertïan le parole grame.
Ma poscia ch'ebber colto lor vïaggio　　　　　　　　　　16
　　su per la punta, dandole quel guizzo
　　che dato avea la lingua in lor passaggio,
udimmo dire: «O tu a cu' io drizzo　　　　　　　　　　19
　　la voce e che parlavi mo lombardo,
　　dicendo 'Istra ten va, più non t'adizzo',

CANTO TWENTY-SEVEN

*Still in the **eighth ditch of Malebolge**, Dante meets another of the **evil counselors**, **Guido da Montefeltro**, who tells of his corruption by **Pope Boniface VIII**, and of his death and damnation.*

The flame had risen upright and was still,
　　for it would speak no more, and went its way,
　　as the sweet poet gave it leave to go,
Whereon another soul who came behind   4
　　turned our eyes to the summit of his flame
　　by the strange garbled noise it spluttered out.
As the Sicilian bull that bellowed first   7
　　with its inventor's cries° —and justly so—
　　who'd smoothed its brazen contours with his file,
Would bellow with the tortured wretch's voice   10
　　so loudly that, though it was made of bronze,
　　the instrument itself seemed pierced in pain;
So here, finding at first the flame entire   13
　　and every passage shut, the wretched words
　　converted to the language of the fire.
But when the voice had traveled all the way   16
　　to the flame's tip, it quivered with that motion
　　the tongue imparted, and we heard it say:
"O you to whom I now direct my voice,   19
　　who spoke in Lombard when you said just now,
　　'Go, then, I won't provoke you any more,'

° *its inventor's cries:* The Athenian Perillus constructed a brazen bull for Phalaris, tyrant of Agrigentum, in Sicily. His clever device was to have victims shut inside the bull and set over a fire; the mouth was so constructed as to turn the cries into bellowing. Fittingly, Perillus himself was the first victim. The story is told in many places, including Ovid, *Tristia* 3.11.41–54.

perch' io sia giunto forse alquanto tardo, 22
   non t'incresca restare a parlar meco;
   vedi che non incresce a me, e ardo!

Se tu pur mo in questo mondo cieco 25
   caduto se' di quella dolce terra
   latina ond' io mia colpa tutta reco,

dimmi se Romagnuoli han pace o guerra; 28
   ch'io fui d'i monti là intra Orbino
   e 'l giogo di che Tever si diserra».

Io era in giuso ancora attento e chino, 31
   quando il mio duca mi tentò di costa,
   dicendo: «Parla tu; questi è latino».

E io, ch'avea già pronta la risposta, 34
   sanza indugio a parlare incominciai:
   «O anima che se' là giù nascosta,

Romagna tua non è, e non fu mai, 37
   sanza guerra ne' cuor de' suoi tiranni;
   ma 'n palese nessuna or vi lasciai.

Ravenna sta come stata è molt' anni: 40
   l'aguglia da Polenta la si cova,
   sì che Cervia ricuopre co' suoi vanni.

La terra che fé già la lunga prova 43
   e di Franceschi sanguinoso mucchio,
   sotto le branche verdi si ritrova.

E 'l mastin vecchio e 'l nuovo da Verrucchio, 46
   che fecer di Montagna il mal governo,
   là dove soglion fan d'i denti succhio.

Le città di Lamone e di Santerno 49
   conduce il lïoncel dal nido bianco,
   che muta parte da la state al verno.

E quella cu' il Savio bagna il fianco, 52
   così com' ella sie' tra 'l piano e 'l monte,
   tra tirannia si vive e stato franco.

Ora chi se', ti priego che ne conte; 55
   non esser duro più ch'altri sia stato,
   se 'l nome tuo nel mondo tegna fronte».

Though I've come somewhat late to take my turn,   22
    let it not vex you to remain and talk.
    You see it does not vex me—and I burn!

If into this blind dungeon you've been spilt   25
    recently from my lovely Italy,
    that sweet land and the scene of all my guilt,

Tell if Romagna is at peace or war,   28
    for I came from the hills between Urbino
    and the peak that sets free the Tiber's flow."

I was still leaning out and looking down   31
    intently, when the poet touched my side.
    "Your turn to talk," he said. "Italian, he."

And I—who had determined what to say,   34
    began to speak. "O spirit down below
    hidden in flame," I said without delay,

"Romagna is not and has never been   37
    free of the war within her tyrants' hearts,
    but I left none in open tyranny.

Ravenna stands as it has stood for years.   40
    The eagle of Polenta's brooding there
    and shadows Cervia with its spreading wings.

Forlì, that passed the trial of long siege   43
    and heaped the slaughtered Frenchmen in the field,
    finds herself once more under the Green Paws.

The mastiff and his puppy from Verrucchio,   46
    who had Montagna slain by treachery,
    suck the blood of their enemies—nothing new.

The Lion Cub in the White Lair controls   49
    the towns on the Lamone and the Santerno,
    who changes parties when the seasons change.

And Cesena, washed by the Savio,   52
    just as it lies between the plains and hills,
    lives neither free nor under tyranny.

And now I ask you, tell me who you are,   55
    do not begrudge me more than I have you—
    so may the world long see your name endure."

Poscia che 'l foco alquanto ebbe rugghiato   58
  al modo suo, l'aguta punta mosse
  di qua, di là, e poi diè cotal fiato:
«S'i' credesse che mia risposta fosse   61
  a persona che mai tornasse al mondo,
  questa fiamma staria sanza più scosse;
ma però che già mai di questo fondo   64
  non tornò vivo alcun, s'i' odo il vero,
  sanza tema d'infamia ti rispondo.
Io fui uom d'arme, e poi fui cordigliero,   67
  credendomi, sì cinto, fare ammenda;
  e certo il creder mio venìa intero,
se non fosse il gran prete, a cui mal prenda!,   70
  che mi rimise ne le prime colpe;
  e come e *quare*, voglio che m'intenda.
Mentre ch'io forma fui d'ossa e di polpe   73
  che la madre mi diè, l'opere mie
  non furon leonine, ma di volpe.
Li accorgimenti e le coperte vie   76
  io seppi tutte, e sì menai lor arte,
  ch'al fine de la terra il suono uscie.
Quando mi vidi giunto in quella parte   79
  di mia etade ove ciascun dovrebbe
  calar le vele e raccoglier le sarte,
ciò che pria mi piacëa, allor m'increbbe,   82
  e pentuto e confesso mi rendei;
  ahi miser lasso! e giovato sarebbe.
Lo principe d'i novi Farisei,   85
  avendo guerra presso a Laterano,
  e non con Saracin né con Giudei,
ché ciascun suo nimico era cristiano,   88
  e nessun era stato a vincer Acri
  né mercatante in terra di Soldano,

After the fire had made its hollow roar,   58
  such as it does, the keen point of the flame
  danced here and there, and breathed out this reply:
"If I believed that my response was heard   61
  by anyone returning to the world,
  this flame would stand and never stir again,
But since no man has ever come alive   64
  out of this gulf of Hell, if I hear true,
  I'll answer, with no fear of infamy.
I was a man of arms, then wore the cord   67
  of a lay friar, thinking to make amends,
  and doubtless my belief would have come true
Had the Great Priest° —may he be dragged to Hell!—   70
  not pitched me back into my former faults.
  Listen to how and why, for I shall tell.
While I yet wore the form of bones and flesh   73
  my mother gave me, all my actions were
  not those that mark the lion, but the fox.
Clever expedients and covered ways—   76
  I worked them all so artfully, my fame
  resounded at the limits of the earth.
Yet when I saw that I had reached the age   79
  at which a man should reel the hawsers in
  and let his sails come down, the deeds which once
I took delight in, now I wearied of,   82
  confessed, repented, gave my freedom over.
  Wretch that I am, it would have done me good!
But the prince of the modern Pharisees—   85
  engaged in battle near the Lateran
  and never against Saracens or Jews,
For all his enemies were Christian men,   88
  and none turned traitor at the siege of Acre,
  or plied his business in the sultan's lands—

° the Great Priest: Pope Boniface VIII.

né sommo officio né ordini sacri 91
   guardò in sé, né in me quel capestro
   che solea fare i suoi cinti più macri.

Ma come Costantin chiese Silvestro 94
   d'entro Siratti a guerir de la lebbre,
   così mi chiese questi per maestro

a guerir de la sua superba febbre; 97
   domandommi consiglio, e io tacetti
   perché le sue parole parver ebbre.

E' poi ridisse: 'Tuo cuor non sospetti. 100
   Finor t'assolvo, e tu m'insegna fare
   sì come Penestrino in terra getti.

Lo ciel poss' io serrare e diserrare, 103
   come tu sai; però son due le chiavi
   che 'l mio antecessor non ebbe care'.

Allor mi pinser li argomenti gravi 106
   là 've 'l tacer mi fu avviso 'l peggio,
   e dissi: 'Padre, da che tu mi lavi

di quel peccato ov'io mo cader deggio, 109
   lunga promessa con l'attender corto
   ti farà trïunfar ne l'alto seggio'.

Francesco venne poi, com' io fu' morto, 112
   per me; ma un d'i neri cherubini
   li disse: 'Non portar, non mi far torto.

Venir se ne dee giù tra ' miei meschini 115
   perché diede 'l consiglio frodolente,
   dal quale in qua stato li sono a' crini;

ch'assolver non si può chi non si pente, 118
   né pentere e volere insieme puossi
   per la contradizion che nol consente'.

Oh me dolente! come mi riscossi 121
   quando mi prese dicendomi: 'Forse
   tu non pensavi ch'io löico fossi!'.

Cared neither for his papal dignity,   91
   his holy orders, nor my friar's cord
   which used to make men leaner in the waist.°

As Constantine once summoned Pope Sylvester   94
   to cure his leprosy on Mount Soracte,
   so this one in the fever of his pride

Called me as his physician for the cure   97
   and asked me for a plan, and I was silent,
   because his words seemed drunken. But he pressed,

'Let your heart not be troubled. In advance   100
   I will absolve you. Show me what to do
   to batter Palestrina to the ground.

I hold the power to bar and unbar Heaven,   103
   you know; for there are two of them, those keys
   my predecessor° did not hold so dear.'

His ponderous words kept pushing me until   106
   silence seemed the more perilous course. Said I,
   'Father, because you cleanse me of that sin

Into which I am falling—well, be long   109
   on promises and short on keeping them.
   This gains the triumph for your lofty throne.'

The day I died, Saint Francis came for me,   112
   but one of the black angels said to him,
   'Don't cheat me now! Don't carry him away!

This one belongs with all my slaves down there,   115
   because he gave his counsel to defraud.
   Since then I've itched to snatch him by the hair!

One who does not repent can't be absolved,   118
   nor can a man repent and will at once:
   the law of contradiction rules it out.'

Ah sorrow! when I woke to my position   121
   and heard him say as he grabbed hold, 'Perhaps
   you hadn't thought that I was a logician.'

° *leaner in the waist:* from fasting, that is. Dante means that the friar's habit used to make a man less
worldly in general. Now, however, the orders are corrupt and no longer observe strict discipline.
° *my predecessor:* Pope Celestine V; see 3.59–60 and note.

A Minòs mi portò; e quelli attorse 124
    otto volte la coda al dosso duro;
    e poi che per gran rabbia la si morse,
disse: 'Questi è d'i rei del foco furo'; 127
    per ch'io là dove vedi son perduto,
    e sì vestito, andando, mi rancuro».
Quand' elli ebbe 'l suo dir così compiuto, 130
    la fiamma dolorando si partio,
    torcendo e dibattendo 'l corno aguto.
Noi passamm' oltre, e io e 'l duca mio, 133
    su per lo scoglio infino in su l'altr' arco
    che cuopre 'l fosso in che si paga il fio
a quei che scommettendo acquistan carco. 136

He bore me off to Minos,° and that judge   124
    twisted his tail eight times round his rough back,
    and biting it in a mad burst of rage
He bellowed, 'To the thieving fire with this,'   127
    so where you see me I am lost forever,
    and garbed in fire, I go in bitterness."
When he had finished what he had to say,   130
    the sorrowing flame departed from us, twisting
    and buffeting the arrow of the fire.
But we continued on, my guide and I,   133
    over the rock ridge up the arch beyond
    which spans the trench in which they pay the fee
Who heap up woe by severing what was joined.   136

° *Minos:* judge of the damned. See 5.4 and note.

Chi poria mai pur con parole sciolte
   dicer del sangue e de le piaghe a pieno
   ch'i' ora vidi, per narrar più volte?
Ogne lingua per certo verria meno
   per lo nostro sermone e per la mente
   c'hanno a tanto comprender poco seno.
S'el s'aunasse ancor tutta la gente
   che già, in su la fortunata terra
   di Puglia, fu del suo sangue dolente
per li Troiani e per la lunga guerra
   che de l'anella fé sì alte spoglie,
   come Livïo scrive, che non erra,
con quella che sentio di colpi doglie
   per contastare a Ruberto Guiscardo;
   e l'altra il cui ossame ancor s'accoglie
a Ceperan, là dove fu bugiardo
   ciascun Pugliese, e là da Tagliacozzo,
   dove sanz' arme vinse il vecchio Alardo;
e qual forato suo membro e qual mozzo
   mostrasse, d'aequar sarebbe nulla
   il modo de la nona bolgia sozzo.
Già veggia, per mezzul perdere o lulla,
   com' io vidi un, così non si pertugia,
   rotto dal mento infin dove si trulla.

4

7

10

13

16

19

22

Canto Twenty-eight

*The poets move on to the **ninth ditch of Malebolge**, where devils slash open the schismatics—sowers of discord on earth. They meet **Mohammed**; the Tuscan leaders **Pier da Medicina** and **Mosca dei Lamberti**; the instigator of Julius Caesar, **Curio**; and the Provençal poet and warrior **Bertran de Born.***

Who could ever—even with words set loose in prose—
    tell in full—though he told it many times—
    of all the blood and wounds I witnessed now?
Certainly every tongue would fall too short   4
    on account of our language and our minds
    which lack the capacity to contain so much.
If you assembled all who ever fell   7
    in the fortune-battered fields of Puglia
    and found the sorrow of bloodshed at the hands
Of Trojans or of Hannibal, who piled   10
    a giant heap of rings from dead men's fingers
    in the long Punic War, as Livy writes,
Who does not stray—and added all who felt   13
    the grievous blows of Robert Guiscard's march,
    with all the men whose bones lie heaped up still
At Ceperan, where every Pugliese chief   16
    turned traitor—and the bones near Tagliacozzo,
    where old Alardo triumphed weaponless,
And had one show his limbs lopped off, and one   19
    his members gored, it would be nothing to
    the fashion of the filth in the ninth ditch.
A barrel with the midstave split apart   22
    is not—as I saw one there—so burst wide,
    from the chin severed down to where we fart.

BERTRAN DE BORN

Tra le gambe pendevan le minugia; 25
   la corata pareva e 'l tristo sacco
   che merda fa di quel che si trangugia.

Mentre che tutto in lui veder m'attacco, 28
   guardommi e con le man s'aperse il petto,
   dicendo: «Or vedi com' io mi dilacco!

vedi come storpiato è Mäometto! 31
   Dinanzi a me sen va piangendo Alì,
   fesso nel volto dal mento al ciuffetto.

E tutti li altri che tu vedi qui, 34
   seminator di scandalo e di scisma
   fuor vivi, e però son fessi così.

Un diavolo è qua dietro che n'accisma 37
   sì crudelmente, al taglio de la spada
   rimettendo ciascun di questa risma,

quand' avem volta la dolente strada; 40
   però che le ferite son richiuse
   prima ch'altri dinanzi li rivada.

Ma tu chi se' che 'n su lo scoglio muse, 43
   forse per indugiar d'ire a la pena
   ch'è giudicata in su le tue accuse?».

«Né morte 'l giunse ancor, né colpa 'l mena», 46
   rispuose 'l mio maestro, «a tormentarlo;
   ma per dar lui esperïenza piena,

a me, che morto son, convien menarlo 49
   per lo 'nferno qua giù di giro in giro;
   e quest' è ver così com' io ti parlo».

Più fuor di cento che, quando l'udiro, 52
   s'arrestaron nel fosso a riguardarmi
   per maraviglia, oblïando il martiro.

«Or dì a fra Dolcin dunque che s'armi, 55
   tu che forse vedra' il sole in breve,
   s'ello non vuol qui tosto seguitarmi,

sì di vivanda, che stretta di neve 58
   non rechi la vittoria al Noarese,
   ch'altrimenti acquistar non saria leve».

His bowels and guts dangled between the legs;   25
    the organs showed, and that repugnant bag
    that turns whatever we gobble into shit.

While my mind clung entirely to this sight,   28
    he looked at me and with his two hands tore
    his chest apart: "See how I split the haunch!

Look at Mohammed and his mangled trunk!   31
    Before me in his weeping goes Ali,
    slashed down the face from cowlick to the chin.

And all the other souls you witness here   34
    sowed scandal, discord, schism when alive,
    and therefore they are cloven as you see.

Behind us is a devil who sets us right,   37
    for to the cruel slicing of his sword
    he subjects every spirit in the file

When we've gone once around the painful road,   40
    and every wound we suffer closes up
    before we come to face the steel again.

But who are you there gazing from the ridge,   43
    maybe to dawdle going to the pains
    they've judged to fit the crimes that *you've* confessed?"

"Death has not caught him yet," my Teacher said,   46
    "nor is he led to torments here by sin,
    but to give him complete experience

I who am dead must lead him into Hell,   49
    down the abyss from one round to the next.
    This is as true as that I speak to you."

When they heard what he said, more than a hundred   52
    stood stock-still in the trench to stare at me,
    forgetting all their tortures as they wondered.

"Well then, tell Fra Dolcin to arm himself—   55
    you who, perhaps, will see the sunlight soon,
    if he'd like not to follow me to Hell

Immediately—with lots of food supplies,   58
    lest snow bring victory to the Novarese
    which wouldn't have come easy otherwise."

Poi che l'un piè per girsene sospese,   61
   Mäometto mi disse esta parola;
   indi a partirsi in terra lo distese.

Un altro, che forata avea la gola   64
   e tronco 'l naso infin sotto le ciglia,
   e non avea mai ch'una orecchia sola,

ristato a riguardar per maraviglia   67
   con li altri, innanzi a li altri aprì la canna,
   ch'era di fuor d'ogne parte vermiglia,

e disse: «O tu cui colpa non condanna   70
   e cu' io vidi in su terra latina,
   se troppa simiglianza non m'inganna,

rimembriti di Pier da Medicina,   73
   se mai torni a veder lo dolce piano
   che da Vercelli a Marcabò dichina.

E fa sapere a' due miglior da Fano,   76
   a messer Guido e anco ad Angiolello,
   che, se l'antiveder qui non è vano,

gittati saran fuor di lor vasello   79
   e mazzerati presso a la Cattolica
   per tradimento d'un tiranno fello.

Tra l'isola di Cipri e di Maiolica   82
   non vide mai sì gran fallo Nettuno,
   non da pirate, non da gente argolica.

Quel traditor che vede pur con l'uno,   85
   e tien la terra che tale qui meco
   vorrebbe di vedere esser digiuno,

farà venirli a parlamento seco;   88
   poi farà sì, ch'al vento di Focara
   non sarà lor mestier voto né preco».

Raising one foot suspended in the air,   61
   Mohammed spoke these words to me, then stretched
   toe to the ground to walk and leave us there.

Another, with a hole bored through his throat   64
   and his nose severed clear up to the eyes,
   and only one ear left, stood in the moat

With all the rest to gape at me in wonder,   67
   but he was first to open up his pipe,
   all red with blood and visible outside,

And said, "O you whom sin does not condemn,   70
   and whom I saw above in Italy,
   unless too close a likeness has deceived me—

Remember me, Pier da Medicina,   73
   if ever you return to the sweet plains
   that from Vercelli slope to Marcabò.

And let the two princes of Fano know,   76
   tell milord Guido and tell Angiolello,
   unless the prophecies of Hell are vain,

They will be pitched out of their boat at sea,   79
   stones hung about their necks near La Cattolica
   by a fierce tyrant° in his treachery.

From Cyprus west all the way to Majolica   82
   Neptune has never seen so great a crime,
   neither by pirates nor by men of Greece.

That treacherous prince who squints out of one eye,   85
   who holds the land whereof one here with me
   would just as soon have fasted from the sight,

Will have them come to parley, then arrange   88
   that they should have no need of prayer or vow
   to get them past Focara's windy cape."°

° *a fierce tyrant:* the one-eyed Malatestino Malatesta, prince of Rimini. *Majolica,* or Majorca, is an island near Spain; the distance from there to Cyprus, in the east, spans almost the whole Mediterranean Sea.

° *Focara's windy cape:* a treacherous headland on the Adriatic, near the town of *La Cattolica.* They will not need to say a special prayer as they round that cape, because they will already have been drowned.

E io a lui: «Dimostrami e dichiara,   91
   se vuo' ch'i' porti sù di te novella,
   chi è colui da la veduta amara».

Allor puose la mano a la mascella   94
   d'un suo compagno e la bocca li aperse,
   gridando: «Questi è desso, e non favella.

Questi, scacciato, il dubitar sommerse   97
   in Cesare, affermando che 'l fornito
   sempre con danno l'attender sofferse».

Oh quanto mi pareva sbigottito   100
   con la lingua tagliata ne la strozza
   Curïo, ch'a dir fu così ardito!

E un ch'avea l'una e l'altra man mozza,   103
   levando i moncherin per l'aura fosca,
   sì che 'l sangue facea la faccia sozza,

gridò: «Ricordera'ti anche del Mosca,   106
   che disse, lasso!, 'Capo ha cosa fatta',
   che fu mal seme per la gente tosca».

E io li aggiunsi: «E morte di tua schiatta»;   109
   per ch'elli, accumulando duol con duolo,
   sen gio come persona trista e matta.

Ma io rimasi a riguardar lo stuolo,   112
   e vidi cosa ch'io avrei paura,
   sanza più prova, di contarla solo;

se non che coscïenza m'assicura,   115
   la buona compagnia che l'uom francheggia
   sotto l'asbergo del sentirsi pura.

Io vidi certo, e ancor par ch'io 'l veggia,   118
   un busto sanza capo andar sì come
   andavan li altri de la trista greggia;

e 'l capo tronco tenea per le chiome,   121
   pesol con mano a guisa di lanterna:
   e quel mirava noi e dicea: «Oh me!».

Di sé facea a sé stesso lucerna,   124
   ed eran due in uno e uno in due;
   com' esser può, quei sa che sì governa.

And I to him: "All right, make clear to me,   91
   if you would have me tell of you above,
   who's he, who hates the sight of Rimini?"

At that he put his hand upon the jaw   94
   of a companion, prying the mouth open,
   shouting, "It's this one here, who doesn't talk.

Driven from Rome, this spirit drowned the doubts   97
   in Caesar, by affirming that a man
   who is prepared delays to his own loss."

Oh how he seemed to me downcast and cold,   100
   with his tongue sliced in half down to the gullet,
   this Curio, whose speech was once so bold!

And one whose hands both left and right were lopped,   103
   raising his dripping stumps in the dark air
   so that the blood that fell befouled his face,

Cried out, "Remember Mosca too, who said,   106
   alas, 'A thing that's done with has an end,'
   which sowed the seeds of ill for Tuscany."

I added, "And brought death to your whole stock,"   109
   at which, accumulating woe on woe,
   he went away as one beset with gloom

And madness. I remained to view the band,   112
   and saw a thing I'd be afraid to tell
   alone, without more proof to back my word,

But my good conscience makes me feel secure,   115
   that trusty friend that frees a man beneath
   the armor of his knowing he is pure.

Clearly I saw, and the sight still comes back,   118
   a trunk without a head come walking on
   just like the others of that sullen pack,

That held the chopped-off head by the long hanks,   121
   hanging like a lantern from his hand,
   and the head gaped at us and said, "Ah, me!"

He made himself a lamp unto himself,   124
   and they were two in one and one in two.
   How that can be, He knows Who steers the helm.

Quando diritto al piè del ponte fue,   127
    levò 'l braccio alto con tutta la testa
    per appressarne le parole sue,

che fuoro: «Or vedi la pena molesta,   130
    tu che, spirando, vai veggendo i morti:
    vedi s'alcuna è grande come questa.

E perché tu di me novella porti,   133
    sappi ch'i' son Bertram dal Bornio, quelli
    che diedi al re giovane i ma' conforti.

Io feci il padre e 'l figlio in sé ribelli;   136
    Achitofèl non fé più d'Absalone
    e di Davìd coi malvagi punzelli.

Perch' io parti' così giunte persone,   139
    partito porto il mio cerebro, lasso!,
    dal suo principio ch'è in questo troncone.

Così s'osserva in me lo contrapasso».   142

When he arrived just at the bridge's foot   127
    he lifted the arm high with the whole head,
    to bring these words the closer to our sides:
"Now look upon the grievous punishment,   130
    you who yet breathe and go to view the dead—
    see whether any is as great as mine!
That you may bring back news about me, know   133
    I am Bertran de Born, the one who gave
    evil encouragement to the English prince.°
I set the father and the son at war;   136
    the wicked goadings of Achitophel
    for Absalom and David did no more.
Because I severed two such persons joined,   139
    severed I carry now my brains, alas,
    from their stem in this trunk. Thus you may see
The rule of retribution work in me."   142

° *the English prince:* Prince Henry of England; see notes.

La molta gente e le diverse piaghe
   avean le luci mie sì inebrïate,
   che de lo stare a piangere eran vaghe.
Ma Virgilio mi disse: «Che pur guate?   4
   perché la vista tua pur si soffolge
   là giù tra l'ombre triste smozzicate?
Tu non hai fatto sì a l'altre bolge.   7
   Pensa, se tu annoverar le credi,
   che miglia ventidue la valle volge.
E già la luna è sotto i nostri piedi;   10
   lo tempo è poco omai che n'è concesso,
   e altro è da veder che tu non vedi».
«Se tu avessi», rispuos' io appresso,   13
   «atteso a la cagion per ch'io guardava,
   forse m'avresti ancor lo star dimesso».
Parte sen giva, e io retro li andava,   16
   lo duca, già faccendo la risposta,
   e soggiugnendo: «Dentro a quella cava
dov' io tenea or li occhi sì a posta,   19
   credo ch'un spirto del mio sangue pianga
   la colpa che là giù cotanto costa».

CANTO TWENTY-NINE

*Before they leave the schismatics, Dante notices the mutilated shade of a kinsman, **Geri del Bello**, threatening him. When the poets come to the **tenth ditch of Malebolge**, where the **falsifiers** are punished by nauseating and detestable diseases, they meet two **alchemists**, **Griffolino** and **Capocchio**. The canto ends with an invective against the stupidity of the Sienese.*

The mob of souls and all their various wounds
    had made my lights so full and drunk with tears,
    I longed to stay a little while and weep.
But Virgil: "What are you still gazing at?   4
    Why does your sight still prop itself down there
    among the dismal amputated shades?
You did not do so at the other moats.   7
    Think, if you're going to number all the spirits,
    twenty-two miles the valley turns about.
The moon's already set beneath our feet;°   10
    the time conceded us is short enough.
    There's more to see which you have not yet seen."
"If you had paid attention to the cause,"   13
    straightaway I responded, "why I gazed,
    you might have granted me a longer pause."
Meanwhile he set out, and I followed him,   16
    my guide, as I was making my reply
    and adding to it, "In that cavity
Where I was keeping at my post to look,   19
    I think a spirit of my own blood mourns
    the wickedness that down there costs so much."

° *The moon's already set beneath our feet:* Thus it is noon—or shortly after—directly above, in Jerusalem.

Allor disse 'l maestro: «Non si franga   22
   lo tuo pensier da qui innanzi sovr' ello.
   Attendi ad altro, ed ei là si rimanga;

ch'io vidi lui a piè del ponticello   25
   mostrarti e minacciar forte col dito,
   e udi' 'l nominar Geri del Bello.

Tu eri allor sì del tutto impedito   28
   sovra colui che già tenne Altaforte,
   che non guardasti in là, sì fu partito».

«O duca mio, la vïolenta morte   31
   che non li è vendicata ancor», diss' io,
   «per alcun che de l'onta sia consorte,

fece lui disdegnoso; ond' el sen gio   34
   sanza parlarmi, sì com' ïo estimo:
   e in ciò m'ha el fatto a sé più pio».

Così parlammo infino al loco primo   37
   che de lo scoglio l'altra valle mostra,
   se più lume vi fosse, tutto ad imo.

Quando noi fummo sor l'ultima chiostra   40
   di Malebolge, sì che i suoi conversi
   potean parere a la veduta nostra,

lamenti saettaron me diversi,   43
   che di pietà ferrati avean li strali;
   ond' io li orecchi con le man copersi.

Qual dolor fora, se de li spedali   46
   di Valdichiana tra 'l luglio e 'l settembre
   e di Maremma e di Sardigna i mali

fossero in una fossa tutti 'nsembre,   49
   tal era quivi, e tal puzzo n'usciva
   qual suol venir de le marcite membre.

Noi discendemmo in su l'ultima riva   52
   del lungo scoglio, pur da man sinistra;
   e allor fu la mia vista più viva

giù ver' lo fondo, là 've la ministra   55
   de l'alto Sire infallibil giustizia
   punisce i falsador che qui registra.

"There is no need," my Teacher said to me,   22
    "to break your thoughts upon him anymore.
    Attend to something else, and let him stay

Where he must stay. I saw him near the bridge   25
    pointing you out and hurling threats at you,
    and heard them call his name: Geri del Bello.

Your mind was then so seized by him who once   28
    was lord of Hautefort,° you didn't look
    in his direction until he had gone."

"My Guide, the violent death he had to die,   31
    which hasn't been avenged by anyone
    who should be party to his shame," said I,

"Makes him indignant, as I guess, and so   34
    he takes his leave and does not speak to me.
    That made me feel more pity for his fate."

So we conversed as we went walking, right   37
    to where the ridge would first reveal the pit
    down to the bottom, if there were more light.

When we arrived at the last cloister of   40
    Pouches of Evil, and our eyes could see
    the lay brothers it housed, I was so stung

With arrows of unusual laments,   43
    they seemed to steel the tips in sympathy—
    and so I blocked my ears up with both hands.

If you threw all the sick in the sick-houses   46
    of Val di Chiana in malaria season,
    and the diseases of Maremma's flats

And of Sardinia, into the same ditch—   49
    such pain was here, and it made just such stink
    as comes from members dying of the rot.

Over the final slope of the long ridge   52
    we two descended, turning still to left,
    and then my power of sight came more alive

Down toward the bottom, where the minister   55
    of God on high, Justice infallible,
    punishes counterfeits whose sins on earth

° *lord of Hautefort:* Bertran de Born.

Non credo ch'a veder maggior tristizia   58
    fosse in Egina il popol tutto infermo,
    quando fu l'aere sì pien di malizia,
che li animali, infino al picciol vermo,   61
    cascaron tutti, e poi le genti antiche,
    secondo che i poeti hanno per fermo,
si ristorar di seme di formiche,   64
    ch'era a veder per quella oscura valle
    languir li spirti per diverse biche.
Qual sovra 'l ventre e qual sovra le spalle   67
    l'un de l'altro giacea, e qual carpone
    si trasmutava per lo tristo calle.
Passo passo andavam sanza sermone,   70
    guardando e ascoltando li ammalati,
    che non potean levar le lor persone.
Io vidi due sedere a sé poggiati,   73
    com'a scaldar si poggia tegghia a tegghia,
    dal capo al piè di schianze macolati;
e non vidi già mai menare stregghia   76
    a ragazzo aspettato dal segnorso,
    né a colui che mal volontier vegghia,
come ciascun menava spesso il morso   79
    de l'unghie sopra sé per la gran rabbia
    del pizzicor, che non ha più soccorso;
e sì traevan giù l'unghie la scabbia,   82
    come coltel di scardova le scaglie
    o d'altro pesce che più larghe l'abbia.
«O tu che con le dita ti dismaglie»,   85
    cominciò 'l duca mio a l'un di loro,
    «e che fai d'esse talvolta tanaglie,
dinne s'alcun Latino è tra costoro   88
    che son quinc' entro, se l'unghia ti basti
    etternalmente a cotesto lavoro».
«Latin siam noi, che tu vedi sì guasti   91
    qui ambedue», rispuose l'un piangendo;
    «ma tu chi se' che di noi dimandasti?».

It enters in its book. No greater gloom 58
    did all the sick of Aegina behold,
    when the air was so full of pestilence
That every living thing down to the worm 61
    dropped dead, all of them, and the ancient folk,
    as the old poets hold for certain truth,
Restored their progeny from the seed of ants, 64
    than was the gloom in that dark valley, where
    the spirits languished in their separate sheaves.
Some on another's stomach or his back 67
    lay sprawled, while others dragged their shifting forms
    on all fours down the melancholy track.
Step by slow step we took our silent way, 70
    listening to and watching the diseased,
    who could not raise their persons from the ground.
I saw two sitting propped, as one fry pan 73
    leans on another fry pan in the oven,
    spotted from head to foot with scabby crusts,
And I've not seen a currycomb so fast 76
    scrubbed by the stable boy whose master's coming,
    or by one waked against his will to hurry,
As did each soul rake himself with the bite 79
    of fingernails in the great maddening itch,
    itch that will never find relief or rest,
And scraped the nails down the long stretch of scab 82
    like a knife slicing scales from off a pike
    or other fish whose scales are bigger yet.
"O you whose fingers strip your sheet mail off," 85
    my guide began to speak to one of them,
    "and sometimes dig the nail to tug and pinch,
Tell us if an Italian in this ditch 88
    is to be found—so may your nail suffice
    to do this labor for eternity."
"We whom you see so laid to waste, we two 91
    are both Italian," said the one, in tears,
    "but you who ask this of us, who are you?"

E 'l duca disse: «I' son un che discendo   94
   con questo vivo giù di balzo in balzo,
   e di mostrar lo 'nferno a lui intendo».

Allor si ruppe lo comun rincalzo;   97
   e tremando ciascuno a me si volse
   con altri che l'udiron di rimbalzo.

Lo buon maestro a me tutto s'accolse,   100
   dicendo: «Dì a lor ciò che tu vuoli»;
   e io incominciai, poscia ch'ei volse:

«Se la vostra memoria non s'imboli   103
   nel primo mondo da l'umane menti,
   ma s'ella viva sotto molti soli,

ditemi chi voi siete e di che genti;   106
   la vostra sconcia e fastidiosa pena
   di palesarvi a me non vi spaventi».

«Io fui d'Arezzo, e Albero da Siena».   109
   rispuose l'un, «mi fé mettere al foco;
   ma quel per ch'io mori' qui non mi mena.

Vero è ch'i' dissi lui, parlando a gioco: 112
   'I' mi saprei levar per l'aere a volo';
   e quei, ch'avea vaghezza e senno poco,

volle ch'i' li mostrassi l'arte; e solo   115
   perch' io nol feci Dedalo, mi fece
   ardere a tal che l'avea per figliuolo.

Ma ne l'ultima bolgia de le diece   118
   me per l'alchìmia che nel mondo usai
   dannò Minòs, a cui fallar non lece».

E io dissi al poeta: «Or fu già mai   121
   gente sì vana come la sanese?
   Certo non la francesca sì d'assai!».

Onde l'altro lebbroso, che m'intese,   124
   rispuose al detto mio: «Tra'mene Stricca
   che seppe far le temperate spese,

And my guide said, "I am one who descends 94
    with this man yet alive from ledge to ledge,
    for I intend to show him all of Hell."

Then they broke off their mutual prop and stay 97
    and each one, trembling, turned to look at me,
    with all who heard it on the ricochet.

Toward my side then the good Teacher drew 100
    and said, "Say anything you want to them,"
    and I began thus, as he wished me to:

"So may your name not steal itself away 103
    from human memory in the former world,
    but live through many turnings of the sun,

Tell me then who you are, and from what city. 106
    Don't let your tedious and repulsive pains
    make you ashamed to show yourselves to me."

"Arezzo was my city," one replied. 109
    "Albert of Siena burnt me at the stake,
    but why I'm damned here isn't why I died.

It's true I said to him, speaking in jest, 112
    'I can rise up into the air and fly!'
    and he, an eager sort with not much brains,

Wanted to learn the art. For this alone— 115
    I did not make him Daedalus!° —he had
    me burned by him who held him as his son.

But Minos, who can never be deceived, 118
    condemned me to this last pouch of the ten
    for alchemy I practiced in the world."

I to the poet: "Now was there ever a folk 121
    as vain and stupid as the Sienese?
    Surely not even Frenchmen, not by far!"

The other leprous spirit overheard 124
    and answered me: "You'd better not count Stricca,
    who had the knack to keep his spending down,

° *Daedalus:* in mythology, the cleverest man alive. He devised the labyrinth for the Minotaur in Crete. Later he fashioned waxen wings for himself and his son Icarus with which to escape from the island.

e Niccolò che la costuma ricca   127
   del garofano prima discoverse
   ne l'orto dove tal seme s'appicca;
e tra'ne la brigata in che disperse   130
   Caccia d'Ascian la vigna e la gran fonda,
   e l'Abbagliato suo senno proferse.
Ma perché sappi chi sì ti seconda   133
   contra i Sanesi, aguzza ver' me l'occhio,
   sì che la faccia mia ben ti risponda:
sì vedrai ch'io son l'ombra di Capocchio,   136
   che falsai li metalli con l'alchìmia;
   e te dee ricordar, se ben t'adocchio,
com'io fui di natura buona scimia».   139

And Niccolò, who was the first above   127
    to sow into that garden lush with weeds
    the luxury of seasoning with the clove,
Nor should you count the Squanderers' Brigade,   130
    among whom Caccia chucked his lands and vines
    and the Bedazzled showed what sense he made.
But if you'd like to know who backs your cry   133
    against the Sienese, sharpen your sight
    until my features give you the reply,
And you will see that I'm Capocchio's shade,   136
    who made false metals by my alchemy,
    and if my eyes see true, you should recall
How fine an ape of Nature's works I was."   139

Nel tempo che Iunone era crucciata
　　per Semelè contra 'l sangue tebano,
　　come mostrò una e altra fiata,
Atamante divenne tanto insano,　　　　　　　　　　　　　4
　　che veggendo la moglie con due figli
　　andar carcata da ciascuna mano,
gridò: «Tendiam le reti, sì ch'io pigli　　　　　　　　　7
　　la leonessa e ' leoncini al varco»;
　　e poi distese i dispietati artigli,
prendendo l'un ch'avea nome Learco,　　　　　　　　　10
　　e rotollo e percosselo ad un sasso;
　　e quella s'annegò con l'altro carco.
E quando la fortuna volse in basso　　　　　　　　　　13
　　l'altezza de' Troian che tutto ardiva,
　　sì che 'nsieme col regno il re fu casso,
Ecuba trista, misera e cattiva,　　　　　　　　　　　　16
　　poscia che vide Polissena morta,
　　e del suo Polidoro in su la riva
del mar si fu la dolorosa accorta,　　　　　　　　　　19
　　forsennata latrò sì come cane;
　　tanto il dolor le fé la mente torta.

Canto Thirty

*Still in the **tenth ditch of Malebolge**, Dante sees two frenzied spirits tearing into the other sufferers; they are the shades of the **impostors Gianni Schicchi** and **Myrrha**. Then the poets meet the hydroptic **Master Adam**, a **counterfeiter**, who finds himself in a scuffle with **Sinon**, the **liar** who played the Trojans false in the affair of the Horse. After Virgil rebukes Dante for evidently enjoying the brawl, the poets leave.*

Back in the days when Juno's wrath was fired
    against the Theban blood by Semele,
    and she avenged herself against them twice,
She made King Athamas grow so insane   4
    that when he saw his wife with either arm
    carrying the burden of his two young sons,
He cried, "Let's lay the nets so I can catch   7
    the lioness and the lion cubs at the pass!"
    And then he thrust his ruthless clutches forth
And snatched the one, Learchus—whirled him round   10
    and brained him on a stone; then with the other
    the mother leapt into the sea and drowned.
And when the wheel of Fortune turned about   13
    to bring Troy down for all its daring pride,
    and king and kingdom were at once wiped out,
Pathetic Hecuba,° in captive gloom,   16
    seeing the strangling of Polyxena
    her daughter, and the sad discovered doom
Of murdered Polydorus on the shore,   19
    frenzied and mad, went howling like a dog,
    so badly had her grief twisted her mind.

° *Hecuba:* queen of Troy; see notes.

Ma né di Tebe furie né troiane   22
    si vider mäi in alcun tanto crude,
    non punger bestie, nonché membra umane,
quant' io vidi in due ombre smorte e nude,   25
    che mordendo correvan di quel modo
    che 'l porco quando del porcil si schiude.
L'una giunse a Capocchio, e in sul nodo   28
    del collo l'assanò, sì che, tirando,
    grattar li fece il ventre al fondo sodo.
E l'Aretin che rimase tremando,   31
    mi disse: «Quel folletto è Gianni Schicchi,
    e va rabbioso altrui così conciando».
«Oh» diss' io lui, «se l'altro non ti ficchi   34
    li denti a dosso, non ti sia fatica
    a dir chi è, pria che di qui si spicchi».
Ed elli a me: «Quell' è l'anima antica   37
    di Mirra scellerata, che divenne
    al padre, fuor del dritto amore, amica.
Questa a peccar con esso così venne,   40
    falsificando sé in altrui forma,
    come l'altro che là sen va, sostenne,
per guadagnar la donna de la torma,   43
    falsificare in sé Buoso Donati,
    testando e dando al testamento norma».
E poi che i due rabbiosi fuor passati   46
    sovra cu' io avea l'occhio tenuto,
    rivolsilo a guardar li altri mal nati.
Io vidi un, fatto a guisa di lëuto,   49
    pur ch'elli avesse avuta l'anguinaia
    tronca da l'altro che l'uomo ha forcuto.
La grave idropesì, che sì dispaia   52
    le membra con l'omor che mal converte,
    che 'l viso non risponde a la ventraia,

But none so fury-ridden in Thebes or Troy   22
    had ever lunged with such ferocity
    to bite at beasts or even rip men's limbs
As I saw two souls, naked, pale as death,   25
    tearing away and snapping as they ran,
    like the tusked swine who's set loose from the sty.
One of them got Capocchio, sank his tusk   28
    into the neck, and as he dragged him off,
    he made him rake his gut on the hard ground.
The Aretine remaining, all a-tremble,   31
    said to me, "That mad demon's Gianni Schicchi,
    who in his frenzy mangles us like that."
Said I, "Oh, let that other swine not stick   34
    its tusks into your back, but tell us, please,
    who it may be, before it dashes off."
"That is the ancient soul of wicked Myrrha,   37
    who strayed beyond the bounds of lawful love,"
    said he, "when she became her father's lover.
This girl went to her father's bed to sin,   40
    falsified in another woman's form;
    that other counterfeiter dared to fake
Buoso Donati at the point of death   43
    so he could win the princess of the stables,
    entering his last will and testament."
When the two shades whom I'd been watching passed   46
    in their furious rage, I turned to look
    upon the others born in evil hour.
I saw one sinner shaped like a fat lute,   49
    or would be, if you chopped off at the groin
    the legs which make a man into a fork.
The heavy dropsy° that distorts the limbs   52
    with ill-drained humors, bloating up the paunch
    so big with fluid that it dwarfs the face,

° *dropsy:* edema. According to medieval medicine, the hydroptic cannot convert nutrients properly. The more food and fluid he takes in, the more swollen he becomes and the thirstier he grows.

faceva lui tener le labbra aperte   55
   come l'etico fa, che per la sete
   l'un verso 'l mento e l'altro in sù rinverte.

«O voi che sanz' alcuna pena siete,   58
   e non so io perché, nel mondo gramo»,
   diss' elli a noi, «guardate e attendete

a la miseria del maestro Adamo;   61
   io ebbi, vivo, assai di quel ch'i' volli,
   e ora, lasso!, un gocciol d'acqua bramo.

Li ruscelletti che d'i verdi colli   64
   del Casentin discendon giuso in Arno,
   faccendo i lor canali freddi e molli,

sempre mi stanno innanzi, e non indarno,   67
   ché l'immagine lor vie più m'asciuga
   che 'l male ond' io nel volto mi discarno.

La rigida giustizia che mi fruga   70
   tragge cagion del loco ov' io peccai
   a metter più li miei sospiri in fuga.

Ivi è Romena, là dov' io falsai   73
   la lega suggellata del Batista;
   per ch'io il corpo sù arso lasciai.

Ma s'io vedessi qui l'anima trista   76
   di Guido o d'Alessandro o di lor frate,
   per Fonte Branda non darei la vista.

Dentro c'è l'una già, se l'arrabbiate   79
   ombre che vanno intorno dicon vero;
   ma che mi val, c'ho le membra legate?

S'io fossi pur di tanto ancor leggero   82
   ch'i' potessi in cent' anni andare un'oncia,
   io sarei messo già per lo sentiero,

cercando lui tra questa gente sconcia,   85
   con tutto ch'ella volge undici miglia,
   e men d'un mezzo di traverso non ci ha.

Puffed up his mouth, as a consumptive man   55
   driven by thirst curls back his upper lip
   and draws the lower one down to touch the chin.
"O you who are without a punishment—   58
   and I don't know why—in this wretched world,"
   said he to us, "behold, and listen to
The miserable state of Master Adam.   61
   Alive, I had all I could want, and now,
   alas, I long for one small water drop.
The little rushing brooks that splash their way   64
   down the green hills of Casentino to
   the Arno, with their streambeds cold and moist,
Are ever before me, and it's not in vain,   67
   for their sweet image dries me out far worse
   than this which wastes the flesh within my face.
The rigid justice sifting me like wheat   70
   has drawn a cause from where my sins took place
   to set my thirsty sighs to faster flight.
There stands Romena castle, where I coined   73
   counterfeit money with the Baptist's stamp,
   for which I left my body burnt above.
But if I could see here the mournful souls   76
   of Guido, Alexander, or their brother—
   for Branda's fountain° I'd not trade that sight!
And if those raving shades that run around   79
   this dungeon tell the truth, one's here already° —
   what good is that to me? My limbs are bound!
Yet if I were still barely light enough   82
   to go but one inch in a hundred years,
   I'd have set out upon the path by now,
Culling him out from all this loathsome dross,   85
   though it's eleven miles around the ditch
   and not less than a half a mile across.

° *Branda's fountain:* probably a spring near the castle.
° *one's here already:* Guido, who died in 1292.

Io son per lor tra sì fatta famiglia;   88
   e' m'indussero a batter li fiorini
   ch'avevan tre carati di mondiglia».

E io a lui: «Chi son li due tapini   91
   che fumman come man bagnate 'l verno,
   giacendo stretti a' tuoi destri confini?».

«Qui li trovai—e poi volta non dierno—»,   94
   rispuose, «quando piovvi in questo greppo,
   e non credo che dieno in sempiterno.

L'una è la falsa ch'accusò Gioseppo;   97
   l'altr' è 'l falso Sinon greco di Troia:
   per febbre aguta gittan tanto leppo».

E l'un di lor, che si recò a noia   100
   forse d'esser nomato sì oscuro,
   col pugno li percosse l'epa croia.

Quella sonò come fosse un tamburo;   103
   e mastro Adamo li percosse il volto
   col braccio suo, che non parve men duro,

dicendo a lui: «Ancor che mi sia tolto   106
   lo muover per le membra che son gravi,
   ho io il braccio a tal mestiere sciolto».

Ond' ei rispuose: «Quando tu andavi   109
   al fuoco, non l'avei tu così presto;
   ma sì e più l'avei quando coniavi».

E l'idropico: «Tu di' ver di questo,   112
   ma tu non fosti sì ver testimonio
   là 've del ver fosti a Troia richesto».

«S'io dissi falso, e tu falsasti il conio»,   115
   disse Sinon. «I' son qui per un fallo,
   e tu per più ch'alcun altro demonio!».

«Ricorditi, spergiuro, del cavallo»,   118
   rispuose quel ch'avëa infiata l'epa,
   «e sieti reo che tutto il mondo sallo!».

On their account I'm in this household here: 88
    they led me on to stamp the florins with
    the three carats of trash instead of gold."

And I to him: "Who are those wretched things, 91
    the two who steam like sweaty hands in winter,
    lying tight on your border at the right?"

"I found them here—they haven't turned once since— 94
    when I rained down into this garbage pot,
    nor do I think they'll ever turn again.

This one's the lying woman° who accused 97
    Joseph; that's the Greek liar, Sinon of Troy.
    Sharp fever burns their grease and makes that stench."

And one of them, who took it as a spite, 100
    perhaps, that he was given so black a name,
    banged with his fist that swollen bag of guts.

It boomed as if it were a kettledrum, 103
    and Master Adam gave him no less back
    but smacked him in the face with a free arm,

And said to him, "Although the heaviness 106
    so weighs my members down that I can't move,
    I have one arm that still can do the job."

And he replied, "Those arms were not so free 109
    when you were strapped and burning at the stake,
    but when you coined, you moved them readily!"

And the hydroptic, "There you do tell truth, 112
    but you were not so true a witness when
    Priam the Trojan asked you for the truth."

"I told a lie, and you lied with your coins," 115
    said Sinon. "I'm here for a single sin,
    but you, for more than any other fiend!"

"Recall, you perjurer,° the Trojan horse," 118
    responded he who had the bloated paunch,
    "and let it pain you that the whole world knows."

° *the lying woman:* Potiphar's wife, who falsely charged the Hebrew Joseph with rape (Gen. 39).
° *you perjurer:* Sinon had called the gods to witness, including the dread gods of the underworld, then lied anyway (*Aen.* 2.154–56).

«E te sia rea la sete onde ti crepa»,   121
  disse 'l Greco, «la lingua, e l'acqua marcia
  che 'l ventre innanzi a li occhi sì t'assiepa!».
Allora il monetier: «Così si squarcia   124
  la bocca tua per tuo mal come suole,
  ché, s'i' ho sete e omor mi rinfarcia,
tu hai l'arsura e 'l capo che ti duole,   127
  e per leccar lo specchio di Narcisso,
  non vorresti a 'nvitar molte parole».
Ad ascoltarli er' io del tutto fisso,   130
  quando 'l maestro mi disse: «Or pur mira,
  che per poco che teco non mi risso!».
Quand' io 'l senti a me parlar con ira,   133
  volsimi verso lui con tal vergogna,
  ch'ancor per la memoria mi si gira.
Qual è colui che suo dannaggio sogna,   136
  che sognando desidera sognare,
  sì che quel ch'è, come non fosse, agogna,
tal mi fec' io, non possendo parlare,   139
  che disïava scusarmi, e scusava
  me tuttavia, e nol mi credea fare.
«Maggior difetto men vergogna lava»,   142
  disse 'l maestro, «che 'l tuo non è stato;
  però d'ogne trestizia ti disgrava.
E fa ragion ch'io ti sia sempre allato,   145
  se più avvien che fortuna t'accoglia
  dove sien genti in simigliante piato:
ché voler ciò udire è bassa voglia».   148

"And let the thirst that cracks your tongue pain you,"   121
    said the Greek, "and that watery rot which makes
    a hedge out of your guts to block your eyes!"

The moneymaker then: "So let your mouth   124
    be gashed to shreds by your disease, as always,
    for if I thirst and fluid stuffs my bag,

You have the burning migraine in the skull,   127
    and you'd need few words to invite you to
    take one lick of Narcissus' glassy pool."°

I was entirely fixed upon those two   130
    when said my Teacher, "You keep looking there
    and in a while *I'll* pick a fight with *you*."

And when I heard the anger in his voice   133
    I turned with such embarrassment and shame
    it haunts my memory still. But as a man

Who dreams disaster or a grievous loss—   136
    dreaming, he longs for it to be a dream,
    yearning for what's the case, as if it weren't—

So was I then, when I could not reply,   139
    wanting to make apology, and I
    apologized indeed—unwittingly.

"Less shame would wash away a greater fault,"   142
    my Teacher said, "than yours has been, and so
    unburden all the sadness from your mind.

Be sure that I am ever at your side   145
    if fortune ever welcomes you again
    where people brawl before the arbiter.

To want to hear it is a base desire."   148

° *Narcissus' glassy pool:* the pool in which the boy Narcissus beheld his lovely image (see Ovid, *Met.* 3.407–510). Sinon, too, longs in vain.

Una medesma lingua pria mi morse,
  sì che mi tinse l'una e l'altra guancia,
  e poi la medicina mi riporse;
così od' io che solea far la lancia 4
  d'Achille e del suo padre esser cagione
  prima di trista e poi di buona mancia.
Noi demmo il dosso al misero vallone 7
  su per la ripa che 'l cinge dintorno,
  attraversando sanza alcun sermone.
Quiv' era men che notte e men che giorno, 10
  sì che 'l viso m'andava innanzi poco;
  ma io senti' sonare un alto corno,
tanto ch'avrebbe ogne tuon fatto fioco, 13
  che, contra sé la sua via seguitando,
  dirizzò li occhi miei tutti ad un loco.
Dopo la dolorosa rotta, quando 16
  Carlo Magno perdé la santa gesta,
  non sonò sì terribilmente Orlando.
Poco portäi in là volta la testa, 19
  che me parve veder molte alte torri;
  ond' io: «Maestro, dì, che terra è questa?».

CANTO THIRTY-ONE

*The poets descend to the **ninth and final circle** of Hell, that of the **traitors**. At the rim of the circle they find the **giants**, punished for their presumption; of these they see **Nimrod** and **Ephialtes**. Finally they are conveyed to the bottom of the sink by **Antaeus**.*

The very tongue that stung me with rebuke
    so that I flushed with shame in either cheek,
    then brought the medicine to soothe the shame,
As I have heard the lance of Peleus   4
    and of his son Achilles used to give
    wounds with the first touch, healing with the next.
We turned our back upon the wretched pit,   7
    with no more conversation as we crossed
    upon the inner ridge that circles it.
Here it was less than night and less than day,   10
    and I could hardly see in front of me,
    but heard instead the deep blast of a horn
Loud enough to make roaring thunder faint,   13
    and as it took its course it turned my eyes
    to focus on the place from which it came.
After the bloody rout, when the great Charles°   16
    had lost his army and the holy war,
    never so terribly in Roncesvalles
Did Roland blow his horn. And when I turned   19
    I soon caught sight, or so it seemed, of towers,
    many and tall. "Teacher, what city is this?"

° *the great Charles:* Charlemagne; see notes.

Ed elli a me: «Però che tu trascorri 22
  per le tenebre troppo da la lungi,
  avvien che poi nel maginare abborri.

Tu vedrai ben, se tu là ti congiungi, 25
  quanto 'l senso s'inganna di lontano;
  però alquanto più te stesso pungi».

Poi caramente mi prese per mano 28
  e disse: «Pria che noi siam più avanti,
  acciò che 'l fatto men ti paia strano,

sappi che non son torri, ma giganti, 31
  e son nel pozzo intorno da la ripa
  da l'umbilico in giuso tutti quanti».

Come quando la nebbia si dissipa, 34
  lo sguardo a poco a poco raffigura
  ciò che cela 'l vapor che l'aere stipa,

così forando l'aura grossa e scura, 37
  più e più appressando ver' la sponda,
  fuggiemi errore e crescémi paura;

però che, come su la cerchia tonda 40
  Montereggion di torri si corona,
  così la proda che 'l pozzo circonda

torreggiavan di mezza la persona 43
  li orribili giganti, cui minaccia
  Giove del cielo ancora quando tuona.

E io scorgeva già d'alcun la faccia, 46
  le spalle e 'l petto e del ventre gran parte,
  e per le coste giù ambo le braccia.

Natura certo, quando lasciò l'arte 49
  di sì fatti animali, assai fé bene
  per tòrre tali essecutori a Marte.

E s'ella d'elefanti e di balene 52
  non si pente, chi guarda sottilmente,
  più giusta e più discreta la ne tene;

I asked, and he replied, "Because you race 22
    ahead too great a distance through the darkness,
    imagination tangles you in knots.

You'll see it well, when you've arrived, how much 25
    your senses have deceived you from afar;
    so spur yourself a bit and hurry on."

He took me by the hand affectionately. 28
    "Before we go much farther you should know,
    lest it should strike you as a shock," said he,

"That those things aren't towers, but giants, sunk 31
    into the basin there behind the banks.
    You can see each one from the navel up."

As when a fog begins to float away, 34
    little by little, sight refigures things
    which had lain hidden in the thickened air,

So in that dark dense vapor, piercing through 37
    as I came near and nearer to the brink,
    my errors fled from me and my fear grew,

For, as upon the circling ramparts of 40
    Montereggion° there stands a crown of towers,
    so here with half their persons high above

The limits of the inner sink of Hell 43
    tower the horrible giants, whom Jupiter
    still menaces° with thundering in the skies.

Then I discerned the face of one indeed, 46
    shoulders and chest and great part of the trunk,
    and both arms hanging at his flanks. No doubt

Nature did very well when she left off 49
    the art of making living things like those,
    depriving Mars of such executors.

And if she still, without regret, creates 52
    the whale and elephant, consider well
    and you will find her wiser and more just,

° *Montereggion:* a fortress near Siena, spiked with sentry towers roundabout. These towers rose over sixty feet from the battlements.

° *still menaces:* as he did when he slew them with his lightning bolts at Phlegra; see 14.58 and note.

ché dove l'argomento de la mente   55
   s'aggiugne al mal volere e a la possa,
   nessun riparo vi può far la gente.

La faccia sua mi parea lunga e grossa   58
   come la pina di San Pietro a Roma,
   e a sua proporzione eran l'altre ossa;

sì che la ripa, ch'era perizoma   61
   dal mezzo in giù, ne mostrava ben tanto
   di sovra, che di giugnere a la chioma

tre Frison s'averien dato mal vanto;   64
   però ch'i' ne vedea trenta gran palmi
   dal loco in giù dov' omo affibbia 'l manto.

«Raphèl maì amècche zabì almi».   67
   cominciò a gridar la fiera bocca,
   cui non si convenia più dolci salmi.

E 'l duca mio ver' lui: «Anima sciocca,   70
   tienti col corno, e con quel ti disfoga
   quand' ira o altra passïon ti tocca!

Cércati al collo, e troverai la soga   73
   che 'l tien legato, o anima confusa,
   e vedi lui che 'l gran petto ti doga».

Poi disse a me: «Elli stessi s'accusa;   76
   questi è Nembrotto per lo cui mal coto
   pur un linguaggio nel mondo non s'usa.

Lasciànlo stare e non parliamo a vòto;   79
   ché così è a lui ciascun linguaggio
   come 'l suo ad altrui, ch'a nullo è noto».

Facemmo adunque più lungo vïaggio,   82
   vòlti a sinistra, e al trar d'un balestro
   trovammo l'altro assai più fero e maggio.

A cigner lui qual che fosse 'l maestro,   85
   non so io dir, ma el tenea soccinto
   dinanzi l'altro e dietro il braccio destro

For where you join to evil will and might   55
    the instrument of reason in the mind,
    no shelter for mankind can ever stand.

I thought his face had the same length and bulk   58
    as the bronze pinecone hanging at Saint Peter's,°
    with a like measure for his other bones;

So the banks of the basin, like a loincloth   61
    from the waist down, still showed enough of him
    above, that if they tried to grab his hair

Three lanky Frisians would have failed their boast,   64
    for I could count thirty great spans of him
    down from the place a man will clasp his cloak.

"Raphèl maì amècche zabì almi,"   67
    the savage mouth began to shout at us;
    no sweeter psalm was fit for such as he.

And my guide turned against him: "Stupid soul!   70
    Grab your horn tight and vent yourself with it
    when wrath or any passion seizes you!

Feel round your neck and there you'll find the strap   73
    that keeps it tied, O spirit of confusion—
    and see it make the stripe across your chest."

To me then, "He incriminates himself.   76
    He's Nimrod;° owing to his evil plan
    there's no one language used in all the world.

Let's leave him and not toss our words away,   79
    for no one's ever heard the tongue he speaks,
    and every tongue is gibberish to him."

So we walked farther onward, to the left,   82
    and at the distance of a crossbow shot
    we found another giant, fiercer far

And mightier in bulk. I cannot say   85
    what sort of craftsman bound him, but a chain
    ran like a belt five times around his body

° *the bronze pinecone hanging at Saint Peter's:* a thirteen-foot statue, perhaps originally cast for the tomb of the emperor Hadrian. It can still be seen today in the Vatican.
° *Nimrod:* according to tradition, the builder of the Tower of Babel (Gen. 10:8–12; 11:1–9); see notes.

d'una catena che 'l tenea avvinto 88
   dal collo in giù, sì che 'n su lo scoperto
   si ravvolgëa infino al giro quinto.

«Questo superbo volle esser esperto 91
   di sua potenza contra 'l sommo Giove»,
   disse 'l mio duca, «ond' elli ha cotal merto.

Fïalte ha nome, e fece le gran prove 94
   quando i giganti fer paura a' dèi;
   le braccia ch'el menò, già mai non move».

E io a lui: «S'esser puote, io vorrei 97
   che de lo smisurato Brïareo
   esperïenza avesser li occhi miei».

Ond' ei rispuose: «Tu vedrai Anteo 100
   presso di qui che parla ed è disciolto,
   che ne porrà nel fondo d'ogne reo.

Quel che tu vuo' veder, più là è molto 103
   ed è legato e fatto come questo,
   salvo che più feroce par nel volto».

Non fu tremoto già tanto rubesto, 106
   che scotesse una torre così forte,
   come Fïalte a scuotersi fu presto.

Allor temett' io più che mai la morte, 109
   e non v'era mestier più che la dotta,
   s'io non avessi viste le ritorte.

Noi procedemmo più avante allotta, 112
   e venimmo ad Anteo, che ben cinque alle,
   sanza la testa, uscia fuor de la grotta.

«O tu che ne la fortunata valle 115
   che fece Scipïon di gloria reda,
   quand' Anibàl co' suoi diede le spalle,

From the neck to the waist, and strapped his arms,   88
    the left pinned tight against his chest, the right
    behind his back. "This piece of arrogance,"

My guide explained, "wanted to try his power   91
    against the power of the highest Jove,
    and this is what he merits for his pains.

He's Ephialtes,° who fought in the great test   94
    when warring giants put the gods to fear.
    The arms he raised, he'll never move again."

And I to him: "If it can be arranged,   97
    I'd like my eyes to have experience
    of Briareus, the immeasurable."

And he responded, "You will see Antaeus   100
    nearby, since he can speak and is unchained.
    He'll set us at the bottom of all crime.

The one you'd like to see is far off there,   103
    and stands in chains, just like this giant here,
    except he's more ferocious in his looks."

No earthquake ever shook so strong a tower   106
    with violence to match Ephialtes
    who on a sudden shook. Then more than ever

I would have feared that I might die—the dread   109
    alone would have sufficed to bring it on,
    had I not seen the bonds that held him bound.

So we proceeded farther, and we came   112
    to where Antaeus rose a good seven yards,
    besides his head, out of the rock-rimmed gulf.

"O you who in that valley° touched by fate—   115
    where Scipio was made the heir of glory
    when Hannibal turned tail with all his troops—

° *Ephialtes:* in mythology, one of the Titans who rebelled—unsuccessfully—against Jupiter, attempting to scale Olympus by piling Mount Pelion upon Mount Ossa. The others mentioned are also Titans; see notes.

° *that valley:* at Zama, near Tunis, in North Africa. There the Roman general Scipio defeated the great Carthaginian Hannibal, to end the Second Punic War. For Antaeus' dwelling, see Lucan, *Phars.* 4.601–2.

recasti già mille leon per preda,   118
    e che, se fossi stato a l'alta guerra
    de' tuoi fratelli, ancor par che si creda

ch'avrebber vinto i figli de la terra: 121
    mettine giù, e non ten vegna schifo,
    dove Cocito la freddura serra.

Non ci fare ire a Tizio né a Tifo: 124
    questi può dar di quel che qui si brama;
    però ti china e non torcer lo grifo.

Ancor ti può nel mondo render fama,   127
    ch'el vive, e lunga vita ancor aspetta
    se 'nnanzi tempo grazia a sé nol chiama».

Così disse 'l maestro; e quelli in fretta   130
    le man distese, e prese 'l duca mio,
    ond' Ercule sentì già grande stretta.

Virgilio, quando prender si sentio,   133
    disse a me: «Fatti qua, sì ch'io ti prenda»;
    poi fece sì ch'un fascio era elli e io.

Qual pare a riguardar la Carisenda   136
    sotto 'l chinato, quando un nuvol vada
    sovr' essa sì, ched ella incontro penda,

tal parve Antëo a me che stava a bada   139
    di vederlo chinare, e fu tal ora
    ch'i' avrei voluto ir per altra strada.

Ma lievemente al fondo che divora   142
    Lucifero con Giuda, ci sposò;
    né, sì chinato, lì fece dimora,

e come albero in nave si levò.   145

Once slew a thousand lions for your prey,   118
    and who, if you had fought in the great war
    beside your brother Titans, some do think
The Sons of Earth would have enjoyed the day,   121
    do not take it in scorn to set us down
    where the cold locks the Cocytus° in ice.
Don't make us seek Typhon or Tityus.°   124
    This man can give you what you long for here,
    so bend and do not turn your face askew,
For in the world he can still bring you fame.   127
    He lives, and looks to live for many years,
    unless grace calls him home before his time."
So said the Teacher, and the giant in haste   130
    reached down those hands which once made Hercules
    feel their hard grip, and took hold of my guide,
And Virgil, when he felt it, said to me,   133
    "Come over here, let me hold on to you,"
    and made one bundle of himself and me.
As it appears to one who stands beneath   136
    the Garisenda tower° that leans, when clouds
    pass by to make the sight impending—so
Antaeus seemed to me who stood intent   139
    to watch him lean; and there were moments when
    I wished we had another road to go.
But softly at the bottom which devours   142
    Judas and Lucifer, he set us down,
    nor did he linger after he had bent
But straightened like a mast upon a ship.   145

° *Cocytus:* the last, icy river of Hell.

° *Typhon or Tityus:* other Titans. Tityus was slain by Apollo for trying to rape Apollo's mother, Latona. Typhon was buried under Mount Aetna by Jupiter after he slew him at Phlegra (Ovid, *Met.* 5.346–53).

° *the Garisenda tower:* a twelfth-century tower in Bologna, over 150 feet high. Again Dante compares the giants to objects of dumb, imposing bulk.

S'ïo avessi le rime aspre e chiocce,
    come si converrebbe al tristo buco
    sovra 'l qual pontan tutte l'altre rocce,
io premerei di mio concetto il suco   4
    più pienamente; ma perch' io non l'abbo,
    non sanza tema a dicer mi conduco;
ché non è impresa da pigliare a gabbo   7
    discriver fondo a tutto l'universo,
    né da lingua che chiami mamma o babbo.
Ma quelle donne aiutino il mio verso   10
    ch'aiutaro Anfïone a chiuder Tebe,
    sì che dal fatto il dir non sia diverso.
Oh sovra tutte mal creata plebe   13
    che stai nel loco onde parlare è duro,
    mei foste state qui pecore o zebe!
Come noi fummo giù nel pozzo scuro   16
    sotto i piè del gigante assai più bassi,
    e io mirava ancora a l'alto muro,

CANTO THIRTY-TWO

*The poets cross the frozen **river Cocytus**. They are in the **ninth circle**, among the **traitors**. Here in the region called **Caina**, frozen in the ice, with their heads bowed, are the **betrayers of kindred**. Dante meets **Camiscion de' Pazzi**, who identifies for him the **brothers of Mangona**, who slew each other. Proceeding to a second zone, **Antenora**, Dante encounters the **betrayers of nation or party**, among whom is the Florentine traitor **Bocca degli Abati**, who betrays for Dante the identities of others there with him.*

Had I the bitter and crack-throated rhymes
    fit for the miserable hole toward which
    all of the other beetling ridges thrust,
I would squeeze out the juice of my invention   4
    more fully, but because I have no such,
    not without fear I bring myself to speak:
It is no jesting enterprise to tell—   7
    not for the tongue that calls "mama" and "dada"—
    about the universal sink of Hell.
But let those Ladies° now assist my verse   10
    who helped Amphion raise the walls of Thebes;
    so may my words not differ from the fact.
You rabble, worst of ill-created things,   13
    who stand fixed in a place which speech abhors—
    better had you been born as sheep or goats!
When we arrived down in that gloomy well°   16
    far lower than the giants' feet above,
    and I was gazing still at the high wall,

° *those Ladies:* the Muses.
° *that gloomy well:* a vast lake of ice, the lowest ring of Hell. The ice suggests the coldheartedness of the traitors it imprisons. It is farthest from the divine fire that sets the stars in motion; it is stasis without peace.

TRAITORS—BOCCA DEGLI ABATI

dicere udi'mi: «Guarda come passi: 19
  va sì, che tu non calchi con le piante
  le teste de' fratei miseri lassi».

Per ch'io mi volsi, e vidimi davante   22
  e sotto i piedi un lago che per gelo
  avea di vetro e non d'acqua sembiante.

Non fece al corso suo sì grosso velo   25
  di verno la Danoia in Osterlicchi,
  né Tanaï là sotto 'l freddo cielo,

com' era quivi; che se Tambernicchi   28
  vi fosse sù caduto, o Pietrapana,
  non avria pur da l'orlo fatto cricchi.

E come a gracidar si sta la rana   31
  col muso fuor de l'acqua, quando sogna
  di spigolar sovente la villana,

livide, insin là dove appar vergogna   34
  eran l'ombre dolenti ne la ghiaccia,
  mettendo i denti in nota di cicogna.

Ognuna in giù tenea volta la faccia;   37
  da bocca il freddo, e da li occhi il cor tristo
  tra lor testimonianza si procaccia.

Quand' io m'ebbi dintorno alquanto visto,   40
  volsimi a' piedi, e vidi due sì stretti,
  che 'l pel del capo avieno insieme misto.

«Ditemi, voi che sì strignete i petti»,   43
  diss' io, «chi siete?». E quei piegaro i colli;
  e poi ch'ebber li visi a me eretti,

li occhi lor, ch'eran pria pur dentro molli,   46
  gocciar su per le labbra, e 'l gelo strinse
  le lagrime tra essi e riserrolli.

Con legno legno spranga mai non cinse   49
  forte così; ond' ei come due becchi
  cozzaro insieme, tanta ira li vinse.

E un ch'avea perduti ambo li orecchi   52
  per la freddura, pur col viso in giùe,
  disse: «Perché cotanto in noi ti specchi?

I heard a voice cry out, "Watch where you step!   19
    Go on, but do not tread upon the heads
    of the exhausted brothers, spirits damned."
At that I turned, and saw before my feet   22
    a lake of ice, which in the terrible cold
    looked not like frozen water, but like glass.
So thick an ice veil never blocks the course   25
    of the Danube in wintry Austria,
    nor of the Don under the frigid sky,
As was this ice; and if Mount Tambernic   28
    had fallen on it, or Mount Pietrapan,°
    even its edge would not have made a creak.
As the frog in the summer sits to croak,   31
    his mug above the pond, while hazy dreams
    of gleaning come upon the peasant girl,
So were the grieving spirits, livid gray,   34
    fixed in the ice up to where shame appears,
    chattering their teeth like storks that snap their bills.
Each held his face down low, while every mouth   37
    gave evidence of the cold, and every eye
    testified to the sorrow in the heart.
When I had looked about awhile, I glanced   40
    down at my feet and saw two spirits so
    tight pressed, their heads of hair had grown ensnarled.
"O you who hold your chests in such a clench,"   43
    said I, "who are you?" And they wried their necks,
    and when they'd raised their faces straight toward me,
Their eyes, which had been moist already, spilled   46
    tears through the eyelids, which the ice froze shut
    back in the sockets with its locking grip.
Never a clamp clamped plank to plank so hard,   49
    for which they were so overcome with wrath
    they butted head to head like two he-goats.
And one whose ears the frost had bitten off   52
    spoke out, although he held his head down low:
    "What mirror are you staring at in us?

° *Mount Tambernic, Mount Pietrapan:* The former probably refers to a mountain in Slovenia; the latter, to one of the peaks near Val di Magra, in Tuscany.

Se vuoi saper chi son cotesti due,   55
    la valle onde Bisenzo si dichina
    del padre loro Alberto e di lor fue.
D'un corpo usciro; e tutta la Caina   58
    potrai cercare, e non troverai ombra
    degna più d'esser fitta in gelatina:
non quelli a cui fu rotto il petto e l'ombra   61
    con esso un colpo per la man d'Artù;
    non Focaccia; non questi che m'ingombra
col capo sì, ch'i' non veggio oltre più,   64
    e fu nomato Sassol Mascheroni;
    se tosco se', ben sai omai chi fu.
E perché non mi metti in più sermoni,   67
    sappi ch'i' fu' il Camiscion de' Pazzi;
    e aspetto Carlin che mi scagioni».
Poscia vid' io mille visi cagnazzi   70
    fatti per freddo; onde mi vien riprezzo,
    e verrà sempre, de' gelati guazzi.
E mentre ch'andavamo inver' lo mezzo   73
    al quale ogne gravezza si rauna,
    e io tremava ne l'etterno rezzo,
se voler fu o destino o fortuna,   76
    non so; ma, passeggiando tra le teste,
    forte percossi 'l piè nel viso ad una.
Piangendo mi sgridò: «Perché mi peste?   79
    se tu non vieni a crescer la vendetta
    di Montaperti, perché mi moleste?».
E io: «Maestro mio, or qui m'aspetta,   82
    sì ch'io esca d'un dubbio per costui;
    poi mi farai, quantunque vorrai, fretta».

If you would like to know who these two are,　　　　55
　　the vale of the Bisenzio was the home
　　both for their father Albert and for them.

From the same womb they came. And you could search　　58
　　all of Caina,° and you'd never find
　　souls fitter to be fixed in aspic here,

Not him whose chest and shadow were gored through　　61
　　by one blow from the hand of Arthur,° not
　　Focaccia, not this one who bothers me

With his head in my way to block my sight,　　64
　　whose name above was Sassol Mascheroni.
　　You'll know of him if you're from Tuscany.

So you won't weary me with talk, I was　　67
　　Camiscion de' Pazzi, and await
　　Carlino, who will make my crime seem less."

After, I saw a thousand faces turned　　70
　　wolfish for cold, at which I shuddered then
　　and shall whenever I see a frozen bog.

And while we went down to the central hole　　73
　　where sinks the whole world's heaviness, and I
　　was trembling in the everlasting chill,

If it was fortune, destiny, or will,　　76
　　who knows, but as I walked among the heads
　　I stubbed my foot hard on one spirit's face.

He wailed and yelled, "Why do you trample me?　　79
　　Unless you come to add to the revenge
　　for Montaperti,° why this injury?"

And I: "My Teacher, wait for me a bit.　　82
　　I want to clear a doubt I have of him;
　　then make me hurry on as you see fit."

° *Caina:* this first of the regions of the treacherous. It freezes those who betrayed kinsmen, and is thus named for the first fratricide, Cain (Gen. 4:8). Fittingly, these two are also brothers.

° *him whose . . . Arthur:* Mordred, treacherous illegitimate son of King Arthur, whom the king slew in his final battle. So mightily did Arthur thrust his sword into Mordred that sunlight shone through the opening when he retracted it.

° *Montaperti:* the massacre in 1260; see note on 10.22. Bocca betrayed the Guelphs by cutting off the hand of their standard-bearer in the middle of the battle, precipitating a panic and rout.

Lo duca stette, e io dissi a colui   85
    che bestemmiava duramente ancora:
    «Qual se' tu che così rampogni altrui?».
«Or tu chi se' che vai per l'Antenora,   88
    percotendo», rispuose, «altrui le gote,
    sì che, se fossi vivo, troppo fora?».
«Vivo son io, e caro esser ti puote»,   91
    fu mia risposta, «se dimandi fama,
    ch'io metta il nome tuo tra l'altre note».
Ed elli a me: «Del contrario ho io brama.   94
    Lèvati quinci e non mi dar più lagna,
    ché mal sai lusingar per questa lama!».
Allor lo presi per la cuticagna   97
    e dissi: «El converrà che tu ti nomi,
    o che capel qui sù non ti rimagna».
Ond' elli a me: «Perché tu mi dischiomi,   100
    né ti dirò ch'io sia, né mosterrolti
    se mille fiate in sul capo mi tomi».
Io avea già i capelli in mano avvolti,   103
    e tratti glien' avea più d'una ciocca,
    latrando lui con li occhi in giù raccolti,
quando un altro gridò: «Che hai tu, Bocca?   106
    non ti basta sonar con le mascelle,
    se tu non latri? qual diavol ti tocca?».
«Omai», diss' io, «non vo' che tu favelle,   109
    malvagio traditor, ch'a la tua onta
    io porterò di te vere novelle».
«Va via», rispuose, «e ciò che tu vuoi conta;   112
    ma non tacer, se tu di qua entro eschi,
    di quel ch'ebbe or così la lingua pronta.
El piange qui l'argento de' Franceschi: 115
    'Io vidi', potrai dir, 'quel da Duera
    là dove i peccatori stanno freschi'.

So my guide paused, and I replied to him   85
    who kept on spitting out his blasphemies,
    "Who are you, slinging such rebuke at others?"
"And who are you who go through Antenora   88
    kicking," he answered, "others' cheeks so hard,
    if I were living, it would be too rough!"°
"*But I'm alive,* and can be good to you,"   91
    was my response, "if you should look for fame:
    I'll make a note of you with all the rest."
And he to me: "I crave the opposite.°   94
    Get lost, then! Don't torment me any more.
    You don't know how to flatter for this pit."
I caught him by the dog hair on his nape   97
    and said, "I think you'd better tell your name,
    or I won't leave a hair left in your scalp!"
And he: "Rip out my locks then, strip me bald!   100
    I still won't tell or show you who I am,
    not if you pounced on me a thousand times!"
I'd wound his hanks already in my hand   103
    and yanked them out in bunches as he yowled
    and huddled his eyes low, when someone yelled,
"Hey, Bocca, what the hell's the fuss? It's not   106
    enough to play the snare drum with your jaws,
    you've got to bark too? What's got into you?"
"Now," said I, "speak no more, it's fine with me,   109
    vile traitor that you are, for I'll bring back
    the truth about you, to your infamy."
"Go away," he replied. "Tell what you like!   112
    But don't keep mum if you get out of here
    about that soul whose tongue was quick to speak.
He weeps for the *argent* he took from France.   115
    'I saw,' you can say, 'the one from Duera
    down where the sinners are kept fresh on ice.'

° *it would be too rough:* that is, "I would not put up with it—I would avenge myself."
° *I crave the opposite:* naturally, since the traitor does not wish his treachery to be revealed.

Se fossi domandato altri chi v'era,   118
    tu hai dallato quel di Beccheria
    di cui segò Fiorenza la gorgiera.
Gianni de' Soldanier credo che sia   121
    più là con Ganellone e Tebaldello,
    ch'aprì Faenza quando si dormia».
Noi eravam partiti già da ello,   124
    ch'io vidi due ghiacciati in una buca,
    sì che l'un capo a l'altro era cappello;
e come 'l pan per fame si manduca,   127
    così 'l sovran li denti a l'altro pose
    là 've 'l cervel s'aggiugne con la nuca.
Non altrimenti Tidëo si rose   130
    le tempie a Menalippo per disdegno,
    che quei faceva il teschio e l'altre cose.
«O tu che mostri per sì bestial segno   133
    odio sovra colui che tu ti mangi,
    dimmi 'l perché», diss' io, «per tal convegno,
che se tu a ragion di lui ti piangi,   136
    sappiendo chi voi siete e la sua pecca,
    nel mondo suso ancora io te ne cangi,
se quella con ch'io parlo non si secca».   139

And if they ask of you, 'Who else was there?'—   118
    here at your side's that son of Beccheria
    whose gullet Florence sliced the axe head through,

And I do think Soldanier's farther on   121
    with Ganelon and Tebaldello, who
    opened Faenza's gates when the town slept."

We had already left him when I saw   124
    two frozen in one hole in such a way
    that one man's head was like the other's hood,

And as a hunk of bread is chewed in hunger,   127
    so did the top soul tear his teeth into
    the other, where the neck adjoins the brain,

Just as Tydeus° in his spiteful rage   130
    gnawed at the temples of his enemy,
    so did he gnaw the brains, the flesh, the skull.

"O you who show by such a beastlike sign   133
    your hatred of the one you feed upon,
    tell me the reason, and I'll set this deal,"

Said I, "that if your hate has a just cause,   136
    knowing his crime and who you are, I will
    make you a good trade in the world above,

Unless my tongue should wither to the root."   139

° *Tydeus:* As he was dying he gnawed at the temples of the dead Melanippus, who had just given him his death wound; see notes.

La bocca sollevò dal fiero pasto
　　quel peccator, forbendola a' capelli
　　del capo ch'elli avea di retro guasto.
Poi cominciò: «Tu vuo' ch'io rinovelli   4
　　disperato dolor che 'l cor mi preme
　　già pur pensando, pria ch'io ne favelli.
Ma se le mie parole esser dien seme   7
　　che frutti infamia al traditor ch'i' rodo,
　　parlare e lagrimar vedrai insieme.
Io non so chi tu se' né per che modo   10
　　venuto se' qua giù, ma fiorentino
　　mi sembri veramente quand' io t'odo.
Tu dei saper ch'i' fui conte Ugolino,   13
　　e questi è l'arcivescovo Ruggieri:
　　or ti dirò perché i son tal vicino.
Che per l'effetto de' suo' mai pensieri,   16
　　fidandomi di lui, io fossi preso
　　e poscia morto, dir non è mestieri;
però quel che non puoi avere inteso,   19
　　cioè come la morte mia fu cruda,
　　udirai, e saprai s'e' m'ha offeso.

CANTO THIRTY-THREE

*Still in **Antenora** among the **betrayers of nation or party**, Dante hears the tale of*
*Count Ugolino, who now takes his revenge by gnawing upon the brains of **Archbishop***
Ruggieri, the man who treacherously imprisoned Ugolino and his four sons in a tower
*and let them starve. The poets continue to the third zone, **Ptolomea,** where souls go,*
*sometimes even before the death of their bodies, when they become **betrayers of guests.***
*Here he finds **Brother Alberigo** and **Ser Branca D'Oria.***

He raised his mouth up from that savage feed,
    the sinner did, and wiped it on the hair
    of the head he was spoiling from behind.
Then he began: "You want me to recount   4
    all the despair and pain that break my heart
    even in thought, before I tell my tale.
But if my words must be the seed to sprout   7
    infamy for this traitor whom I gnaw,
    you'll see me weeping, speaking through my tears.
I don't know who you are or by what way   10
    you've come down here, but from the speech I hear
    you surely seem to be a Florentine.
Then you should know I was Count Ugolino,   13
    and this here is Ruggieri, the archbishop.
    I'll tell you now why I'm so close to him.
That on account of his malicious plots,   16
    trusting myself to him, I was first seized
    then put to death, there is no need to say,
Yet what you can't have heard a thing about,   19
    the cruelty of the death I suffered, now
    you'll hear, and know if he has done me wrong!

UGOLINO

Breve pertugio dentro da la Muda,   22
    la qual per me ha 'l titol de la fame,
    e che conviene ancor ch'altrui si chiuda,

m'avea mostrato per lo suo forame   25
    più lune già, quand' io feci 'l mal sonno
    che del futuro mi squarciò 'l velame.

Questi pareva a me maestro e donno,   28
    cacciando il lupo e ' lupicini al monte
    per che i Pisan veder Lucca non ponno.

Con cagne magre, studïose e conte   31
    Gualandi con Sismondi e con Lanfranchi
    s'avea messi dinanzi da la fronte.

In picciol corso mi parieno stanchi   34
    lo padre e ' figli, e con l'agute scane
    mi parea lor veder fender li fianchi.

Quando fui desto innanzi la dimane,   37
    pianger senti' fra 'l sonno i miei figliuoli
    ch'eran con meco, e dimandar del pane.

Ben se' crudel, se tu già non ti duoli   40
    pensando ciò che 'l mio cor s'annunziava;
    e se non piangi, di che pianger suoli?

Già eran desti, e l'ora s'appressava   43
    che 'l cibo ne solëa essere addotto,
    e per suo sogno ciascun dubitava;

e io senti' chiavar l'uscio di sotto   46
    a l'orribile torre; ond' io guardai
    nel viso a' mie' figliuoi sanza far motto.

Io non piangëa, sì dentro impetrai: 49
    piangevan elli; e Anselmuccio mio
    disse: 'Tu guardi sì, padre! che hai?'.

Perciò non lagrimai né rispuos' io   52
    tutto quel giorno né la notte appresso,
    infin che l'altro sol nel mondo uscìo.

Come un poco di raggio si fu messo   55
    nel doloroso carcere, e io scorsi
    per quattro visi il mio aspetto stesso,

A little peephole in the Eagle Cage,   22
   now called the Tower of Hunger after me,
   a tower which shall be barred for others yet,
Had shown me through its hole the passing moon   25
   several times over, when a nightmare came
   and tore in two the veil of things to come.
This one appeared to me as lord and master,   28
   chasing the wolf and wolf pups to the hills
   obstructing Lucca from the Pisan's sight.
Leading his famished bitches in the hunt,   31
   the Gualandi, Sismondi, and Lanfranchi°
   took their positions and assumed the front.
A short run—then the father and his sons   34
   appeared exhausted, and I dreamed I saw
   the fangs of hounds ripping their sides apart.
When I awoke before the break of dawn   37
   I heard my small sons sobbing in their dreams,
   for they were with me, and they asked for bread.
You must be cruel if you don't grieve now,   40
   thinking of what my heart foretold—and if
   now you don't weep, when do you weep at all?
Then they awakened, and the hour drew near   43
   when food was always brought us, but we grew
   afraid, as each of us recalled his dreams;
And I could hear them nailing up the door   46
   of the horrible tower, and gazed upon
   the faces of my sons, and spoke no more.
I did not weep, I had so turned to stone;   49
   they wept. And my little Anselm said,
   'Father, why do you stare like that? What's wrong?'
Therefore I did not weep or make reply   52
   all that long day and all the night to follow,
   until the next sun came into the world.
When a weak glint of daylight made its way   55
   into our prison of sorrow, and I saw
   my own face in the four that looked at me,

° *Gualandi, Sismondi, and Lanfranchi:* families allied with Ruggieri.

ambo le man per lo dolor mi morsi;   58
    ed ei, pensando ch'io 'l fessi per voglia
    di manicar, di sùbito levorsi

e disser: 'Padre, assai ci fia men doglia   61
    se tu mangi di noi: tu ne vestisti
    queste misere carni, e tu le spoglia'.

Queta'mi allor per non farli più tristi;   64
    lo dì e l'altro stemmo tutti muti.
    Ahi dura terra, perché non t'apristi?

Poscia che fummo al quarto dì venuti,   67
    Gaddo mi si gittò disteso a' piedi,
    dicendo: 'Padre mio, ché non m'aiuti?'.

Quivi morì; e come tu mi vedi,   70
    vid' io cascar li tre ad uno ad uno
    tra 'l quinto dì e 'l sesto; ond' io mi diedi,

già cieco, a brancolar sovra ciascuno,   73
    e due dì li chiamai, poi che fur morti.
    Poscia, più che 'l dolor, poté 'l digiuno».

Quand' ebbe detto ciò, con li occhi torti   76
    riprese 'l teschio misero co' denti,
    che furo a l'osso, come d'un can, forti.

Ahi Pisa, vituperio de le genti   79
    del bel paese là dove 'l sì suona,
    poi che i vicini a te punir son lenti,

muovasi la Capraia e la Gorgona,   82
    e faccian siepe ad Arno in su la foce,
    sì ch'elli annieghi in te ogne persona!

Che se 'l conte Ugolino aveva voce   85
    d'aver tradita te de le castella,
    non dovei tu i figliuoi porre a tal croce.

Innocenti facea l'età novella,   88
    novella Tebe, Uguiccione e 'l Brigata
    e li altri due che 'l canto suso appella.

Noi passammo oltre, là 've la gelata   91
    ruvidamente un'altra gente fascia,
    non volta in giù, ma tutta riversata.

I bit both hands for grief; and they, who thought   58
   I must be longing for some food to eat,
   suddenly rose and came to me and said,
'Father, for us it would be much less pain   61
   if you ate us instead! You clothed us with
   this wretched flesh, now strip it off again.'
I calmed myself lest they grow sadder still.   64
   That day and all the next we did not speak.
   Ah hard earth, why did you not open up!
And when we had arrived at the fourth day,   67
   my Gaddo fell outstretched before my feet,
   saying, 'Papa, why don't you help me?' There
He died. As clearly as you see me here   70
   I watched the other three drop, one by one,
   the fifth and sixth days. Then I flung myself,
Already blind, groping upon each one—   73
   two days I called their names, when they were dead.
   Then hunger did what sorrow could not do."
Having said that, he turned his eyes askance   76
   and took the wretched skull between his teeth,
   tough as a dog's that gnaws down to the bone.
Ah Pisa, vile disgrace of all the folk   79
   in the sweet land where *sì* is uttered! Since
   your neighbor towns are slow to punish you,
May the isles of Capraia and Gorgona   82
   uproot themselves to plug the Arno's mouth,
   that everyone who dwells in you may drown!
For if Count Ugolino suffered blame,   85
   having betrayed you of your fortresses,
   you for your part should not have nailed his sons
To such a cross! O Thebes° renewed and young,   88
   their tender ages made them innocent—
   Brigata, Hugh, and the other two my song
Remembers here. We passed on, where the ice   91
   swaddles another clan in its coarse wrap—
   their heads not bowed, but all turned up and back.

° *Thebes:* classical locus of unnatural wickedness and cruelty.

Lo pianto stesso lì pianger non lascia,   94
    e 'l duol che truova in su li occhi rintoppo,
    si volge in entro a far crescer l'ambascia;

ché le lagrime prime fanno groppo,   97
    e sì come visiere di cristallo,
    rïempion sotto 'l ciglio tutto il coppo.

E avvegna che, sì come d'un callo,   100
    per la freddura ciascun sentimento
    cessato avesse del mio viso stallo,

già mi parea sentire alquanto vento;   103
    per ch'io: «Maestro mio, questo chi move?
    non è qua giù ogne vapore spento?».

Ond' elli a me: «Avaccio sarai dove   106
    di ciò ti farà l'occhio la risposta,
    veggendo la cagion che 'l fiato piove».

E un de' tristi de la fredda crosta   109
    gridò a noi: «O anime crudeli
    tanto che data v'è l'ultima posta,

levatemi dal viso i duri veli,   112
    sì ch'ïo sfoghi 'l duol che 'l cor m'impregna,
    un poco, pria che 'l pianto si raggeli».

Per ch'io a lui: «Se vuo' ch'i' ti sovvegna,   115
    dimmi chi se', e s'io non ti disbrigo,
    al fondo de la ghiaccia ir mi convegna».

Rispuose adunque: «I' son frate Alberigo;   118
    i' son quel da le frutta del mal orto,
    che qui riprendo dattero per figo».

«Oh», diss' io lui, «or se' tu ancor morto?».   121
    Ed elli a me: «Come 'l mio corpo stea
    nel mondo sù, nulla scïenza porto.

Cotal vantaggio ha questa Tolomea,   124
    che spesse volte l'anima ci cade
    innanzi ch'Atropòs mossa le dea.

E perché tu più volontier mi rade   127
    le 'nvetrïate lagrime dal volto,
    sappie che, tosto che l'anima trade

Weeping itself forbids the souls to weep,   94
    and pain which finds a barrier in their eyes
    turns back within to make the agony grow;
For the first teardrops form an icy knot,   97
    and as a helmet visor of hard glass
    they fill the sockets full beneath the brow.
And even though, as in a callus, all   100
    sensation ceased to linger in my face
    because of the great cold, I felt a trace
Of a breeze striking me, and so I said,   103
    "Teacher, what makes this motion of the air?
    I thought that every wind was spent down here."
And he to me: "You will come soon enough   106
    where your own eyes will give you the reply,
    seeing what makes this blast of wind come down."
One of the wretches in the frosty crust   109
    cried to us then, "O cruel souls, so wicked
    that you are given the lowest place of all,
Lift the hard veils from off my face, that I   112
    may vent the grief my heart has soaked me with,
    one moment, till the tears freeze up again."
So I to him: "You'd like my help, then tell   115
    your name. If I don't clear your eyes, may I
    go to the bottom of this icy Hell!"
So he replied, "I'm Brother Alberigo,   118
    the man who served the fruit in the bad garden.
    Here I'm paid back with interest, date for fig."
"Oh," said I, "are you dead already then?"   121
    And he responded, "How my body stands
    up in the world above, I do not know.
Such privilege has this realm of Ptolomea,   124
    that oftentimes the soul drops down to Hell
    before the Fates have cut the thread of life.
And that you may, with greater will, scrape off   127
    the tears hardened to glass upon my face,
    know that as soon as any soul betrays

come fec' ïo, il corpo suo l'è tolto   130
   da un demonio, che poscia il governa
   mentre che 'l tempo suo tutto sia vòlto.

Ella ruina in sì fatta cisterna;   133
   e forse pare ancor lo corpo suso
   de l'ombra che di qua dietro mi verna.

Tu 'l dei saper, se tu vien pur mo giuso: 136
   elli è ser Branca Doria, e son più anni
   poscia passati ch'el fu sì racchiuso».

«Io credo», diss' io lui, «che tu m'inganni;   139
   ché Branca Doria non morì unquanche,
   e mangia e bee e dorme e veste panni».

«Nel fosso sù», diss' el, «de' Malebranche,   142
   là dove bolle la tenace pece,
   non era ancora giunto Michel Zanche,

che questi lasciò il diavolo in sua vece   145
   nel corpo suo, ed un suo prossimano
   che 'l tradimento insieme con lui fece.

Ma distendi oggimai in qua la mano;   148
   aprimi li occhi». E io non gliel' apersi;
   e cortesia fu lui esser villano.

Ahi Genovesi, uomini diversi   151
   d'ogne costume e pien d'ogne magagna,
   perché non siete voi del mondo spersi?

Ché col peggiore spirto di Romagna   154
   trovai di voi un tal, che per sua opra
   in anima in Cocito già si bagna,

e in corpo par vivo ancor di sopra.   157

As I betrayed, his body's snatched away   130
    and taken by a demon, who controls it
    until the time arrives for it to die.

The soul then falls headlong into this tank.   133
    Perhaps his body still appears above,
    the shade who chirps his winter song behind me;

You may well know, for you have just come down.   136
    He is Ser Branca d'Oria; many years
    have passed since he was thus encased in ice."

Said I, "I think you play me for a fool!   139
    For Branca d'Oria never died, but eats
    and drinks and sleeps and puts his woolens on."

"Up in the trench," said he, "of Evilclaws,°   142
    the pocket with the sticky bubbling pitch,
    judge Michel Zanche hadn't yet arrived

Before Ser Branca left his body for   145
    a devil—and a kinsman did the same,
    one who assisted in the treachery.

But now reach out your hand, open my eyes."   148
    And so I did not open them: to be
    villainous to him was a courtesy.

Ah Genoese, you aliens to all   151
    morality and full of every taint,
    why have you not been scattered from the world?

For with the wickedest soul Romagna bore°   154
    I found such one of yours who for his works
    already bathes his soul in Cocytus,

Whose body up above still seems alive.   157

° *the trench . . . of Evilclaws:* That of the grafters; see Cantos 21–22.

° *the wickedest soul Romagna bore:* Alberigo.

«*Vexilla regis prodeunt inferni*
  verso di noi; però dinanzi mira»,
  disse 'l maestro mio, «se tu 'l discerni».

Come quando una grossa nebbia spira,   4
  o quando l'emisperio nostro annotta,
  par di lungi un molin che 'l vento gira,

veder mi parve un tal dificio allotta;   7
  poi per lo vento mi ristrinsi retro
  al duca mio, ché non li era altra grotta.

Già era, e con paura il metto in metro,   10
  là dove l'ombre tutte eran coperte,
  e trasparien come festuca in vetro.

Altre sono a giacere; altre stanno erte,   13
  quella col capo e quella con le piante;
  altra, com' arco, il volto a' piè rinverte.

Quando noi fummo fatti tanto avante,   16
  ch'al mio maestro piacque di mostrarmi
  la creatura ch'ebbe il bel sembiante,

d'innanzi mi si tolse e fé restarmi,   19
  «Ecco Dite», dicendo, «ed ecco il loco
  ove convien che di fortezza t'armi».

CANTO THIRTY-FOUR

*The poets arrive at the sinkhole of Hell, **Judecca**, where the **betrayers of benefactors** are punished, most of them completely encased in ice. Here Dante beholds **Satan** himself, chewing, in his three mouths, **Judas Iscariot, Brutus**, and **Cassius**. With Dante on his back, Virgil climbs down Satan's matted hide, reaches the **center of the earth**, and wheels about. The poets are now on the far side of the center, toward the Southern Hemisphere. They exit through a cavern and look upon the stars again.*

"*The standards of the king of Hell advance*
    toward us, and therefore look ahead and see,"
    my Teacher said, "if you can make him out."
A turning windmill far off would appear,   4
    when a thick fog begins to lift away
    or night descends upon our hemisphere,
Like the strange edifice I then descried;   7
    but as there was no shelter from the wind
    so cold, I huddled back behind my guide.
With fear I set these words in verse! It was   10
    where the shades are all covered up in ice,
    and clearly seen, like wisps of straw in glass.
Some souls lie prone and some stand straight; of those   13
    some have their heads up, others have their soles,
    and some bend over, face to feet, like bows.
When we'd walked far enough to reach the place   16
    where my instructor thought it well to show me
    the creature who once had the lovely face,
He stopped me, stepped away from where I stood,   19
    saying, "Behold there, Dis!° Behold the place
    where you must arm yourself with fortitude."

° *Dis:* Satan.

THE JUDECCA—LUCIFER

Com' io divenni allor gelato e fioco,   22
   nol dimandar, lettor, ch'i' non lo scrivo,
   però ch'ogne parlar sarebbe poco.
Io non mori' e non rimasi vivo.   25
   Pensa oggimai per te, s'hai fior d'ingegno,
   qual io divenni, d'uno e d'altro privo.
Lo 'mperador del doloroso regno   28
   da mezzo 'l petto uscia fuor de la ghiaccia;
   e più con un gigante io mi convegno,
che i giganti non fan con le sue braccia: 31
   vedi oggimai quant' esser dee quel tutto
   ch'a così fatta parte si confaccia.
S'el fu sì bel com' elli è ora brutto,   34
   e contra 'l suo fattore alzò le ciglia,
   ben dee da lui procedere ogne lutto.
Oh quanto parve a me gran maraviglia   37
   quand' io vidi tre facce a la sua testa!
   L'una dinanzi, e quella era vermiglia;
l'altr' eran due, che s'aggiugnieno a questa   40
   sovresso 'l mezzo di ciascuna spalla,
   e sé giugnieno al loco de la cresta:
e la destra parea tra bianca e gialla;   43
   la sinistra a vedere era tal, quali
   vegnon di là onde 'l Nilo s'avvalla.
Sotto ciascuna uscivan due grand' ali,   46
   quanto si convenia a tanto uccello:
   vele di mar non vid' io mai cotali.
Non avean penne, ma di vispistrello   49
   era lor modo, e quelle svolazzava,
   sì che tre venti si movean da ello:
quindi Cocito tutto s'aggelava.   52
   Con sei occhi piangëa, e per tre menti
   gocciava 'l pianto e sanguinosa bava.
Da ogne bocca dirompea co' denti   55
   un peccatore, a guisa di maciulla,
   sì che tre ne facea così dolenti.

How faint I then became, how turned to ice,
    Reader, ask not; I will not write it down,
    for any words I used would not suffice.

I did not die, did not remain alive.
    Think for yourself, if wisdom buds in you,
    what I became, deprived of life and death.

The emperor of the reign of misery
    from his chest up emerges from the ice:
    I and a giant are more near in stature

Than are a giant and that creature's arm,
    and if one limb is so enormous, you
    can see how vast the rest must be. If once

He was as fair as he is ugly now,
    and raised his brow against his Maker still,
    he well is made the source of every woe.

But when I saw three faces in his head,
    how great a marvel it appeared to me!
    One face in front, and it was ruddy red;

The other two were joined to it upon
    the middle of the shoulder on each side,
    and joined above, where the cock sports his crown;

And the right was a kind of yellowish white,
    and where the Nile comes rolling to the plains,
    men's faces are the color on the left.

Beneath each face extended two huge wings,
    large enough to suffice for such a bird.
    I never saw a sail at sea so broad.

They had no feathers, but were black and scaled
    like a bat's wings, and those he flapped, and flapped,
    and from his flapping raised three gales that swept

Cocytus, and reduced it all to ice.
    With his six eyes he wept, and down three chins
    dribbled his tears and slaver slick with blood.

In every mouth he gnashed his teeth to grind
    a sinner, as a thresher crushes flax,
    so there were three he put to such great pain.

22

25

28

31

34

37

40

43

46

49

52

55

A quel dinanzi il mordere era nulla   58
    verso 'l graffiar, che talvolta la schiena
    rimanea de la pelle tutta brulla.
«Quell'anima là sù c'ha maggior pena»,   61
    disse 'l maestro, «è Giuda Scarïotto,
    che 'l capo ha dentro e fuor le gambe mena.
De li altri due c'hanno il capo di sotto,   64
    quel che pende dal nero ceffo è Bruto:
    vedi come si storce, e non fa motto!;
e l'altro è Cassio, che par sì membruto.   67
    Ma la notte risurge, e oramai
    è da partir, ché tutto avem veduto».
Com' a lui piacque, il collo li avvinghiai;   70
    ed el prese di tempo e loco poste,
    e quando l'ali fuoro aperte assai,
appigliò sé a le vellute coste;   73
    di vello in vello giù discese poscia
    tra 'l folto pelo e le gelate croste.
Quando noi fummo là dove la coscia   76
    si volge, a punto in sul grosso de l'anche,
    lo duca, con fatica e con angoscia,
volse la testa ov' elli avea le zanche,   79
    e aggrappossi al pel com' om che sale,
    sì che 'n inferno i' credea tornar anche.
«Attienti ben, ché per cotali scale»,   82
    disse 'l maestro, ansando com' uom lasso,
    «conviensi dipartir da tanto male».
Poi uscì fuor per lo fóro d'un sasso   85
    e puose me in su l'orlo a sedere;
    appresso porse a me l'accorto passo.
Io levai li occhi e credetti vedere   88
    Lucifero com' io l'avea lasciato,
    e vidili le gambe in sù tenere;
e s'io divenni allora travagliato,   91
    la gente grossa il pensi, che non vede
    qual è quel punto ch'io avea passato.

For him in front the bites were nothing to   58
   the scraping claws that peeled away his back
   and often left it nude of any skin.
"The soul up there whose punishment is worst,"   61
   the Teacher said, "is Judas Iscariot,
   whose feet stick out and who is chewed headfirst.
Of the two others with their heads hung down,   64
   the one who hangs from the black snout is Brutus.
   See how he writhes, and does not speak a word!
Cassius the last, who looks so squarely built.   67
   But night is rising, and it's time to leave,
   for Hell has nothing more for us to see."
Just as he wished, I clasped him round the neck,   70
   and then he chose the moment and the place,
   just when the wings were open far enough,
To grapple to the devil's matted side,   73
   clambering down from clump to clump between
   the fur in tangles and the frozen crust.
When we had reached the joint that turns the thigh,   76
   just at the thickening of the hip, my guide,
   with struggle, with his breath in agony,
Reversed his head to face the devil's shanks,   79
   and he clutched at the fur like one who climbs.
   I thought we must be turning back to Hell.
"Hold on tight now, for by such stairs as these,"   82
   my Teacher panted, like a weary man,
   "one must depart from so much wickedness."
He came out through a fissure in a rock   85
   and set me down upon a ledge to sit,
   then joined me with a quick and careful step.
I raised my eyes and thought that I would see   88
   Lucifer as I'd left him, but I saw
   his legs held straight up in the air before me,
And if I was bewildered then, let those   91
   fog-headed people judge who do not see
   what was that point° which I had passed beyond.

° *that point:* the center of the earth.

«Lèvati sù», disse 'l maestro, «in piede: 94
   la via è lunga e 'l cammino è malvagio,
   e già il sole a mezza terza riede».

Non era camminata di palagio   97
   là 'v' eravam, ma natural burella
   ch'avea mal suolo e di lume disagio.

«Prima ch'io de l'abisso mi divella,   100
   maestro mio», diss' io quando fui dritto,
   «a trarmi d'erro un poco mi favella:

ov' è la ghiaccia? e questi com' è fitto   103
   sì sottosopra? e come, in sì poc' ora,
   da sera a mane ha fatto il sol tragitto?».

Ed elli a me: «Tu imagini ancora   106
   d'esser di là dal centro, ov' io mi presi
   al pel del vermo reo che 'l mondo fóra.

Di là fosti cotanto quant' io scesi;   109
   quand' io mi volsi, tu passasti 'l punto
   al qual si traggon d'ogne parte i pesi.

E se' or sotto l'emisperio giunto   112
   ch'è contraposto a quel che la gran secca
   coverchia, e sotto 'l cui colmo consunto

fu l'uom che nacque e visse sanza pecca;   115
   tu haï i piedi in su picciola spera
   che l'altra faccia fa de la Giudecca.

Qui è da man, quando di là è sera;   118
   e questi, che ne fé scala col pelo,
   fitto è ancora sì come prim' era.

Da questa parte cadde giù dal cielo;   121
   e la terra, che pria di qua si sporse,
   per paura di lui fé del mar velo,

"Come on," my Teacher said. "Up on your feet.   94
    The way is long, the road is difficult,
    the sun already shines in the third hour."
That was no palace hall or entryway   97
    we took then, but a cavern nature carved,
    where the footing was bad and the light dim.
"Before I pull my roots out of the pit,   100
    Teacher," I said when I could stand upright,
    "to clear an error speak with me a bit:
Where is the ice? The Devil, why is he   103
    fixed upside down? How has the sun so soon
    gone all the way to morning?" "You believe
You're on the far side of the center still,   106
    there where I grabbed the hide of the evil worm,"°
    said he, "who gnaws a hole into the world.
And so you were, as long as I climbed down,   109
    but when I turned, you passed beyond the point
    toward which all weight from every side is drawn.
You're underneath the hemisphere which lies   112
    opposite that which spans the earth's dry land,°
    under whose zenith He was put to death,
He who was born and who lived without sin.°   115
    You have your feet upon a little sphere
    which constitutes Judecca's other side.
Whenever it's morning here, it's evening there,   118
    and he who made a ladder with his hide
    is there still fixed just as he was before.
He fell from Heaven on this side of the earth,   121
    and all the land that once was here took flight
    in fear of him, shrouded him in the sea,

° *evil worm:* Satan.
° *that which spans the earth's dry land:* the Northern Hemisphere, covering Europe and most of Africa and Asia.
° *He who was born and who lived without sin:* Christ.

e venne a l'emisperio nostro; e forse   124
   per fuggir lui lasciò qui loco vòto
   quella ch'appar di qua, e sù ricorse».
Luogo è là giù da Belzebù remoto   127
   tanto quanto la tomba si distende,
   che non per vista, ma per suono è noto
d'un ruscelletto che quivi discende   130
   per la buca d'un sasso, ch'elli ha roso,
   col corso ch'elli avvolge, e poco pende.
Lo duca e io per quel cammino ascoso   133
   intrammo a ritornar nel chiaro mondo;
   e sanza cura aver d'alcun riposo,
salimmo sù, el primo e io secondo,   136
   tanto ch'i' vidi de le cose belle
   che porta 'l ciel, per un pertugio tondo.
E quindi uscimmo a riveder le stelle.   139

And fled north to our hemisphere,° and maybe   124
   the land we're walking on fled from him too,
   leaving the hole below us when it rose."
As far as you can go from Beelzebub°   127
   inside the cavern tomb,° there is a place
   where not by sight, but by its sound one finds
A little rushing stream that courses down   130
   a hollow it has eaten in a rock,
   taking a winding way, with easy slope.
Upon this hidden path my guide and I   133
   entered, to go back to the world of light,
   and without any care to rest at ease,
He first and I behind, we climbed so high   136
   that through a small round opening I saw
   some of the turning beauties of the sky.
And we came out to see, once more, the stars.   139

° *fled north to our hemisphere:* Satan's plunge into the sea dispersed the land below it, causing it to rise as a continent in the north, and perhaps to rise as this mountain here. See Is. 14:9: "Hell from beneath is moved for thee to meet thy coming."

° *Beelzebub:* "Lord of the Flies"—that is, Satan.

° *inside the cavern tomb:* There is a vast cavity (his "tomb") surrounding Satan. One leaves the farthest end of the hole by means of an underground passage eroded by this mysterious stream.

Appendix A

Virgil, from the *Aeneid*

It is worth learning Latin merely to hear the rich, melancholy cadences of Virgil, the greatest writer in that venerable tongue, and to feel the rhythms of his meditation on human suffering, and passion, and duty, and resignation to the mysteries of fate. Dante captures the gravity and the generosity of his Roman mentor; yet he sees that Virgil's underworld was a shadow of the true eternal realms, as Virgil's Rome, celebrated in that underworld, found its highest purpose as the stage for a Prince of Peace whom Virgil himself never knew. Hence Dante's many adaptations of and borrowings from book 6 of the *Aeneid*, which recounts Aeneas' journey below, are a great tribute to Virgil that at the same time, gently but firmly, point out the limitations of the man who knows the natural law and no more.

The following excerpts are from book 6. The reader will note how often Dante echoes lines and borrows motifs from Virgil—and if he is careful, he will note how often Dante places their radical revisions in the mouth of Virgil himself. The translation is by Robert Fitzgerald (New York: Random House, 1983).

Aeneas approaches the Sibyl's cave

> Aeneas,
> In duty bound, went inland to the heights
> Where overshadowing Apollo dwells
> And nearby, in a place apart—a dark
> Enormous cave—the Sibyl feared by men.
> In her the Delian god of prophecy
> Inspires uncanny powers of mind and soul,
> Disclosing things to come. Here Trojan captains
> Walked to Diana of the Crossroads' wood
> And entered under roofs of gold. They say
> That Daedalus, when he fled the realm of Minos,

Dared to entrust himself to stroking wings
And to the air of heaven—unheard-of path—
On which he swam away to the cold North
At length to touch down on that very height
Of the Chalcidians. Here, on earth again
He dedicated to you, Phoebus Apollo,
The twin sweeps of his wings; here he laid out
A spacious temple. In the entrance way
Androgeos' death appeared, then Cecrops' children
Ordered to pay in recompense each year
The living flesh of seven sons. The urn
From which the lots were drawn stood modeled there.
And facing it, upon the opposite door,
The land of Crete, emergent from the sea;
Here the brutish act appeared: Pasiphae
Being covered by the bull in the cow's place,
Then her mixed breed, her child of double form,
The Minotaur, got of unholy lust.
Here, too, that puzzle of the house of Minos,
The maze none could untangle, until, touched
By a great love shown by a royal girl,
He, Daedalus himself, unravelled all
The baffling turns and dead ends in the dark,
Guiding the blind way back by a skein unwound.
In that high sculpture you, too, would have had
Your great part, Icarus, had grief allowed.
Twice your father had tried to shape your fall
In gold, but twice his hands dropped.

Aeneas asks the Sibyl to take him below

"No novel kinds of hardship, no surprises
Loom ahead, Sister. I foresaw them all,
Went through them in my mind. One thing I pray for:
Since it is here they say one finds the gate
Of the king of under world, the shadowy march
That wells from Acheron, may I have leave
To go to my dear father's side and see him.
Teach me the path, show me the entrance way . . .

Pity a son and father, gracious lady,
All this is in your power. Hecate
Gave you authority to have and hold
Avernus wood. If Orpheus could call
His wife's shade up, relying on the strings
That sang loud on his Thracian lyre; if Pollux
Redeemed his brother, taking his turn at death,
So often passing back and forth; why name
The heroes, Theseus and Hercules?
By birth I too descend from Jove on high—"

While in these terms he prayed and pressed the altar,
Breaking in, the Sibyl said:
                              "Offspring
Of gods by blood, Trojan Anchises' son,
The way downward is easy from Avernus.
Black Dis's door stands open night and day,
But to retrace your steps to heaven's air,
There is the trouble, there is the toil. A few
Whom a benign Jupiter has loved or whom
Fiery heroism has borne to heaven,
Sons of gods, could do it. All midway
Are forests, then Cocytus, thick and black,
Winds through the gloom . . ."

They enter the underworld

She flung herself wildly into the cave-mouth,
Leading, and he strode boldly at her heels.
Gods who rule the ghosts; all silent shades,
And Chaos and infernal Fiery Stream,
And regions of wide night without a sound,
May it be right to tell what I have heard,
May it be right, and fitting, by your will,
That I describe the deep world sunk in darkness
Under the earth.
                  Now dim to one another
In desolate night they walked on through the gloom,
Through Dis's homes all void, and empty realms,
As one goes through a wood by a faint moon's

Treacherous light, when Jupiter veils the sky
And black night blots the colors of the world.

Before the entrance, in the jaws of Orcus,
Grief and avenging Cares have made their beds,
And pale Diseases and sad Age are there,
And Dread, and Hunger that sways men to crime,
And sordid Want—in shapes to affright the eyes—
And Death and Toil and Death's own brother, Sleep,
And the mind's evil joys; on the door sill
Death-bringing War, and iron cubicles
Of the Eumenides, and raving Discord,
Viperish hair bound up in gory bands.
In the courtyard a shadowy giant elm
Spreads ancient boughs, her ancient arms where dreams,
False dreams, the old tale goes, beneath each leaf
Cling and are numberless. There, too,
About the doorway forms of monsters crowd—
Centaurs, twiformed Scyllas, hundred-armed
Briareus, and the Lernaean hydra
Hissing horribly, and the Chimaera
Breathing dangerous flames, and Gorgons, Harpies,
Huge Geryon, triple-bodied ghost.
Here, swept by sudden fear, drawing his sword,
Aeneas stood on guard with naked edge
Against them as they came. If his companion,
Knowing the truth, had not admonished him
How faint these lives were—empty images
Hovering bodiless—he had attacked
And cut his way through phantoms, empty air.

The path goes on from that place to the waves
Of Tartarus' Acheron. Thick with mud,
A whirlpool out of a vast abyss
Boils up and belches all the silt it carries
Into Cocytus. Here the ferryman,
A figure of fright, keeper of waters and streams,
Is Charon, foul and terrible, his beard
Grown wild and hoar, his staring eyes all flame,
His sordid cloak hung from a shoulder knot.

Alone he pokes his craft and trims the sails
And in his rusty hull ferries the dead,
Old now—but old age in the gods is green.

Here a whole crowd came streaming to the banks,
Mothers and men, the forms with all life spent
Of heroes great in valor, boys and girls
Unmarried, and young sons laid on the pyre
Before their parents' eyes—as many souls
As leaves that yield their hold on boughs and fall
Through forests in the early frost of autumn,
Or as migrating birds from the open sea
That darken heaven when the cold season comes
And drives them overseas to sunlit lands.
There all stood begging to be first across
And reached out longing hands to the far shore.

But the grim boatman now took these aboard,
Now those, waving the rest back from the strand.
In wonder at this and touched by the commotion,
Aeneas said:
         "Tell me, Sister, what this means,
The crowd at the stream. Where are the souls bound?
How are they tested, so that these turn back,
While those take oars to cross the dead-black water?"

Briefly the ancient prophetess answered him:

"Cocytus is the deep pool that you see,
The swamp of Styx beyond, infernal power
By which the gods take oath and fear to break it.
All in the nearby crowd you notice here
Are pauper souls, the souls of the unburied.
Charon's the boatman. Those the water bears
Are souls of buried men. He may not take them
Shore to dread shore on the hoarse currents there
Until their bones rest in the grave, or till
They flutter and roam this side a hundred years;
They may have passage then, and may return
To cross the deeps they long for."

                    Anchises' son

Had halted, pondering on so much, and stood
In pity for the souls' hard lot.

They cross the Acheron

      Now from the Stygian water
The boatman, seeing them in the silent wood
And headed for the bank, cried out to them
A rough uncalled-for challenge:
                    "Who are you
In armor, visiting our rivers? Speak
From where you are, stop there, say why you come.
This is the region of the Shades, and Sleep,
And drowsy Night. It breaks eternal law
For the Stygian craft to carry living bodies.
Never did I rejoice, I tell you, letting
Alcides cross, or Theseus and Pirithous,
Demigods by paternity though they were,
Invincible in power. One forced in chains
From the king's own seat the watchdog of the dead
And dragged him away trembling. The other two
Were bent on carrying our lady off
From Dis's chamber."
              This the prophetess
And servant of Amphrysian Apollo
Briefly answered:
              "Here are no such plots,
So fret no more . . ."

Minos and the dead

Now voices crying loud were heard at once—
The souls of infants wailing. At the door
Of the sweet life they were to have no part in,
Torn from the breast, a black day took them off
And drowned them all in bitter death. Near these
Were souls falsely accused, condemned to die.
But not without a judge, or jurymen,
Had these souls got their places: Minos reigned
As the presiding judge, moving the urn,
And called a jury of the silent ones
To learn of lives and accusations. Next
Were those sad souls, benighted, who contrived
Their own destruction, and as they hated daylight,
Cast their lives away. How they would wish
In the upper air now to endure the pain
Of poverty and toil! But iron law
Stands in the way, since the drear hateful swamp
Has pinned them down here, and the Styx that winds
Nine times around exerts imprisoning power.
Not far away, spreading on every side,
The Fields of Mourning came in view, so called
Since here are those whom pitiless love consumed
With cruel wasting, hidden on paths apart
By myrtle woodland growing overhead.
In death itself pain will not let them be.

The Sibyl describes for Aeneas the eternal punishments of the wicked

But at Aeneas' side the Sibyl spoke,
Warning him briefly:
                    "Night comes on, Aeneas,
We use up hours grieving. Here is the place
Where the road forks: on the right hand it goes
Past mighty Dis's walls, Elysium way,
Our way; but the leftward road will punish
Malefactors, taking them to Tartarus."

... A massive gate
With adamantine pillars faced the stream,
So strong no force of men or gods in war
May ever avail to crack and bring it down,
And high in air an iron tower stands
On which Tisiphone, her bloody robe
Pulled up about her, has her seat and keeps
Unsleeping watch over the entrance way
By day and night. From the interior, groans
Are heard, and thud of lashes, clanking iron,
Dragging chains. Arrested in his tracks,
Appalled by what he heard, Aeneas stood.

"What are the forms of evil here? O Sister,
Tell me. And the punishments dealt out:
Why such a lamentation?"
                              Said the Sibyl:
"Light of the Teucrians, it is decreed
That no pure soul may cross the sill of evil.
When, however, Hecate appointed me
Caretaker of Avernus wood, she led me
Through heaven's punishments and taught me all.
This realm is under Cretan Rhadamanthus'
Iron rule. He sentences. He listens
And makes the souls confess their crooked ways,
How they put off atonements in the world
With foolish satisfaction, thieves of time,
Until too late, until the hour of death.
At once the avenger girdled with her whip,
Tisiphone, leaps down to lash the guilty,
Vile writhing snakes held out on her left hand,
And calls her savage sisterhood. The awaited
Time has come, hell gates will shudder wide
On shrieking hinges. Can you see her now,
Her shape, as doorkeeper, upon the sill?
More bestial, just inside, the giant Hydra
Lurks with fifty black and yawning throats.
Then Tartarus itself goes plunging down
In darkness twice as deep as heaven is high
For eyes fixed on etherial Olympus.

Here is Earth's ancient race, the brood of Titans,
Hurled by the lightning down to roll forever
In the abyss. Here, too, I saw those giant
Twins of Aloeus who laid their hands
Upon great heaven to rend it and to topple
Jove from his high seat, and I saw, too,
Salmoneus paying dearly for the jape
Of mimicking Jove's fire, Olympus' thunder:
Shaking a bright torch from a four-horse car
He rode through Greece and his home town in Elis,
Glorying, claiming honor as a god—
Out of his mind, to feign with horses' hoofs
On bronze the blast and inimitable bolt.
The father almighty amid heavy cloud
Let fly his missile—no firebrand for him
Nor smoky pitchpine light—and spun the man
Headlong in a huge whirlwind.
                      One had sight
Of Tityos, too, child of all-mothering Earth,
His body stretched out over nine whole acres
While an enormous vulture with hooked beak
Forages forever in his liver,
His vitals rife with agonies. The bird,
Lodged in the chest cavity, tears at his feast,
And tissues growing again get no relief.
As for the Lapiths, need I tell: Ixion,
Pirithous, and the black crag overhead
So sure to fall it seems already falling.
Golden legs gleam on the feasters' couches,
Dishes in royal luxury prepared
Are laid before them—but the oldest Fury
Crouches near and springs out with her torch,
Her outcry, if they try to touch the meal.
Here come those who as long as life remained
Held brothers hateful, beat their parents, cheated
Poor men dependent on them; also those
Who hugged their newfound riches to themselves
And put nothing aside for relatives—
A great crowd, this—then men killed for adultery,

Men who took arms in war against the right,
Not scrupling to betray their lords. All these
Are hemmed in here, awaiting punishment.
Best not inquire what punishment, what form
Of suffering at their last end overwhelms them.
Some heave at a great boulder, or revolve,
Spreadeagled, hung on wheel-spokes. Theseus
Cleaves to his chair and cleaves to it forever.
Phlegyas in his misery teaches all souls
His lesson, thundering out amid the gloom:
'Be warned and study justice, not to scorn
The immortal gods.' Here's one who sold his country,
Foisted a tyrant on her, set up laws
Or nullified them for a price; another
Entered his daughter's room to take a bride
Forbidden him. All these dared monstrous wrong
And took what they dared try for. If I had
A hundred tongues, a hundred mouths, a voice
Of iron, I could not tell all of the shapes
Their crimes had taken, or their punishments."

The Elysian Fields

He saw, how vividly! along the grass
To right and left, others who feasted here
And chorused out a hymn praising Apollo,
Within a fragrant laurel grove, where Po
Sprang up and took his course to the world above,
The broad stream flowing on amid the forest.
This was the company of those who suffered
Wounds in battle for their country; those
Who in their lives were holy men and chaste
Or worthy of Phoebus in prophetic song;
Or those who bettered life, by finding out
New truths and skills; or those who to some folk
By benefactions made themselves remembered.
They all wore snowy chaplets on their brows.

Anchises names for Aeneas the destiny and genius of the Roman people

"Others will cast more tenderly in bronze
Their breathing figures, I can well believe,
And bring more lifelike portraits out of marble;
Argue more eloquently, use the pointer
To trace the paths of heaven accurately
And accurately foretell the rising stars.
Roman, remember by your strength to rule
Earth's peoples—for your arts are to be these:
To pacify, to impose the rule of law,
To spare the conquered, battle down the proud."

Appendix B

From the *Visio sancti Pauli* (*The Vision of Saint Paul*)

In his second letter to the Corinthians, after reminding the philosophers of the church at Corinth that unless Christ did rise from the dead, the Christian faith is vain, Saint Paul describes a mystical experience whereby he was granted a glimpse of the life to come (12:1–5). Although such a vision was beyond Paul's words, his intimation roused the curiosity of pious believers in the early Church, one of whom was obliging enough to provide for his fellow Christians his own account of what Paul saw. The noncanonical *Vision of Saint Paul*, probably written in the middle of the third century, was the result. Although it was condemned by the Church, its orthodox, if simplistic, theology and its immediacy of detail helped it remain popular for many centuries. The following excerpts describe the state of the damned.

The translation, by Montague R. James, ed., is from J. K. Elliott, *The Apocryphal New Testament* (Oxford: Clarendon Press, 1993).

———

The angel answered and said to me, "Do you understand why you go hence?" And I said, "Yes, sir." And he said to me, "Come and follow me, and I will show you the souls of the godless and sinners, that you may know what manner of place it is . . ."

And I saw there a river boiling with fire, and in it a multitude of men and women immersed up to the knees, and other men up to the navel, others even up to the lips, others up to the hair. And I asked the angel and said, "Sir, who are those in the fiery river?" And the angel answered and said to me, "They are neither hot nor cold, because they were found neither in the number of the just nor in the number of the godless. For those spent the time of their life on earth passing some days in prayer, but others in sins and fornications, until their death." And I asked him and said, "Who are these, sir, immersed up to their knees in fire?" He answered and said to me, "These are they who when they have gone out of church occupy themselves with idle disputes. Those who are immersed up to the navel are those who, when they have taken the body and blood of Christ, go and fornicate and do not cease from their sins till they die. Those who are immersed up to the lips are those who slander each other when they assemble in the church of God; those up to the eyebrows are those who nod to each other and plot spite against their neighbor."

And I saw to the north a place of various and diverse punishments full of men and women, and a river of fire ran down into it. I observed and I saw very deep pits and in them several souls together, and the depth of that place was about three thousand cubits, and I saw them groaning and weeping and saying, "Have pity on us, O Lord!" and no one had pity on them. And I asked the angel and said, "Who are these, sir?" And the angel answered and said to me, "These are they who did not hope in the Lord, that they would be able to have him as their helper." And I asked and said, "Sir, if these souls remain for thirty or forty generations thus one upon another, I believe the pits would not hold them unless they were dug deeper." And he said to me, "The Abyss has no measure, for beneath it there stretches down below that which is below it; and so it is that if perchance anyone should take a stone and throw it into a very deep well after many hours it would reach the bottom, such is the abyss. For when the souls are thrown in there, they hardly reach the bottom in fifty years."

When I heard this, I wept and groaned over the human race. The angel answered and said to me, "Why do you weep? Are you more merciful than God? For though God is good, he knows that there are punishments, and he patiently bears with the human race, allowing each one to do his own will in the time in which he dwells on the earth."

I observed the fiery river and saw there a man being tortured by Tartaruchian angels having in their hands an iron instrument with three hooks with which they pierced the bowels of that old man; and I asked the angel and said, "Sir, who is that old man on whom such torments are imposed?" And the angel answered and said to me, "He whom you see was a presbyter who did not perform his ministry well: when he had been eating and drinking and committing fornication he offered the host to the Lord at his holy altar."

And I saw not far away another old man led on by evil angels running with speed, and they pushed him into the fire up to his knees, and they struck him with stones and wounded his face like a storm, and did not allow him to say, "Have pity on me!" And I asked the angel, and he said to me, "He whom you see was a bishop and did not perform his episcopate well, who indeed accepted the great name but did not enter into the witness of him who gave him the name all his life, seeing that he did not give just judgement and did not pity widows and orphans, but now he receives retribution according to his iniquity and his works."

And I saw another man in the fiery river up to his knees. His hands were stretched out and bloody, and worms proceeded from his mouth and nostrils, and he was groaning and weeping, and crying he said, "Have pity on me! For I am hurt more than the rest who are in this punishment." And I asked, "Sir, who is this?" And he said to me, "This man whom you see was a deacon who devoured the oblations and committed fornication and did not do right in the sight of God; for this cause he unceasingly pays this penalty."

And I looked closely and saw alongside of him another man, whom they delivered up with haste and cast into the fiery river, and he was in it up to the knees; and the angel who was set over the punishments came with a great fiery razor, and with it he cut the lips of that man and the tongue likewise. And sighing, I lamented and asked, "Who is that, sir?" And he said to me, "He whom you see was a reader and read to the people, but he himself did not keep the precepts of God; now he also pays the proper penalty."

And I saw another multitude of pits in the same place, and in the midst of it a river full with a multitude of men and women, and worms consumed them. But I lamented, and sighing asked the angel and said, "Sir, who are these?" And he said to me, "These are those who exacted interest on interest and trusted in riches and did not hope in God that he was their helper."

. . . And I observed and saw another pool in the pit and its appearance was like blood, and I asked and said, "Sir, what is this place?" And he said to me, "Into that pit stream all the punishments." And I saw men and women immersed up to the lips, and I asked, "Sir, who are these?" And he said to me, "These are the magicians who prepared for men and women evil magic arts and did not cease till they died."

And again I saw men and women with very black faces in a pit of fire, and I sighed and lamented and asked, "Sir, who are these?" And he said to me, "These are fornicators and adulterers who committed adultery, having wives of their own; likewise also the women committed adultery, having husbands of their own; therefore they unceasingly suffer penalties."

And I saw there girls in black raiment, and four terrifying angels having in their hands burning chains, and they put them on the necks of the girls and led them into darkness; and I, again weeping, asked the angel, "Who are these, sir?" And he said to me, "These are they who, when they were virgins, defiled their virginity unknown to their parents; for which cause they unceasingly pay the proper penalties."

And again I observed there men and women with hands cut and their feet placed naked in a place of ice and snow, and worms devoured them. Seeing them I lamented and asked, "Sir, who are these?" And he said to me, "These are they who harmed orphans and widows and the poor, and did not hope in the Lord, for which cause they unceasingly pay the proper penalties."

... And I saw other men and women covered with dust, and their countenance was like blood, and they were in a pit of pitch and sulphur running in a fiery river, and I asked, "Sir, who are these?" And he said to me, "These are they who committed the iniquity of Sodom and Gomorrah, the male with the male, for which reason they unceasingly pay the penalties."

And I observed and saw men and women clothed in bright garments, but with their eyes blind, and they were placed in a pit, and I asked, "Sir, who are these?" And he said to me, "These are heathen who gave alms, and knew not the Lord God ..."

... And after that I saw men and women clothed with rags full of pitch and fiery sulphur, and dragons were coiled about their necks and shoulders and feet, and angels with fiery horns restrained them and smote them, and closed their nostrils, saying to them, "Why did you not know the time in which it was right to repent and serve God, and did not do it?"

... And he carried me to the north and placed me above a well, and I found it sealed with seven seals; and the angel who was with me said to the angel of that place, "Open the mouth of the well that Paul, the well-beloved of God, may see, for authority is given him that he may see all the torments of hell." And the angel said to me, "Stand far off that you may be able to bear the stench of this place." When the well was opened, immediately there arose from it a disagreeable and evil stench, which surpasses all punishments; and I looked into the well, and I saw fiery masses glowing on all sides and anguish, and the mouth of the well was narrow so as to admit one man only. And the angel answered and said to me, "If any man has been put into this well of the abyss and it has been sealed over him, no remembrance of him shall ever be made in the sight of the Father and his Son and the holy angels." And I said, "Who are these, sir, who are put into this well?" And he said to me, "They are those who do not confess that Christ has come in the flesh and that the Virgin Mary brought him forth, and those who say that the bread and the cup of the Eucharist of blessing are not the body and blood of Christ."

And I looked from the north to the west and I saw there the worm that never rests, and in that place there was gnashing of teeth; and the worms were one cubit long, and had two heads, and there I saw men and women in the cold gnashing their teeth. And I asked and said, "Sir, who are these in this place?" And he said to me, "These are they who say that Christ did not rise from the dead and that this flesh will not rise again." And I asked and said,

"Sir, is there no fire nor heat in this place?" And he said to me, "In this place there is nothing else but cold and snow." And again he said to me, "Even if the sun should rise upon them, they do not become warm on account of the excessive coldness of that place and the snow."

Appendix C

Thomas Aquinas, from the *Summa theologiae* (**Summa of Theology**)

The Gothic cathedrals, *The Divine Comedy*, and the *Summa theologiae* of Thomas Aquinas stand as the greatest artistic and intellectual achievements of the Middle Ages, and among the greatest of any age. They share a desire to incorporate all that human beings are, and do, and know into a vast but intelligible and coherent system. Just as the Gothic masons could find a place for anything in their stone-and-glass compendia of life, from plants and animals to angels, so too the work of Aquinas, though it soars to the consideration of Deity, grips its roots down into the humble and everyday. It is meant to be more than logical: it is meant to be reasonable, fully in accord with human experience. In the excerpts below, chosen for their relevance to various sections of the *Inferno*, Thomas analyzes the nature of virtues and vices and their sometimes everlasting effects upon man. Though he believes that Scripture speaks truly on these matters, he proves his arguments not by referring to that authority but by reasoning from what anyone can see, experientially or logically. The translation is that of the Dominican Fathers (London: Burns, Oates, and Washbourne, 1927), edited lightly for contemporary idiom.

———

On free will

Man has free will: otherwise counsels, exhortations, commands, prohibitions, rewards and punishments would be in vain. In order to make this evident, we must observe that some things act without judgement: as a stone moves downwards, and in like manner act all things which lack knowledge. And some act from judgement, but not a free judgement—brute animals, for instance. For the sheep, seeing the wolf, judges it a thing to be shunned, from a natural and not a free judgement, because it judges not from reason but from natural instinct.... But man acts from judgement, because by his apprehensive power he judges that something should be avoided or sought. But because this judgement, in the case of some particular act, is not from a natural instinct but from some act of comparison in the reason, he acts from free judgement and retains the power of being inclined to various things. For reason in contingent matters may follow opposite courses, as we see in dialectic syllogisms and rhetorical arguments. Now particular operations are contingent, and therefore in such matters the judgement of reason may follow opposite courses, and is not determinate to one. And since man is rational it follows necessarily that man has a free will.

(First part, q. 83, art. 1)

On the distinction between mortal and venial, or pardonable, sins

Now the difference between venial and mortal sin results from the diversity of that inordinateness which constitutes the notion of sin. For inordinateness is twofold, one that destroys the principle of order, and another which, without destroying the principle of order, implies inordinateness in the things which follow the principle. Thus, in an animal's body, the frame may be so out of order that the vital principle is destroyed; this is the inordinateness of death. On the other hand, saving the vital principle, there may be disorder in the bodily humours; and then there is sickness. Now the principle of the entire moral order is the last end. . . . Therefore when the soul is so disordered by sin as to turn away from its last end, [that is] God, to Whom it is united by charity, there is mortal sin; but when it is disordered without turning away from God, there is venial sin.

(Second part, part one, q. 72, art. 5)

On sins meriting eternal punishment

Sin incurs a debt by disturbing an order. But the effect remains so long as the cause remains. So as long as the disturbance of the order remains the debt of punishment must needs remain also. Now disturbance of an order is sometimes reparable, sometimes irreparable: because a defect which destroys the principle is irreparable, but if the principle is saved, defects can be repaired by virtue of that principle. For instance, if the principle of sight be destroyed, sight cannot be restored except by Divine power; but if the principle of sight is preserved, though certain impediments to the use of sight may arise, these can be remedied by nature or by art. Now in every order there is a principle whereby one takes part in that order. Consequently if a sin destroys the principle of the order whereby man's will is subject to God, the disorder will be such as to be considered in itself irreparable, although it is possible to repair it by the power of God. Now the principle of this order is the last end, to which man adheres by charity. Therefore whatever sins turn man away from God so as to destroy charity, considered in themselves, incur a debt of eternal punishment.

... It is just that he who has sinned against God in his own eternity should be punished in God's eternity. A man is said to have sinned in his own eternity, not only by continual sinning throughout his life, but also because, from the very fact that he fixes his end in sin, he has the will to sin everlastingly. That is why Gregory [the Great] says that *the wicked would wish to live without end, that they might abide in their sins forever* (*Dialogues* 4.44).
(Second part, part one, q. 87, art. 5)

On sins of weakness and passion

Weakness of the soul is when the soul is hindered from fulfilling its proper action on account of a disorder in its parts. Now as the parts of the body are said to be out of order when they fail to comply with the order of nature, so too the parts of the soul are said to be inordinate when they are not subject to the order of reason, for reason is the ruling power of the soul's parts. Accordingly, when the concupiscible or irascible power is so affected by any passion contrary to the order of reason that an impediment arises ... to the due action of man, it is said to be a sin of weakness. Hence the Philosopher (*Ethics* 7.8) compares the incontinent man to an epileptic, whose limbs move in a manner contrary to his intention.
(Second part, part one, q. 77, art. 3)

Whether sins of deliberate will-to-evil are graver than sins committed in a state of passion

A sin committed through deliberate malice is more grievous than a sin committed through passion, for three reasons. First, as sin consists chiefly in an act of the will, it follows that, other things being equal, a sin is all the more grievous according as the movement of the sin belongs more to the will. Now when a sin is committed through deliberate malice, the movement of sin belongs more to the will, which is then moved to evil of its own accord, than when a sin is committed through passion, when the will is impelled to sin by something extrinsic. ... Second, the passion which incites the will to sin soon passes away, so that man repents of his sin and soon returns to his good intentions; whereas the habit through which a man sins is a permanent quality,

so that he who sins through deliberate malice abides longer in his sin. . . . Third, he who sins through deliberate malice is ill-disposed towards the end itself, which is the principle in matters of action; and so the defect is more dangerous than in the case of the man who sins through passion, whose purpose tends toward a good end, although this purpose is interrupted for the time being on account of the passion. Now the worst of all defects is defect of principle. Therefore it is evident that a sin committed through deliberate malice is more grievous than one committed through passion.
(Second part, part one, q. 78, art. 4)

Whether pride is the beginning of all sin

Some say pride is to be taken in three ways. First, as denoting inordinate desire to excel; and thus it is a special sin. Second, as denoting actual contempt of God, to the effect of not being subject to His commandment; and thus, they say, it is a generic sin. Third, as denoting an inclination to this contempt, owing to the corruption of nature; and in this sense they say that it is the beginning of every sin, and that it differs from covetousness, because covetousness regards sin as turning toward the mutable good by which sin is, as it were, nourished and fostered, for which reason covetousness is called the *root*; whereas pride regards sin as turning away from God, to Whose commandment man refuses to be subject, for which reason it is called the *beginning*, because the beginning of evil consists in turning away from God.
(Second part, part one, q. 84, art. 2)

Whether one beyond the age of discretion can be guilty of original sin but not mortal sin

It is impossible for venial sin to be in anyone with original sin, and without mortal sin. The reason for this is that before a man comes to the age of discretion, the lack of years hinders the use of reason and excuses him from mortal sin. Thus all the more does it excuse him from venial sin, if he does anything which is such generically. But when he begins to have the use of reason, he is not entirely excused from the guilt of venial or mortal sin. Now the first thing that occurs to a man then is to deliberate about himself. **And if he then direct himself to the due end, he will, by means of grace, receive the remission of original sin** [emphasis added]. But if he is capable of discretion at that age, he will sin mortally, by failing to do what is in his power to do. And so from then on there cannot be venial sin in him without mortal, until all sin is remitted to him through grace.

(Second part, part one, q. 89, art. 6)

On grace as the only remedy for sin

Man by himself can in no way rise from sin without the help of grace. For since sin is transient as to the act and abiding in its guilt, . . . to rise from sin is not the same as to cease the act of sin. To rise from sin means that man has restored to him what he lost by sinning. Now man incurs a triple loss by sinning: . . . stain, corruption of natural good, and debt of punishment. He incurs a stain, inasmuch as he forfeits the lustre of grace through the deformity of sin. Natural good is corrupted, inasmuch as man's nature is disordered by man's will not being subject to God's; and once this order is overthrown the whole nature of sinful man remains disordered. Last, there is the debt of punishment, inasmuch as by sinning man deserves everlasting damnation.

Now it is manifest that none of these three can be restored except by God. For since the lustre of grace springs from the shedding of Divine light, this lustre cannot be brought back unless God sheds His light anew. Hence a habitual gift is necessary, and this is the light of grace. Likewise, the order of nature can only be restored, i.e., man's will can only be subject to God when God draws man's will to Himself. . . . So, too, the guilt of eternal punishment can be remitted by God alone, against Whom the offence was committed and Who is man's Judge. And thus for man to rise from sin he needs the help of grace, both as regards a habitual gift, and as regards the internal motion of God.

(Second part, part one, q. 109, art. 7)

On the sinfulness of unbelief

Unbelief may be taken in two ways; first, by way of pure negation, so that a man be called an unbeliever, merely because he has not the faith. Secondly, unbelief may be taken by way of opposition to the faith, in which sense a man refuses to hear the faith, or despises it. . . . It is this that completes the notion of unbelief, and it is in this sense that unbelief is a sin.

If, however, we take it by way of pure negation, as we find it in those who have heard nothing about the faith, it bears the character not of sin but of punishment, because such ignorance of Divine things is a result of the sin of our first parent. **If such unbelievers are damned, it is on account of other sins** [emphasis added], which cannot be taken away without faith, but not on account of their sin of unbelief.

(Second part, part two, q. 10, art. 1)

On whether unbelievers may be saved

Many of the gentiles received revelations about Christ, as is clear from their predictions. . . . Yet if any were saved without receiving any revelation, they were not saved without faith in a Mediator. For even if they did not believe in Him explicitly, they still did have implicit faith through believing in Divine Providence, since they believed that God would deliver mankind in whatever way was pleasing to Him, and according to the revelation of the Spirit to those who knew the truth.

(Second part, part two, q. 2, art. 7)

On the proper object of human hope

The hope we speak of attains God by leaning on His help in order to obtain the hoped-for good. Now an effect must be proportionate to its cause. So the good which we ought to hope for from God, properly and chiefly, is the infinite good, which is proportionate to the power of our Divine Helper, since it belongs to an infinite power to lead anyone to an infinite good. Such a good is eternal life, which consists in the enjoyment of God Himself. For we should hope from Him for nothing less than Himself, since His goodness, whereby He imparts good things to His creature, is no less than His Essence. Therefore the proper and principal object of hope is eternal happiness.

(Second part, part two, q. 18, art. 2)

On hope in the damned

Just as it is a condition of happiness that the will should find rest therein, so is it a condition of punishment that what is inflicted should go against the will. Now since what is not known can neither be restful nor repugnant to the will, Augustine says (*Commentary on Genesis* 11) that the angels could not be perfectly happy in their first state before their confirmation, or unhappy before their fall, since they had no foreknowledge of what would happen to them. For perfect and true happiness requires that one should be certain of being happy forever, else the will would not rest.

Similarly, since the everlastingness of damnation is a necessary condition of the punishment of the damned, it would not be truly penal unless it went against the will, and this would be impossible if they were ignorant of the everlastingness of their damnation. Hence it belongs to the unhappy state of the damned that they should know that they cannot by any means escape from damnation and obtain happiness.

(Second part, part two, q. 18, art. 3)

Peace as the proper effect of charity

Peace implies a twofold union. . . . The first is the result of one's own appetites being directed to one object; the other results from one's appetite being united with the appetite of another. Each of these unions is effected by charity [which is the state of friendship with God]. The first is effected insofar as man loves God with his whole heart, referring all things to Him, so that all his desires tend to one object; the second, insofar as we love our neighbor as ourselves, so that we wish to fulfill our neighbor's will as though it were ours.

(Second part, part two, q. 29, art. 3)

The lawfulness of vengeance

Vengeance consists in the infliction of a penal evil on one who has sinned. Accordingly, in the matter of vengeance, we must consider the mind of the avenger. For if his intention is directed chiefly to the evil of the person on whom he takes vengeance, and rests there, then his vengeance is altogether unlawful, because to take pleasure in another's evil belongs to hatred, which is contrary to the charity whereby we are bound to love all men. Nor is it an excuse that he intends the evil of one who has unjustly inflicted evil on him, as neither is a man excused for hating one that hates him. For a man may not sin against another just because the latter has already sinned against him, since this is to be overcome by evil. . . .

If, however, the avenger's intention is directed chiefly to some good to be obtained by punishing the person who has sinned (for instance that the sinner may amend, or at least that he may be restrained and others not be disturbed, that justice may be upheld, and God honored), then vengeance may be lawful, provided other due circumstances are observed.

(Second part, part two, q. 108, art. 1)

The relationship of zealous love and vengeance

Fortitude disposes one to vengeance by removing an obstacle to it, namely, fear of an imminent danger. Zeal, as denoting the fervor of love, signifies the primary root of vengeance, insofar as a man avenges the wrong done to God and his neighbor, because charity makes him regard them as his own. Now every act of virtue proceeds from charity as its root. . . .

Two vices are opposed to vengeance: one by way of excess, namely, the sin of cruelty or brutality, which exceeds the measure in punishing; while the other is a vice by way of deficiency and consists in being remiss in punishing. That is why it is written (Prov. 13:24): *He that spareth the rod hateth his son.*

(Second part, part two, q. 108, art. 2)

On the support which anger gives to fortitude

The Stoics excluded anger and all other passions of the soul from the mind of a wise or good man, while the Peripatetics, of whom Aristotle was the chief, ascribed to virtuous men both anger and the other passions of the soul, albeit modified by reason. And possibly they differed not in reality but in their way of speaking. For the Peripatetics . . . gave the name of passions to all the movements of the sensitive appetite, however they may comport themselves. And since the sensitive appetite is moved by the command of reason, so that it may cooperate by rendering action more prompt, they held that virtuous persons should employ both anger and the other passions of the soul, modified according to the dictate of reason. On the other hand, the Stoics gave the name of passions to certain immoderate emotions of the sensitive appetite, and so they called them sicknesses or diseases, and severed them altogether from virtue.

Accordingly the brave man employs moderate anger for his action, but not immoderate anger.

(Second part, part two, q. 123, art. 10)

On magnanimity and honor

Magnanimity by its very name denotes the stretching forth of the mind to great things. Now virtue bears a relationship to two things, first to the matter which is the field of its activity, second to its proper act, which consists in the right use of such matter. And since a virtuous habit is so named chiefly by its act, a man is said to be magnanimous chiefly because he is minded to do some great act.

... The things which come into man's use are external. Among these honor is the greatest simply, both because it is the most akin to virtue, since it attests to a person's virtue ... and because it is offered to God and to the best; and also because, to obtain honor even as to avoid shame, men set aside all other things. Now a man is called magnanimous in respect of things that are great absolutely and simply, just as a man is said to be brave in respect of things that are difficult simply. It follows therefore that magnanimity is about honors.

(Second part, part two, q. 129, art. 1)

On pusillanimity

Anything contrary to a natural inclination is a sin, because it is contrary to a law of nature. Now everything has a natural inclination to accomplish an action commensurate with its power, as is evident in all natural things, animate or inanimate. Now just as presumption makes a man exceed what is proportionate to his power, by striving to do more than he can, so pusillanimity makes a man fall short of what is proportionate to his power.... And so, just as presumption is a sin, so is pusillanimity. Hence it is that the servant who buried in the earth the money he had received from his master, and did not trade with it through fainthearted fear, was punished by his master (Matt. 25, Luke 19).

(Second part, part two, q. 133, art. 1)

On the goodness of the sexual act, as opposed to lust

A sin, in human acts, is what is against the order of reason. Now the order of reason consists in ordering everything to its end in a fitting manner. So it is no sin if, by the dictate of reason, one makes use of certain things in a fitting manner and order for the end to which they are adapted, provided that this end be something truly good. Now just as the preservation of the bodily nature of one individual is a true good, so too is the preservation of the nature of the human species a very great good. And just as the use of food is directed to preserve life in the individual, so is the use of venereal acts directed to preserve the whole human race. Hence Augustine says, *"What food is to a man's well being, such is sexual intercourse to the welfare of the whole human race"* (*The Good Wife* 16). Therefore, just as the use of food can be without sin, if it is taken in due manner and order, as required for the welfare of the body, so too the use of venereal acts can be without sin, as long as they are performed in due manner and order, in keeping with the end of human procreation. (Second part, part two, q. 153, art. 2)

On sinful and justified anger

Chrysostom says, *"He that is angry without cause, shall be in danger; but he that is angry with cause, shall not be in danger: for without anger, teaching will be useless, judgments unstable, crimes unchecked."* Therefore to be angry is not always an evil.

. . . Properly speaking, anger is a passion of the sensitive appetite, and gives its name to the irascible power. . . . Now as for the passions of the soul, we should note that evil may be found in them in two ways. First, by reason of the passion's very species, which is derived from the passion's object. Thus envy, in respect of its species, denotes an evil, since it is displeasure at another's good, and such displeasure is in itself contrary to reason. . . . Now this does not apply to anger, which is the desire for revenge, since revenge may be desired both well and ill. Second, a passion may be evil because of the passion's quantity, that is, by its excess or deficiency. In this way evil may be found in anger, when, to wit, one is angry more or less than right reason demands. **But if one is angry in accordance with right reason, one's anger is deserving of praise** [emphasis added]. (Second part, part two, q. 158, art. 1)

On the sin of acedia or "sloth"

It is written: *The sorrow of the world worketh death* (2 Cor. 7:20). But such is sloth; for it is not sorrow *according to God,* which is different from the sorrow of the world. Therefore it is a mortal sin.

. . . Mortal sin is so called because it destroys the spiritual life which is the effect of charity, whereby God dwells in us. So any sin which by its very nature is contrary to charity is a mortal sin per se. And such is sloth, because the proper effect of charity is joy in God, ... while sloth is sorrow about spiritual good. ...

Sloth is opposed to the precept about hallowing the Sabbath-day. For this precept, insofar as it is a moral precept, implicitly commands the mind to rest in God: and sorrow of the mind about the Divine good is contrary to that.
(Second part, part two, q. 35, art. 3)

On blasphemy

The word *blasphemy* seems to denote the disparagement of some surpassing goodness, especially that of God. Now God ... is the very essence of true goodness. Hence whatever befits God pertains to His goodness, and whatever does not befit Him is far removed from the perfection of goodness which is His Essence. Consequently whoever either denies anything befitting God, or affirms anything unbefitting Him, disparages the Divine goodness.

Now this may happen in two ways: first, by an opinion in the intellect; second, by the union of this opinion to a certain detestation in the affections (just as, on the contrary, faith in God is perfected by love of Him). Accordingly this disparagement of the Divine goodness is either in the intellect alone, or in the affections also. If it is in thought only, it is blasphemy of the heart, but if it betrays itself outwardly in speech it is blasphemy of the tongue. It is in this sense that blasphemy is opposed to confession of faith.
(Second part, part two, q. 13, art. 1)

The blasphemy of the damned

Detestation of the Divine goodness is a necessary condition of blasphemy. Now those who are in hell retain their wicked will which is turned away from God's justice, since they love the things for which they are punished, would wish to use them if they could, and hate the punishments inflicted on them for those same sins. They regret indeed the sins which they have committed, not because they hate them, but because they have been punished for them. Accordingly this detestation of the Divine justice is, in them, the interior blasphemy of the heart: and we may well believe that after the resurrection they will blaspheme God with the tongue, even as the saints will praise Him with their voices.
(Second part, part two, q. 13, art. 4)

On sexual sins against nature

Just as the ordering of right reason proceeds from man, so the order of nature is from God Himself. That is why, in sins contrary to nature, whereby the very order of nature is violated, an injury is done to God, the Author of nature. Hence Augustine says, "Those foul offences that are against nature should be everywhere and at all times detested and punished, such as were those of the people of Sodom, which should all nations commit, they would all stand guilty of the same crime, by the law of God, which hath not so made men that they should so abuse one another. For even that very intercourse which should be between God and us is violated, when that same nature, of which He is the Author, is polluted by the perversity of lust" (*Confessions* 3.8).

Vices against nature are also against God . . . and are so much more grievous than the depravity of sacrilege, as the order impressed on human nature is prior to and firmer than any subsequently established order.
(Second part, part two, q. 154, art. 12)

On hypocrisy

The outward deed is a natural sign of the intention. Thus when a man does good works pertaining in themselves to the service of God, and seeks by their means to please not God but man, he simulates a right intention which he does not have. That is why Gregory says that *"hypocrites make God's interests subservient to worldly purposes, since by making a show of saintly conduct they seek, not to turn men to God, but to draw to themselves the applause of their approval"* (*Moral Teachings* 31). So they pretend to have a good intention which they do not have, although they do not pretend to do a good deed without doing it.

The habit of holiness, for instance the religious habit, signifies a state whereby one is bound to perform works of perfection. So when a man puts on the habit of holiness with the intention of entering the state of perfection, if he fails through weakness, he is not a dissembler or a hypocrite, because he is not bound to disclose his sin by laying aside the habit of holiness. But if he were to put on the habit of holiness in order to make a show of righteousness, he would be a hypocrite and a dissembler.
(Second part, part two, q. 111, art. 2)

On pride as the worst of sins

Two things are to be observed in sin, conversion toward a mutable good (this is the material part of sin) and aversion from the immutable good. . . . On the part of the aversion, pride is very grave, because in other sins man turns away from God, either through ignorance or through weakness or through desire for any other good whatever; whereas pride denotes aversion from God simply through being unwilling to be subject to God and His rule. Hence Boethius says that *"while all vices flee from God, pride alone withstands God."* And so it is specially stated that *"God resisteth the proud"* (Jas. 4:6). Thus aversion from God and His commandments, which is a consequence as it were in other sins, belongs to pride by its very nature, for its act is the contempt of God.

(Second part, part two, q. 162, art. 6)

From *The Compendium of Theology*

These excerpts from the *Compendium* were translated by Cyril Vollaert, S.J. (Saint Louis: Herder, 1947).

Chapter 104: The End of the Intellectual Creature

A thing may be in potency in two ways: either naturally, that is, with respect to perfections that can be reduced to act by a natural agent; or else with respect to perfections that cannot be reduced to act by a natural agent but require some other agent. This is seen to take place even in corporeal beings. The boy grows up to be a man; the spermatozoon develops into an animal. This is within the power of nature. But that lumber becomes a bench or that a blind man receives sight, is not within the power of nature.

The same is the case with our minds. . . . [But] man's last end cannot consist [merely in the cognition of objects presented to the senses]. The reason is that, once the ultimate end has been reached, natural desire ceases. But no matter how much we may advance in this kind of understanding, whereby we derive knowledge from the senses, there still remains a natural desire to know other objects. For many things are quite beyond the reach of the senses. We can have but a slight knowledge of such things through information based on sense experience. We may get to know that they exist, but we cannot know what they are, for the natures of immaterial substances belong to a different genus from the natures of sensible things and excel them, we may say, beyond all proportion.

Moreover, as regards objects that fall under sense experience, there are many whose nature we cannot know with any certainty. Some of them, indeed, elude our knowledge altogether; others we can know but vaguely.

Hence our natural desire for more perfect knowledge ever remains. But a natural desire cannot be in vain.

Accordingly we reach our last end when our intellect is actualized by some higher agent than an agent connatural to us, that is, by an agent capable of gratifying our natural, inborn craving for knowledge. So great is the desire for knowledge within us that, once we apprehend an effect, we wish to know its cause. Moreover, after we have gained some knowledge of the circumstances investing a thing, our desire is not satisfied until we penetrate to its essence. Therefore our natural desire for knowledge cannot come to rest within us until we know the first cause, and that not in any way, but in its very essence. This first cause is God. Consequently the ultimate end of an intellectual creature is the vision of God in His essence.

From Chapter 174: Wretchedness Flowing from the Punishment of Loss

Since the wretchedness to which vice leads is opposed to the happiness to which virtue leads, whatever pertains to wretchedness must be understood as being the opposite of all that we have said about happiness. We pointed out above that man's ultimate happiness, as regards his intellect, consists in the unobstructed vision of God. And as regards man's affective life, happiness consists in the immovable repose of his will in the first Good. Therefore man's extreme unhappiness will consist in the fact that his intellect is completely shut off from the divine light, and that his affections are stubbornly turned against God's goodness. And this is the chief suffering of the damned. It is known as the punishment of loss.

APPENDIX D

Dante, from *De monarchia* (*On Monarchy*)

In this treatise exhibiting both the tight logic of the schoolmen and the allegorical fancy of the medieval exegete, Dante argues boldly for his belief that the state, like the Church, was created and ordained by God, with its own proper responsibilites and sphere of activity. Let the reader not assume that Dante was therefore modern in his understanding of an autonomous state and a merely privately chosen or privately avoided Church. Both powers are essential for man's achievement of his end, the "good of the intellect." The Church shows us the path to go and gives us the spiritual food to sustain the journey, while the state curbs our vices and punishes us when we stray too far. The *De monarchia* was written in response to the broad claims made by Boniface VIII in *Unam sanctam,* to wit that the pope was not only the chief spiritual authority but also the chief temporal authority in the world. Yet we should note that for Dante, as for Boniface, all authority derives from God, and is legitimate only insofar as it helps men achieve the intellectual good for which they have been made.

The translation is by Prue Shaw (Cambridge: Cambridge University Press, 1996).

———

On the necessity of the Monarchy

Now it has been sufficiently explained that the activity proper to mankind considered as a whole is constantly to actualize the full intellectual potential of humanity, primarily through thought and secondarily through action (as a function and extension of thought). And since what holds true for the part is true for the whole, and an individual human being "grows perfect in judgment and wisdom when he sits at rest," it is apparent that mankind most freely attends to this activity—an activity which is almost divine, as we read in the psalm: "Thou hast made him a little lower than the angels"—in the calm tranquillity of peace. Hence it is clear that universal peace is the best of those things which are ordained for human happiness. That is why the message which rang out from on high to the shepherds was not wealth, nor pleasures, nor honours, nor long life, nor health, nor strength, nor beauty, but peace; for the heavenly host said: "Glory to God on high, and on earth peace to men of good will. . . ."

. . . Now [Aristotle] states in [the *Politics*] that when a number of things are ordered to a single end, one of them must guide or direct, and the others be guided or directed; and it is not only the author's illustrious name which requires us to believe this, but inductive reasoning as well. For if we consider a single person, we shall see that what happens in the individual is this: while all the faculties are directed towards happiness, it is the intellectual faculty which guides and directs all the others; otherwise happiness is unattainable. If we consider a household, whose purpose is to prepare its members to live the good life, there must be one person who guides and directs, who is called the "pater familias" or his representative, in line with Aristotle's observation that "every household is governed by the eldest," and his role, as Homer says, is to guide everyone and impose rules on the others. Hence the proverbial curse: "May you have an equal in your house." If we consider a small community, whose purpose is neighborly support in relation both to people and to goods, there must be one person who guides the others, either appointed by someone from outside or emerging as leader from among their number with the agreement of the others; otherwise not only will they fail to achieve that neighborly collaboration, but sometimes, if a number of people contest the leadership, the whole community is destroyed. If we consider a city, whose purpose is to be self-sufficient in living the good life, there must be one ruling body, and this is so not only in just government, but in perverted forms of government as well; if this should not be the case, not only is the purpose of social life thwarted, but the city itself ceases to be what it was. Lastly, if we consider an individual kingdom—and the purpose of a kingdom is the same as that of a city, but with greater confidence that peace can be maintained— there must be one king who rules and governs; otherwise not only do those who live in the kingdom not achieve their purpose, but the kingdom itself falls to ruin, in accordance with those words of the infallible Truth: "Every kingdom divided against itself shall be laid waste." . . . Now it is agreed that the whole of mankind is ordered to one goal. . . . There must therefore be one person who directs and rules mankind, and he is properly called "Monarch" or "Emperor." And thus it is apparent that the well-being of the world requires that there be a monarchy or empire.

(From I.iv–v)

On the divine origin and purpose of the Monarchy

And every thing is in a good (indeed, ideal) state which is in harmony with the intention of the first mover, who is God; and this is self-evident, except to those who deny that divine goodness attains the summit of perfection. It is God's intention that every created thing should show forth His likeness in so far as its own nature can receive it. For this reason it is said: "Let us make man in our image, after our likeness"; for although "in our image" cannot be said of things lower than man, "after our likeness" can be said of anything, since the whole universe is simply an imprint of divine goodness. So mankind is in a good (indeed, ideal) state when, to the extent that its nature allows, it resembles God. But mankind most closely resembles God when it is most a unity, since the true measure of unity is in him alone; and for this reason it is written, "Hear, O Israel, the Lord thy God is one." But mankind is most a unity when it is drawn together to form a single entity, and this can only come about when it is ruled as one whole by one ruler, as is self-evident. Therefore mankind is most like God when it is ruled by one ruler, and consequently is most in harmony with God's intention; and this is what it means to be in a good (indeed, ideal) state, as we established at the beginning of this chapter.

(From I.viii)

Connection of the Roman Empire with Christ

All the arguments advanced so far are confirmed by a remarkable historical fact: namely the state of humanity which the Son of God either awaited, or himself chose to bring about, when he was on the point of becoming man for the salvation of mankind. For if we review the ages and the dispositions of men from the fall of our first parents (which was the turning-point at which we went astray), we shall not find that there ever was peace throughout the world except under the immortal Augustus, when a perfect monarchy existed. That mankind was then happy in the calm of universal peace is attested by all historians and by famous poets; even the chronicler of Christ's gentleness [Luke] deigned to bear witness to it; and finally Paul called that most happy state "the fullness of time." . . .

(From I.xvi)

On the illegitimacy of the Donation of Constantine

Again, some people maintain that the Emperor Constantine, cured of leprosy by the intercession of Sylvester who was then supreme Pontiff, made a gift to the church of the seat of empire (i.e., Rome), along with many other imperial privileges. From this they argue that since that time no one can take on those imperial privileges unless he receives them from the church, to whom (they say) they belong; and it would indeed follow from this that the one authority was dependent on the other, as they claim.

... [But] Constantine was not in a position to give away the privileges of empire, nor was the church in a position to accept them. And if they stubbornly insist, my point can be proved in this way: nobody has the right to do things because of an office which he holds which are in conflict with that office, otherwise one and the same thing would oppose itself in its own nature, which is impossible; but to divide the empire is in conflict with the office bestowed on the emperor, since his task is to hold mankind in obedience to a single will ...; therefore the emperor is not allowed to divide the empire. Thus if certain privileges had been taken away from the empire by Constantine, as they maintain, and had passed into the control of the church, that seamless garment would have been torn which even those who pierced Christ the true God with their lance dared not divine. Moreover, just as the church has its foundation, so too the empire has its own. For the foundation of the church is Christ; hence the Apostle in *Corinthians* says: "For other foundation can no man lay than that is laid, which is Jesus Christ." He is the rock on which the church is built. But the foundation of the empire is human right....

Moreover, all jurisdiction is prior to the judge who exercises it, for the judge is appointed for the sake of the jurisdiction, and not vice versa.... From this it is clear that the emperor, precisely as emperor, cannot change it, because he derives from it the fact that he is what he is.... [Moreover], for a donation to be legitimate requires a suitable disposition not just in the giver, but in the recipient as well.... But the church was utterly unsuited to receiving temporal things because of the command which expressly forbade it, as we gather from these words in *Matthew:* "Provide neither gold, nor silver, nor brass for your purses, nor scrip for your journey...."

(From III.x)

APPENDIX E

Dante, from *Il convivio*

The *Convivio* is a fascinating, far-ranging work—by turns a treatise in praise of the vernacular, a polemic against avarice, an argument in favor of empire, and the allegorical explication of songs written in honor of a lovely lady, whom Dante identifies as Philosophy. In the following short section on moral virtue, we see Dante adapting, from Aristotle's *Ethics,* the notion of virtue as occupying a mean between defect and excess. This mean is not to be thought of as a mathematical splitting of the difference, but as the best, most decorous ordering of the passion in question.

The translation is by Philip Wicksteed (London: J. M. Dent, 1912).

—

Our most proper fruits are the moral virtues, because in every direction they are in our power. And they have been distinguished and enumerated diversely by divers philosophers, but inasmuch as wherever the divine opinion of Aristotle has opened its mouth, methinks that every other's opinion may be dropped, purposing to declare what they are I will briefly pass through them in discourse according to his opinion. These are the eleven virtues named by the said philosopher.

The first is called courage, which is weapon and rein to control rashness and timidity in things which bring destruction to our life.

The second is temperance, which is rule and rein to our gluttony and our excessive abstinence in things which preserve our life.

The third is liberality, which is the moderator of our giving and of our taking of temporal things.

The fourth is munificence, which is the moderator of great expenditures, making the same and arresting them at a certain limit.

The fifth is consciousness of greatness, which is moderator and acquirer of great honors and fame.

The sixth is proper pride, which moderates and regulates us as to the honors of this world.

The seventh is serenity, which moderates our wrath and our excessive patience in the face of external evils.

The eighth is affability, which makes us pleasant in company.

The ninth is called frankness, which moderates us in speech from vaunting ourselves beyond what we are, or depreciating ourselves beyond what we are.

The tenth is called *eutrapelia,* which moderates us in sports, causing us to play them in due measure.

The eleventh is justice, which disposes us to love and to do righteousness in all things.

And each of these virtues has two collateral foes, namely vices, the one in excess and the other in defect. And they themselves are the means between them; and they all spring from one principle, to wit from the habit of our right selection. Wherefore it may be said generally of all of them that they are an "elective habit consisting in the mean."

(From book 4, chapter 17)

Appendix F

Boniface VIII, *Unam sanctam* (1302)

It may surprise the modern reader to learn that the Catholic Church has never repudiated (indeed, given its understanding of the papacy, can never repudiate) the doctrine of subordination of all authority to that of the vicar of Christ, a doctrine here set forth by Dante's enemy Boniface VIII. From the pope's point of view, the bull was meant as a reassertion of the Church's independence from outside manipulation; for Philip IV of France had attempted to tax churchmen and church lands in order to finance his own ambitions to unite all French lands under his control. Dante and Boniface disagree not in the manner of their reasoning, nor about the ends to which human life is created, but about exactly what Scripture does say about the relationship between temporal and spiritual authority. To be sure, Dante believed that in interpreting Scripture, Boniface was misled by his own hunger for power. What Boniface believed about Dante's passions is not recorded. Happily, motives are not germane to the merits of an argument.

The following translation is from Philip Schaff, *A History of the Christian Church*, Vol. VI (Grand Rapids: Eerdmans, 1910), pp. 25–27.

Urged on by our faith, we are obliged to believe and hold that there is one holy, catholic, and apostolic Church. And we firmly believe and profess that outside of her there is no salvation nor remission of sins, as the bridegroom declares in the Canticles, "My dove, my undefiled, is but one; she is the only one of her mother; she is the choice one of her that bare her." And this represents the one mystical body of Christ, and of this body Christ is the head, and God is the head of Christ. In it there is one Lord, one faith, one baptism. For in the time of the Flood there was the single ark of Noah, which prefigures the one Church, and it was finished according to the measure of one cubit and had one Noah for pilot and captain, and outside of it every living creature on the earth, as we read, was destroyed. And this Church we revere as the only one, even as the Lord saith by the prophet, "Deliver my soul from the sword, my darling from the power of the dog." He prayed for his soul, that is, for himself, head and body. And this body he called one body, that is, the Church, because of the single bridegroom, the unity of the faith, the sacraments, and the love of the Church. She is that seamless shirt of the Lord which was not rent but was allotted by the casting of lots. Therefore, this one and single Church has one head and not two,—for had she two heads, she would be a monster,—that is, Christ and Christ's vicar, Peter and Peter's successor. For the Lord said unto Peter, "Feed my sheep." "My," he said speaking generally and not particularly, "these and those," by which it is to be understood that all the sheep are committed unto him. So, when the Greeks or others say that they were not committed to the care of Peter and his successors, they must confess that they are not of Christ's sheep, even as the Lord says in John, "There is one fold and one shepherd."

That in her and within her power are two swords, we are taught in the Gospels, namely, the spiritual sword and the temporal sword. For when the Apostles said, "Lo, here,"—that is, in the Church,—are two swords, the Lord did not reply to the Apostles "it is too much," but "it is enough." It is certain that whoever denies that the temporal sword is in the power of Peter, hearkens ill to the words of the Lord which he spake, "Put up thy sword into its sheath." Therefore, both are in the power of the Church, namely, the spiritual sword and the temporal sword; the latter is to be used for the Church, the former by the Church; the former by the hand of the priest, the latter by the hand of princes and kings, but at the nod and sufferance of the priest. The one sword must of necessity be subject to the other, and the temporal authority to the spiritual. For the Apostle said, "There is no power but of God, and the powers that be are ordained of God"; and they would not have been ordained unless one sword had been made subject to the other, and even as the lower is subjected by the other for higher things. For, according to Dionysius, it is a divine law that the lowest things are made by mediocre things to attain to the highest. For it is not according to the law of the universe that all things in an equal way and immediately should reach their end, but the lowest through the mediocre and the lower through the higher. But that the spiritual power excels the earthly power in dignity and worth, we will the more clearly acknowledge just in proportion as the spiritual is higher than the temporal. And this we perceive quite distinctly from the donation of the tithe and functions of benediction and sanctification, from the mode in which the power was received, and the government of the subjected realms. For truth being the witness, the spiritual power has the functions of establishing the temporal power and sitting in judgment on it if it should prove to be not good. And to the Church and the Church's power the prophecy of Jeremiah attests: "See, I have set thee this day over the nations and the kingdoms to pluck up and to break down and to destroy and to overthrow, to build and to plant."

And if the earthly power deviate from the right path, it is judged by the spiritual power; but if a minor spiritual power deviate from the right path, the lower in rank is judged by its superior; but if the supreme power [the papacy] deviate, it can be judged not by man but by God alone. And so the Apostle testifies, "He which is spiritual judges all things, but he himself is judged by no man." But this authority, although it be given to a man, and though it be exercised by a man, is not a human but a divine power given by divine word of mouth to Peter and confirmed to Peter and to his successors by Christ himself, whom Peter confessed, even him whom Christ called the Rock. For the Lord said to Peter himself, "Whatsoever thou shalt bind on earth," etc. Whoever, therefore, resists this power so ordained by God, resists the ordinance of God, unless perchance he imagine two principles to exist, as did Manichæus, which we pronounce false and heretical. For Moses testified that God created heaven and earth not in the beginnings but "in the beginning."

Furthermore, that every human creature is subject to the Roman pontiff,— this we declare, say, define, and pronounce to be altogether necessary to salvation.

Appendix G

Bertran de Born, *"Be'm platz lo gais temps de pascor"*

The joy of combat has seldom been rendered so vigorously as by this minor nobleman and poet. It is attractive to suppose that he himself has provided Dante much of the language of the circle of the sowers of discord, in Canto 28. The following is a fairly free translation of one of Bertran's most famous poems. I hope the muscularity of the original is more than faintly suggested.

How I do love the merry spring,
the Eastertide, that brings the leaf and flower,
and love to hear the bold birds sing,
echoing through the woods and everywhere,
and how I love to see meadows strewn
with tents and with pavilions staked in place—
how it makes my heart race
to see ranged over the countryside aright
gallant horsemen and horses armed to fight!

How I love watching the chargers rush
to set the folk and all their train to flee—
and then the soldiers at one push
come at them, in a mass of infantry!
Does my heart good to see great castles laid
siege, the ramparts cracked and smashed,
the huge host penned behind a palisade
at the edge of a trench
hemmed round by fortifications, ditch on ditch.

And yes, how I love to see that lord
first to race forth against the enemy—
armed, on his horse, no trace of fear,
stirring the hearts of his own men with his sheer

valor and nobility—
and when the hosts are clashing, let each man
stand eager to follow wherever he goes,
for no man's prized a damn
till he's taken and given back his share of blows.

When the fight's under way we'll see
the gaily painted helmets and the swords,
maces and shields to fling away
all cut to shreds,
vassals striking together, and aimlessly
galloping horses of the dead and hurt.
And once he enters the fight
let any man proud of his birth
think only of cracking an arm, splitting a head,
for a man's worth
less beaten and alive than dead.

Neither to sleep nor drink nor eat,
I tell you, is so sweet
to my taste, as to hear both armies cry
"At them, at them!" and the horses neigh
riderless in the gloom,
with calls of "Help, help," as I see men fall
dead on the fields, the great, the small,
with silken-tasseled stubs
of lances in their ribs.
Brave lords, put all your lands in hock,
all of your towns and fortresses, before
you ever cease your going forth to war!

Papiols, if you please,
hurry and go to my lord Will-He Won't-He,
and tell the man he's lived too long in peace.

Notes

The following notes are intended as an aid for the general reader. I have, therefore, provided such historical background as I judged was quite necessary. The *Inferno* is rich enough to warrant many pages of notes to one page of text; but my task, I think, was to guide the reader out of the dark woods and not lead him into another. I have also flagged most of Dante's adaptations of four ancient poets: Virgil, Ovid, Lucan, and Statius, the most important poetic influences upon the *Comedy*. Although much of Dante's mythology is treated more fully in the work of the Greek poets Homer and Hesiod, these were not available to Dante, and so the notes do not refer to them. One source I have been careful to note: the Bible (from the Douay-Rheims version, the closest English counterpart to the Latin Vulgate, which Dante knew). To ignore that source is to turn Dante's work into an interesting cultural artifact, a literary museum piece, mummified in a living death. But the *Comedy* is alive as no other poem is, except perhaps the *Odyssey;* and it is alive because, like the *Odyssey,* it records the living wisdom of a man who had thought deeply about the whole cosmos, from Deity to the earth beneath our feet. For Dante, that wisdom is a gift from God, at one with that other gift, faith. I have taken care, in the notes referring to Scripture, to suggest the depth, the subtlety, and the comprehensiveness of that faith.

I am most grateful for the penetrating and wise edition of Umberto Bosco and Giovanni Reggio, to my taste the best of many fine modern editions. To that work I am deeply indebted. I am also especially indebted to the editions of C. M. Grandgent, Charles Singleton, Natalino Sapegno, and Giuseppe Vandelli, and to the notes of those English translators who have gone before, particularly the magnificent John Ciardi.

CANTO ONE

We are apt to think of allegory as a dead system of symbols, for which one must apply some kind of standard decoder. This notion is what caused the great allegorists Dickens and Tolkien to deny that they wrote allegory at all. As for Dante, his first canto is one of the most "allegorical" in the *Comedy*, yet we should pause to note what that common critical observation does and does not mean. For what meets Dante in this first canto are real beasts, really intending to devour him: the lion "seemed to strike tremors in the very air." Like the mysterious "waters of my heart," the beasts hover and flicker between objects of body and objects of mind. That is as it should be. Dante's allegory is not one genre among others, but a habit of viewing the whole universe; and that habit is justified, he would remind us, because in fact the universe itself is one great system of coruscating and interreflecting signs. It is not that, for example, believers found it convenient to compare the pelican to Christ, but that one of the reasons why God from all eternity created the pelican was precisely that it should be a sign of Christ. Dante's literary wolf is a sign of avarice because, in part, that is what all wolves are.

P. 3, L. 2. *dark wilderness:* This wilderness, or *selva oscura*, represents the confusion of choices in a life not obedient to reason and thus not oriented toward man's happiness. Says Dante: "So the youth, who enters into the wandering woods of this life, would never know the right way to go, were it not shown to him by his elders" (*Conv.* 4.24). Such a forest is made all the rougher for corruption in the papacy and the empire, for then there are no reliable spiritual guides to direct us on the right path and no temporal authorities to check us when we wander from it. In these opening lines Dante accuses himself of a spiritual straying, the precise nature of which is much disputed, although most critics agree that it involved his abandoning the quest for theological truth, symbolized by Beatrice (see note on line 122 below). The events of the poem occur exactly halfway through Dante's pilgrimage of life: "The sum of our years is seventy" (Ps. 90:10). Since Dante was born in 1265, we are in the year 1300. Dante is also paraphrasing the ailing King Hezekiah's cry unto the Lord: "In the midst of my days I shall go to the gates of Hell" (Is. 38:10). The good king was cured, and granted longer life.

P. 3, L. 3. *straight and true:* The adjectives render the Italian *diritta*, "direct," "just," "right." Dante associates straightness with justice, that is to say with a thing's true aim, the fulfillment of the purpose inherent in its creation. For the strait (and straight) path, recall the words of Christ: "How narrow the gate and close the way that leads to life! And few there are who find it" (Matt. 7:14).

P. 3, L. 7. *bitter:* The pleasures of the unredeemed life are only apparent. That life is actually "more bitter than death" (Eccl. 7:26).

P. 3, L. 11. *sleep:* spiritual torpor, dullness of soul, forgetfulness of oneself and of one's Maker. In Isaiah, such sleepiness characterizes sin and is one of its most severe punishments: "For the Lord hath mingled for you the spirit of a deep sleep, he will shut up your eyes, he will cover your prophets and princes, that see visions" (Is. 29:10).

P. 3, L. 18. *that leads all men aright on every road:* The sun represents grace but also lights the path men must take to reach their goal. It shines upon a hill whose light and freedom soar above the murk of the wood. See Ps. 121:1–2: "I lift my eyes to the mountains: whence shall help come to me? My help is from the Lord, who made heaven and earth."

P. 3, L. 20. *the waters of my heart:* literally, "the lake of my heart," that chamber in the heart that was thought to house the blood for our strongest emotions.

P. 5, L. 30. *firmer foot:* allegorically, the left foot (of the will), the one more beholden to the appetites. Dante's climb is tentative. Burdened by original sin, he cannot free himself: "I do not the good that I wish, but the evil that I do not wish, that I perform" (Rom. 7:19).

P. 5, L. 32. *leopard:* the first of the three beasts to block Dante's ascent. The beasts are part of Jeremiah's condemnation of unjust and hardhearted Jerusalem: "A lion out of the wood hath slain them, a wolf in the evening hath spoiled them, a leopard watcheth for their cities" (Jer. 5:6). Their significance is debated. Following the beast symbolism of their day, medieval commentators identified the *leopard* with lust, the *lion* with pride, and the *wolf* with avarice. Others, referring to Dante's description of Florence as proud, envious, and avaricious (6.74; 15.68), identify the leopard (actually a lynx, traditionally keen-sighted) with envy—and envy, or *invidia*, is, literally, the seeing of things askance or inside out. Still others, noting 11.81, suggest that the beasts represent the three dispositions of the soul that Heaven abhors: incontinence (leopard), bestiality (lion), and malice (wolf). The first interpretation has the advantage of dividing all sins into the three classes that theologians had derived from the account of Satan's temptation of Christ: the World (wolf), the Flesh (leopard), and the Devil (lion). Dante concludes with the World because of his insistence that avarice, or greed for power, in both the Church and the state, and particularly in Florence, has destroyed many a human soul and is the most pernicious disease that ails Christendom.

P. 5, L. 37. *The hour:* This cosmos is the stage of God's creation and of his redemption of fallen man. Fittingly, then, it is the vernal equinox, and the sun is in Aries, as it was when, according to tradition, the universe was created. It is shortly before the morning of Good Friday, thought to be the same date as that of the Creation. In general, Dante's view of time is not ours: Time is not an amoral fourth dimension in a four-dimensional space-time continuum. It is the moving image of eternity. All times are impregnated with God's being and his eternal purposes. To know the time is to know one's relation to the Creator of time, and thus to see the end, or purpose, of time as present in the here and now. "For [God] hath given me the true knowledge of the things that are: to know the disposition of the whole world, and the virtues of the elements, the beginning, and ending, and midst of the times, and alterations of their courses, and the changes of seasons, the revolutions of the year, and the dispositions of the stars" (Wis. 7:17–19).

P. 7, L. 65. *Mercy:* Latin *miserere.* The word recalls the liturgical prayer *Miserere mei* (Ps. 51).

P. 7, L. 69. *Mantua:* The speaker is Virgil (70–19 B.C.), the greatest of Roman poets, author of the *Aeneid,* the epic poem that celebrates the founding of the Roman people by Aeneas, a Trojan who fled the city after the night of its destruction. For Dante, Virgil is a symbol of human reason unaided by divine revelation; he is the best the pagan world has to give. That best, we will see, is still not good enough, for man cannot redeem himself. Of course, Virgil is more than a symbol; he is one of the greatest characters ever drawn by a poet. He is a stern but kind father, the great-souled man who shows his pupil the ways of virtue. He is also a patriot who celebrated the greatness of his native land, a land destined to become, in the twin institutions of empire and papacy, the ruler of Christendom. He is Dante's fellow poet and friend, a little touchy on points of honor, a little overconfident at times, but always large of heart and attentive to his charge. He who unknowingly anticipated the reign of peace brought in by Christ and prepared for by Augustus Caesar, he who knew Christ neither as Savior nor as Messiah to come, must lead the younger poet Dante, who was privileged to know Christ but who has forgotten the way of truth.

P. 7, L. 72. *cheating gods:* Quiet disappointment is never far from Virgil's noble mind. He above all poets longed for the truth, and will never see it face-to-face.

P. 7, L. 87. *the style:* the tragic style, proper to epics and to moral allegories of high sublimity. Some critics say Dante claims an honor that he only anticipates winning, since, after all, at this point the *Comedy* has but begun. Perhaps he is claiming the honor for those most cosmically allusive portions of his allegorical biography of love, *La vita nuova.* In any case, the poetry of Virgil has prepared the way for Dante's journey, just as reason lays the groundwork for revelation.

P. 9, L. 101. *the Greyhound:* Sometimes identified as Cangrande (Big Dog) della Scala, Dante's Veronese friend and patron, the Greyhound is probably best seen as an unnamed, providential savior of lowly (or humbled) Italy, one sustained by the Trinity itself in power, wisdom, and love. His birthplace is, literally, "between felt and felt," or for some, "between the towns of Feltre and [Monte]feltro." Political interpretations are quite possible: Cangrande's Verona lies between Feltre and Montefeltro, and ballots to elect a new Holy Roman Emperor were placed in urns lined with felt. My translation here prefers the suggestive: the *felt* is a sign of secret, humble beginnings. The Greyhound's victory is to be seen in apocalyptic terms, for the beast's fornications recall those of the whore of Babylon: "All the nations have drunk of the wrath of her immorality, and the kings of the earth have committed fornication with her" (Rev. 18:3; see *Inf.* 19.106–8).

P. 9, LL. 107–8. *Camilla ... Nisus, Turnus, and Euryalus:* warriors in the *Aeneid* who died in the battles between the Trojans and the native Italic peoples. *Camilla* was the Latin maiden who, like Homer's Penthesilea, chose warfare instead of the feminine arts (see 7.803–11). *Turnus,* Aeneas' principal rival, was betrothed to Lavinia, King Latinus' daughter, before the king gave her instead to Aeneas, provoking Turnus to war (7.403–44). *Nisus* and *Euryalus* are two young Trojan friends—Nisus the elder, Euryalus the protégé—who are captured and slain after a mad night raid on the Latin camp (9.176–445). These are all presented, Trojan and Latin alike, as Italian heroes and patriots, yet all were caught by what Virgil calls *dira cupido,* "dreadful desire" (9.185).

P. 9, L. 111. *envy:* that of Satan for Adam and Eve. "By the envy of the devil, death came into the world" (Wis. 2:24).

P. 9, L. 117. *second death:* damnation, as in Scripture: "And hell and death were cast into the pool of fire. This is the second death" (Rev. 20:14). Yet the souls cry out *for* that death, as if it could annihilate them and thus end their suffering. In that sense theirs is a death ever-dying, a passing away that cannot pass away.

P. 9, L. 122. *another soul:* Beatrice, the sainted woman who will lead Dante through Paradise. She is, on the human level, the soul of Beatrice Portinari (1266–90), a young woman with whom Dante fell in love—that is, if we mean by love nothing less than the chaste, idealized, wondrous admiration he describes in *La vita nuova.* Allegorically, Beatrice represents what her name suggests: that blessedness which is a free gift from God. Since God's revelation of himself is also such a gift, and since revelation is meant to lead to blessedness, Beatrice also represents theology, man's grateful meditation upon and study of that gift.

P. 9, L. 125. *rebel:* Virgil did not possess the true faith, and so with all the rest of unredeemed mankind he remained in a state of war against God. It is faith and not reason that ushers the soul beyond the threshold of Paradise, into that true and only City whereof the Roman Virgil could but dream. Virgil's words testify to his paganism, and are mingled with a wistful regret that it was not otherwise.

CANTO TWO

Fortitude, says Thomas Aquinas in his winningly direct way, has primarily to do with death and danger. It is, of course, the virtue one had better have if one is about to descend body and soul into Hell. But as Dante begins this canto, he has his doubts. These are practical enough. He recalls other men who visited the hereafter, Aeneas and Saint Paul, and compares himself unfavorably with both their persons and their missions. Now, Virgil could give a practical response: he could remind Dante of his perilous state and inform him, again, that his only hope for salvation lies in the journey. Actually, he does so, but in the form of a love story that wins Dante's heart before it persuades his intellect. The master of the Latin tongue uses his artistry—just as, in his story itself, Beatrice has requested him to do—to take Dante's cool hesitancy by storm. As art is more than rule and line and precept, although art will use rule and line and precept, so, while fortitude may calculate advantages and act accordingly, it is more than that practical wisdom. Fortitude is the virtue that deals primarily with death and danger. It is faith put to the test.

P. 13, L. 5. *the pity of my heart:* Dante must learn to accept the judgments of God. His spirited pity, occasionally stirred by a sinner or his punishment, must bow to both reason and faith.

P. 13, L. 7. *O Muses, O high genius:* Dante invokes the Muses in passing; his emphasis is rather on his own ingenuity. For Purgatory and Paradise it will not be so. Human art suffices to describe most of Hell and its misery. For blessedness we require the Muses, or the Holy Spirit, indeed.

P. 15, L. 27. *his triumph . . . the pope:* Aeneas' descent to the underworld (see Appendix A) leads to the founding of Rome and, ultimately, to the institutions of the empire and the papacy, whose corruption by avarice has ruined Dante's native land. Saint Paul's journey, "caught up to the third heaven" (2 Cor. 12:2), brought back assurance of the resurrection (what Paul saw he does not say, but the anonymous writer of the *Visio sancti Pauli* provided the details, which entered into the popular imagination; see Appendix B). Dante's journey to the other world is meant both to set Church and empire right and to strengthen his reader's faith. In his disclaimer Dante shows that he really does intend to play the roles of Aeneas and Saint Paul.

P. 15, L. 35. *mad and foolish:* Italian *folle,* "mad," "foolish," "presumptuous." Dante would defuse the charge of blasphemy—for who can pretend to know the secrets of the other world? For a truly presumptuous voyage, see that of Ulysses, Canto 26.

P. 15, L. 44. *greathearted man:* Italian *magnanimo,* rendering the *megalopsychos* of Aristotle: the great-minded or great-souled who possesses a just estimation of his superiority. Even in Hell, Dante admires those whose deeds are brave and whose thoughts are serious and sublime (see note on 10.27). The Christian faith is not for the faint of heart. The opposite of the magnanimous man is the petty-souled coward, whom we will meet below (3.33–69).

P. 17, L. 61. *not a fortune-friend:* not a man I have befriended by accident or for my own profit. Perhaps, too, the phrase suggests that Fortune has been no friend of Dante's.

P. 17, L. 71. *love makes me speak:* Beatrice speaks the language of a lady in troubadour love poetry (see Dante's description of the motive behind his own poetic style, *Purg.* 24.52–54). Without contradiction, Dante is also thinking here of God, "the Love that moves the sun and the other stars." He is saved not because he loves but because he is loved.

P. 17, L. 76. *power:* Italian *virtù,* "power," "virtue," "peculiar strength"; here, probably the particular virtue, or power, symbolized by Beatrice, that of theology: reflection upon what God has revealed.

P. 19, L. 96. *rigid sentence:* divine judgment, which mercifully and justly suffers itself to be won over by divine mercy. "Mercy triumphs over justice" (Jas. 2:13).

P. 19, L. 105. *common crowd:* Inspired by love, Dante withdrew from total dedication to political action or any other worldly enterprise, giving himself to a poetry infused by the eternal longings of man.

P. 19, L. 110. *to seize his profit or to flee his harm:* The materialist Epicurus asserted that these motives, basically self-interested, were the only motives for human friendship; Cicero treated the assertion with contempt (*On Friendship* 9.30–32). Love is speedier than these.

P. 21, L. 140. *teacher:* Italian *maestro,* Latin *magister,* "teacher," in the sense of wise master or rightful authority.

CANTO THREE

I have long thought that the most chilling words upon the portal of Hell are not those that shut the door on the fulfillment of human longings: ABANDON ALL HOPE, YOU WHO ENTER HERE. These crush with their finality, but they do not possess the shocking irony of the simple signature of the architect: DIVINE OMNIPOTENCE CREATED ME, THE HIGHEST WISDOM, AND THE PRIMAL LOVE. Of course, it is a Trinitarian signature. Still, the sonorous ending on *amore,* Love, should give us pause. How can Love fashion a realm of groaning and wailing, of utter agony and alienation? Theology can take us far: the just punishment of the wicked, says Thomas, is an act of charity toward them (justice and charity cannot finally be at odds), even when that punishment does not or cannot result in their correction. At the least it restrains them from deeper depravity. One may suppose, too, that punishment respects the dignity of the sinner, to grant him what his own disordered love has merited and has longed for. For such a lover, the only place more agonizing than Hell would be Heaven. Indeed, the one place hotter than Hell is Heaven, as Dante imagines it: without grace, the fires of Love in Paradise would be unendurable. Perhaps, then, the inscription over the gates of Hell is meant to teach as much about Love as about Hell. For Love, as Dante saw, is no mere sentiment, no habit of ease. It is a consuming fire.

P. 23, LL. 5–6. OMNIPOTENCE ... WISDOM ... LOVE: Hell is created, as an act of justice, by the Trinity: the Father (omnipotence), the Son (wisdom; see 1 Cor. 1:24, John 1:1–3, Prov. 8:22–30), and the Holy Spirit (love). And it is his likeness to these three that man subverts by sin. Grasping, in his foolish and disordered loves, at godlike power, man sentences himself to the impotence, ignorance, and alienation of Hell—that city of Lucifer crammed with many crowds, and no communion.

P. 23, LL. 7–8. NO CREATED THINGS BUT THOSE THAT LAST FOREVER: Only the angels and the incorruptible heavens had been created before Hell. It is the fall of the rebellious angels that occasions the creation of Hell: "For God did not spare the angels when they sinned, but dragged them down by infernal ropes to Tartarus, and delivered them to be tortured and kept in custody for judgment" (2 Pet. 2:4).

P. 23, L. 9. ABANDON ALL HOPE: In this most memorable of verses Dante adapts the warning of Virgil's Sibyl, who advises Aeneas that it is easy to go to the world below; the difficult thing is to get back out (*Aen.* 6.128–29). But what Dante has chiefly in mind is the theological virtue of hope, standing between the longing of love and the faith that the longing will be fulfilled. Hope is the state proper to man not yet blessed. To have neither fulfillment nor hope is to be lost, utterly.

P. 23, L. 18. *good of intellect:* The sight of God, who alone is truth, alone can satisfy our natural and sacred desire to know: "Now I know in part, but then I shall know even as I have been known" (1 Cor. 13:12).

P. 25, L. 35. *those sad souls:* the pusillanimous, or petty-souled, too smallmindedly selfish in life to devote their hearts either to God or to evil. They are more contemptible than the souls below, who surpass them in wickedness. Having taken no sides in the warfare of life, they now follow, mindlessly, the blank standard of their band. The neutral angels Dante mentions have no firm basis in revelation, although the idea of loathsome neutrality is manifest in the condemnation of the Laodicean Church: "Because thou art lukewarm and neither cold nor hot, I am about to vomit thee out of my mouth" (Rev. 3:16).

P. 27, L. 60. *the craven one:* The most solid candidate is Celestine V, a saintly monk who was elevated to the papacy, an office beyond his physical and political powers. He abdicated in 1294, cajoled to do so by his successor, Boniface VIII, who had cagily persuaded him that no man could mix himself up with the affairs of the world without falling into grave sin. For Dante, Boniface's assumption of the papacy was a moral and political disaster (see 19.52–57 and 27.85–111, and notes). Celestine was canonized in 1313—a fact that Dante boldly ignores. In life Celestine wanted only to be a hermit; here in Hell, Dante recognizes him immediately.

P. 27, L. 83. *an old man:* Charon, classical ferryman of the dead (see *Aen.* 6.298–304). He is the first of several guardians of the rings of Hell, and the first of several who grow indignant at Dante's presence. His flaming eyes associate him with the demonic.

P. 27, L. 84. *crooked souls:* A literal rendering of the Italian *anime prave.* The souls are depraved, bent ruins of the erect creatures they were made to be. We are erect that we might behold our destiny, the heavens above—or (what I hope is poignant literalism) that we might behold *the sky.* That most human of glances these souls will never enjoy again.

P. 29, L. 103. *Hurled blasphemy:* paraphrasing the suffering Job: "Let the day perish wherein I was born, and the night in which it was said: 'A man child is conceived'" (Job 3:3). The souls' curse encompasses all, from God to the entire material creation that has led to the particulars of their birth. They feel the brunt of Christ's condemnation: "It were better for that man if he had not been born" (Mk. 14:21).

P. 29, L. 112. *As in the fall:* a lovely and elegaic simile, adapted by Milton in his description of the fallen angels (*Paradise Lost* 1.301–4) and deriving from Virgil (*Aen.* 6.309–12). The image owes its power not only to the frailty and helplessness of the leaves, whose gentle fall is compared to the flinging of human souls into eternal torment, but also to the somber awareness that none of it need ever have come to pass.

P. 29, L. 126. *their desire:* That is no ironic cruelty on God's part. Hell is what some men finally and irrevocably desire, and now they receive it, shorn of its delusive glamour. It is the terrible object of their love.

CANTO FOUR

What of the virtuous men and women who never knew Christ? The Calvinist reply is to deny that any have ever really existed. The modern reply is to assert that it does not matter anyway, either since there is no God or since God will save everyone who exceeds a certain modest level of virtue, usually a level slightly below that of the asserter. The first option (available to Dante in the writings of Augustine and Bernard of Clairvaux) Dante rejects, good Aristotelian that he is, as flatly contradicted by the evidence of our senses. There were heroes, practical and intellectual, who did not know Christ, and their heroism was real, not specious; so real that here in Limbo it merits distinction granted by Heaven. The second option is flatly contradicted by the Scriptures and would make Christ's atoning death and resurrection utterly unnecessary. Not compromising either his honesty or his faith, Dante imagines a place of both mercy and unyielding justice for those to whom, in the mysterious providence of God, it was not given to find the Truth.

P. 33, L. 24. *first belt:* Limbo, from Latin *limbus,* "edge," "rim." Theologians had conceived of two Limbos, one for the Jewish patriarchs awaiting the Messiah, and the other for unbaptized babies. Dante makes Limbo a portion of Hell proper. His Limbo is the place whence the patriarchs were taken when, after his death and before his resurrection, Christ "was brought to life in the spirit, in which also he went and preached to those spirits that were in prison" (1 Pet. 3:18–19). It is inhabited by the unbaptized, both infants and all those who lived according to the four cardinal virtues but who lacked the three theological virtues of faith, hope, and charity (see *Purg.* 7.34–36). Because of the taint of original sin they are damned, yet their punishment consists only in knowing that they will never be able to look upon the Lord. Dante's struggle with the question of their fate involves him in deep probings into the nature of divine justice, and is resolved only by faith, in Paradise (*Par.* 19.67–81; 20.67–138). For Thomas Aquinas's views, see Appendix C.

P. 37, L. 72. *people to be honored:* Human achievement in the arts and sciences merits honor even among those just men who will never see God: so precious is that intellect whereby we can truly be said to have been made in God's image. But this is the only place in Hell where light fends off the gloom. All other light in Hell is murky, or is shed by the fires of torment.

P. 37, L. 88. *Homer:* The great poets of antiquity are here presented as the emblematic artists of various forms of poetry. In hierarchical order, then: *Homer,* writer of the *Iliad* and the *Odyssey* (whom Dante knew only at second hand, by discussions of his work in Latin writers such as Cicero), is the supreme epic poet, and thus he carries a sword, symbol of warfare and of authority. *Horace* is the poet of satire (Dante knew his epistles and conversation poems but probably did not know his odes). *Ovid* is the poet of lyric (though Dante loved and drew heavily upon Ovid's epic *Metamorphoses,* here he is thinking of Ovid's elegaic verses, such as the *Amores*); and *Lucan* (author of the *Pharsalia,* an unfinished poetic account of civil strife in ancient Italy—that strife which broke out into civil war between Julius Caesar and Pompey) is the poet of historical narrative.

P. 39, L. 102. *and made me sixth:* False modesty is but a small-minded form of pride, and Dante, like the other great-souled men in his narrative, will have none of it.

P. 39, L. 106. *noble castle:* Dante and Virgil enter a region reserved for the noble leaders and thinkers of pagan antiquity and of the "gentile" (that is, Muslim) world. The imagery of this place derives from that of the classical Elysian Fields, the green and pleasant underworld for the just (see *Aen.* 6.637–77). Yet the place is also a medieval castle, a stronghold of learning, guarded by a moat and seven walls. The castle is commonly held to represent knowledge, with the walls or the seven turns of the stream representing the seven branches of learning in the medieval school: the trivium (grammar, logic, rhetoric) and the quadrivium (music, arithmetic, geometry, astronomy). The souls within are marked by the same decorum and gravity we see in Virgil and his fellow poets.

PP. 39–41, LL. 121–28. *Electra . . . Cornelia:* a list of mythical and historical progenitors and heroes of ancient Rome. *Electra* (not the daughter of Oedipus) was the mother of Dardanus, who sired the Trojan race and thus, through his descendant Aeneas, the Romans themselves. *Hector* was the greatest of the Trojan warriors, slain by Achilles in the tenth year of the war. *Aeneas* was, in Virgil, second to Hector in prowess, first among the Trojans in his devotion to his fatherland and its gods. *Julius Caesar,* with his hawklike eyes, is the great initiator of the Roman Empire. *Camilla* and *Penthesilea* were mythical warrior women who fought, respectively, against the Trojans in Italy and for them in Troy. *King Latinus* was the ruler in Italy who wished to unite his people with the Trojans by marrying his daughter *Lavinia* to Aeneas. *Brutus* is not the slayer of Caesar (for that Brutus, see below, 34.64–66), but Lucius Junius Brutus the Liberator, who ended the rule of Etruscan kings in Rome when he drove the last of them, Tarquin the Proud, into exile. Brutus then became the first consul of the Roman Republic. *Lucretia* and the three women who follow are the feminine exemplars of Roman honor. *Lucretia* was indirectly responsible for the founding of the republic. Raped by the son of Tarquin the Proud, she revealed the crime to her husband and to Brutus, and then—in an act condemned by Saint Augustine (*City of God* 1.19) as selfish and prideful, but apparently approved by Dante for its bold devotion to purity—slew herself. In retribution for this crime, Brutus seized control of the state (Livy, *History of Rome* 1.56–60). *Julia* was Caesar's daughter and Pompey's first wife. *Martia* was the wife of Cato of Utica, in Lucan a model of wifely devotion and obedience (*Phars.* 2.328–91; see also *Purg.* 1.79); and *Cornelia* was either the mother of the land-reforming tribunes Tiberius and Gaius Gracchus or, far more likely, the second wife of Pompey; Lucan portrays her as noble, greathearted, and loyal (*Phars.* 5.728–815).

P. 41, L. 129. *Saladin:* Salah ad-Din, sultan of Egypt from 1174 to 1193, the man who defeated the Crusaders led by Richard the Lionhearted; renowned in the West for his wise rule and his magnanimity (see Boccaccio, *Decameron* 10.9). As an Arab and a Muslim he sits apart from the Roman pagans.

P. 41, L. 132. *his wisdom-seeking family:* or his "philosophic band." Dante exalts the philosophers because, as lovers of wisdom, they seek the highest goal of human life; the practical virtue of the noble men and women we have just seen is superseded by the intellectual virtue Dante celebrates here. *Aristotle* is, for Dante as for his teacher Thomas Aquinas, and indeed for the Arabs who translated and commented upon his works and reintroduced them into the West, the greatest of the philosophers. Aristotle's empirically founded but nonmaterialist examination of physical cause and effect was well suited for what the thinkers of the high Middle Ages took to be their greatest task: to reconcile the earthly with the divine. For Dante, here, he is the great teacher of physics and metaphysics, and is followed by *Plato* and *Socrates,* considered as moral philosophers. The rest include thinkers with whose ideas Dante does not necessarily agree. The atomist *Democritus* (460–370? B.C.) and the Cynic *Diogenes* (400–325?) lead a series of philosophers known to Dante by reputation only, including *Zeno* (either the Stoic or Zeno of Elea, the deviser of paradoxes—we cannot tell) and the natural philosophers *Empedocles* of Agrigentum (490?–430), *Thales* of Halicarnassus (sixth century B.C.), *Anaxagoras* (500–428?), and *Heraclitus* (c. 500 B.C.). The philosophers are followed by men learned in other arts. From ancient Greece and Rome come the collector of medicinal plants *Dioscorides* (first century A.D.); *Orpheus,* mythical inventor of poetry (see Ovid, *Met.* 10.1–85, 11.1–66); *Marcus Tullius Cicero,* the Roman orator and amateur philosopher; the Roman historian *Livy* (59 B.C.–A.D. 17, though most editions read *Lino,* "Linus," another mythical poet, like Orpheus); the moral philosopher *Seneca* (4? B.C.–A.D. 65); the mathematician *Euclid* (365?–300? B.C.) and the astronomer *Ptolemy* (A.D. 100?–170); and the physicians *Hippocrates* (460?–377 B.C.) and *Galen* (A.D. 130?–200?). From the Muslim world come the Persian physician and philosopher *Avicenna* (Ibn Sina, 980–1037) and the greatest of the Arab philosophers, the Spanish *Averroes* (Ibn Rushd, 1126–98), the quasimaterialist whose commentary on Aristotle became a textbook in the universities and a source of theological controversy.

CANTO FIVE

The Prince of Darkness, we are told, appears as an angel of light. A predictable strategy on the part of the Prince of Darkness, that. Yet there ought to remain some sooty tinge to that beauty, some Miltonic etching of fire upon the face, some hectic compulsion in the eye. Now here, in his treatment of lust, Dante could have contented himself with ugly brutality, with the rutting and snorting of our animal natures. A lesser poet would have made the all-lecherous Semiramis the queen of this canto. Instead, our paradigmatic sinner is the courtly and lovely Francesca, and her sin has every worldly justification you can name. Her husband is crippled in body and soul; her brother-in-law, the young Paolo, is noble and handsome. She and Paolo fall in love almost as in a dream, caught up by the fabulous beauty of the greatest of romances, the story of Lancelot and Guinevere. We are meant to respond to Francesca's beauty and to the beauty of her tragic love. That is true beauty indeed—but like Lucifer's, it is beauty spoiled; and we can note in Francesca the traces of gracious manipulativeness and self-excuse. As the brightest and most glorious of the angels fell, so may fall those whose hearts should have been quickest to respond in sympathy with the words of the courtly evangelist John: "God is love."

P. 43, L. 4. *Minos:* legendary king of Crete whose father, Zeus, had assumed the form of a bull to rape Minos' mother, Europa. Minos was known for his iron justice and for the Minotaur, the man-bull given birth to by his lecherous queen, Pasiphae (Dante's portrait of Minos borrows some of the characteristics of that monster). In Homer and Virgil, Minos is one of the rigid justices of the underworld. Therefore Dante has him judge the realm in Hell fit for every sinner: each soul is flung to its proper place, defined forever by the sin to which it gave its allegiance on earth.

P. 47, L. 31. *cyclone:* Those who subjected reason to the storm of passion now suffer that storm whether they will or no. Aquinas says that reason must direct the will by informing it of the good or evil of a choice. The sin of lust—like the other sins against temperance (gluttony, avarice, wrath, and sloth, punished below)—reverses that order. For example, Francesca (see line 103) assumes not only the will's primacy but its irresistibility. For such, reason halts behind, devising clever rationalizations to justify what has already been willed. In their willfulness these sinners once denied the freedom of the will. Now all freedom, even the physical freedom to stay in one place for more than a few moments, is taken away. Since the human body is worthier than is food or material wealth, immoderate enjoyment of its delights is less grave a sin than is gluttony or avarice; hence lust is punished on this upper ring.

P. 49, L. 58. *Semiramis:* legendary Assyrian queen notorious for her insatiable and bestial libido. She was the wife (some traditions also say the incestuous daughter) of King Ninus of Babylon. Dante paraphrases a line from Paulus Orosius' *History* (1.4): Semiramis decreed that all that was *libitum* (pleasurable) was to be considered *licitum* (licit)—as if moral law could follow upon a pun.

P. 49, LL. 63–67. *Cleopatra ... Tristan:* A list of noble men and women ruined by carnal desire. *Cleopatra,* princess of Egypt (69–30 B.C.), had three of the greatest men of Rome for her lovers: Julius Caesar, Pompey, and Marc

Antony. She slew herself after Antony lost the battle of Actium, for she did not wish the victor, Octavian (the future Augustus Caesar), to lead her in triumph through Rome. In the *Aeneid* (8.685–713) she is an exemplar of the lush, emasculating excess of the barbaric East. *Dido* is, in the *Aeneid*, the Phoenician woman whose husband, *Sychaeus*, was murdered by her own brother. Following the instructions of his ghost, Dido fled Phoenicia with a hoard of treasure and some loyal followers and landed in North Africa, where she founded Carthage. When Aeneas is shipwrecked on her coast, she takes him in, for she is a woman of piety who herself has known suffering. But when she falls in love with Aeneas, her piety fails. She breaks her vow to the dead Sychaeus that she would never marry again, and then slays herself when, telling her that the gods are compelling him to leave for Italy, Aeneas ends their affair. Before she dies she utters a curse of everlasting enmity between Carthage and Rome. *Helen of Troy* was the lovely queen of Sparta whose kidnapping by the Trojan Paris (a kidnapping not resisted by Helen) brought about the ten-year-long Trojan War. According to one tradition, *Achilles*, the greatest of the Greek warriors, did not die from an arrow in the heel. Rather, he fell in love with Polyxena, one of the daughters of King Priam of Troy, and she lured him into a trap: he entered the temple of Apollo, intending to betray the Greeks and turn Trojan, and Paris cut him down. *Paris*, one of Priam's fifty sons, was chosen as arbiter by the goddesses Hera, Athena, and Aphrodite, who were quarreling over which of them was the most beautiful. Paris allowed his judgment to be suborned, taking a bribe from Aphrodite, who promised him the loveliest woman in the world. Thus even before he sailed to Sparta and saw Helen, Paris had committed the sin for which he is here condemned. *Tristan* was the woodsman and knight of Celtic romance who fell in love with the Irish princess Iseult when he was sent to bring her back as the betrothed of his uncle King Mark of Cornwall. Later he left Cornwall for France, where he married Iseult of the White Hands, whom he finally abandoned to see the Cornish queen again. There in Cornwall he was slain by Mark.

P. 49, L. 71. *the courtly ladies and the knights of old:* Dante reconsiders the tradition of love poetry represented by the French troubadours and romance writers he so admired, and by the artists of the *dolce stil novo* (the "sweet new style") in Italy, of whom he himself was the most excellent. According to the literary code of courtly love, a knight must devote himself entirely to the service of a lady, inevitably a lady already married to someone else. This feature of the love poetry was reconcilable with Christian piety only in the form of chaste self-sacrifice. It is this sort of sublimated courtesy that flourishes in Dante's love for Beatrice. But the more common courtly lover in medieval literature was rather like Paris, Tristan, or Lancelot. There are dangers inherent in the sweetest poetry of love, if that poetry is not guided by virtue. Revisiting some of the work of his own youth, Dante gives us one of the damned, the gracious and noble lady Francesca, who will tell how reading the tale of Lancelot was the occasion for her eternal loss.

P. 51, L. 91. *Were He who rules the universe our friend:* Notice the subjunctive. The fact is, the courtly Francesca does not pray for Dante. The damned do not, cannot, pray for anyone. No love is possible in Hell: for charity itself is none other than friendship with God, as Aquinas says (*Summa theologiae* 2.2 . q. 23, art. 1). That fact surely forms part of the womanly Francesca's suffering. Then why suggest the prayer? Francesca's empty yet involuted attempt to win Dante's goodwill is of a piece with the rest of her speech. It is sweet, but it hides a self-justifying lie. The speaker is Francesca da Polenta; she is with her kinsman Paolo Malatesta. She had married the prince of Rimini, the crippled Gianciotto Malatesta, to settle a long feud between Ravenna and Rimini. But she fell in love with her noble and young brother-in-law Paolo, and the two of them, caught in flagrante delicto (as Guinevere and Lancelot almost are, in Chrétien's *Knight of the Cart*), were murdered by her husband. Report of the murder spread immediately; Dante was a young man when it happened.

P. 51, L. 100. *Love:* Dante himself had written a sonnet, "Love and the noble heart are both one thing" (*La vita nuova* 20), echoing the older poet Guido Guinizelli: "Love makes its dwelling in the noble heart / As a bird in the green leaves of the wood." Francesca's brilliant apostrophes to love show how deeply she longs to see love as an irresistible, amoral force—for in her own will she did not desire the freedom to resist it. Her sentiment is typical of the courtly love literature: "Love will not deny anything to the lover." That is rule twenty-six in Andreas Capellanus's *Treatise on Love;* but book 3 of the same treatise is a vigorous rejection of all sexual love not sanctioned by marriage.

P. 53, LL. 121–23. *There . . . misery:* Francesca paraphrases Boethius: "In the midst of adversity, the worst misfortune of all is to have once been happy" (*Consolation of Philosophy*, 2.p.4). Assuming that the Teacher she refers to is not Boethius but Virgil, we are reminded of the hopelessness of Virgil's condition in Limbo, compared with the happiness, earthly and shadowy though it was, that he enjoyed while alive. But Francesca, too, remembers: she remembers what it was to love. It is certain, theologically, that in Hell she cannot love, and that she and Paolo must forever be reminders of the everlasting harm they visited upon each other. Poetically, I am not so sure; perhaps a terrible ray of love yet flickers in their hearts.

P. 53, L. 128. *Lancelot:* Arthur's greatest knight, who in his affair with Queen Guinevere betrayed his friend and lord. For Chrétien de Troyes (*The Knight of the Cart*) and the unknown Cistercian monk who wrote the *Quest of the Holy Grail,* Lancelot is the naturally "gentle," or noble, man whose sins of love bring him to the edge of perdition.

P. 53, L. 137. *pander:* literally, Galahault, Guinevere's seneschal, who urged her to kiss her hesitant lover. In Italian the name came to refer to a go-between.

CANTO SIX

In this, the shortest of all the cantos of *The Divine Comedy,* critics have noted the unsettling reticence of the central figure, the glutton Ciacco. That silence may be by way of punishment for the disordered or false conviviality of his life in "the sweet world" above, yet it also suggests something about his own world now, where no love can dwell. In a remarkable little sonnet from his youth, Dante imagines that he and two of his poet friends are placed in a boat by a magician, with the ladies they love beside them, and what do they do all day while the fantastic boat guides itself but talk—talk about love. No such easy and blessed chat can be had in Hell, where talk so often is a means to torment and alienate. Terrible are the cries of anguish, "the wailing and gnashing of teeth," that stunned the ear of our pilgrim as he was about to enter the abyss. More terrible still are the silences below.

P. 55, L. 8. *cold:* We eat to keep our bodies warm and strong. The gluttons who abused that purpose will never be warm again: they are among the most sluggish and inactive souls in Hell. Ciacco, their representative in this canto, evidently finds even a short speech a tremendous effort. From that we can judge what longing he still feels for the greatest good thing he knew in life: his native land.

P. 55, L. 13. *Cerberus:* in mythology, the three-headed, serpent-tailed hound of Hades. In the *Aeneid* (6.417–23) he is the watchdog of the infernal regions. Here, as a semicanine symbol of mindless greed for food, he guards the circle of the gluttons, who are themselves described as dogs, drowning themselves in the pasty mess of taste and smell.

P. 55, L. 21. *desecrating wretches:* Italian *profani,* "profane." They have polluted their bodies, the temples of the Holy Spirit (1 Cor. 6:19), turning their bellies into gods. So Scripture condemns "Esau, who sold his birthright for a mess of pottage" (Heb. 12:16).

P. 59, L. 26. *mud:* In the *Aeneid,* Cerberus is placated by a honey cake. Dante has changed the feed to stinking mud, to tear the illusory veil from immoderate use of food and drink.

P. 59, L. 36. *emptiness:* The souls in Hell are quasisubstantial bodies (how that can be so, the poet Statius will explain to Dante in Purgatory; *Purg.* 25.31–108). Sometimes, for poetic effect or to underscore a theological point, Dante will focus instead upon their insubstantiality. To highlight the banality of this particular sin, Dante imagines a blurry confusion of souls mired in the everlasting slops.

P. 59, L. 52. *Ciacco:* a Florentine of Dante's youth; we are not sure who. One tradition says he was a convivial companion of the gentlemen at court, a mordant wit. His speech here is detached yet profoundly sad.

P. 61, L. 65. *the backwoods side:* Ciacco refers to the Blacks and the Whites, the two factions of the Guelphs (usually but by no means always a pro-papal party) ruling in Florence at the time. The Whites, followers of the Cerchi family, were merchants who had grown rich and had settled in Florence fairly recently; hence, they are from *the backwoods* and known for their rough manners. In 1301 they drove the Blacks, followers of the Donati family, out of the city. But by the machinations of Pope Boniface VIII and his delegate, Charles of Valois, the Blacks returned to power in 1302 and banished hundreds of the Whites, including Dante. For the next nineteen years until his death in 1321, Dante would never return to Florence.

Ciacco's prophecy is the first of many throughout the *Comedy.* Naturally, few readers now will care deeply about the fortunes of Blacks or Whites, Guelphs or Ghibellines. We should remember, however, that Dante's vision—the incarnational vision of Christianity—was never, and could never be, a vision that ignored the goodness of this very world that Christ entered to save. Florence is part of that world; then even Florence plays a part in the divine plan.

P. 61, L. 73. *Two men:* perhaps Dante and someone else; critics have ventured various suggestions. Dante is probably comparing Florence to Sodom, which God agreed to spare if but ten just men could be found in it (Gen. 18:23–33).

P. 61, L. 74. *Avarice, pride, and envy:* See 1.32 and note; also the rebuke of Florence by Brunetto Latini, 15.68.

P. 61, LL. 79–80. *Tegghiaio ... Mosca:* Florentine patriots, now damned. In many ways these men were admirable and had "merited well" from their city. They suggest a theme that Dante will develop in Paradise (*Par.* 15.97–148), that of

Florence's degeneracy from a noble, courtly past. *Farinata*, the moniker of Manente degli Uberti, was a chief of the Ghibelline (usually pro-imperial and anti-papal) party; we will meet him below in Canto Ten, in the circle of the heretics. *Tegghiaio Aldobrandi* and *Jacopo Rusticucci* are to be found in the circle of the Sodomites (Canto 16); in life they brokered peace between the Tuscan towns of Volterra and San Gimignano, and were important political leaders in Tuscany during the early thirteenth century. *Mosca dei Lamberti,* chief of Reggio d'Emilia, now dwells among the sowers of discord (Canto 28). The identity of *Arrigo* has not been certified.

P. 63, L. 95. *trump of doom:* the blast that summons up the resurrected dead for the Last Judgment. See Matt. 24:31, 1 Cor. 15:52, 1 Thess. 4:16.

P. 63, L. 111. *perfect:* Man's end is to dwell, body and soul, in the presence of God, enjoying the intellectual vision of the Deity (*Par.* 14.43–51). That is the Christian belief, expressed in the teleological language of Aristotelian philosophy as adapted by Thomas Aquinas. The souls of the damned will not attain that end. Yet since they will be reunited with their bodies, they will be more properly human then, and thus more keenly sensible of pain. And since the bodies they now possess are formed of circumambient air by the influence of the soul (*Purg.* 25.91–108), their resurrected bodies of flesh and bone will, naturally, feel what these bodies now feel, but with full corporeal vigor.

CANTO SEVEN

When Adam named the beasts, it was his privilege as man to do so, man made in the image and likeness of the god who had given him this creative and divine authority. It was but one part of his obeying the command "Fill the earth and subdue it." The beasts and the things of earth were to be tended by man and used for his profit, and even after the fall this remained true, though that profit would now include the eating of animal flesh. What makes men avaricious, then, is not love for the profitable things of this earth. Those things are good, and they merit an appropriate attention. In *Purgatory,* Dante will go so far as to misquote Virgil, asking, "Why do you, holy hunger after gold, / Not guide the appetites of mortal men?" (*Purg.* 22.40–41). But the avaricious man so loves these things that they become his idols, for as Christ says, "No man can love God and Mammon" (Matt. 6:24). That idolatry subjects our divine authority to mere earth, and in ignorance we fall before the dust of palaces and cathedrals. Hence the punishment in this canto removes all trace of our divine authority: the "nothing-knowing souls" have lost their own names, and the only thing that distinguishes some of them, to their shame, is the haircut that was supposed to have served as a sign of their submission to God.

P. 65, L. 1. *Pape Satan ... aleppe:* As is clear from this near gibberish, Plutus is a demon of shocking stupidity, and that befits the mindless nameless avaricious souls that inhabit this ring. His words are a sudden cry to Satan, perhaps even to Papa Satan, with *aleppe* suggesting aleph, the first letter of the Hebrew alphabet, and hence signifiying Plutus' god (for God calls himself "the Alpha and the Omega," Rev. 22:13). Plutus is enraged to see the living Dante treading through Hell; hence Virgil's rebuke.

P. 67, L. 22. *Charybdis:* in mythology, the name for a dangerous whirlpool in the straits between Italy and Sicily, where the waters of the Ionian and Tyrrhenian seas clash (see Virgil, *Aen.* 3.420–25; Ovid, *Met.* 7.62–65). Opposite Charybdis were the shipwrecking cliffs inhabited by the ravenous monster Scylla (*Met.* 13.898–14.74). The reference to Charybdis is apt, since Dante's conception of avarice is Aristotelian (see *Conv.* 4.17; Aristotle, *Ethics* 4.1): men must make proper use of the goods of the earth and avoid the opposed vices of greed and prodigality.

P. 69, L. 64. *For all the gold:* It was a commonplace in classical literature that our wants, not our needs, can grow insatiable. Dante's phrasing derives from Boethius: "If free-handed Plenty should dispense riches from her cornucopia as plentiful as the sands cast up by the storm-tossed sea, or as the stars that shine in heaven on clear nights, men still would not stop crying their miserable complaints" (*Cons.* 2.m.2).

P. 69, L. 78. *guide:* Fortune, conceived not as the capricious, even malevolent pagan goddess spinning her wheel (for that famous image, see Boethius, *Cons.* 2.p.1, adapted by Dante himself in *Conv.* 4.11.6) but as an agent of divine providence. Much has been said about the radical change Dante has made in the iconography of Fortune. It should be understood, however, that for Boethius, to mistake an earthly and partial good for one's ultimate and complete good, which can be found only in God and which indeed is God, is to experience as blind Fortune what the virtuous experience as the working out of divine providence. Fundamentally, then, Boethius and Dante agree.

P. 73, L. 121. *Sullen:* These souls gave their hearts not to explosions of anger but to acedia, one of the seven deadly sins and somewhat misleadingly translated as "sloth." The sin is not physical but spiritual torpor, a willful inability to take delight in what is meant for our pleasure or—intriguingly— an inability to grow angry at what should legitimately arouse anger. Thomas

Aquinas (see Appendix C) aptly calls acedia the sin against the Sabbath—the sin against festivity itself. That notion may have motivated Dante's choice of words here: the sullen gargle a *hymn* of futility.

CANTO EIGHT

Children love justice because they are innocent, said Chesterton, while adults are sinners and therefore prefer mercy. Without sentimentalizing what was often a brutal age—as Dante's own parade of malefactors gives witness—there is a sense in which his day, compared with ours, enjoyed a keener hunger for justice and greater confidence that right was right and wrong was wrong. Justice is a characteristic of God and thus ought to be hungered for; and since we are creatures of body and soul, made up of all manner of passions, that hunger for justice will be no cool, detached, intellectualized assent to this or that proposition, but a full-bodied hunger, stirring all the flame of true anger. Thus when Dante says of Filippo Argenti in this canto, "I've got a hankering to see them dunk that spirit in this swill," the language is so full of gusto that he inspires that hankering in the reader, too. And that desire will be fierce indeed, but not cruel, so long as the reader is still innocent enough to feel the pleasure of seeing things set right.

P. 75, L. 19. *Phlegyas:* In mythology, Phlegyas, son of the war god, Ares, set fire to the oracle at Delphi to avenge himself against Apollo, who had seduced his daughter. In Virgil, he shouts a warning to all, that they learn justice and fear the gods (*Aen.* 6.618–20).

P. 79, L. 30. *other souls:* which others, Dante does not say. We have already heard that the soul is flung below as soon as it is judged by Minos (5.15), but perhaps that flinging can be figurative, and many souls do assume that those traveling through their circles are descending until they reach their adjudged place (see 28.43–45).

P. 79, L. 32. *a spirit:* Filippo Argenti, a member of the Black party, whose family, the Adimari, profited from the goods confiscated when Dante was exiled. Boccaccio said that he was called Argenti because he had his horse shod with silver (Italian *argento*), and that he was prone to fits of anger at the slightest provocation.

P. 79, L. 44. *Indignant soul:* Virgil's warm praise is roused by the warmth of Dante's righteous anger. For Dante, wrath is the sinful surrendering of one's entire being to what is essentially a good and necessary faculty of the soul. In that way it is intemperate, just as are lust, gluttony, and avarice—sins that also involve the disordered or idolatrous use of a created good.

Dante's quick anger is the proper response to a spirit as brusquely obnoxious as Argenti, who is infuriated at having been recognized, to the spoiling of his reputation on earth. Had Dante failed to respond so, he might justly be taxed with sluggishness of soul—exactly the sin punished *under* the Stygian swamp. Virgil's exclamation daringly adapts that of the woman in the gospels who praised Jesus: "Blessed is the womb that bore thee" (Lk. 11:27).

P. 81, L. 68. *Dis:* one of the names of Hades (Pluto), god of the underworld, and like the name Hades, sometimes used to designate the place, or the "city," itself (see Virgil, *Aen.* 6.127; Ovid, *Met.* 4.438). The city of Dis is the infernal counterpart of the new Jerusalem, the City of Peace, the heavenly City of God (Rev. 21:2). Dis houses the most depraved of sinners, as Virgil explains (11.79–90), and is conceived as a medieval citadel, with the sinners swallowed up in separate moats. Its turrets are the minarets of mosques, those edifices sacred to medieval Christendom's fiercest and most determined enemy, Islam.

P. 81, L. 91. *his mad way:* The demons, seeking to inspire despair, echo Dante's own fear (2.34–35).

P. 83, L. 98. *seven times and more:* The language is formal and biblical; see Eccl. 11.2.

P. 83, L. 115. *adversaries:* punning again on Hebrew *satan,* "adversary."

P. 83, L. 125. *a less secret gate:* Virgil refers to Christ's harrowing of Hell, popularly conceived in the Middle Ages as his commanding the gates of Hell to be opened, against the flimsy and foolish resistance of the devils. Says a traditional prayer during the service of the Easter Vigil: "Today our Savior has burst at once the bars and gates of death." See Ps. 107:16: "For he hath broken the gates of brass, and cut the bars of iron in sunder."

CANTO NINE

It is a strange paradox that the prince of this world is powerless; stranger still that the most powerless creature of all is prince of this world. As Dante and Virgil wait for the messenger from Heaven who will overcome the recalcitrance of the devils within and open the gates of Dis, they experience both the tremendous power and the utter impotence of evil. Dante, we must understand, is in real danger. When Virgil covers his charge's face with his hands lest he see the Gorgon and be turned to stone, we must not think it idle. Dante himself, with great solemnity, pauses in the narrative to address the reader: "O you whose intellects see clear and whole, gaze on the doctrine that is hidden here beneath the unfamiliar verses' veil." Whatever the danger is (despair?), we are to remember that its approach to Dante might well cause the loss of his eternal soul. For providence requires us to use our will and our wits. Yet from the eternal vantage, not only is evil weak, but it has already failed utterly, and in hopeless ignorance and incorrigibility it continues to fail utterly. Virgil—whose reason here struggles at the threshold of faith—knows that matters have been decided and that Dante will come through safely, and sure enough we see the messenger of God open the gates with the most effortless amen.

P. 89, L. 23. *Erichtho:* In Lucan (*Phars.* 6.508–830) the hideous witch Erichtho animates a mangled corpse with a soul dragged from the dead, to predict Pompey's defeat at Pharsalia. Her using Virgil to summon a soul punished at the bottom of Hell, *Judas' ring,* explains how Virgil can know the terrain.

P. 89, L. 38. *Furies:* in Greek mythology, hideous underworld goddesses who drove particularly heinous sinners mad with remorse. Dante found them portrayed in the *Aeneid* (6.570–72, 7.324–29, 12.845–48). Below, Dante uses their Greek name, *Erinyes.* Their individual names are also traditional; *Alecto,* for one, plays an instigating role in the *Aeneid.*

P. 91, L. 52. *Medusa:* in mythology, the youngest of the three Gorgons. The sight of Medusa's face, with its serpent locks, would turn the beholder to stone. She was slain by Perseus, yet even after her head was cut off, it retained its petrifying power (see Ovid, *Met.* 4.739–45).

P. 91, L. 63. *the unfamiliar verses' veil:* Dante suspends his narrative to ask the reader to consider the allegorical, or supraliteral, import of this scene (he will do so again at *Purg.* 8.19–21). Scripture, according to Augustine, possesses as many as four levels of meaning. Dante himself, in a famous letter to his friend and patron Cangrande della Scala, explaining that his own poem must be read by a similar method, showed how the four levels could be divined from a single biblical verse, *"In exitu Israel de Aegypto"* ("When Israel went out of Egypt," Ps. 114:1; Dante uses the verse in *Purg.* 2.46): "If we inspect the letter alone the departure of the children of Israel from Egypt in the time of Moses is presented to us; if the allegory, our redemption wrought by Christ; if the moral sense, the conversion of the soul from the grief and misery of sin to the state of grace is presented to us; if the anagogical [that is, having to do with eternal destiny], the departure of the holy soul from the slavery of this corruption to the liberty of eternal glory." But in this chilling moment Dante counsels against faintness of heart. The petrifying danger is despair, thought by many of the fathers to be the unforgivable "sin against the Holy Spirit" alluded to by Christ (Matt. 12:31–37). In fact, from the moroseness of the sullen we move to the tense silence of waiting that characterizes this canto. However terrible it may be to travel through Hell, it is worse to stand still there.

P. 93, L. 89. *little wand:* The scene is a reprise of Christ's harrowing of Hell. The gates simply open, by the will of God.

P. 93, L. 97. *butt your heads at fate:* Fate, literally "what has been spoken," here implies providential design. The question echoes Christ's reproach of the recalcitrant Saul: "It is hard for thee to kick against the goad" (Acts 26:14).

P. 93, L. 98. *Cerberus did so:* When the Fates sent Hercules down into Hades, he put an iron collar and chain around Cerberus' neck and dragged him out (see *Aen.* 6.395–96).

P. 93, L. 112. *Arles:* Dante refers to a large ancient Roman cemetery at Arles, near the mouth of the Rhône, in Provence. According to legend it was the burial ground for the Christians in Charlemagne's army who had died fighting the Saracens in Spain. Their bodies were miraculously transported there from across the Pyrenees. Another large necropolis lay near *Pola,* a city across the Adriatic from northeastern Italy.

CANTO TEN

With manly directness and gravity of purpose, Farinata rises in his tomb to learn from Dante the hard fortune of his city and his family. His sudden appearance and his decisive words—including his final dismissal, "About the rest I have no more to say"—portray him as one for whom any frivolity, any foolish vanity or softness, would be an offense. Dante, kindred spirit, holds his own; and we might note that as Farinata suffers, so Dante writes, sensing that authority, like the deepest suffering, better expresses itself in few words than in many. For in this strange canto of clipped speeches and interruptions we look with awe upon the unbending Farinata, and at best with pity upon the weeping Cavalcante, who, misunderstanding Dante's words, speaks too much and feels too freely to be corrected. In portraying the grief of Farinata in a single stroke or two—"He shook his head a little, with a sigh"—Dante shows at once what it is to be the consummate artist and the consummate man. In this he has learned well from his master Virgil, whose Aeneas thus describes, tersely and bravely, the grief he has endured: "Hard work and manhood learn from me, my son; / good fortune you can learn from someone else" (*Aen.* 12.435–36).

P. 97, L. 11. *Jehosophat:* the biblical site of the resurrection of the dead and the Last Judgment: "I will gather together all nations, and will bring them down into the Valley of Josaphat" (Joel 3:2). This canto fittingly begins and ends with reference to that day of doom, for the only heretics Dante attends to are those who deny the immortality of the soul. Such heretics are more culpable than are those who distort divine revelation, since the soul's immortality, according to the scholastic theologians, is discoverable by unaided reason. Those who believed in death—and the two heretics we meet possessed prodigious intellects—are made to witness their own ignorance, dwelling in graves eternally. It is as if their doctrine were death to the mind. For these souls the most poignant thing about the Last Judgment is that there will be a judgment at all.

P. 97, L. 14. *Epicurus:* the ancient philosopher (340–271 B.C.), known to Dante through his condemnation by the Church Fathers. Epicurus held that all things in the universe were made of atoms and empty space, and that even the soul, being corporeal, would decay and die. (It is not clear why Democritus, Epicurus' predecessor in atomism, is allowed a place in Limbo; perhaps Dante did not know that Democritus also believed in the death of the soul.) Though Epicurus himself lived simply, even austerely, and considered the pleasures of the body as slight compared with the pleasures of the mind, he was unfortunate in some of his disciples, and his name quickly became associated with hedonistic excess: "For he was Epicurus owene sonne," says Chaucer of the food-loving Franklin. Impressively enough, Dante does not follow the popular slander (in *Conv.* 4.6 he states, quite fairly, the Greek's view of pleasure). Dante's Epicureans are his own contemporaries, especially the Ghibellines, whose politics or intellectual enterprises might suggest that they founded all their hopes on this world alone; and it is that sort of Epicureanism which medieval commentators complained about when they said that this heresy was rampant in Florence. It was a philosophy that could appeal not to the slack libertine but to those fearless men who were too proud to stoop to the common faith.

P. 101, L. 27. *I may have punished once too bitterly:* The speaker is Manente degli Uberti (?1203–64), called Farinata, a Ghibelline leader in Florence during the civil strife of the thirteenth century. His party ousted the Guelphs in 1248, only to see them return in 1251 after the death of the emperor Frederick II—another Epicurean punished in this circle. Following seven years of conflict, his family and the other leading Ghibelline families were exiled from the city. Their desire to avenge themselves led to the battle of Montaperti in 1260. There, with the vile assistance of the Guelph traitor Bocca degli Abati (see 32.79–111), the Ghibellines slaughtered the Guelphs.

Shortly afterward, the heads of the families met at Empoli, prepared to raze Florence to the ground. Farinata resisted them, proudly and openly, and they yielded to his counsel. In 1264, a few years after Farinata's death, the Florentine Guelphs reversed their fortunes for good at the battle of Benevento, and once more banished the Uberti. As for Farinata's heresy, our direct evidence is his posthumous exhumation and excommunication in 1283, but that may have been politically motivated—for in addition, the goods of his sons and grandsons were seized. But it seems unlikely that Dante would draw this impressive figure entirely other than as those who knew him remembered him to be. And to say that the charge of heresy had to do with politics is, perhaps, not to say much, since the men of Dante's day did not distinguish clearly between those who opposed the doctrines preserved by the vicar of Christ and those who set themselves against that vicar's legitimate rule. Be that as it may, Dante, a Guelph, came to sympathize with the Ghibelline suspicion of papal encroachment into the temporal affairs of the empire. Like Virgil, Farinata is presented as a *magnanimo* of a notably Roman sort: grave, senatorial, fiercely loyal, almost impassive. His valorous deeds and his crimes never bore the taint of pettiness. Dante addresses him with the deferential pronoun *voi*.

P. 101, L. 42. *your family:* Even in death, Farinata is defined by the familial and the political. That is not to condemn him, exactly. Love of family, love of native city, and love of fatherland are commanded by God under the general admonition "Honor thy father and thy mother" and take their worthy places in the symphony of love that animates the universe. In Paradise, Dante will be allowed to rejoice in his ancestry and in the courtly past of his native city when he meets his great-souled ancestor Cacciaguida (*Par.* 15–17). But Cacciaguida was a Crusader: and Farinata, having denied the life of this life, effectively made his family and his party into his gods.

P. 101, L. 53. *a shadow:* Cavalcante de' Cavalcanti, a Guelph and the father of Dante's friend and fellow poet Guido Cavalcanti (1250–1300). He is placed here with Farinata because they were parties to the same conflict and because, in order to resolve the differences between their families, Cavalcanti's son Guido married Farinata's daughter Beatrice. Their sharing one tomb must be a peculiar source of displeasure for each. Indeed, Farinata does not deign once to refer to his in-law. Ancient sources, not all dependent upon Dante, portray Cavalcanti as a follower of Epicurus (that rumor is also broached by Boccaccio, *Decameron* 6.9, whose anecdote treats the old man with great reverence and leaves the matter of his heresy undecided). Cavalcanti, like Farinata, is absorbed in the fortunes of his family; in Cavalcanti's case it is not patriotism but a doting father's pride in his son's genius and fame.

P. 103, L. 60. *where is my son:* The second interruption in this solemn canto is a dramatic cry of futile affection. Guido Cavalcanti, "the glory of the Latin tongue" (*Purg.* 11.98), wrote love poetry whose philosophy seems to assert the doctrine of determinism taught by the Muslim philosopher Averroes (see 4.144 and note). Guido suggests that love is irresistible, and that our individual intellects are mere movements in the Agent Intellect that governs the cosmos. Averroism denies both free will and the individual nature of the soul's immortality—the soul merely participates in the all-absorbing immortality of the Agent Intellect. Hence it is fitting that Guido should be recalled in this scene, yet with judgment suspended. Writing years after Guido's death in August 1300 (a few months later than the purported time of this journey to the underworld), Dante still must have held out hope that his brilliant and earnest friend at last found the truth for which he had searched in vain. Guido's mistaken scorn of *one,* as I take it, cannot be the scorn of Virgil (what true Italian poet could do that?) or of reason (in that case Averroes would fall under the same condemnation) or of God (the charge of blasphemy seems out of place here). Rather, it is Beatrice herself he may have scorned, in her allegorical role as theology—the study of divine revelation; and therefore his error would be Dante's own, the error that led Dante into the dark wilderness and thus became the occasion for the journey.

Why is the father so anxious? Since we have learned, from Charon and Ciacco, that the souls can see into the future, we can gather that Cavalcanti knows that in a few years his son will no longer be beholding *the sweet sunlight.* Yet he does not know Guido's state in the present. The father's confusion strikes Dante as odd, and raises a doubt that Farinata will resolve, below. Whether Guido is alive or dead, Cavalcanti's question is strange, and his solicitousness, though emotionally coherent and powerful, is illogical. Now that he knows—he is in Hell—that the soul is immortal, why would the loving father care so much whether his son still dwells on earth? Souls in Purgatory pray unceasingly for those they have left behind; they pray for their salvation, not necessarily for their continued stay on earth. And why would Cavalcanti rejoice to see his son where *he* is now? It never occurs to him that Dante might be a sinner nearly lost. The father assumes that all human worth is a matter of human genius: grace plays no role at all. His own sentence proves otherwise.

P. 103, L. 76. *But went on speaking:* Notice that Farinata does not show the slightest emotion at the mention of his own son-in-law Guido. This gravity bespeaks a man of intense passions and iron will. When he does sigh, later, we must conclude that he is troubled to the depths of his being.

P. 103, L. 81. *before you find how hard that is to learn:* Farinata refers to the exile of Dante and his fellow Whites, an exile that for our poet became permanent in 1304. The Uberti will never return to the city, and neither will Dante. Poet and warrior, of opposing parties, are united now by their city's ingratitude.

P. 103, L. 86. *blushed the river Arbia red with blood:* the river near Montaperti, where the Guelphs were slaughtered in 1260. According to contemporary accounts, Dante's description of the river is no exaggeration.

P. 103, L. 93. *her sole defender:* Farinata does not apologize for what he did; he took the actions he thought were necessary. It pains him that his decision has meant banishment for his family, since he did love Florence. Here he acknowledges, as before, that he may have punished his city too bitterly. Yet he asserts, with just pride, that he alone of all the Ghibelline leaders defended Florence when everyone was prepared to destroy her. Apparently Florence has forgotten that. But Dante the Guelph responds with a gracious prayer for peace for the Uberti family.

P. 105, L. 98. *what time will bring:* Now Dante asks the question that has troubled him. Farinata answers, revealing one of the laws governing knowledge in Hell: the souls can see a great part of the future but lapse into oblivion when events draw near. It is an ironic reversal of how men on earth know: we see clearly what is before us now, and perceive but dimly what is to come. Moreover, we are made for hope, for an eternal flourishing of knowledge, for the vision of Truth that fulfills our love: "We see now through a mirror in an obscure manner, but then face to face. Now I know in part, but then I shall know even as I have been known. So there abide faith, hope and charity, these three; but the greatest of these is charity" (1 Cor. 13:12–13). But the damned suffer a containment and constriction, and to use the words of Christ, "from him who does not have, even that which he thinks he has shall be taken away" (Lk. 8:18). With terrible sadness this punishment of the mind is revealed by the heretic, who suffers the greatest loss from it.

P. 105, L. 119. *Frederick the Second and the Cardinal:* Frederick II, Holy Roman Emperor from 1212 to 1250, called Stupor Mundi, or Wonder of the World, for his intellectual accomplishments and for the high and noble culture of his court. He is reported to have boasted that he could use the

Scriptures themselves to prove the soul's mortality. His relationships to a series of popes, especially the great Innocent III, were tempestuous, and he was excommunicated twice. This Epicurean of the empire is linked, fittingly, with an Epicurean of the Church, Cardinal Ottaviano degli Ubaldini, bishop of Bologna from 1244 to 1273 and uncle of the archbishop Ruggieri to be found deep in Hell below (33.14). The Cardinal, as he was simply known, fought for the pope against Frederick, though in general he opposed the anti-imperial Guelphs. He is reported to have said, "If there is a soul, I've lost it for the Ghibelline party."

CANTO ELEVEN

Will there be organization in Hell? It could not be Hell without it. The logic is inexorable: Hell was created by God, and all things created by God are good. Therefore Hell is good, and since it was made by the supreme Artist, it must possess its appropriate order, the order of justice. What that order is, Virgil explains at length, revealing what must strike the first-time reader as a surprising variety of sinners below, all categorized and subcategorized as if in a medieval compendium of evil. So far we have followed, roughly, the seven deadly sins on our way down into Hell: lust, gluttony, avarice, wrath, and, as I interpret the sullen of Canto Eight, sloth. Now, when it is time to touch upon the great spiritual sins of envy and pride, Dante turns rather to bestiality and malice, in all their ramifying abjectness. Of course, envy and pride (and wrath, too) are the seeds of these most wicked sins, as Dante will show. Thus one categorizing of sins is embedded within the other, and within each category of sin there is ordering, too, for neither God nor Dante is the author of confusion.

P. 109, L. 8. *Pope Anastasius:* Anastasius II, pope from 496 to 498. Actually, Anastasius was no preacher of heresy but too great a lover of concord. He sent delegates to Constantinople to try to reach some understanding with the newly risen Monophysites. Opposing themselves to the Arian heretics, who preached that Jesus was not truly divine, the Monophysites insisted that Christ possessed a single nature that fused the human and the divine. Unfortunately, that meant Christ was truly neither. Anastasius invited the Monophysite deacon Photinus to see him, in an attempt to sway the leader of the sect, Acacius, and to lead him back into union with the Church. Anastasius is mentioned last among the heretics because, as Dante saw it (taking his history from the *Decretals* of pseudo-Gratian, 1.19.9, which said that Anastasius was stricken by God for having given communion to Photinus), his sin is the most reprehensible of all, his charge as pope having been to safeguard the truth. It is possible, however, that Dante is confusing Pope Anastasius with Emperor Anastasius (who ruled 491–518), whom in fact Photinus did persuade.

P. 109, L. 22. *malice:* Italian *malizia,* a term from moral philosophy. Here it denotes not the improper love of something good but the deliberate love of something evil. This malice can turn men into ferocious beasts, or it can, in the case of fraud, corrupt the intelligence that distinguishes man from beast. Since man's end is the good of the intellect, Dante reasons that fraud is a greater evil than violence, afflicting man at the core of that for which he was made. Note that malice is not hate per se, although love of evil implies hatred of the good. God himself justly hates evil: "Thou hatest all who do wickedly" (Ps. 5:6). The intellectual sin of heresy—a twisted misapprehension of the truth—stands fittingly between misuse of the good and love of the evil.

P. 111, L. 25. *fraud's an evil owned by man alone:* Beasts can use violence, but only man can deceive, perverting his most divine faculty. Cicero agreed, saying that fraud merited greater loathing (*On Duties* 1.13).

P. 111, L. 47. *denying it in one's heart:* "The fool says in his heart, 'There is no God'" (Ps. 14:1). Saint Augustine glossed this psalm by insisting that the fool was committing blasphemy rather than expressing a sincere belief, since the existence of God is manifest to all men who do not wish to cloak their evil.

P. 113, L. 80. *Ethics:* Aristotle's *Nicomachean Ethics* 7.1, which Dante had studied closely. Of the three evil propensities, incontinence—the immoderate use of things that are good by nature, such as food and drink, sex and wealth—does not have injustice as its conscious end. Malice does. Malice is divided here into two categories, the malice that is proper to men (fraud) and the malice or *deranged bestiality* that turns men into beasts (violence).

P. 115, L. 109. *the usurer takes a different path:* The usurer does not reap the fruits of his own labor, as God commands (Gen. 2:15, 3:19; 2 Thess. 3:8), but takes advantage of the sweat of other men's brows, using money itself to make more money, in a kind of unnatural financial procreation. Dante seems to condemn all brokerage, whereas his master Aquinas admitted that, as all goods command a just price, so could the use of money.

CANTO TWELVE

Violence is about the only sin that modern man still recognizes, and fitfully at that. That is because sin, which is to trespass upon the rights of God, has collapsed into coercion, which is to trespass upon the rights of the almighty individual will. We must strain to consider it violent if two men freely decide to kill each other, and we are on the verge of forgetting how to formulate any sort of argument against suicide. But for Dante, as for most philosophers, religious teachers, and poets before him and after him, the wickedness of violence is seen less in what it does to others than in what it does to the violent, not as a consequence but in the very act. To kill, rape, maim, and pillage is to be as heartless and ferocious as a tiger. It is unworthy of man. For the Christian, it violates the rights of God (as all sin does), for it turns the created world into an arena of destruction.

P. 117, L. 12. *the infamy of Crete:* The Minotaur (Ovid, *Met.* 8.152–82) is a fit symbol for the bestiality of violence, conceived as he was by the queen of Crete, Pasiphae, who had concealed herself within a wooden cow that she might be mounted by a certain bull, the object of her unnatural desires. The Minotaur was set in a palace labyrinth by King Minos, who sacrificed seven Athenian lads and seven Athenian maidens to its appetite every year, as Athens' tribute to Crete. But Theseus, duke of Athens, aided by a *clue,* or ball of yarn, given to him by the loving princess Ariadne, esaped the labyrinth and slew the Minotaur. Dante imagines him as a bull with the head of a man, rather like the centaurs to follow, and not as a man with the head of a bull, as was pictured by the ancients. Dante's creature seems the more ferocious.

P. 119, L. 41. *love:* Dante refers to the doctrine of Empedocles, the Sicilian philosopher (see 4.137) who believed that the cosmos was born when chaos, a confused mass of all the matter in the world, was energized by Strife and separated itself into its distinct components. Love would recombine these things into the same original chaos. In Dante's vision here, it is as if even the soil of Hell trembles with passion when it is pressed by the feet of its Maker, Christ. Consequently, many of the walls and bridges of Hell have fallen to ruin (5.34, 21.107, 23.136). The earthquake Dante refers to occurred at the time of Christ's death (Matt. 27:51).

P. 121, L. 56. *centaurs:* Again Dante's imagery stresses the bestiality of violence, for the centaurs, half human, half equine, gallop about like beasts on the hunt for beastlike men. Note that the centaurs speak but the men do not: the centaurs, with their twin natures, had more excuse for their violence than had the men.

P. 121, L. 65. *Chiron:* the tutor of Achilles, to whom he taught not only warfare but music, astronomy, and other noble arts. In Statius' *Achilleid,* Chiron is a noble and wise old teacher, whose gravity contrasts with the recklessness of other centaurs. Dante preserves much of that portrayal here.

P. 121, L. 67. *Nessus:* a centaur who fell in love with Hercules' wife, *Deianira.* He ferried her on his back across the river Evenus and then tried to gallop off with her. After Hercules wounded him mortally with a poisoned arrow, Nessus avenged himself by giving Deianira his robe, soaked with his own poisoned blood, saying that she should give it to Hercules as a charm if ever she felt that his love for her was flagging. When Deianira suspected (correctly) that Hercules had fallen in love with the girl Iole, she gave him the shirt, and he died in a frenzy of pain and madness (Ovid, *Met.* 9.101–272).

P. 121, L. 72. *Pholus:* one of the centaurs whose drunken lust and rage reduced the wedding feast of Pirithous and Hippodamia to carnage (the story is told in Ovid, *Met.* 12.210–535). The brawl between the centaurs and the Lapiths (the clan attending the feast), sculpted in relief on the pediment of the Parthenon, is the classical exemplum of the struggle between reason and appetite.

P. 123, L. 107. *Alexander:* probably Alexander the Great (356–23 B.C.), possibly the Thessalian Alexander of Phares, proverbial for his cruelty (see Cicero, *On Duties* 2.7.25). Of the Macedonian, the ancient Christian historian Paulus Orosius said that he slew all his relatives and neighbors before embarking on his war against Persia (*History* 3.16). Lucan called him "a thief and spoiler of peoples" (*Phars.* 10.28–36).

P. 123, L. 107. *Dionysius:* the famous tyrant of Syracuse, who ruled from 405 to 367 B.C.

P. 123, L. 110. *Azzolino:* Ghibelline ruler (1223–59) of the Marca Trevigiana in northern Italy, popularly called a son of Satan. The Guelphs said that Azzolino blinded his enemies and seized their property, at one time burning to death eleven thousand citizens of Padua.

P. 123, L. 111. *Obizzo:* or Opizzo II d'Este, of Ferrara, slain by his son Azzo VIII, as rumor had it. Dante calls Azzo a *figliastro,* denoting either an unnatural or an illegitimate son. The word *bastard* should cover both possibilities. Dante can hardly believe what he hears, but Virgil's words assure him that Nessus is telling the truth.

P. 123, L. 119. *That spirit:* Guy de Montfort. His father, Simon, had been slain in a rebellion against the English king Henry III. Guy avenged the death by murdering Prince Henry, the late king's nephew, in a church (*the lap of God*) in the Tuscan town of Viterbo. The prince's body was removed to England.

Dante's contemporaries say that the heart was preserved in a golden chalice, where it became a devotional relic.

P. 125, L. 134. *Attila the Hun:* the infamous nomadic chieftain (r. 433–53) whose marauding in the West earned him the name Scourge of God.

P. 125, L. 135. *Pyrrhus:* possibly the brutal son of Achilles, who slew Priam of Troy on the altar in the king's palace (Virgil, *Aen.* 2.526–58); possibly also Pyrrhus of Epirus (319–272 B.C.), who waged war against the Romans in southern Italy; he was a tyrant to foe and subject alike.

P. 125, L. 135. *Sextus:* Sextus Pompeius, son of Pompey the Great. His piracy was put down by Octavian and Antony (see Lucan, *Phars.* 6.420–22).

P. 125, L. 137. *Rinier Pazzo and Rinier Corneto:* more marauders. The latter was a highwayman in the Maremma, at that time a dismal swampland in western Tuscany; the former, a Ghibelline excommunicated by Clement IV in 1268 for attacking and slaying a bishop and most of the clergymen in his entourage.

CANTO THIRTEEN

"Eat of the fruit of this tree," said the serpent, "and ye shall be as gods." Somewhere in every sin, no matter how small, this first of sins is repeated. I am a creature, but I wish to be the Creator. Specifically, I wish to be my own creator, creature and creator both, dividing myself from myself and disposing with myself as I see fit. In our canto here, it is the practical atheism of the suicide. I wish to pretend—in order to justify its destruction—that I have created a life that I have manifestly not created. And let us understand that for Dante the fact that one is a creature has to do not only with one's origins but with one's present being and one's destiny. For God does not create in vain. All things that are made, notes Aristotle, are made with an end, a purpose—they are made *for* something. Now if, as Dante believed, God is the Creator, then all things, including human bodies, were made by God and endowed with their generic forms and features that they might be precisely those sorts of things, serving certain purposes, just as a carpenter might fashion a stool with three legs so that someone would be able to sit on it without falling over. God, says Scripture, is the Potter—and we know what that makes us. Pride whispers otherwise.

P. 127, L. 8. *between Corneto and Cecina:* the Maremma flatlands in western Tuscany, a dense expanse of stunted trees and thickets, inhabited by wild animals.

P. 131, L. 33. *Why do you hack at me:* The souls of the suicides are touchingly solicitous for their unnatural, immobile "bodies." That is fit punishment for their having murdered their own. The motif of the bleeding tree comes to Dante through Virgil (*Aen.* 3.22–48). When, having disembarked on the coast of Thrace, Aeneas tried to uproot a shrub for kindling, he discovered blood welling up from the ground—the blood of Polydorus, one of the sons of Priam, now buried beneath the shrub. Polydorus tells Aeneas how he was treacherously murdered by the king of Thrace, Polymnestor, after he had been sent to Thrace by Priam to ask for aid. He advises Aeneas to flee that place of impiety, and asks for a proper burial. Dante's suicides, however, combine in one both Trojan prince and Thracian king: the impiety of the murderer and the grief and unfulfilled longing for justice of the murdered.

The speaker is Pier della Vigna (1190?–1249), one of the finest poets of the Sicilian school—those who had adopted the rhetorical and stylistic traditions of the most polished of the French troubadours. Pier was a trusted minister at the court of Frederick II from 1230 to the year of his death. As he says, for a few years he was indeed Frederick's closest counselor—his secretary, if you will, the safeguarder of his secrets. But his enemies began to accuse him of being richer than the emperor himself, and framed him in what was made to look like a plot against his king. He was arrested in 1247 and had his eyes put out. Shortly afterward, in prison, he killed himself, dashing his brains against a wall. Dante condemns him for the crime even as he vigorously asserts that the old poet, victim of the same envy that has set Florence in such turmoil, never did betray his lord.

Pier's stylized speech befits a graceful courtier and man of letters, and echoes the style of his own poetry. It also suggests, in its high artifice, the fundamental illogic and falsity of suicide, which violates the instinct of any living thing to preserve itself. What is most true about Pier is still his warm loyalty to Frederick, as is reflected in his direct style when he speaks about that. For then he is seen as more than a courtier and a poet—he is a man.

P. 133, L. 59. *who held the keys:* quoting Is. 22:22: "And I will lay the key of the house of David upon his shoulder; and he shall open, and none shall shut; and he shall shut, and none shall open."

P. 133, L. 66. *death for all mankind:* "By the envy of the devil, death came into the world" (Wis. 2:24).

P. 133, L. 72. *just, unjust:* The juxtaposition reveals the self-contradiction of suicide, as does the strained phrase *me against myself* (Italian *me contra me*) and the curious conflict of Pier's noble and bitterly righteous scorn with the envious scorn of his enemies.

P. 135, L. 98. *Wherever Fortune's crossbow slings it:* The souls are flung carelessly away, as those persons once flung away their bodies. The wild, tough growth of the trees is a proper punishment for them: they are animals, living beings created to move about and sense the world around them, but now they are imprisoned in plants—rational souls united with vegetative souls, as it were, without the animal soul to make sense out of the union. They, too, says Pier, will be reunited with their bodies on the last day, as will every soul, but for them this reunion will be a peculiar source of pain and longing and regret. For they will not quite be reunited. Their bodies will be slung over the thorny branches of the trees, a testament to the unnaturalness of the soul's dividing itself from the body to which it belongs. Says Saint Paul: "For no one ever hated his own flesh; on the contrary he nourishes and cherishes it, as Christ also does the Church" (Eph. 5:29).

P. 135, L. 118. *Run quickly, quickly, death:* The speaker is probably one Lano da Squarcia of Siena. He belonged to the Squanderers' Brigade (see 29.125 and note). Reduced to poverty in life, he sought death; now he seeks death forever, in vain. The other soul is Jacopo da Sant' Andrea, assassinated in 1239. Many anecdotes tell of his nihilistic self-destructiveness. According to one story, he amused his companions while crossing the Po River by throwing gold coins overboard, one after the other. Also he was said to have stuffed one of his houses with his own goods and set fire to it, because he wanted his guests to behold something really magnificent.

P. 137, L. 143. *My city changed its patron:* Through the words of the anonymous Florentine suicide, Dante decries his city's loss of courtly valor and the emergence of a mercantile society whose main engine is greed. The last remains of a statue upon the Ponte Vecchio—the Old Bridge over the Arno—washed away in a flood in 1333. It was thought to have been part of a statue of the war god, Mars.

CANTO FOURTEEN

There is no circle of Hell for those who speak Anglo-Saxon, not even when the words are of that short quaint variety heard alongside docks and quarries. Obscenity and blasphemy are not the same. Still, they do both assume what is clean, untouchable, forbidden, set apart—all meanings of the Latin *sanctus,* "holy." Now God is holy, and that means more than that he is good. It means that, like Moses before the burning bush, men must take the sandals from their feet as they stand before him. The holy bursts the bounds of what men can know and appropriate; it is an attribute of the terrible mystery of God. Like the strewer of obscenities, the blasphemer lays hands upon a holiness not his own and treads it beneath his feet. Yet in a way, obscenity, precisely because of its acknowledged filth, pays indirect homage to the forbiddenness and holiness of what it sullies. Blasphemy pays no such homage.

P. 139, L. 4. *Already faint:* The suicides can express themselves only through open, running wounds.

P. 139, L. 8. *flat moor:* The sulfurous flats under the rain of fire recall God's punishment of Sodom for its unnatural wickedness (Gen. 18:16–19:28), a punishment attendant on a direct offense against God's majesty (see Ezek. 38:22). Blasphemy and sodomy are linked by a common contempt for the Deity: the former, for the Deity per se, the latter, for Nature, the instrument of the Deity. Yet Dante could have found both sins in the story of Sodom, for when the angels of the Lord came to visit Lot and warned him of the impending doom, "the men of Sodom, all the people from every quarter, both young and old, surrounded the house, and called to Lot, and said to him, 'Where are the men who came to your house tonight? Bring them out that we may abuse them' " (Gen. 19:4–5). More explicit still, Scripture links the blasphemous rebellion of the wicked angels with the sin of Sodom: "And the angels also that did not preserve their original state, but forsook their abode, he has kept in everlasting chains under darkness for the judgment of the great day. Just as Sodom and Gomorrah, and the neighboring cities which like them committed sins of immorality and practiced unnatural vice, have been made an example, undergoing the punishment of eternal fire" (Jude 6–7).

P. 139, L. 15. *Cato:* The account is in Lucan (*Phars.* 9.371–396). Cato of Utica (whom Dante will meet in Purgatory) was on the march with the armies of Pompey the Great.

P. 141, LL. 22–24.*Some . . . continually:* Among the offenders against God there are hierarchies of sinfulness and of punishment. The blasphemers, worst of all, lie supine, immobile except to writhe, directly facing the god they scorned. The usurers, vile and petty, must sit, yet they can use their hands to brush off the flames. The sodomites walk and apparently receive some measure of relief from doing so. In some ways the particulars of the punishments link these sinners to others in Hell: in their immobility the blasphemers recall the tyrants and suicides of the previous cantos, and poetically it is therefore fitting that they should be treated first; the never-resting movement of the sodomites recalls the tempest-tossed flying of the souls of the lustful; and the usurers, sitting at the edge of the precipice that separates this circle from the next, suggest the fraud of the sinners to come, and are fittingly treated last.

P. 141, L. 32. *Alexander:* A letter to Aristotle attributed to the philosopher's pupil Alexander the Great tells of a snowstorm so heavy that the general ordered his troops to stamp upon the fallen snow to make the terrain passable. This storm was directly followed by a rain of fire, which the soldiers put out with their coats. In Dante's medieval source the two events merged into one. The simile is one of the most stupendous in the poem, as the quiet, cool snowfall sets the terrible rain of fire in stark relief; yet that fire falls as inexorably and invariably as the snow.

P. 141, L. 46. *that huge one:* Capaneus—and his hugeness refers not only to his massive size but to his impressive defiance of God. In mythology, Capaneus was one of the seven kings who besieged Thebes in its civil war after the death of King Oedipus. In Statius' *Thebaid,* Capaneus boasts that his god is his own manhood and the sword he draws (3.615–16). He blasphemes: "Fear it was that first fashioned gods upon the earth" (3.661). Scaling the walls of Thebes, he, like the Titans at Phlegra, threatens war against the throne of Jupiter himself, provoking the incensed deity to run him through with a thunderbolt just as he is about to climb over the ramparts. Capaneus falls flaming to the earth, hurling out blasphemies to the last, and scorning the lightning even as it kills him (10.827–930). Note that while Virgil treated Farinata—"who seemed to hold all Hell in scorn"—with respect, here he adds his wrath to the wrath of God and informs Capaneus that the Greek's own *mad rage* is the worst of the fire raining down upon him.

P. 143, L. 58. *the Phlegran battlefield:* in Thessaly, on the plains of Phlegra. There Jove put down the revolt of the Titans, who, led by the giants Ephialtes and Otus, had tried to scale Mount Olympus by piling Mount Ossa upon Mount Pelion (Virgil, *Georgics* 1.278–83; Ovid, *Met.* 1.151–62). Dante will see some of those presumptuous Titans below, in Canto 31. Capaneus thus links himself with the great mythological exemplars of blasphemous pride.

P. 143, L. 79. *Bulicame:* hot sulfur springs near Viterbo. It is said that whores who set up for themselves near the springs would divert some of the hot water for their own use. The reddish springs there do indeed bubble.

P. 143, L. 89. *this river:* Virgil now explains to Dante the origin of the rivers in Hell. They all derive from the trickling tears of the Old Man of Crete, a gigantic statue under the hollowed steeps of Mount Ida. Dante's inspiration for this statue, a symbol of sinful mankind, was the dream of Nebuchadnezzar: "Thou, O king, sawest, and behold there was as it were a great statue. This statue, which was great and high, tall of stature, stood before thee, and the look thereof was terrible. The head of this statue was of fine gold, but the breast and the arms of silver, and the belly and the thighs of brass, and the legs of iron, the feet part of iron and part of clay" (Dan. 2:31–33). The symbol works in at least three ways. First, the image of Nebuchadnezzar's dream refers to various kingdoms to follow the Babylonian; and in this way the Old Man of Crete rightly looks to Rome, in longing, as the just seat of both temporal and spiritual authority. Second, the hierarchy of metals in the statue suggests man's degeneracy from the Golden Age, a common motif among the writers of antiquity (see Ovid, *Met.* 1.89–150). This myth is compatible with the biblical account of man's fall from grace, as Dante himself says (*Purg.* 28.139–44). The older we grow as a race, the more we degenerate, lapsing from sin to sin, moving from innocence in the Age of Gold to the utter frailty of terra-cotta—and it is ominous that the Old Man rests more weight on that foot than on the other. Finally, the Old Man is Saint Paul's "old man": the man of flesh, the man of sin. That man longs to die in the baptism of Christ: "Put off the old man which is being corrupted through its deceptive lusts. But be renewed in the spirit of your mind, and put on the new man, which has been created according to God in justice and holiness of truth" (Eph. 4:22–24).

P. 145, L. 113. *trickling tears:* Man was made to be golden, incorrupt. His grief, occasioned by sin, breaks him, gnaws a hole into the world (see 34.108). Aptly is it said that the rivers of Dante's Hell flow with human tears.

P. 147, L. 138. *when their repented sins are wiped away:* Lethe, the river of forgetfulness, will appear at the top of the Mountain of Purgatory, where it will be used for the sacral purpose of washing away all the bitterness of remembered sin.

CANTO FIFTEEN

High culture availeth a man nothing. It is interesting to note the gentility of the sinners in this ring. As Ser Brunetto says, "they were scholars all, great men of letters, clerks of wide renown." Nor does Dante scorn that gentility and that learning. He expresses admiration and sympathy for Ser Brunetto here and for the three noble Florentines he will meet in the next canto. Conversely, he is no sentimentalist when it comes to the rude and uncouth, as we will find when we hear him laugh at the famously stupid people of Siena. The tragedy is rather that so learned and decorous a man as Ser Brunetto should have given himself wholly over to a vice that Dante, with quiet delicacy, chooses not to describe. Hence the terrible disappointment in his voice when he recognizes his old and beloved mentor.

As for the sinfulness of the homosexual act, it follows from Scripture and from Dante's understanding of created nature, about which I have spoken in the headnote to Canto 13. Then let it be credited to his honesty that Dante does not spare his own friends for the sins that some members of his class tended to commit.

P. 149, L. 12. *whoever he might be:* Dante does not say that God made them. Perhaps we are observing the craftsmanship of Lucifer.

P. 153, L. 21. *as an old tailor threads the needle's eye:* The images in this tercet derive from common experience in town life and thus prepare us to meet one of Dante's townsmen and to hear from him a harsh appraisal of that town. Also, this initial difficulty in seeing will be dispelled by a sudden shock of recognition, as Dante and his old mentor in city politics, Brunetto Latini, find each other. Sharp-sightedness, spryness, nobility, honesty, courtesy—all are marred in the old man by his devotion to one sin, the sin that damns him.

P. 153, L. 30. *Ser Brunetto:* Only if words were tears could any translation do justice to this moment. Dante is appalled, disappointed, grieved, surprised—and overwhelmed with affection and reverence for his elder. He grants him the honorific title of a notary, "Ser," and as he had done with Farinata and as he will do for no one else in Hell, he addresses him with the polite pronoun *voi.* Dante's words convey something like this: "Are you, you whom I revere, you of all people, here, here of all places, my worthy Ser Brunetto?"

Brunetto Latini (1220?–94) was a notary in Florence, a member of the Guelph party active in the city's political struggles, and a poet whose main interests lay in putting his moral wisdom and rhetorical skills at the service of the state. As a writer he is known for one vast, didactic work, *Li Livres dou tresor* (*The Books of the Treasury*), a planless thesaurus of bits of medieval wisdom, written in French, and in France, during the Ghibelline rule of Florence after the battle of Montaperti. The work was allegorical in structure, leading some critics to suggest that Dante may have derived from it his initial plan for the *Comedy.* From this work Brunetto culled selections for a book of Italian verses called the *Tesoretto* (*Little Treasury*). He is Dante's mentor, but not as a poet, exactly—Virgil was that, and for Italian letters, Dante will call the love poet Guido Guinizelli his "father" (*Purg.* 26.97–99). Rather, Brunetto was the elder statesman who showed Dante how the man of letters might also be the man of political action. Fittingly, the two do not discuss writing at all, but the state and service to the state. Brunetto died when Dante was twenty-nine years old and coming into his own as a leader in Florence. About his sin we have no other reports—yet reports there must have been, for Dante to have placed his old instructor here. By all accounts Brunetto was intelligent, patriotic, and scrupulously honest in the things of this world.

P. 155, L. 62. *came down from Fiesole:* Dante is suggesting that the true founders of the Florence he knows were not the noble Romans but the uncouth Fiesolans. See note on line 77 below.

P. 155, L. 64. *Will grow to hate you:* another prophecy of Dante's exile; see 10.79–81.

P. 155, L. 71. *both sides:* probably the Whites and the Blacks, the two divisions among the ruling Guelphs of Dante's day. It is not clear in the Italian—the ambiguity is certainly deliberate—whether both sides are eager to enlist Dante as one of their own or, with the treacherous envy that marked Florentine politics, wish like beasts to seize upon Dante and devour him.

P. 155, L. 77. *those old Romans:* Most of the noble Florentine families, including Dante's, held that they stemmed from the Romans and not from the hill people, the Fiesolan partisans of the traitor Catiline. After Julius Caesar destroyed Faesulae, the mountain town overlooking the Arno River, the Romans built a new town, Florence, below. The surviving Fiesolans then moved into that new town, and according to Dante's view, it has been strife ever since. *Vice and greed* is my attempt to specify, for this occasion, the Italian *malizia,* "malice."

P. 155, L. 85. *How man achieves an everlasting name:* Italian *come l'uom s'etterna,* "how man makes himself eternal," echoing Brunetto's *Treasury,* 2.120.1. I have translated so as to avoid the obvious heresy, for man cannot make himself live a single day, let alone eternally. What Dante means is that Brunetto showed him how a man may win glory and fame for his virtuous deeds in life, for meriting well from his grateful city (if he has a grateful city). Again, we are talking about Dante the patriot, not Dante the immortal poet.

P. 157, L. 99. *One who takes note has listened well:* Dante's courage pleases Virgil, who sees that his pupil has heeded his advice (10.127–32).

P. 157, L. 109. *Pedagogue Priscian:* Only the name Priscian appears in the Italian. I have added *pedagogue* because of the traditional association, in the Middle Ages, of sodomy with teachers of boys—pedagogues. Priscian was the great Latin grammarian of the sixth century, whose works were standard fare for schoolboys.

P. 157, L. 110. *Francis d'Accorso:* famous Florentine teacher of law at the universities of Bologna and Oxford (1225–93).

P. 159, L. 122. *race for the green banner:* A yearly race was held at Verona. The winner would receive the green flag, while the man who came in dead last would be given a rooster and would become the butt of playful jokes about town. Brunetto's pace is swift: Dante's words associate him with victory, yet it is in a race he has no choice but to run, to his everlasting loss.

CANTO SIXTEEN

People have always sensed that the world is falling apart, because of course it always has been. If Dante was a herald of the Renaissance, as historians used to like to say, then he was a man not before but after his time, as were the men of the Renaissance themselves. Like them, Dante looked behind his own age to a previous one of imagined virtue and grace. In his conversation with the noble Florentines in this canto, Dante blames that great destroyer of culture, prosperity, for Florence's present strife. He was not so far wrong. The "outsiders and their sudden wash of wealth"—the merchants who, unlike the landed aristocracy, could capitalize upon new trade routes, venturing from Britain to India and even China—set the stage for the emerging nation-states and the withering away of that empire to which Dante was devoted.

P. 161, L. 22. *naked champions:* In antiquity, wrestlers competed nude, as Dante would have known from various writers, not to mention from the Bible's reference to the gymnasia ("nuditoriums," as it were) in the days of the Greek occupation of Israel (1 Macc. 1:14). The sodomites of the previous canto were clerics and scholars; in this canto they are politicians and warriors. Here the three Florentines make a kind of ring of themselves that they may stop and speak to Dante while yet remaining in motion—for as Ser Brunetto has said, if they stop they must remain immobile for a hundred years, unable "to fan away the flames that strike" (15.39). Yet in speaking to Dante they must also turn their necks his way, regardless of the direction of their feet. The unnatural motion seems to strain Dante's powers of description—and that, I think, is deliberate on Dante's part and appropriate to the sin.

P. 163, L. 33. *scraping securely:* Throughout the sinner's speech we sense a vigorous awareness of, and even a self-accusing emphasis upon, the lowly sand that scorches their feet, and a hardly repressed shame for their sin. As with

Ser Brunetto, the poignancy of it all is that men so courteous and noble-minded could so stoop.

P. 163, L. 38. *Guido Guerra:* a Florentine Guelph (?1220–72), exiled after Montaperti (1260). He earned renown in battle and helped his Guelphs triumph at Benevento (1267) and return to power. His grandmother *Gualdrada* was a legendary exemplar of womanly modesty and domestic virtue.

P. 163, L. 41. *Tegghiaio Aldobrandi:* A political leader in Arezzo, he recommended against the attack that led to the disaster at Montaperti.

P. 163, L. 44. *Jacopo Rusticucci:* a Florentine patriot, sent as a delegate to the other Tuscan cities to conclude a treaty. We know nothing about his stubborn wife.

P. 165, L. 61. *I leave the chaff and go for the sweet fruit:* Dante's words recall an image used by Saint Paul and seized upon by writers in the Middle Ages when they wished to describe the nature of allegory. As the letter of the law, which is the only thing the carnal man can understand, kills, so that which lies beneath the hull of the letter, the "fruit" or spirit, gives life (see John 12:24; 1 Cor. 15:35–58; 2 Cor. 3:6). It is not dualistic rejection of the earth but a reordering of Dante's heart: he now seeks the sweet fruit of grace (Rom. 6:21–23).

P. 165, L. 67. *courtesy and valor:* the noble and generous ideals of Florence's courtly past, now supplanted by the appetites of a new mercantile class, the *outsiders* to whom Dante will refer.

P. 165, L. 70. *Borsiere:* Guglielmo Borsiere, a Florentine about whom we know little. He was said to be a man of frank and courtly generosity (Boccaccio so portrays him in *Decameron* 1.8), who saw at court the decline in customs, which he now mourns.

P. 165, L. 73. *sudden wash of wealth:* Dante paraphrases Lucan here, who says that the very same thing (*opes nimias*) destroyed the moral backbone of the Roman Republic, when "poverty fled, she who gives birth to virile men" (*Phars.* 1.160–66).

P. 165, L. 85. *speak about us:* As did Ciacco (6.88–90), the noblemen ask from Dante the only extension of their lives they can know, that of being remembered well on earth, especially in their native land. Rusticucci's phrasing tactfully echoes that of Aeneas, encouraging his men to persevere through their troubles: "Maybe someday you will find pleasure in remembering even this" (*Aen.* 1.203).

P. 165, L. 87. *amen:* literally, "So be it." Dante fulfills their request in his recording of it here.

P. 167, L. 106. *a rope:* Whatever this belt is (some say the belt of a lay brother of the Franciscans), one thing is clear: Dante placed some confidence in it, and now, without explanation, Virgil asks him to take it off and then casts it into the abyss. Dante will not be girded again until, at Cato's instruction, Virgil takes him to the shores of Purgatory Mountain and binds a humble reed about his waist (*Purg.* 1.133). Perhaps the point is cautionary. One should not be too confident in one's own ability to conquer sin, generally—and specifically, one should not expect to outsmart and snare the inventors of lies. Indeed, we will meet sinners below whose lies are but snares for themselves.

CANTO SEVENTEEN

Even a liar wants those around him to tell the truth. And so there is something fundamentally absurd, self-contradictory, and even chaotic about the lie. While it is true that no murderer wishes to be murdered, still the act of murder is not necessarily predicated upon self-preservation, nor does it use some special means of self-preservation as its instrument. But the lie does so contradict itself. There could be no lies, as Kant observed, unless there were a reasonable expectation that people tell the truth. Upon this expectation the liar depends, and he uses language, the special means of truth telling, as his instrument. Where the murderer abandons his humanity out of wrath or greed, the liar perverts reason itself, using it as a tool for undermining reason's purpose. Hence, as we are about to descend into the ditches of fraud on the back of the monster Geryon, we prepare ourselves by observing the contemptible usurers, whose labor was to pervert the purpose of labor. To such as these Dante shows neither sympathy nor respect.

P. 171, L. 1. *the beast:* Geryon, monstrous guard over the circle of fraud (see *Aen.* 6.289). In mythology he was a giant with three bodies (that is, three heads, six arms, six legs), who ruled as a king in Spain. It was one of Hercules' labors to slay him. The tradition developed in the Middle Ages that he was a hypocrite who beamed kindly upon his guests and then slew them. His triform body, as outlandish as a gargoyle's, unctuously surmounted by the face of a just man, suggests the contradictions and intricacies of fraud. His stench *sickens the world* because he corrupts what separates man from beast: reason, language, intelligence. Spurred by greed, the fraudulent man corrupts Church and empire, the two divinely ordained institutions of law on earth. We are drawing ever closer to Satan, "the father of lies" (John 8:44).

P. 171, L. 16. *Not Turks nor Tartars:* known not only for their carpets woven with fantastic geometric intertwinings, but also for their cruelty.

P. 171, L. 18. *Arachne:* In mythology, she challenged Athena to a contest in weaving. Athena defeated her, and for her presumptuousness she turned Arachne into a spider—whose web is also a nice symbol for the complicated and cold plottings of liars.

P. 173, L. 27. *like a scorpion's flail:* Commenting on the armed locusts of Revelation, who had "tails like those of scorpions, and there were stings in their tails" (9:10), Aquinas says that the tails of scorpions are smooth, so that people may be fooled into touching them. The serpentine quality of fraud echoes that of the original tempter: "Now the serpent was more cunning than any beast of the field" (Gen. 3:1).

P. 173, L. 39. *that crew:* the usurers. Dante considers these sinners, like the avaricious of Canto Seven, too vile to name. The pettiness of their money-grubbing is aptly revealed by their lowbrow, feral manners. They feed upon their purses as horses plunge their noses into the trough. Since their schemes for enriching themselves involve dishonesty (for how can money be made to produce money, without a substantial lie?), they serve as a nice bridge from the violent to the fraudulent below. Their purses bear the animal heraldry of their families—now, their banking houses. None of these men were induced by poverty to practice usury. They, like the Florentines in general (13.143–44), have turned courtly coats of arms into symbols of profit.

P. 173, L. 57. *gorge his eyes:* See Eccl. 4:8: "Neither are his eyes satisfied with riches."

P. 175, L. 68. *Vitaliano:* Vitaliano del Dente was a Paduan politician with a reputation for generosity; perhaps we do not know to which Vitaliano Dante refers.

P. 175, L. 72. *the sovereign knight:* Giovanni di Buiamonte dei Becchi. His coat of arms displayed three black goats in a field of gold. He was an able broker who rose to the highest positions of authority in Florence, but he was convicted of embezzlement in 1308 and was forced to cede all his possessions to his creditors and to the Church. Apparently he had a taste for gambling, and that destroyed him. In him we see personified the degradation of the courtly ideal—his knighthood disdained or put to use in the pursuit of money.

P. 175, L. 75. *like an ox that licks its nose:* a gross sign of scorn: "Upon whom have you jested? Upon whom have you opened your mouth wide, and put out your tongue? Are not you wicked children, a false seed?" (Is. 57:4).

P. 177, L. 106. *Phaëthon:* The famous tale is told by Ovid (*Met.* 2.19–324). The lad Phaëthon, doubting that he was the son of Apollo, pleaded with the sun god to prove it by allowing him to drive the sun's chariot. But unable to control the horses, Phaëthon veered out of the proper track, and the sun began to sear the sky and threatened to burn the earth to a cinder. Jupiter answered the pleas of the terrified Earth and struck Phaëthon down with a thunderbolt, pitching him in flames to his death. The still-scorched region of the sky is the Milky Way.

P. 177, L. 109. *Icarus:* Son of the inventor Daedalus, who with his father, the creator of the labyrinth for King Minos, tried to escape from Crete by flying with waxen wings. When Icarus flew too close to the sun, the wax melted and he plunged to his death in the Aegean Sea (Ovid, *Met.* 183–235). Both Phaëthon and Icarus, straying from the track, were considered emblems of heedless ambition, the intoxication of glory. Both disregarded the words of their fathers; but here Dante keeps close to his "father," Virgil, who commands the beast and guards Dante from the menace of its tail.

P. 179, L. 129. *without catching sight of call or prey:* The falcon was trained to keep flying until it caught something, or until the master called it by the sight of its lure. Thus a falcon that descends in the manner Dante describes does so from sheer exhaustion.

CANTO EIGHTEEN

Dante has been called the great poet of the disgusting, and critics who have called him so must have been thinking of this canto, wherein he describes the punishment of flatterers. But their praise is unfair. If we look at medieval paintings of Hell, such as the great fresco in the cathedral complex at Pisa, we can see the popular imagination at work, relishing the pouring of molten gold down the throats of the greedy, or the serving of lumps of excrement to sinners at a table, with the garçon-devils gleefully grinning. Dante's *Inferno* is rather remarkable for the absence of anything so puerile. Thus when he does describe the flatterers as "plunged deep in just the sort of dung you dump from human privies and latrines," that is because he wishes to show with devastating acuity just how abject and groveling the sin of flattery is. From the dunes of the usurers just above us all the way to the lowest sink of Hell, a new and harsher note is sounded, that of reductive sarcasm, of irony against the frauds; and more and more will the sinners feel the brunt of that irony, in loathsome ways, upon their own bodies.

P. 181, L. 16. *rock-ribs:* These are natural bridges, stone arches crossing the ten ditches from different directions, like the spokes of a wheel, then converging at the hub—the "well," or basin, of Cocytus, sinkhole of Hell. There is a conscious irony, I think, in Dante's having the liars (usually, not always, lying in the quest for riches or power) pocketed up in ditches like so much filthy lucre or like so much trash.

P. 183, L. 23. *handlers of the lash:* figuratively, punishers, but in fact here the sinners—panderers and seducers—really are flogged, appropriately so, since in life they instigated others, applying the goad to their desires.

P. 183, L. 28. *jubilee:* A jubilee is a holy year of amnesty, proclaimed after the seventh sabbatical year of seven—that is, at the beginning of each fiftieth year. During the jubilee year, those who have lost their inheritances may redeem them, and those who have become slaves because of debt are released (see Lev. 25). It is an interesting custom to remember here, as we are introduced to ten pockets of racketeers, swindlers, influence peddlers, and so forth. In 1300, Pope Boniface VIII declared a year of jubilee, granting a plenary indulgence (the remission of all punishment due in Purgatory to sins confessed and repented) to all who came as pilgrims to Rome to pray at each of the basilicas and to repent of their sins. To accommodate the crowds, the Romans divided their bridges in just the way we drivers of automobiles have divided our roads.

P. 183, L. 50. *Venedico Caccianemico:* a Bolognese politician (1228?–1301?) of the Guelph party. He arranged a political marriage between his sister and one of the Estes (the ducal family) in Ferrara. Dante considers the act to be the fraudulent spurring on of the sister for the procuring of political gain and (ever in Dante's eyes the vilest of motives) money.

P. 185, L. 78. *walking the same way:* The poets turn to watch the souls who had been facing in their direction. These souls occupy the inner half of the first ditch: they are the seducers, and since their motives were more selfish (the panderers instigate for others), their sin is the more serious.

P. 185, L. 86. *Jason:* captain of the Argonauts, who led his men to Colchis on the Black Sea to fetch the golden fleece. Dante portrays him as a great-hearted man, like Farinata, a man of great determination and courage. In his quest for the fleece, Jason availed himself of the witchcraft of Medea, who had fallen in love with him. When he broke his promise to marry her, she avenged herself by slaying their two young sons. This deception of his is recounted by Ovid (*Met.* 7.1–158; *Heroides* 6).

P. 187, L. 92. *Hypsipyle:* When the women of Lemnos neglected to worship the goddess Aphrodite, she cursed them by giving them a sickening odor.

Naturally, the menfolk of the island began to avoid them. Avenging themselves for that affront, the women of Lemnos murdered them all, including even their own fathers, sons, and brothers. Hypsipyle, their leader, deceived the rest by allowing her own father to live. Her story, including her jilting by Jason, is told at length in book 6 of Statius' *Thebaid*.

P. 187, L. 104. *people who whimpered:* the flatterers. The link between their sin and excrement needs no comment. The flatterer lies to curry favor; it is no act of charity.

P. 187, L. 122. *Alessio Interminei:* We know nothing of this personage. Dante treats him to caustic wit, and Interminei's slapstick self-accusation is a fit reply.

P. 189, L. 133. *Thaïs:* a character in Terence's play *The Eunuch*. In the actual scene (which Dante probably had never read), the braggart soldier Thraso asks his go-between whether Thaïs was thankful for the slave he sent to her, and the go-between responds, "Immensely!" Cicero (*On Friendship* 26) considered the response an example of *adsentatio* (think of the immediate and insincere assent of yes-men), typical of parasites; it is opposed to true friendship, which allows one to admonish and be admonished (25.1). From Cicero's quotation of this passage it is not clear who is speaking to Thaïs. Dante evidently thought it was the lover himself.

CANTO NINETEEN

God himself will not put a man in Hell who is still alive on earth, but Dante manages to do it several times, in this canto using the motif of prophetic knowledge granted to the damned. We are informed, by the shade of Pope Nicholas III, that Boniface VIII, very old but very much alive in 1300 when this journey to the other world is said to take place, will be joining him in Hell in a few years. That is one of the two or three most dramatic moments in a poem persistently and intensely dramatic. It occurs only because Nicholas's "up is down," fixed headfirst in a hole in the floor of Hell; and that is so because Nicholas has inverted the purpose of the ecclesial hierarchy of which he was the head. Nowadays Nicholas might be a very ordinary executive, ambitious for himself and for his family, gaining power and enjoying it. But Christ had something else in mind for the "Servant of Servants" when he instructed his apostles in a leadership that the world would see as upside down: for they were to wash one another's feet, becoming the greatest by becoming least of all.

P. 191, L. 2. *The things of God:* holy orders and church offices; also, surely, the sacred objects in the Temple and the consecrated food (see Lev. 21:22, 22:2; 1 Chr. 28:11–19). To sell a church office is as repugnant as to pawn the candlesticks.

P. 191, L. 5. *foul them for silver:* The Church is the Bride of Christ (see Eph. 5:32, Rev. 21:2), but the simonists treat her as would the pimps of the previous canto. The Italian *avolterate* means either "adulterate" or "turn away from one's vows"; I have split the verb into two, *pander* and *foul*. Images of pandering and whoring are prominent in this canto.

P. 191, L. 14. *holes:* like the holes in the old stone Baptistery of Saint John in Florence. Critics are not sure which holes Dante means: either cubicles wherein the priest would stand, immersing the child in a large central font, or, as I take it, holes for immersion itself. Dante says he once had to smash one of these receptacles to save a boy who had gotten caught in it (head-first, for he was in danger of drowning or smothering). Apparently the poet's enemies used the incident to accuse him of sacrilege. The reverse is true, says Dante: his opponents and their opportunistic abettor, Boniface VIII, abuse the things of God, taking what should be conduits of grace and turning them into means for scrambling up wealth or, in the case of Boniface, temporal power.

The scene to follow is one of shameful sacramental inversion. In baptism, the sacrament of entry to the Church, "the one gate to the faith" (4.36), the sacrament whereby the stain of original sin is wiped away, the child's head is anointed with chrism. He is thus strengthened to become like Christ, the Anointed One: the anointing is proper to his role as a member of "a chosen race, a royal priesthood, a holy nation, a purchased people" (1 Pet. 2:9). Oil is also used in the sacrament of holy orders, a ritual harking back to the Law of Moses (Lev. 8). But here, the oil is applied to the basest part of the priest's body, the soles of the feet ("He who has bathed has no need to wash, except for his feet," says Jesus, adopting what came to be seen as a priestly function, washing the feet of his disciples; see John 13:1–20). It punishes those who, by looking to the earth and not to the heavens, inverted the purpose of baptism itself and used the power of the Church to divide, not to unite.

P. 195, L. 31. *that one:* Nicholas III, pope from 1277 to 1280. Simoniacs include not only the ordained but laymen who profit from the sin. Nevertheless, the worst of such sinners will be those whose offices were highest: the members of the pontifical order, that is, the bishops, direct successors of the apostles.

P. 195, L. 33. *licked by redder flame:* With cruel lightness the flame dances and does not consume the flesh. One might think here of flames that signaled the births of both empire and Church: the flame descending upon the head of Aeneas' son, Ascanius (Virgil, *Aen.* 2.681–86), and the tongues of flame descending upon the heads of the apostles at Pentecost (Acts 2:1–4).

P. 195, L. 51. *to hold off death awhile:* Dante's words reveal a barely hidden anger. The ridiculing inversion of adverbs—you *whose up is down*—reflects the savagely ironic reversal of roles. In leaning over and straining to hear the words of the man buried upside down, Dante assumes, by necessity, the role of a friar administering the sacrament of penance to a *faithless* (Italian *perfido*) *assassin.* The ordained is the layman—and an assassin, no less—and the layman, ordained. The irony captures the essence of what Dante considered to be simony. Dante believed in two coequal realms of influence, two powers ordained by providence to guide men's affairs on earth: the temporal, to check the evil and reward the good; and the spiritual, to direct us in the true faith. Our poet believed that most of the evils of his day rose from the confusion of these two powers, or their encroachment one upon the other (*Purg.* 16.94–114).

P. 195, L. 53. *Boniface:* Boniface VIII, pope from 1294 to 1303. Though far from the holiest of the men to occupy the papal chair, Boniface was no seller of church offices. The simony Dante accuses Boniface of is hard to distinguish from this pope's attempts to assert the Church's rights as regards temporal authority and the Church's freedom from control by local princes. The caustic and impolitic Boniface confirms positions already staked out by his predecessors Innocent III and Saint Gregory VII (notable omissions from Dante's accounts of the hereafter). It is possible that Boniface was indirectly responsible for Dante's exile from Florence in 1302. Here Dante manages to consign Boniface to Hell even though, at the time of this journey (1300), Boniface was not yet dead. So he will also manage to do for Clement V, below.

P. 197, L. 70. *Orsini:* Nicholas's sin is not that he used his office to amass wealth but that he used it to advance the power and prestige of his family.

P. 197, L. 82. *a filthier work:* Clement V (r. 1305–14), who in his elevation to the papacy benefited from his alliance with Philip IV of France. As soon as Clement was elected he moved the papal see to Avignon, near the confines of Philip's territory, beginning what Petrarch would call the Babylonian Captivity of the Church. It is said that in return for Philip's influence, Clement promised that cash-needy king all the tithes of the Papal States for five years. The two also suppressed the order of Knights Templar, to seize their wealth (see *Purg.* 20.91–93).

P. 197, L. 85. *Jason:* high priest of Judea; he bought his office from the Greek king Antiochus IV Epiphanes (2 Macc. 4:7–8). How heinous a crime that was can be deduced from the fact that it was Antiochus who placed the Abomination of Desolation (a statue of Zeus) in the Holy of Holies in the Temple, and who ordered prostitute priestesses to perform their rites at the altar.

P. 199, L. 92. *the keys:* symbols of papal and apostolic authority (Matt. 16:19).

P. 199, L. 95. *Matthias:* The apostles prayed and drew lots between Matthias and Barsabbas, to replace the traitor Judas as a member of their brotherhood (Acts 1:15–26).

P. 199, L. 98. *guard those evil-gotten coins:* Dante assumes the role of the first pope, Peter, who said to Simon Magus, "Thy money go to destruction with thee" (Acts 8:20).

P. 199, L. 99. *Anjou:* Charles of Anjou (1226–85), son of Louis VIII of France, and king of Naples and Sicily. For most of his reign he and the popes got on quite well, but Nicholas reversed that state of affairs. Dante accuses Nicholas of having accepted money as part of a plot against Charles. That plot resulted in a bloody revolt known as the Sicilian Vespers.

P. 199, L. 113. *idolater:* While Moses was on Mount Sinai receiving the Ten Commandments from God, the Israelites below were fashioning for themselves a golden calf to worship (Ex. 32). This pope has done worse: he pays homage to every gold coin he can snatch. Dante's phrasing is biblical: "Of their silver and their gold they have made idols to themselves, that they might perish" (Hos. 8:4).

P. 199, L. 116. *Donation:* Legend had it that Constantine lay ill with leprosy on Mount Soracte and called Pope Sylvester I (r. 314–365) to pray over him. The pope did so, baptized him, and he was cured. In gratitude, when he moved his capital from Rome to Byzantium, Constantine donated temporal control over central Italy to the pope and his successors. Though the document describing this Donation of Constantine was later shown to be an early medieval forgery (of the eighth century, as it happens), it was considered genuine by men in the Middle Ages, including Dante. The legend did have a slight basis in fact, for when Constantine moved the capital of the empire to the eastern port of Byzantium (Constantinople), he began what would be a centuries-long process of ceding authority over charitable and even judicial matters to the Christian bishops in the West, who were generally more reliable than the degraded Italian senates. In *De monarchia* (3.10, 3.13), Dante argues that Constantine had no right to dispose of the empire's power in this way, since, like the papacy, the empire was instituted by God. It was not Constantine's private possession. Moreover, the riches of the pope violate the very meaning of the Church. Dante cites the words of Christ commissioning his disciples to go forth and preach: "Take no gold, nor silver, nor copper in your belts" (Matt. 10:9).

CANTO TWENTY

Sometimes the obvious is the most terrible thing of all. The diviners attempted to see the future, or at least to persuade paying customers that they could see the future. Therefore they are punished by having their heads screwed on backward. They cannot now even see what stones may lie in the path before their feet. Of course, with his talent for the visually precise, Dante tells us that the tears of those weeping sinners would trickle down the crack in the buttocks. And that trickling is as inevitable, as obvious, as the form of the punishment itself.

P. 205, L. 27. *Even now:* Virgil adapts Jesus' rebuke of Peter: "Are you also even yet without understanding?" (Matt. 15:16).

P. 205, L. 28. *Here pity lives the best when it is dead:* stupendous verse. *Pietà* (piety) lives the best when *pietà* (pity) is dead. *Here* denotes Hell, generally; and as he proceeds downward, Dante must learn to conform his will to that of God, hardening his heart against the sinners and their punishments. Virgil did not reproach Dante when Francesca's story moved him to tears (5.117), yet *here* in this pouch he does, reserving a special scorn for the diviners. Despite Virgil's fears, Dante is not really weeping for the sinners but for the terrible distortion of that work of beauty the human body. He will not weep again in Hell.

P. 205, L. 30. *make God's judgment yield to human force:* an obscure verse, variously interpreted. I have assumed that Virgil attacks the presumptuousness of fortune-telling—as if one could use human cleverness to compel providence divine (that is what Thessalian witches do in Lucan, *Phars.* 6.492–99). We should note also that none of the soothsayers speak. Perhaps the wrenching of the throat forbids it.

P. 205, L. 34. *Amphiaraus:* one of the seven kings who besieged Thebes. His wife, Eriphyle, took a bribe and revealed his whereabouts to Polynices, the leader of those attempting to take the city. Amphiaraus had foreseen that he would not survive the war. He was right: the earth swallowed him up (Statius, *Thebaid* 7.809–23, 8.84–122).

P. 205, L. 40. *Tiresias:* the famous diviner of Thebes. The incident Dante refers to can be found in Ovid (*Met.* 3.316–31). Tiresias used his walking stick to separate two snakes in the act of copulation. At that he was transformed into a woman, so that he might settle an argument among the gods, as to which sex derived the greater pleasure. So he remained, until seven years later he separated the snakes once again. The story is another instance of the leitmotif of this canto: things contrary to nature and propriety.

P. 205, L. 46. *Aruns:* in Lucan's *Pharsalia* (1.586–638), a soothsayer who predicts the disaster of civil war but for his own sake hides his prediction in ambiguities. His cave dwelling is his contribution to this lineup of the bizarre. He did not look upon the stars that he might dwell among them—only that he might the better divine what was going to happen on earth.

P. 205, L. 55. *Manto:* daughter of Tiresias (in book 4 of Statius' *Thebaid*, she assists her father in his soothsaying) and legendary foundress of Mantua. The following account of the founding of Virgil's native city may strike the reader as long-winded and irrelevant (Dante himself shows a little impatience: lines 100–105). Two things should be kept in mind. First, Virgil loves his homeland, and in Dante's works patriotism is never scorned. Yet this love can coincide with a confession of the unprepossessing, dare we say inauspicious, birth of one's city, as a check against foolish pride. Second, Dante allows Virgil to inveigh against Manto in order to clear his own name. The tradition had arisen in the Middle Ages that Virgil himself was a magician. It probably arose from two sources: Virgil's fourth eclogue was considered an unwitting prophecy of the birth of Christ (see *Purg.* 22.70–72); and the practice grew, in late classical times, of treating the *Aeneid* as holy writ, opening it at random and allowing the first passage lit upon to dictate one's course of action. This was called the *sortes Virgilianae*, the "Virgilian lots." Dante implies that Virgil was inspired by the Holy Spirit in the former case, and that he was not at all responsible in the latter. In clearing his master, Dante will go so far as to adjust what Virgil himself reveals about the founding of Mantua (*Aen.* 10:198–201), for the elder poet had said that Ocnus, son of Manto and the river Tiber, founded the city and named it after his mother. Some readers may suspect, however, that Virgil is a trifle too energetic in his implicit self-defense.

P. 207, L. 81. *it grows rank:* as it still does. Like Aruns, Manto has chosen an inhospitable place to live.

P. 207, L. 87. *empty corpse:* Empty because the soul has fled; but the Italian *vano* also suggests the vanity and futility of Manto's life.

P. 209, L. 93. *drawing no lots:* Thus the only connection between Virgil's city and actual soothsaying is the mere name of Manto.

P. 209, LL. 95–96. *Casalodi ... Pinamonte:* Mantua was not free of the civil strife that plagued Florence. Pinamonte dei Bonacolsi, a Ghibelline, persuaded the count Alberto da Casalodi to cast into exile most of his rival aristocratic families. Then, when Casalodi was thoroughly detested by the wealthy, Pinamonte allied himself with the party of the middle class and drove Casalodi from the city. Having done that, he seized power and drove out the rest of the noble families—Guelphs.

P. 209, L. 112. *Eurypylus:* Dante says that Eurypylus and the soothsayer Calchas advised the Greeks about when to leave for Troy. In the *Aeneid* (2.114–15), the liar Sinon says that Eurypylus was sent to Delphi to ask Apollo why the Greeks could not sail back toward home. Since Calchas also figures prominently in Sinon's lie, it seems that Dante has interpreted Virgil as meaning that Eurypylus was a soothsayer too—either that or Dante is subtly revising the *Aeneid* again.

P. 209, L. 116. *Michael Scot:* famous alchemist and natural scientist at the court of Frederick II. To him were attributed various prophecies concerning the cities of Italy. He wrote commentaries on books of astrology and alchemy, translated Aristotle and Avicenna, and acquired a powerful reputation as a magician.

P. 209, L. 118. *Bonatti:* Guido Bonatti, an astrologer from Forlì, hired by Guido da Montefeltro (see Canto Twenty-seven). He wrote ten treatises on astrology. The story goes that he would ascend to the bell tower in Forlì while Count Guido had all his forces mustered below. At the most auspicious moment Bonatti would give the sign, and Guido would attack.

P. 209, L. 118. *Toothless:* Benvenuto, a shoemaker from Parma, nicknamed Asdente, "Toothless"; well known for his predictions.

P. 209, L. 121. *women:* witches, leaving their natural work to try to harm others by means of potions and dolls. For Dante all of this soothsaying falls under the category of fraud—all lies, even when the liars themselves come to believe the lies.

CANTO TWENTY-ONE

There can be no joy in Hell, but whoever said anything about fun? For this canto and the next, the sheer relish of the Evilclaws overshadows both Dante and Virgil. No gargoyle chewing a sinner atop Notre Dame can compare with the brusque and muscular entry of the demon in this canto, shouting to his chums at the sin works, "Stick this one under while I go for more!" If there is a fun that is itself punishment, frenzied, compulsive, nerve-jarring, breathless, debasing, then these devils suffer it. Theirs is the game of the naked and shifty against the armed and stupid, world without end.

P. 213, L. 7. *the Arsenal of Venice:* The bustle of the shipmen sets the tone for the next two cantos: energetic, lowbrow, physically comic—befitting the petty sin of running about to skim money or to wheedle bribes and kickbacks. As these sinners had sticky fingers in life, so now they are unceremoniously plunged in boiling tar.

P. 215, L. 30. *a devil:* This unnamed demon introduces us to the punishers in this pouch. They are the grinning, malevolent, half-moronic demons of the popular imagination, always loudly and stupidly setting themselves against the will of God, always embarrassingly defeated. But even at that, Dante's demons are much more. Note, for instance, the ferocity and gusto of this one as he flings the sinner down and can't wait to go back for more; and note the vicious wit as he does so. Here demon and damned never rest, always at the vain game of trying to outsmart each other.

P. 215, L. 41. *Bonturo:* known as the greatest bribe taker of them all—though as leader of the popular party in Lucca, he boasted of having done away with the corrupt practices of his predecessors once he came into power. The demon's taunt suggests otherwise.

P. 215, L. 42. *of course:* Latin *ita,* "aye," mocking the legal language of documents and elections.

P. 217, L. 59. *go squat behind some rock:* Dante, himself no stranger to the hard knocks of city politics and also falsely accused by his enemies, here allows his persona to cut a comic figure, too.

P. 219, L. 95. *Caprona:* As a young man Dante apparently accompanied other Guelphs from Florence, Siena, and Pistoia to assist Nino Visconti (see *Purg.* 8.50) in his attempt to retake the castle of Caprona, which had been won for the Ghibellines of Pisa by Guido da Montefeltro (the speaker in Canto 27). The Guelphs took the castle, and the Pisan soldiers were given leave to return to their homes ummolested, as part of a deal worked out between the principals.

P. 219, L. 105. *Crumplehead:* The Italian names of the demons, with my wild-guess, Screwtape-like English renderings, are as follows: Malacoda (Evil-tail), Scarmiglione (Crumplehead), Alichino (Harlequin), Calcabrina (Tramplefrost), Cagnazzo (Larddog), Libicocco (Stormbreath), Barbariccia (Curlybeard), Draghignazzo (Dragonsnout), Ciriatto (Swinetooth), Graffi-acane (Dogscratcher), Farfarello (Gobgoblin), and Rubicante (Redfroth). It is intriguing, too, to suppose that Dante's names echo the family names or nicknames of brigands and politicians of his day.

P. 219, L. 113. *one thousand and two hundred sixty-six:* Jesus died in the year 34, on Good Friday. Thus, if Jesus died at midday (the phrasing of Lk. 23:44 is ambiguous), it is now 7 A.M. on Holy Saturday.

P. 221, L. 139. *a bugle of his arse:* one musical note in Hell, as it were.

CANTO TWENTY-TWO

When Eviltail makes a bugle of his arse, he sounds a note that brings his platoon of frequently rebelling and squabbling devils to temporary order. That's what military signals are for, after all; and Dante begins this canto with a marvelous mock-epic catalog of other military signals he has seen, and wouldn't you know it, he's never seen one quite like *that.* Yet the action befits both the buffoonery of the devils and the sin they punish. Grafting (or barratry, that is, the "bartering" of money or other goods for political favors) establishes a false union that compromises the social unity the political officeholder is supposed to foster. The devils and their chief are "united" in signs of mutual contempt; and just as the platoon seem to work together but fall out among themselves, so did the grafters in life and so do they still. Here, the harpooned sinner says that he and his fellows collude to tell one another when the devils are out of sight, yet he promises to whistle to get his own mates in trouble. I think it safe to suppose that he is not the first to do that.

P. 223, L. 5. *O Aretines:* At the battle of Campaldino (1289), Dante saw raiding forays undertaken by the cavalry, and may himself have taken part.

P. 225, L. 46. *man in tar:* traditionally identified as one Ciampolo (Jean-Paul). He is a petty peddler of influence at court. Note his proneness to fear of physical pain, appropriate to the pusillanimous.

P. 225, L. 53. *Thibault:* king of Navarre (r. 1253–70) and son-in-law of the French king Louis IX (who was canonized for his piety and his courage in fighting for Christendom). Thibault accompanied Louis on a Crusade against the Muslims at Tunis.

P. 225, L. 54. *pay the reckoning:* The sinner paraphrases Christ, in the parable of the corrupt servant: "Make an accounting of thy stewardship, for thou canst be steward no longer" (Lk. 16:2).

P. 227, L. 81. *Friar Gomita:* a friar of Sardinia who governed the district of Gallura (1275–96) as the delegate of judge Nino Visconti. The man apprehended several of Visconti's enemies but set them free in exchange for money. When Visconti learned the truth of the matter, he had Gomita hanged.

P. 227, L. 88. *Michel Zanche:* Some evidence suggests that when his king, Enzio of Naples (son of Frederick II), was taken prisoner of war, he arranged a divorce for the queen, Adelasia of Logodoro (Logodoro, like Gallura, is a region in Sardinia), so that he could marry her himself and take control of the province. He was treacherously murdered by his son-in-law Ser Branca d'Oria (33.136–47).

P. 227, L. 85. *scot-free:* Friar Gomita has let them off *di piano* (Latin *de plano*), meaning with a summary legal proceeding, or in this case, without any legal proceeding at all. The words are legalese for his scornful act of legal corruption.

P. 231, L. 135. *so he could start a brawl:* Note that the devils' energy and hatred cannot sate itself upon the sinners but must spill over in a riot of anarchy even among themselves.

P. 231, L. 136. *the barterer:* Italian *barattier*, "barrator" or "cheater." The English word "barter" is related. The sense is of someone who swindles you in an exchange.

CANTO TWENTY-THREE

The devil Screwtape sips a glass of vintage Pharisee, bemoaning the fact that you can't get anything like it anymore, what with the great drab sins of the modern world. What makes Pharisee so delightful is that tang of righteousness. God can bring good out of evil; what hypocrites do is to bring evil out of good by reducing good to the mere face of good, the polished, gentle-spoken, bowed-head appearance of good. It is not wholly an act; they are not mere dissemblers. The hypocrites in part believe they are righteous, and even in Dante's Hell they retain their modest gestures and their high-toned habits of speech. How hollow it all is can be seen in the malevolent witticism with which the hypocritical friar Catalano ends the canto.

P. 233, L. 6. *the frog and mouse:* a fable attributed to Aesop. A mouse wanted to cross a stream, and the frog agreed to carry him over, tying one of his own feet to one of the mouse's and planning to drown him when they reached midstream. But a kite, catching sight of the mouse struggling at the surface of the water, swooped down and seized it in its talons—and, of course, with the mouse the frog. The malice of Tramplefrost results only in his own scorching beside Harlequin in the boiling tar.

P. 237, L. 38. *a mother:* We have seen Virgil play the role of father (and Dante calls him so, with tremendous reverence and affection; see especially *Purg.* 30.50). He is the stern but loving authority who gives of himself quietly that Dante may walk the paths of righteousness. Here he is the mother whose care for her child's safety is more immediate and decisive than even her womanly modesty. Wisely, Virgil does not pause to consider.

P. 239, L. 58. *a painted populace:* The hypocrites wear leaden cloaks painted with gold, just as in life they cloaked their malice under the guise of goodwill. Their slow steps impress us the more after the frenzy of the last two cantos, and as their sin was to keep the truth to themselves, so their punishment here is inward, cutting to the heart with remorse. The gold of their cloaks may derive from a false etymology: it was thought that "hypocrite" was a compound of *hyper* and *chrysos,* that is, "over gold." As for the difference between their inside and their outside, critics cite Christ's condemnation of the Pharisees: "Woe to you, Scribes and Pharisees, hypocrites! because you are like whited sepulchres, which outwardly appear to men beautiful, but within are full of dead men's bones and all uncleanness" (Matt. 23:27). Dante calls them *long-faced hypocrites* (Italian *triste,* "sad") after another saying of Jesus: "And when you fast do not look gloomy like the hypocrites, who disfigure their faces in order to appear to men as fasting" (Matt. 6:16). Hypocrites on earth assume the airs of sadness, for their own ostensible suffering or for the suffering of others, that men may praise their piety. It is no accident that every soul Dante names in this ring was a cleric, as grasping and sad-faced as the Pharisees Jesus rebuked. The occupation attracts not only the pious but those who very much wish to seem so.

P. 239, L. 63. *Cluny:* the great Benedictine monastery in Provence. Cluny had grown so prosperous that the easy life of the monks there was a byword as early as the eleventh century. Saint Bernard of Clairvaux inveighed against their opulence; he, along with others who wished to live a genuine life of monastic disciple and poverty, joined the Cistercians, a new order of reforming Benedictines.

P. 239, L. 66. *Frederick:* Frederick II was rumored (it may have been a malicious lie spread by pro-papal enemies, though Dante accepts the report as true) to have compelled traitors against the king to wear a robe of lead over their naked flesh. Then he is said to have placed them in a cauldron over the fire; the lead would melt into their skin. The cloaks these hypocrites wear would make those leaden ones feel like straw.

P. 239, L. 86. *did not say a word:* Even in death the speech and bearing of the hypocrites are cautious, sly, and ironical. They say less than they intend.

P. 241, L. 103. *Jolly Friars:* Italian Frati Godenti, members of a religious order called the Knights of the Blessed Virgin Mary. Loderingo was one of the founders of the order in 1260. They were supposed to go about in habits reminiscent of the cavalry, defending the faith and establishing peace among Christians. In actuality, they quickly grew quite worldly—hence the faintly pejorative nickname Jolly Friars, which nevertheless contrasts bitterly with the silent weariness of the sinners here. Although members of the order were forbidden to hold public office, Catalano (1210?–85) and Loderingo (1210?–93) were invited to rule strife-torn Florence in a sort of dual mayoralty—for Catalano was a Guelph, Loderingo a Ghibelline. This was in 1266, when the Guelphs were taking heart again after their victory over the Ghibellines at Benevento. Initially, the friars settled tempers among the embattled citizens and, as a measure of reform, established a council of elders called the Thirty-six Good Men. As it turns out, however, their actions were being orchestrated by Pope Clement IV. He compelled them to bring back the exiled Guelph families and to confiscate the goods of the Ghibellines. Some of the houses of these Ghibellines were in the *Gardingo,* a locale near what is now the Piazza della Signoria. Note how severely Dante condemns these churchmen who meddled in political affairs, even when the meddling benefited Dante's own party.

P. 241, L. 109. *your evil deeds:* or perhaps "your sufferings." Dante is about to launch into a reproof (as I take it) or into a statement of mock sympathy for their pains—fit irony for the hypocrites.

P. 241, L. 117. *to martyr one man for the people's sake:* Said Caiaphas: "Nor do you reflect that it is expedient for us that one man die for the people, instead of the whole nation perishing" (John 11:50). Caiaphas did not say, explicitly, that Jesus should be put to death; such is the manner of hypocrites. Yet though hypocrites usually intend more than they will say, in this case Caiaphas spoke more than he intended, and was the victim of his own irony. For Jesus was slain for the people, but not as the priest supposed: "This, however, he said not of himself; but being high priest that year, he prophesied that Jesus was to die for the nation; and not only for the nation, but that he might gather into one the children of God who were scattered abroad" (John 11:51–52). For his lying in the road, see the prophet Isaiah: "Thou hast laid thy body as the ground, and as a way to them that went over" (51:23); also the psalm of suffering whose first words, "My God, my God, why hast thou forsaken me?" were uttered by Christ from the cross: "But I am a worm, and no man; the reproach of men and the outcast of the people" (Ps. 22:6).

P. 241, L. 123. *the seeds of evil for the Jews:* Medieval Christians held the Jews particularly responsible for Christ's death, citing the curse of the crowds before Pilate: "His blood be on us and on our children" (Matt. 27:25). They saw the fulfillment of this curse in Titus's destruction of Jerusalem in A.D. 70 (see Lk. 23:27–31; Dante accepts the interpretation, *Par.* 6.91–93) and, with shame be it said, in the Jews' subsequent diaspora and their mal-treatment at the hands of Christians.

P. 243, L. 140. *a bad account of things:* Here Dante reveals Eviltail's petty, mali-cious lie: there was no further bridge over which the poets could have crossed. It is Virgil's second surprise in this canto, and both do him credit. Petty lying and hypocrisy do not occur to the magnanimous man. The friar's reply is vicious. Adopting a pose of consideration, he enjoys Virgil's embarrassment, informing him, in an ironical anticlimax, that he did once learn, in those theology lectures he heard at the University of Bologna, that the devil is, you see, the father of lies (see John 8:44). But Dante loves Vir-gil all the better for that embarrassment, as his last lines show.

CANTO TWENTY-FOUR

Ovid was the great poet of change, and Dante was the great poet of order, and here and in the next canto Dante's moral order and his poetic craftsman-ship defeat Ovid at his own game. The metamorphoses of the thieves fasci-nate not only because of Dante's superb ability to see how such things might transpire—one recalls one sinner's sprouting a pair of paws out of his *mem-brum virile*—but because, unlike Ovid, Dante has placed the metamorphoses in the context of an absolutely stable moral order. That causes his changes to appear not as exceptions, miraculous and usually disastrous interventions of the gods into the lives of men, but as the working out of unchanging rules. In a real sense, Dante's sinners may exchange bodily forms (and Dante excels Ovid in his description of that), but they themselves do not change, nor can they change.

P. 247, L. 52. *Get up, then:* We shake off the weariness of the last canto. Virgil's words are not just pagan exhortations to courage. For Dante, as for Aquinas, the virtues make use of our passions, necessarily so. Virgil appeals to Dante's "spirit," or ambition, that Dante may fulfill what reason has shown to be his task (for the diligence required of a poet, see Horace, *Ars Poetica* 2.3.412–13). Moreover, Virgil encourages Dante by spurring his hope for a still more ar-duous climb. Dante will not be condemned to Hell, and that means, as we will see, that he must scale the Mountain of Purgatory. Interestingly, in Scripture the wicked use the same imagery Virgil does, in order to con-clude that one should seek pleasure alone, since youth is fleeting and fame a mere mist: "The breath in our nostrils is smoke . . . Which being put out, our body shall be ashes, and our spirit shall be poured abroad as soft air, and our life shall pass away as the trace of a cloud . . . And our name in time shall be forgotten. . . . Come, therefore, and let us enjoy the good things that are present" (Wis. 2:2–4, 6).

P. 249, L. 85. *Libya:* In the rest of this scene Dante strives to outdo the poets to whom the scene is indebted: Lucan and Ovid. In the *Pharsalia* (9.708–26), Lucan describes various serpents that infest the North African sands. I have tried to find English equivalents for the evocative Latin and Greek names: *jaculi* (*spearers*), *phareas* (*slitherers*), *hot chelydri, cenchri erect,* and *twin-head amphisboenes.* Why should thieves be punished by serpents? First, there is a connection between the sly-minded of the previous canto and the shifty-handed of this. Says Jesus to the Pharisees whom he has just called hypocrites: "Serpents, you brood of vipers, how are you going to escape the judgment of hell?" (Matt. 23:33). Also, as these thieves are the most under-handed of the fraudulent, Dante recalls what was said about the deceitful serpent in Eden: "Now the serpent was more cunning than any beast of the field" (Gen. 3:1).

P. 251, L. 93. *antidote:* literally, "heliotrope," a fabulous stone that in the Middle Ages was thought to cure snakebites and make the bearer invisible (see one of the farcical Calandrino tales in Boccaccio, *Decameron* 7.3). For both reasons, these thieves, of all people, would find the heliotrope useful.

P. 251, L. 105. *returned to what it was:* The first of several metamorphoses of thieves. Their punishment is appropriate and degrading. That which is most proper to ourselves, the body, is snatched from the thieves, who in life never considered too deeply what did or did not belong to them.

P. 251, L. 107. *the Phoenix:* In mythology, this bird, unique in all the world, would live for five hundred years, then burn herself in her own nest, coming to life again immediately as the new Phoenix (see Ovid, *Met.* 5:391–407; Dante fairly steals Ovid's line describing the Phoenix's food). For obvious reasons, the bird came to be associated with Christ. Yet we have just witnessed no true resurrection, only a meaningless snatching away followed by a meaningless restitution.

P. 251, L. 125. *Vanni Fucci:* bastard son of Fuccio de' Lazzari of Pistoia. Dante *knew him as a man of wrath and blood* indeed: Vanni plundered and wrecked his adversaries' estates, and his adversaries were the Pistoian Whites, Dante's party. He is here for a sacrilegious, and thus particularly vile, theft of vestments from the cathedral of Pistoia. Originally *the blame was wrongly laid on someone else;* then the culprits were discovered, but not before Vanni had fled. His calling himself *Beast* is no mark of honesty—apparently that is what his contemporaries called him. Every detail about this sinner reveals him to be as snarling and as vicious as a trapped animal. Dante has caught him, and he can neither escape nor deny his deeds.

P. 253, L. 143. *Pistoia will first slim itself of Blacks:* Here is what Vanni is predicting. In 1301 the Whites of Pistoia, with assistance from their allies in Florence, expelled the Blacks from the city. But the Blacks removed to Florence, where they and the Florentine Blacks, under the leadership of the *war god* Charles of Valois, drove out the Whites. The key battle was at *Piceno.*

CANTO TWENTY-FIVE

"Pistoia, Pistoia!" cries Dante, "why should you not destroy yourself!"
Here and elsewhere we see another habit of mind that separates Dante from us. People of his day lived in towns, and those towns were organisms of their own. Each was born, and each perhaps would die. Each had its history, its people, its genius, or native talent (the Sienese seemed to have a genius for lavish idiocy), its patron saint, perhaps even its guardian angel. They were not arbitrarily defined geographical areas. No one in America will be crying out against Anaheim or Long Beach. That is because, essentially, Anaheim and Long Beach are legal fictions rather than places. Only a man who felt the genius of a place—that hill, this stream, those towers—could love or hate a place enough to wish it reduced to rubble.

P. 255, L. 12. *your seed:* Pistoia was said to have been settled by the followers of Catiline, the notorious Roman traitor.

P. 255, L. 18. *Where's that rebel:* Literally, "Where is that bitter one?" Even the feral centaur is enraged by Vanni Fucci and relishes the possibility of punishing him for it. Vanni resents Dante for his having revealed the theft of the vestments, and resents God for having provided the opportunity for the sacrilege. He is a common, spiteful, foulmouthed political sneak, who nevertheless utters prophecy and hurls Hell's foulest blasphemy in the face of God.

P. 257, L. 25. *Cacus:* He stole the herds of Hercules and dragged them by the tails, backward, into his cave, so that the footprints would face the wrong way. Hercules discovered the theft when he heard mooing coming from inside. The tale is told in the *Aeneid,* 8.190–267.

P. 257, L. 43. *Cianfa:* The sinners in this scene are the cattle thief *Cianfa* Donati (the little serpent who now appears), the disguise artist *Agnello* Brunelleschi (the thief who is bitten in the cheek), Francesco de' Cavalcanti (the second serpent, on whose account *Gaville* mourns), *Buoso* (we do not know which Buoso; he is the one bitten in the navel), and *Puccio the Lame* (Italian, Puccio Sciancato), *the only soul that did not suffer change.*

P. 259, L. 69. *neither two nor one:* a fit condition for sinners who never respected what is proper to (what is the property of) the individual or family. Now their own boundaries blur in a hideous defacing of the body: a false union, an "impropriety," so to speak. Dante's description owes much to the story of the fusing together of the nymph Salmacis with her lover, Hermaphroditus (Ovid, *Met.* 4.369–79), but where Ovid's nymph is moved by love, Dante's thieves are moved by covetousness and spite.

P. 259, L. 89. *he yawned:* Notice throughout this scene the strange defenselessness of the thieves after they have been bitten. We might as well be watching chemical reactions in a beaker.

P. 261, L. 95. *Sabellus and Nasidius:* from the *Pharsalia* (9.761–804). Sabellus was bitten by a snake and began to dissolve into a heap of ash. Nasidius was bitten and swelled so large he burst his breastplate and exploded.

P. 261, L. 97. *Arethusa:* In the *Metamorphoses,* Ovid tells of how *Cadmus,* founder of Thebes, was transformed into a serpent, along with his wife (4.575–603), and how the nymph Arethusa was transformed into a fountain (5.572–641). Ovid's account of the former is whimsical and, in a bizarre way, charming, as Cadmus' wife pleads to be transformed along with her husband. Dante's thieves, however, stand in icy silence.

P. 261, L. 100. *I hold no grudge:* Literally, "I do not envy it" or "I do not look at it askance." Dante borrows heavily from Lucan and Ovid even as he asserts that he has witnessed a more astonishing metamorphosis than ever they described. The transmutation of natures is not a mere transformation of bodies, since the snake assumes the form of the man while the man assumes the form of the snake.

P. 263, L. 151. *Gaville:* The people of the castle of Gaville murdered the plunderer Francesco de' Cavalcanti, and his family avenged it with a massacre.

CANTO TWENTY-SIX

What is there that a man may not know? The question admits only roundabout answers. In Paradise the souls of the just, those who see most deeply into the providence of God, will admit to Dante that there are some mysteries even they cannot plumb. Yet human beings are made to know God and to love him. Our desire to know is blessed; our acting upon this desire is also blessed, so long as we wisely seek to be guided by God, the fount of wisdom.

That is where the intellectual Ulysses failed. It may seem harsh that Dante, who journeys to Hell of all places, will finally ascend to Paradise, while Ulysses must remain in Hell, and all he wanted to do was sail to the Southern Hemisphere. Naturally, that is not the point, for Ulysses is an emblem of the desire to know without acknowledging anything or any One higher than oneself. Scripture puts it bluntly: the beginning of wisdom is fear of the Lord.

P. 265, L. 7. *dreams before the dawn:* commonly thought to be prophetic (see Horace, *Satires* 1.10.32–33). Dante adopts the severity of an Old Testament prophet who longs, with mingled wrath and sadness, to see justice visited upon his native land. *Prato* is a small town near Florence. Perhaps Dante implies that even little Prato suffered because of the city's bad government. Some say that Dante refers rather to an ambassador of the good Pope Benedict XI, one Niccolò da Prato, who forbade celebration of the sacraments in Florence because of the intransigent quarreling of its leaders.

P. 265, L. 21. *my genius:* Dante's inborn talents. In this pouch Dante meets sinners of tremendous intellect. In the case of Ulysses, those gifts led him to an act of presumptuous audacity. In the case of Guido da Montefeltro in the next canto, they led him to think he could outwit the Almighty. Dante's own gifts were great, and he knew it (see *Purg.* 13.133–38). He has already worried about the presumptuous folly of his proceeding down into Hell (2.35). But for the grace of God, Ulysses' sin, Dante sees, might well have been his own.

P. 267, L. 25. *a peasant resting on a hill:* The lovely simile, taken from the simple life of the peasant, belies the ferocious penalty visited upon the ever-striving minds of these sinners.

P. 267, L. 34. *that prophet:* Before his master, Elijah, was swept away, Elisha asked him for a double portion of his power; yet that was power justly requested and justly used. Cunning speech is like a fire: "So the tongue also is a little member, but it boasts mightily. Behold, how small a fire—how great a forest it kindles!" (Jas. 3:5).

P. 267, L. 47. *every flame:* Flames are fit punishments for those who misuse their genius, since fire is the most rarefied of the elements, given to ascend to the heavens above, its proper and native place. And we are meant to ascend to the heavens, too, to enjoy the good of the intellect. Fire is also the medium by which the Holy Spirit bestowed his gifts upon the apostles at Pentecost—tongues of flame descended upon them, conferring upon them, among other gifts, eloquence and the wisdom and courage to use it (Acts 2). To abuse that power to fashion words that move men to action—to conceal oneself within the brilliance of one's speech—that is the sin of evil counsel. Note that the flames *stow away* the souls, for these sinners were also thieves, of a sort; Ulysses stole the Palladium but also stole away the minds of his companions.

P. 269, L. 75. *they were Greek:* The intellectual pride of the sinners is evinced by a taint of snobbishness (attributed to them by Virgil, for we see no trace of it directly). Ulysses might scorn to speak to Dante, not because Virgil immortalized him as the *inventor scelerum,* the "inventor of wicked deeds" (*Aen.* 2.164) but because Dante would not be addressing them in the noblest tongue. Diomedes and Ulysses are content to be named in Virgil's *lofty verse,* that their fame as consummate strategists, evil or no, might never die.

P. 271, L. 84. *where you went to die:* Dante's account of Ulysses' death is an astonishing invention. Our poet knew of the *Odyssey* only at second hand; yet so well he has captured Ulysses' restlessness of mind, his nobility, and his rhetorical genius that succeeding generations have embraced it and adjoined it to the older myths. Structurally, Ulysses' journey beyond the Straits of Gibraltar and into the Southern Hemisphere reflects Dante's own journey to the hereafter, also a journey from which no man is supposed to return. Moreover, Ulysses' journey is motivated not by idle boasting but by the noblest force in human life, the longing to know. Dante likewise travels that he might be no longer blind (*Purg.* 26.58), and it is surely a serious kind of sloth that would dampen our natural yearning to behold and know the beautiful. Yet we should note the differences between their journeys, too. Ulysses' is mad, presumptuous, exactly what Dante fears his own will prove to be. By that fear, Dante shows his humility; and Virgil persuades him to go only when he reveals to him that the journey has been prompted by heavenly grace. To answer Cavalcanti's question again (10.59), if Dante had been going to Hell *by means of genius at its height,* he would be going to Hell, but he would not be leaving it anytime soon. Yet that is what Ulysses does. Proud, avaricious for knowledge, he abandons his legitimate ties in Ithaca (unlike Dante, he is not exiled) and thinks to gain *experience* (the lowest form of knowledge) of the other hemisphere all by himself. That other hemisphere turns out to be the Mountain of Purgatory, a lone island in the southern sea, exactly opposite Calvary on the globe. Not that Ulysses and his men are allowed to land there—for that, as he admits now, is a realm opened by the will of God and not by human intelligence.

P. 271, L. 91. *Circe:* the witch who turned Ulysses' men into swine and attempted to do so to him, too. In his *little speech* below, Ulysses reminds his men that they are men, not beasts; and the noblest of men, too, for they are

Greeks. In doing so, he performs a Circean metamorphosis, turning his men, in their own minds anyway, into demigods.

P. 271, LL. 98–99. *to . . . learn of every human vice, and human worth:* in a way, the goal of Dante's own journey. But Dante is guided by reason and enabled by grace. Dante's lines echo Horace, who describes Ulysses' wide experience by paraphrasing the first few lines of the *Odyssey (Ars Poetica* 141–42).

P. 271, L. 102. *my friends:* Dante likely did not know that Ulysses returned to Ithaca alone. Still, the presence of his friends here is critical. Those friends are what makes Ulysses the giver of evil counsel. His speech will appeal to the same manhood, the same nobility, to which Virgil so often appeals when he encourages Dante; and Ulysses does so in a cause that resembles a genuinely noble and blessed search for truth. But Ulysses betrays these friends, capitalizing upon their loyalty.

P. 273, L. 120. *the good in mind and deed:* Italian *virtute e canoscenza,* "virtue and knowledge," or perhaps more accurately, "manhood and knowledge." The quest for truth is not for the fainthearted. I have translated so as to suggest the Aristotelian telos, or final cause, for the rational being, man: for that is none other than the highest virtue in both the active and the intellectual life. Says Dante: "Inasmuch as knowledge is the distinguishing perfection of our soul, wherein consists our distinguishing blessedness, all of us are naturally subject to the longing for it" (*Conv.* 1.1).

P. 273, L. 122. *this little speech:* all the more powerful because little. It is instructive to compare it with Peter's little speech converting the thousands on Pentecost, after the descent of the tongues of flame. While Ulysses sees death as the end of all and so races to know and experience as much as he can before he dies, Peter speaks of the foreknowledge of God and the resurrection of Jesus (Acts 2:14–36).

CANTO TWENTY-SEVEN

If this world is to make any sense at all, the law of noncontradiction must hold. It states simply that a thing cannot be and not be, in the same place, at the same time, in the same manner. God cannot exist and simultaneously not exist, if by "exist" we mean the same thing in both parts of the sentence. This law is not one of reason but of being itself, and reason takes it as self-evident. The trouble with Guido da Montefeltro in this canto is not, finally, that he was a bad reasoner, but that he was a bad man, whose habits of equivocation caused him to confuse words with things. Of course he was aware of the law of noncontradiction. He knew quite well that no one can repent and simultaneously not repent, if the word "repent" means the same thing in both phrases. But caught in the tangles of his own cleverness, he failed to see that that most obvious law applied to the evil counsel he was giving to Boniface and to the empty absolution that Boniface was giving to him. Logic he knew; himself he did not.

P. 275, L. 20. *who spoke in Lombard:* Virgil was from Mantua, considered in Dante's day a part of Lombardy. Dante imagines him speaking in a dialect similar to that used in medieval Mantua. Fittingly, we return now to the milieu of civic life in Italy. But why would Virgil address Ulysses in a Lombard dialect, when he has told us that those souls might ignore a man unless he spoke Greek? Perhaps Dante wants to show the astuteness of the speaker, Guido da Montefeltro. Yet I cannot help but suspect a slight dismissiveness in Virgil's words and tone.

P. 277, L. 29. *I came from the hills:* The peak is Mount Coronaro; the speaker is Guido da Montefeltro (1220–98), count of Montefeltro. He was indeed famed for his shrewdness as a military and political tactician. For most of his life he was a Ghibelline, ably frustrating papal designs in Romagna. As punishment for that he was excommunicated twice and forced to submit to the pope, a fact that Boniface VIII will use to force his hand, as we shall see. He died with the odor of sanctity, having left his worldly life to become a Franciscan friar, revered by the neighboring peoples and praised by Dante himself for having learned humility in his old age (*Conv.* 4.28). But now, we suspect, Dante has better information. He reveals that Guido never really left his devious ways. Dante's story is, in fact, corroborated by an early chronicler. Guido shows in clear form a certain legalistic and hypocritical deal making and corner cutting with God and his laws; and that is the same presumptuous fraud that characterizes, in dimmer form, many another of Dante's political and ecclesiastical sinners.

P. 277, L. 40. *Ravenna:* Dante summarizes the situation of the various cities of Romagna, using heraldic symbols in place of personal names (in his reply, Guido will do something similar, adopting for himself the heraldry of the fox). Here are the players: *Ravenna* is ruled by Guido il Vecchio da *Polenta* (*the eagle*) and controls the rich port of *Cervia.* Defended by Guido himself, *Forlì* had withstood a siege by papal armies and allied troops from France. The Frenchmen were slaughtered in one of Guido's stunningly courageous ploys: he mustered a sudden sortie against the enemy, drove them back, then rapidly reentered the city, trapping behind the gates those Frenchmen who had been tricked into going in. Now, however, it is ruled by *the Green Paws,* the insignia of Sinibaldo degli Ordilaffi. The *mastiff from Verrucchio* is

Malatesta il Vecchio, ruler of Rimini; the *puppy* is his son Malatestino. Dante calls them mastiffs for their cruelty (see, for example, 28.76–90). The *Lion Cub* is Maghinardo Pagani da Susinana, who controlled the towns of Faenza and Imola; his family treated with both Guelphs and Ghibellines, depending on the situation. The moderately free *Cesena,* like most of the smaller cities, was prone to being controlled by various bosses from the outside.

P. 279, L. 66. *I'll answer:* Because Guido appeared to die a saint, he does not want anyone to know the truth about him. The irony is rich. Guido fooled the people and thought he could wheedle his way around divine law; now he is about to ruin his reputation on earth forever. Two things motivate him: pride and an irrepressible hatred for Boniface VIII, the man whose threats and promptings tempted him to sin. Guido relishes talking about his trickery. Though he was a man of valor, he loved his intelligence more. Boniface, too, required not the old man's courage but his wiles, and that is why Guido is damned here.

P. 279, L. 68. *amends:* the key word (see also *Purg.* 20.65–69), suggesting the sacrament of penance—which attempt at amendment the pope, highest minister of that sacrament, corrupts.

P. 279, L. 85. *prince of the modern Pharisees:* Boniface VIII. The charge of hypocrisy is interesting, coming from a man who himself only appeared to be holy and who was tripped up by his own legalism. The *battle near the Lateran* to which Guido refers was Boniface's conflict with the Colonna family, who had contested the legitimacy of Boniface's election. The Lateran is the cathedral of the pope in his office as bishop of Rome and was at that time the pope's residence. Far from trying to win back the Holy Land, Boniface, worse than any Saracen, wages a "Crusade" against a rival family a few miles away. And these are fellow Christians, not renegades who helped the Saracens take the last Crusader fortress in the Holy Land, at *Acre* (1291), nor those who compromised the faith by making money in lands controlled by the sultan.

P. 281, L. 94. *Constantine:* A wickedly ironic allusion. For the legend of Constantine and Pope Sylvester, see 19.115–17 and note. Here it is Boniface, the pope, dying of a *fever*—no real fever, only the heat of avarice, the lust for power—who comes to Guido, the worldly man turned friar, for a *cure,* that is to say for a piece of strategy that will allow him to destroy *Palestrina,* the seat of the Colonna family. It is as if the pope is pleading for extreme unction, the sacrament given to a man in extremis, to heal him in body and soul. That may be thought still another sacrament corrupted by Boniface, whose actions here will leave Guido overconfident and unrepentant on his own deathbed. Between the two of them, Boniface is the giver of wickeder counsel.

P. 281, L. 104. *those keys:* given by Christ to Peter (Matt. 16:19), symbols of authority and of the forgiving and retaining of sins (see 19.92). Boniface uses this power as leverage. Critics say he is threatening Guido, slyly, with a third excommunication—and thus with dire consequences, for Guido is old and cannot live long. It is enough to appeal to Guido's vulpine mind. Boniface's *predecessor* is the saintly but weak Celestine V, whom he urged to abdicate (see 3.58–60).

P. 281, L. 107. *silence seemed the more perilous course:* Guido never ceases to calculate profit and loss to himself. Could the holy man think of nothing to reply?

P. 281, LL. 109–10. *be long on promises:* Boniface took the advice. He promised pardon to his enemies, inviting them to his court at Rieti, where he absolved them of their excommunication. In the meantime he had Palestrina (Latin Praeneste, a suburb of Rome) destroyed and recommenced persecuting the Colonna family anyway.

P. 281, L. 112. *Saint Francis came for me:* Guido did become a Franciscan, after all, and died in the cathedral of Assisi. For a moment we are in the realm of popular piety: it was common in the drama of the time to show a tussle between an angel and a devil over the soul of the deceased. From this point on, the great intellect of Guido da Montefeltro is cut to shreds. For he is not so smart after all. The devil reminds him of the law of contradiction (a thing cannot simultaneously be and not be), exactly as a teacher would remind a child of his alphabet. With this difference: the devil (literally a "cherub," one gifted in knowledge) is even more malevolent than a pedagogue in his superiority.

CANTO TWENTY-EIGHT

It is hard for us to imagine anyone ever believing that the family and the city were bodies as real as these flesh-and-blood affairs we bear about with us. When Aristotle famously said, "Man is a political animal," he did not mean to describe that unfortunate penchant man has for meddling. He meant that man is the sort of living creature whose physical, moral, and intellectual fulfillment can be realized only in a polis, that is, as a free man in the self-governing city-state. In this sense the polis is natural to man, and man is a political animal. That fairly sunny view of the state was adopted by Thomas

Aquinas and is shared by Dante. Sowers of discord, such as we see suffering in this canto, do not cause trouble among individuals. They slash at a natural organism; they divide a real, not notional, not metaphorical, body. Hence their indecorous punishment, the slashing of their own bodies, laying bare what in a well-ordered body remains hidden and protected: a windpipe, a nostril, intestines.

P. 285, L. 1. *Who could ever:* The following verses are disjointed, deliberately so, since Dante wishes to illustrate the unnaturalness of the sin here castigated, namely the conscious, self-serving sowing of discord. He takes his imagery from war, our most flagrant form of discord or schism (literally, "cutting"). The dismembered limbs recall that prime metaphor for Christian unity: "For as the body is one and has many members, and all the members of the body, many as they are, form one body, so also is it with Christ" (1 Cor. 12:12). The various killing fields Dante refers to are as follows. The *Trojans* under Aeneas fought in central and southern Italy (Apulia, called *Puglia* here) against the native Latins; but perhaps, instead, Dante refers to the Samnite wars between the Romans and the native tribes south of Rome (343–290 B.C.). *Hannibal* fought a guerrilla war against Rome for almost twenty years (219–202 B.C.); the heaped-up rings were gathered from the many thousands of dead Romans after the battle of Cannae (Livy, *History of Rome* 23.12). The Norman *Robert Guiscard* (1015–85) was a Guelph warlord who attempted to conquer southern Italy in the eleventh century; Dante places him in heaven among the great Crusaders (*Par.* 18.48). *Ceperan* (Ceprano) is a mountain defile on the border between the Papal States and the kingdom of Naples. It lies near Benevento, where in 1266, Manfred, son of Frederick II, was slain by Charles of Anjou; many of his Pugliese troops had abandoned him. *Alardo,* or *Erard de Valéry,* was an old French general whose strategy of holding troops in reserve helped Charles defeat the imperial armies again in 1268, at *Tagliacozzo.*

P. 289, L. 31. *Mohammed:* prophet of Islam (560–633). Mohammed is presented here as a schismatic, one who fostered division in the Church. Legend had it that Islam was born when Mohammed, a disgruntled bishop, failed to be elected pope. That legend aside, there is a sense in which Islam, with its rejection of the Incarnation and the Trinity, can be considered a unitarian heresy. Nor should the modern reader underestimate how gravely the Church and Christendom were threatened by Muslim incursions along the Mediterranean coasts and up the Danube River. *Ali* (597–660) was Mohammed's son-in-law and successor (and ironically, the occasion of the great schism within Islam itself, between the Sunni and the Shi'a). Between the two of them, Mohammed and Ali complete the schism, as their punishments, taken together, cleave the body in half.

P. 289, L. 55. *tell Fra Dolcin to arm himself:* It is a brotherly thing to give a man advice lest he meet one's own fate. That is not the case here. Mohammed (like Pier da Medicina, below) knows quite well what will happen, since the sinners in Hell are granted a vision of the future (see 10.100–102). His advice, then, is a cloak for ironic malice. Thus even in death do the sowers of discord mangle and divide the bonds of trust upon which any social body must rely. The self-styled *Fra Dolcin* (no friar of any recognized order) was a follower of a sect called the Apostolic Brothers, who preached communion of goods and of wives, in a misguided swerve away from the worldliness of those increasingly mercantile times. Dolcino became the leader of the sect and was persecuted for proselytizing in northern Italy. When Pope Clement V summoned a crusade against him, he fled to the mountains, withstanding a siege led by troops from nearby Vercelli and Novara, until one harsh winter forced him to surrender. He and his wife, his "sister in Christ" Margherita, were burned at the stake, fiercely unrepentant, in 1307.

P. 291, L. 73. *Pier da Medicina:* About Pier and his sowing of civil discord we know little. *Marcabò* was a fortress built by the Venetians to help them control mercantile traffic on the Po; *Vercelli* is a city in the hills west of Milan. The *two princes of Fano* are *Guido* del Cassero and *Angiolello* da Carignano. They were called to parley by Malatestino Malatesta, duke of Rimini (see 27.46–48 and note), but he gave the sailors instructions to drown them en route. Of this event we have no corroborating evidence.

P. 291, L. 84. *men of Greece:* literally, "men of Argos." Dante is thinking either of the Greek destruction of Troy, perpetrated by a fraud, or of the theft of the golden fleece by the Argonauts.

P. 293, L. 102. *Curio:* Gaius Curio, who, according to Lucan, took a bribe and joined Caesar's army in the civil war against Pompey. When Caesar hesitated to cross the Rubicon with his army—an act tantamount to declaring war on the Roman Senate—Curio spoke up: "Do not delay; putting a thing off always harms those who are prepared" (*Phars.* 1.281). In so doing Curio severed Caesar from Pompey, who was married to Caesar's daughter, and divided the state. Dante believed that Caesar's victory was providentially ordained; still, that did not justify Curio's incitement. He echoes Lucan's judgment: Curio was "bold of speech, with a venal tongue" (1.269).

P. 293, L. 106. *Mosca:* Mosca dei Lamberti (d. 1243), mentioned above (6.80), leader of an important Ghibelline family. In 1216 one Buondelmonte dei Buondelmonti broke off his betrothal to a young girl in the Amedei family and married a Donati instead. The insulted Amedei and their allies the Lamberti met to decide what to do about it. Mosca advised them, saying, *"cosa fatta capo ha"—a thing that's done with has an end*—basically meaning that half measures were useless and that the man should die. According to popular belief, this incident sparked decades of warfare between the Guelphs and Ghibellines in Florence. Dante's laconic riposte is sympathetic but stern: the Lamberti, even the women and children, were eventually driven from Florence for good. The man whose god was his family honor now hears that he himself has caused that family's disintegration.

P. 295, L. 132. *see whether any is as great as mine:* See Lamentations: "O all ye that pass by the way, attend, and see if there be any sorrow like to my sorrow" (1.12), a verse traditionally used in the liturgy of Good Friday to describe Christ's passion and death. The speaker is *Bertran de Born* (d. 1215?), a renowned poet of Provence whom Dante once praised for his military verses and for his liberality. Bertrand was rumored to have urged the son of the English king Henry II to rebel against his father. That father was the young man's king, his head: hence the strikingly unnatural schism Bertran suffers now.

P. 295, L. 137. *Achithophel:* The parasite encouraged *Absalom* to rebel against his father, King *David* (2 Sam. 15:12–17:14). Note that most of the sinners in this ring may also be said to be evil counselors.

P. 295, L. 142. *rule of retribution:* Italian *contrapasso*, Latin *contrapassum* (see Aquinas, *Summa theologiae* 2.2.61.4)—what one suffers in just exchange for one's wrong. The principle is biblical: "Eye for eye, tooth for tooth, hand for hand, foot for foot" (Ex. 21:24). So is its extension to mean that the sin itself will provide its own punishment: "By what things a man sinneth, by the same also he is tormented" (Wis. 11:17). "Thou hast also greatly tormented them who in their life have lived foolishly and unjustly, by the same things which they worshipped" (Wis. 12:23). The punishments in Dante's Hell are meant to fit the crime, in the sense that they provide a painfully obvious emblem of, and sealing of, the sin. What the sinners did in life they now become, with the mists of self-deception stripped away.

CANTO TWENTY-NINE

Master dramatist that he is, once again Dante shifts from the solemn and dreadful to the contemptible and comic, for we are moving from those whose sins can set a city or nation at war to the ragtag refuse of city life. The last of the Evil Pouches is stuffed full of confidence men, quacks, charlatans, impostors, and assorted clever artists of various bunk. They are the dry rot of a people. Afflicted with this or that lingering and nauseating disease, in Hell they now sit propped against one another like pans in an oven, or they scratch themselves ceaselessly like flea-ridden dogs. Clever folks like these need dupes to prey upon, and so the canto ends with a devastating satire against what for a Florentine was fertile ground for fools: Siena. Perhaps the charlatans now wish, with mingled scorn and resentment, that the Sienese had not been quite so stupid.

P. 297, L. 10. *The moon's already set:* The moon is directly below the poets, halfway on its course around the earth. If the moon were full, the sun would be directly above them. It would, then, be noon in the city lying on a straight line between them and the zenith of the heavens—Jerusalem. But the moon was full when Dante was in the dark woods, two days past. Since the moon after it's full rises later every day, it is now about two P.M. on Holy Saturday.

P. 297, L. 20. *a spirit of my own blood:* Dante accepts the rules regarding family honor. It is a defect in love and courage if one fails to exact a just payment for an outrage committed against a kinsman. (The Old Testament sanctioned and regulated such avenging—see Num. 35:19—and the law allowed for it in Dante's own time.) The problem is, how to avenge without falling into mere vengeance ("Vengeance is mine; I will repay, says the Lord," Rom. 12:19), as did Mosca dei Lamberti (28.103–11). The spirit here is *Geri del Bello,* Dante's cousin, about whose discord-sowing and death we know little except that he provided occasion for decades of strife between the Alighieri family and the Sacchetti. Dante's friend Forese Donati (whom Dante will meet in Purgatory, Canto Twenty-four) addressed verses to Dante, twitting him for having left the death unavenged.

P. 299, LL. 47–49. *Val di Chiana . . . Maremma . . . Sardinia:* places infested with malaria. The sinners in this group—confidence men, impostors, charlatans— were like counterfeit coins, not whole and sound, not ringing true. Hence the degrading diseases that corrupt them now.

P. 301, L. 58. *in its book:* that wherein our deeds are written: "And another scroll was opened, which is the book of life; and the dead were judged out of those things that were written in the scrolls, according to their works" (Rev. 20:12).

P. 301, L. 59. *the sick of Aegina:* Ovid tells of this pestilence on the Greek island (*Met.* 7.523–660). When Juno learned that Jupiter had lain with a young girl (also named Aegina), she visited a terrible plague upon the Aeginetans. The island was repopulated when Aeacus, the sole survivor and the child of

Aegina and Jupiter, prayed to his father for help. Jupiter then transformed the ants on the ground nearby into men: the so-called Myrmidons, or "ant race."

P. 301, L. 89. *so may your nail suffice:* Notice the ambiguity of Virgil's wish, for the nails, ever scraping, do not relieve the itch at all.

P. 303, L. 109. *Arezzo was my city:* The speaker is the alchemist Griffolino, burned at the stake for heresy circa 1272. He told *Albert* he could fly, and the simpleton wanted to learn how, too, and paid him money for it. Predictably disappointed, Albert accused Griffolino of heresy and had the bishop, his protector, burn him at the stake. But Griffolino was no heretic; and God, with Minos as his instrument, flings him where he belongs.

P. 303, L. 120. *alchemy:* The sense of this word ranged from mineralogy to quackery. There is no sin in studying minerals. Griffolino, however, falsified metals in order to separate others from their money. Chaucer writes of a similar charlatan in the Canon's Yeoman's Tale.

P. 303, L. 122. *Sienese:* known by Florentines for their foolish grandiosity (see *Purg.* 13:151–53).

P. 303, L. 125. *Stricca:* Here follows a list of *vain and stupid* Sienese. We do not know which *Stricca* Dante intended. *Niccolò* Salimbeni may have been one of the founders of the *Squanderers' Brigade;* the clove was imported from the East at a great price. Niccolò was said to have seasoned roast game with it. The brigade itself consisted of twelve young men devoted to squandering all they owned, having placed it in a common pool. *The Bedazzled* was the nickname of Bartolomeo dei Folcacchieri (d. 1300), a Sienese political leader. We know little about him, but he was fined in 1278 for getting drunk in a tavern.

P. 305, L. 136. *Capocchio:* a genius of a falsifier, punished here for alchemy. The story goes that one day Dante caught him painting the passion of Christ, with painstaking lifelikeness, on his fingernails. When Dante surprised him and asked him what he was doing, Capocchio licked the drawings away. Capocchio was burned at the stake in Siena in 1293; he thus has good reason to hold a grudge against the Sienese. The *ape* is a medieval symbol for the subhuman—a mere diabolical imitation of a man.

CANTO THIRTY

If comedy is the genre that allows us to laugh at the vices of those beneath us, then this canto is brutally comic. We learn, with the pleasant distance afforded by moral and intellectual superiority, of the great trick pulled off by the impostor Gianni Schicchi, and we appreciate his cleverness while we remain free of taint ourselves. Then when Master Adam and Sinon (they who have for years borne each other's diseases with scorn and nausea) go at their insults like professionals, we stand assuredly and calmly in Dante's shoes, enjoying the fray. Until Virgil catches us, that is—and then we may be reminded, forcibly and with embarrassment, of another meaning of "comedy," the one that Dante accepted. For the passage of a man from sin to redemption, from depravity to the straight and true, is comic in that sublime sense. Our pilgrim poet will not make that mistake again.

P. 307, L. 1. *Juno's wrath:* The goddess avenged herself against Jove's beloved *Semele* by a campaign against Thebes (Ovid, *Met.* 4.512–30). In his madness *Athamas* forgets who he is—an appropriate emblem for the maddened impostors of this canto.

P. 307, L. 14. *Troy:* For the pride of Troy, a byword in medieval literature, see 1.75; *Purg.* 11.61–63.

P. 307, L. 16. *Hecuba:* queen of Troy, made a widow when King Priam was slain in the sacking of the city. Hecuba was taken captive and led into slavery. She witnessed the sacrifice of *Polyxena* at the tomb of Achilles and, on the coast of Thrace, discovered the corpse of her son *Polydorus,* treacherously murdered by the king, Polymnestor (see 13.33 and note.). Ovid tells of how Hecuba then went mad, tearing out Polymnestor's eyes and barking like a dog (*Met.* 13.399–575).

P. 309, L. 32. *Gianni Schicchi:* One *Buoso Donati* had died (some contemporaries say that the conspirators helped him along, by suffocation), but his nephew Simone persuaded Gianni Schicchi, a member of the Cavalcanti family, to impersonate the old man on his deathbed, dictating a will to the benefit of Simone. Gianni's take turned out to be the prize mare of Donati's stables, as he included that in the false will, too. A great haul it was, for the whimsical but mortal sin.

P. 309, L. 37. *Myrrha:* Ovid (*Met.* 10.298–502) tells of this princess of Cyprus who fell in love with her father, Cinyras, and, after struggling in near madness with her incestuous desires, impersonated another woman to go to bed with him.

P. 311, L. 61. *Master Adam:* As did Bertran de Born (28.126), Master Adam begins his plea by crying out a verse from Lamentations (1:12). He was probably an Englishman, living in Bologna in the 1270s. The counts *Guido* and *Alexander* persuaded him to counterfeit florins by adulterating the gold with three carats of dross. Since the florin was supposed to be pure gold, twenty-four carats, the result would have been a profit of 14.3 percent for the conspirators. For all his physical grotesqueness, the personality of Master Adam is strangely appealing. His words make us see the lovely splashing streams he longs for. He makes us imagine the agony of crawling at the rate of one inch per century, crossing all those miles to take ferocious delight in seeing his fellows in crime damned. It is no surprise that Dante (who had a taste for the sport) should find himself fascinated by the slashing insult match between Master Adam and Sinon.

P. 313, L. 98. *Sinon of Troy:* Virgil (*Aen.* 2.57–198) tells how the Trojans, unsure what to do, were persuaded to bring the wooden horse into the city. Advised by Ulysses, the inventor of frauds, Sinon lets himself be captured by the Trojans and pretends to be fleeing from the Greeks and the all too believable machinations of Ulysses. According to Sinon, Ulysses has bribed the prophet Calchas to say that the Greeks would not be able to set sail for their homelands unless there was a human sacrifice—namely, Sinon. The complexity and sheer audacity of the lie astound: it relies upon the Trojan belief that Ulysses would be capable of any treachery and deceit. Asked what they should do about the horse, Sinon tells the Trojans that if they bring it into the city before the Greeks return, the Trojans will prevail, but if the horse remains outside the city, the Greeks will use it to sack the town when they get back. Master Adam's epithet, Sinon *of Troy,* is keenly insulting, for Priam had told Sinon, with all human sympathy, that he should consider himself one of theirs, a Trojan.

P. 313, L. 109. *And he replied:* This sparring match (in which, by the way, Master Adam trounces the Greek) is in the style of the tenzon, a poem of invective; Dante himself wrote tenzons. In Purgatory, Dante will allude to this tradition with remorse (*Purg.* 24.115–18), but for a few moments here he allows himself a malicious delight. The pattern of the match echoes that of a poet and insulter, Cecco Angiolieri, who in a sonnet to Dante wrote with characteristically crude gusto, "If I have lunch off someone else, you dine—/ If I eat fat, you have to suck the lard." Virgil, for whom, as a poet, personal invective was quite foreign, does not enjoy the scene and recalls Dante to his better self.

P. 315, L. 144. *unburden all the sadness:* paraphrasing Scripture: "Have pity on thy own soul, pleasing God, and contain thyself; gather up thy heart in his holiness, and drive away sadness far from thee" (Ecclus. 30:24).

CANTO THIRTY-ONE

There are two things that every child needs to know about giants: they are very big and they are stupid. For some reason, wishful thinking perhaps, the stupidity of giants is a common motif in folklore. Think of the gullible Teutonic ogres, the swaggering Goliath, and the monstrous and unimaginative race of Titans, the siblings of Cronus, who (with the notable exception of Prometheus) were perfectly content to have the whole human race subsist on acorns and berries, like ignorant beasts. If Lucifer wished to overthrow the Almighty by his greatness, the Titans in Greek mythology wished to overthrow Zeus by their bigness—and with astonishing astuteness, Dante has recognized the difference and has portrayed it in his contemptuous treatment of the Greek Ephialtes and the Hebrew Nimrod. Put it another way: Lucifer wished to match his intellect against that of his Creator. The giants wished to shoulder the Deity aside, corporeally, and for that they suffer the snuffing out of intellect itself.

P. 317, L. 4. *lance of Peleus:* For this healing weapon, see Ovid (*Met.* 13.171–72). It was a commonplace in the poetry of Dante's day to compare the kiss of one's beloved to the touch of this lance.

P. 317, L. 19. *his horn:* According to the legend, memorably recounted in the *Song of Roland*, Charlemagne's rearguard, led by his nephew Roland, was ambushed by Saracens as the emperor was crossing the Pyrenees back into France. After having fought valiantly, when all was lost, Roland finally blew his horn to call for help (1753–67). He blew with such force, according to the chronicles, that he burst the bruised veins in his neck and temples. That terrible blast of the horn places us in the midst of an apocalyptic battle between light and darkness. It is a fitting entry to the last ring, the circle of the traitors, where, among others, we will find Ganelon himself, the Frenchman who conspired with those Saracens to betray his hated stepson.

P. 319, L. 44. *giants:* These monstrous creatures, whom Dante does not allow a single verbal expression of intelligence, are a conflation of the Titans (the *sons of earth* who rebelled against the sky father, Zeus; see Ovid, *Met.* 1.151–62) and the mysterious giants (Nephilim) roaming the earth in the days of Noah (Gen. 6:4). Dante's giants have betrayed their rightful ruler; yet there is little about them that soars, other than their earthy, stupid, outsize bulk. They prepare us for the ultimate traitor, Lucifer, who also does not speak, and whose vast, shaggy body will be used by the poets for a ladder. The giants' size helps to set off their angry impotence.

P. 321, L. 61. *loincloth:* Latin *perizoma,* referring to the clothes Adam and Eve, rebels against God, made for themselves out of fig leaves (Gen. 3:7).

P. 321, L. 67. *Raphèl maì amècche zabì almi:* gibberish of a Hebrew sort. The angry babbler is *Nimrod,* the "mighty hunter before the Lord" (Gen. 10:9). According to the patristic writers, Nimrod was the presumptuous one who tried to build the Tower of Babel to stretch unto Heaven (Gen. 11:1–9), just as the Greekish giants piled Mount Ossa upon Mount Pelion in their attempt to storm Olympus. Nimrod's horn is a symbol of his being that mighty hunter and empire builder—or of being nothing more than a childish fool. God punished the presumption by confusing the language of the builders (Gen. 11:7); many, including Dante, thought that this original language must have been Hebrew (later, however, Dante would assert that the language of Adam had already suffered change by the time of the tower; see *Par.* 26.124–38). Nimrod's stupidity reflects the folly of his sin, as if reaching Heaven were a matter of constructing a big staircase.

P. 323, L. 99. *Briareus:* Another of the Titans, traditionally portrayed with fifty heads and a hundred arms (Statius, *Thebaid* 2.595–601). Dante has quietly dropped this detail from his portrait, preserving our view of the giants as very large, and very foolish, manlike creatures.

P. 323, L. 100. *Antaeus:* One of the *Sons of Earth,* Antaeus lived in a cave in North Africa and fed upon the lions of the desert. His mother, Earth, gave him the power to renew his strength every time he touched her. Hercules crushed the life out of him while holding him aloft (Lucan, *Phars.* 4.593–660). Antaeus was born too late to take part in the rebellion against Zeus; therefore he is not chained.

P. 325, L. 120. *some do think:* some, but not Virgil. He appeals to Antaeus' pride, that the giant may do what the poets require.

CANTO THIRTY-TWO

When Dante rams his foot against the face of Bocca degli Abati, it is a sign that his will and his passions are growing conformed to the will of God. We cannot be sure that he intended to do it (Dante winks at us and leaves the matter undecided), but we can be sure that had he known it was Bocca, he would have intended it, and that will do just as well. Are we not to pray for our enemies? According to some strains of Christian folklore, Mary, in the throes of an invincible motherliness, prays for the souls in Hell, winning for them a respite from their pains, the so-called *refrigerium.* There is no *refrigerium* here, although there is a lot of ice; nor may one pray for the sinners so as to contradict God's will. Pray for them we may indeed—that they be shown the only good thing that they can now know, which is justice. Strange as it may seem, Dante's yanking of hair from Bocca's head is an act of zealous love for God's justice and love for his own native city, nor does it violate Christ's command regarding love of enemies.

P. 327, L. 1. *Had I the bitter and crack-throated rhymes:* Dante signals a separation from what has gone before. We are now in the realm of ultimate evil, where only the poetry of harshness and dissonance will serve. Therefore the poet's language must be the product of intense intellectual and emotional strain.

P. 331, L. 20. *do not tread:* The warning is ironic. These are traitors, with whom there can be no brotherhood. Accordingly, any warning of this sort must appear made to be disobeyed, and in fact Dante will tread upon one of the heads, and will, in righteous anger, do worse (32.76–105).

P. 331, L. 23. *a lake of ice:* If evil is nothing in itself but the absence of or corruption of good, then the fittest punishment for the worst sinners should be not fire but ice. For fire is an image of the divine potency, while ice is an image not of rest but of inert stasis, as far from the freedom and power of God as a thing can be. As Hell grows narrower, the souls grow more cramped, until finally all power to move is taken away. Scripture, too, lends justification for this view: "But snow and ice endured the force of fire, and melted not" (Wis. 16:22).

P. 331, L. 37. *down low:* Souls in Caina can weep reasonably freely; not so the souls to follow.

P. 331, L. 44. *who are you:* Dante's question reminds them of what stings them with anger and remorse. For they are two who should have been united in soul, not ensnarled by the hair: they were brothers, Napoleone and Alessandro degli Alberti, counts of Mangona. The civil discord of the cities in northern Italy drove them apart, too, for Napoleone was a Ghibelline and Alessandro a Guelph. They slew each other. These brothers recall, horribly, the union of the lovers Paolo and Francesca in the circle of the carnal, above (5.105). Some critics say that their tears here freeze them together, and in a burst of wrath and hatred they butt heads to break free of each other.

P. 333, L. 63. *Focaccia:* Nickname of Vanni de' Cancellieri, a member of the White party in Pistoia, who in the midst of a feud within his family killed one of his own kin.

P. 333, L. 65. *Sassol Mascheroni:* a Florentine said to have murdered his cousin, a small boy, to gain an inheritance. For punishment he was rolled about in a cask of nails, then beheaded. Now his head only gets in the eternal way of the speaker's line of sight.

P. 333, LL. 68–69. *Camiscion ... Carlino:* Camiscion betrayed and murdered his in-law Ubertino de' Pazzi to seize sole control of several fortresses. Carlino de' Pazzi betrayed his castle in 1301 to the Blacks, for money and permission to return to his city. Many Whites were slain as a result. For Dante, treason against one's nation or one's party is more heinous than treason against one's kin, and that is why Carlino's crime will make Camiscion's seem the less by comparison.

P. 333, L. 76. *fortune, destiny, or will:* a false question; surely it is all three.

P. 335, L. 88. *Antenora:* the second zone of the final ring, where traitors to their party or nation are punished. Antenor was a Trojan prince. One version of the story of Troy, common in the Middle Ages, had it that Antenor secured his escape from the city by handing over the Palladium to Ulysses and Diomedes (see 26.63).

P. 335, L. 106. *Hey, Bocca:* With malicious elan the traitors now rat on one another. Their wickedness overpowers even their desire to remain anonymous. *Bocca* is Bocca degli Abati, a Guelph who, at the battle of Montaperti, cut off the hand of the standard-bearer of his own party, causing a panicked retreat and rout. He then cooperated with the Ghibellines when they took control of Florence. The Guelphs merely exiled him when they returned to power, since, apparently, his guilt was not certain. That explains Bocca's stubborn refusal to tell his name and Dante's stubborn insistence that he do so.

P. 335, L. 116. *the one from Duera:* Buoso da Duera, who in 1265 was commissioned by Manfred, son of Frederick II, and the Ghibellines of Lombardy to raise an army to oppose Charles of Anjou, who was marching into Italy with a French army. Instead, he took money (*argent,* says Bocca, using a scornful Gallicism) from France and allowed the French troops free passage.

P. 337, L. 119. *that son of Beccheria:* Tesauro dei Beccheria, abbot and papal legate to Tuscany, beheaded in 1258 in Florence for working to return the exiled Ghibellines to the city. After confessing under torture, he was beheaded in one of the public squares, for which act the whole city for a time was placed under interdict, forbidden the ordinary reception of the sacraments.

P. 337, L. 121. *Soldanier:* Gianni de' Soldanier, a Florentine of the Ghibelline party who went over to the Guelphs during the discord roused by the friars Catalano and Loderingo (see 23.103 and note). Some people in Dante's day considered Soldanier a great patriot. But for Dante, love of one's city does not justify treachery.

P. 337, L. 122. *Ganelon:* the traitor who plotted with the Saracens to have Roland and his rearguard ambushed at Roncesvalles (see 31.16–19).

P. 337, L. 122. *Tebaldello:* Tebaldello Zambrasi, a Ghibelline who avenged himself on the Bolognese Ghibellines for a prank they had played against him. Exiled from Bologna and living in refuge in Faenza along with his fellow party members, Tebaldello secretly opened the city gates to an expedition of Bolognese Guelphs.

P. 337, L. 127. *a hunk of bread:* "Who devour my people as they eat bread" (Ps. 14:4).

P. 337, L. 130. *Tydeus:* Given a mortal wound in battle by the Theban Melanippus, whom he had himself wounded mortally, the ever-wrathful Tydeus called for his half-dead slayer to be dragged to him. He watched him die, then spent his last furious moments sinking his teeth into Melanippus' skull (Statius, *Thebaid* 8.716–66).

P. 337, L. 133. *such a beastlike sign:* Ironically, the bestiality of this act endows the aggressor, Count Ugolino, with an impressive tenacity, while the victim, like a mute beast, suffers the cruelty he once practiced on his foe.

P. 337, L. 139. *Unless my tongue should wither:* "Let my tongue cleave to my palate, if I remember thee not, if I place not Jerusalem above all my joy" (Ps. 137:6).

CANTO THIRTY-THREE

Man's apprehension of infinity, some have thought, suggests that his soul cannot die with the body, spatially and temporally finite. Nowhere in the *Inferno* is man's natural capacity for transcendence so powerfully illustrated as it is in this canto, with the unfathomable and everlasting hatred of Ugolino for the man who betrayed him and his sons. He is locked in ice now as he was once imprisoned in Ruggieri's castle; and as—in those terrible days of starvation, when he saw his sons pass into eternity one by one—he brooded upon his own evil and the evil done to him, so now that evil forms the sole subject of his thought. His hatred is as profound as his range of physical and intellectual motion is constricted. If there is an eternal form of hatred, as immutable as number and as cold as space, Ugolino's hatred touches upon it and, in its own way, testifies to the transcendent grandeur of justice.

P. 339, L. 4. *You want me to recount:* Ugolino's story will move us to indignation just as Francesca's moved us to pity. Both speakers echo the words of Aeneas to Dido as he prepares to describe the treachery that brought about the fall of Troy (*Aen.* 2.3).

P. 339, LL. 13–14. *Ugolino . . . Ruggieri:* The speaker is Ugolino della Gherardesca (d. 1289); his victim, Ruggieri degli Ubaldini, archbishop of Pisa. In 1284, Ghibelline Pisa, besieged by a league of powerful Guelph cities, chose the Guelph Ugolino as the podesta (governor) for ten years, hoping that he might secure a fair truce from the enemy. Ugolino secretly conceded several of Pisa's castles to the Guelphs, probably out of diplomatic prudence or necessity. At this time, Ugolino's grandson Nino Visconti (see note for 22.81; *Purg.* 8.53) came of age and set himself as a rival to his grandfather for control of the city. Although their factions broke into armed conflict, grandfather and grandson afterward managed an uneasy resolution. Then, in 1288, seeing the successes of the Ghibellines outside of Pisa, Ugolino decided to work with them as a way of shoring himself up against his upstart kinsman. He and Archbishop Ruggieri, along with the Ghibellines of the *Gualandi, Lanfranchi,* and *Sismondi* families, agreed to have Nino expelled from Pisa. Ugolino retired to a country villa to await his grandson's banishment, doing nothing when Nino appealed for help.

Now podesta himself, Ruggieri called Ugolino to return to Pisa. Infuriated when he saw that his own treachery had placed the archbishop in the office he had craved, Ugolino returned with troops; but he was defeated by the Ghibellines and the rabble, who were goaded by the accusation that Ugolino had betrayed Pisa's castles. Ugolino and his sons and grandsons were finally imprisoned in the tower, as he tells us below, and the office of podesta passed to Guido da Montefeltro. After several months the family was left to starve.

P. 343, L. 38. *my small sons:* In fact, they were grown men, and two of them, Brigata and Anselm, were grandsons. Dante has made Ruggieri's crime the crueler, and Ugolino's anguish the more severe—and that anguish includes the pain of remorse, since Ugolino knows that his own treachery has rendered him powerless to help those innocent fellow sufferers, his sons, for whom he would gladly give his life. More than politician, he is a father, and he exerts all his self-control to keep from revealing to his sons the depth of his grief. Yet his collapse is as inevitable as their death.

P. 343, L. 49. *turned to stone:* "His heart died within him, and he became as a stone" (1 Sam. 25:37).

P. 343, L. 51. *Father:* Again restrained by the innocence of his sons, Ugolino must allow his grief, his self-accusation, and his wrath to gnaw him inwardly. The sons' request is not rhetorical nor quaintly pious. They long to die.

P. 345, L. 71. *one by one:* With what terrible inexorability must he see his sons die, not all at once but slowly, one after the other, and yet he must bear it in silence. All that pent-up passion he now exercises eternally, tearing in never-sated hunger at the malevolent brain of his betrayer and tormentor.

P. 345, L. 75. *Then hunger did what sorrow could not do:* What Ugolino means is left in doubt. Perhaps he died of hunger, when he had longed to die of grief; or he lost control of himself in hunger, when he had remained stonily silent in grief; or he was driven to eat the flesh of his own sons, a wholly animal and insane hunger overpowering every last trace in him of grief and humanity.

P. 347, L. 94. *Weeping itself forbids the souls to weep:* They are not allowed the outlet of tears. Their punishment is greater because their sin was greater: betraying those who, as guests or hosts, were particularly vulnerable. They are to be compared to the Egyptians who enslaved the Israelites: "For they exercised a more detestable inhospitality than any. Others indeed received not strangers unknown to them, but these brought their guests into bondage that had deserved well of them" (Wis. 19:13–14).

P. 347, L. 116. *If I don't clear your eyes:* Dante has benefited from the mutual treachery of Bocca degli Abati and Buoso da Duera. Now he practices what looks like treachery of his own. His words are coolly ambiguous. After all, Dante plans to descend to the center of Hell. The traitor, who believes Dante to be an even greater traitor than he, surely can expect nothing reliable. Yet he does, and we enjoy seeing the cheater cheated of his expectation. Treachery deserves no better; Dante is but acting as the instrument of a promise-keeping justice of God, and his anger is laudable: "For the creature serving thee the Creator, is made fierce against the unjust for their punishment" (Wis. 16:24). The sinner is *Brother Alberigo,* a Guelph of Faenza. He invited several of his relatives, with whom he had been feuding bitterly, to dinner, and at a signal—a call for fruit—his servants came forth and assassinated them.

P. 347, L. 124. *Ptolomea:* The region is named for Ptolemy, governor of Jericho, who invited Simon Maccabeus and his sons to a banquet and then slew them (1 Macc. 16:11–17).

P. 349, L. 131. *taken by a demon:* Dante imagines that such a sinner is slain at once by God, before the death of the body. Critics suggest that Dante is thinking of the entry of Satan into the heart of Judas, during, appropriately enough, the Last Supper (John 13:27).

P. 349, L. 137. *Branca d'Oria:* A Genoese Ghibelline who died at least twenty-five years after the purported date of this journey to the underworld, and at least four years after Dante himself died. He and his grandson invited judge *Michel Zanche* (see 22.88) to dinner and then had him and all his companions hacked to death.

CANTO THIRTY-FOUR

At the center of evil there is nothing but a small, hard, cold kernel of self, transcendentally small, a something just this side of emptiness. Despite his apparent power in the world, that is what Lucifer finally is, and despite his threatening size, that is how Dante has portrayed him. That he flaps his wings everlastingly only underscores his impotence. He is the "evil worm" who "gnaws a hole into the world." For Dante, escape from sin is escape from that tight little hole, to breathe the air of freedom and humanity, and to look upon those vast realms above—realms meant for the fire of love, and therefore also meant for man.

P. 351, L. 1. The standards of the king of Hell advance: Latin, *Vexilla regis prodeunt inferni*. Virgil is playing a change on the first line of the ancient hymn *Vexilla regis prodeunt*, "The standards of the king advance," written by Venantius Fortunatus in the sixth century and sung during Holy Week. It became a crusading hymn; the standards of the Crusaders were marked with a red cross. But the image at the bottom of Hell is not that of the solemn and terrible Cross. It is of the useless, ceaselessly whirling wings of Satan, as great and as tedious as the arms of a windmill.

P. 351, L. 11. *all covered up in ice:* a still severer punishment than that of Ptolomea. We are in Judecca now.

P. 355, L. 36. *he well is made the source of every woe:* for his ingratitude, that is.

P. 355, L. 37. *three faces:* Satan is an anti-Trinity. The power, wisdom, and love of God are inverted here into impotence, ignorance, and hate. The colors of the faces seem to correspond with the colors of the men of the three continents Dante knew: ruddy (European), yellowish (Asian), and dusky (African).

P. 355, L. 52. *reduced it all to ice:* Satan's action locks him in place. What should be a symbol of freedom—the flapping of wings—is the engine of his imprisonment. He who would be free of God is bound by his own will and shackled into a dumb, mechanical dullness.

P. 357, L. 62. *Judas Iscariot:* The betrayer of Christ is placed between the two betrayers of Caesar; here for the final time in *Inferno* Dante returns to the theme of the two powers, spiritual and temporal, ordained by God to govern the world (see *De Mon.* 3.16). We also see Dante's typical Thomistic division and subdivision: Judas receives the worst punishment of the three, since all his vision can ever comprehend will be the maw of Satan. His kicking legs, too, should remind us of those of the simoniacs, also in their way betrayers of Christ. Finally, we see signs of the magnanimous man in Brutus, who will not express his pain in word or cry. He suffers the more for that.

P. 357, L. 79. *Reversed his head:* Virgil has climbed down the devil's side. When he reaches the earth's center of gravity, he must turn around to climb "up"—though he is still climbing in the same direction, away from the devil's waist.

P. 359, L. 105. *morning:* The poet is confused because he does not know that he and Virgil have passed beyond the earth's center, and thus it is morning, when a moment ago—as they were facing the other side of the earth—it was night. The poets are about to ascend again to the surface of the earth, where they will find themselves at the base of the Mountain of Purgatory, exactly opposite Jerusalem and the mount of Calvary. Christ climbed that mountain that we might climb the other. It will take them as long to do so as it took them to descend to the center of Hell. Since, however, they have gained half a day by the reorientation toward the Southern Hemisphere, it will be twelve hours later than when they began their descent. Thus they emerge from the underworld just before the dawn, on Easter morning.

P. 359, L. 121. *fell from Heaven:* "I was watching Satan fall as lightning from heaven" (Lk. 10:18; see Is. 14:12; Rev. 12:9).

A NOTE ON THE TYPE

The principal text of this Modern Library edition
was set in a digitized version of Janson, a typeface that
dates from about 1690 and was cut by Nicholas Kis,
a Hungarian working in Amsterdam. The original matrices have
survived and are held by the Stempel foundry in Germany.
Hermann Zapf redesigned some of the weights and sizes for
Stempel, basing his revisions on the original design.

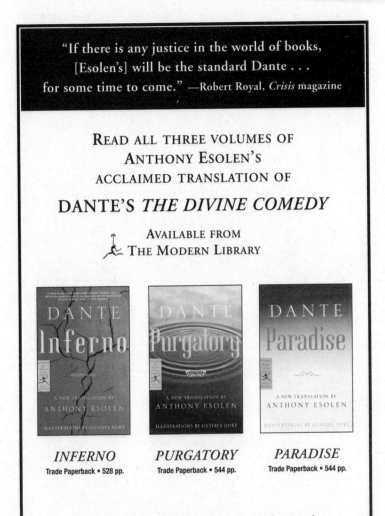

MODERN LIBRARY IS ONLINE AT
WWW.MODERNLIBRARY.COM

MODERN LIBRARY ONLINE IS YOUR GUIDE
TO CLASSIC LITERATURE ON THE WEB

THE MODERN LIBRARY E-NEWSLETTER

Our free e-mail newsletter is sent to subscribers, and features sample chapters, interviews with and essays by our authors, upcoming books, special promotions, announcements, and news.

To subscribe to the Modern Library e-newsletter, send a blank e-mail to: **sub_modernlibrary@info.randomhouse.com** or visit **www.modernlibrary.com**

THE MODERN LIBRARY WEBSITE

Check out the Modern Library website at
www.modernlibrary.com for:

- The Modern Library e-newsletter
- A list of our current and upcoming titles and series
- Reading Group Guides and exclusive author spotlights
- Special features with information on the classics and other paperback series
- Excerpts from new releases and other titles
- A list of our e-books and information on where to buy them
- The Modern Library Editorial Board's 100 Best Novels and 100 Best Nonfiction Books of the Twentieth Century written in the English language
- News and announcements

Questions? E-mail us at **modernlibrary@randomhouse.com**
For questions about examination or desk copies, please visit
the Random House Academic Resources site at
www.randomhouse.com/academic